THE AUTHOR   Professor Daniel J. McInerney teaches United States history at Utah State University. His research interests focus on cultural and intellectual history particularly in the nineteenth century. He is the author of *The Fortunate Heirs of Freedom: Abolition and Republican Thought*. His articles have appeared in *Civil War History* and the *Journal of the Early Republic*. He is currently studying the popular nineteenth-century phenomenon of mnemonics as a social and cultural movement in America.

Other Titles in the Series

A Traveller's History of France
A Traveller's History of Paris
A Traveller's History of Spain
A Traveller's History of Italy
A Traveller's History of Russia and the USSR
A Traveller's History of Scotland
A Traveller's History of England
A Traveller's History of London
A Traveller's History of Ireland
A Traveller's History of Turkey
A Traveller's History of Greece
A Traveller's History of India
A Traveller's History of Japan
A Traveller's History of India
A Traveller's History of China
A Traveller's History of North Africa
A Traveller's History of the Caribbean
A Traveller's History of Australia

THE TRAVELLER'S HISTORY SERIES

'Ideal before-you-go reading' *The Daily Telegraph*

'An excellent series of brief histories' *New York Times*

'I want to compliment you ... on the brilliantly concise contents of your books' *Shirley Conran*

Reviews of Individual Titles

A Traveller's History of France

'Undoubtedly the best way to prepare for a trip to France is to bone up on some history. *The Traveller's History of France* by Robert Cole is concise and gives the essential facts in a very readable form.' *The Independent*

A Traveller's History of China

'The author manages to get 2 million years into 300 pages. An excellent addition to a series which is already invaluable, whether you're travelling or not.' *The Guardian*

A Traveller's History of India

'For anyone ... planning a trip to India, the latest in the excellent Traveller's History series ... provides a useful grounding for those whose curiosity exceeds the time available for research.' *The London Evening Standard*

A Traveller's History of Japan

'It succeeds admirably in its goal of making the present country comprehensible through a narrative of its past, with asides on everything from bonsai to *zazen*, in a brisk, highly readable style ... you could easily read it on the flight over, if you skip the movie.' *The Washington Post*

A Traveller's History of Ireland

'For independent, inquisitive travellers traversing the green roads of Ireland, there is no better guide than *A Traveller's History of Ireland*.' *Small Press*

A Traveller's History of the USA

For Re, with love

A Traveller's History of the USA

DANIEL J. McINERNEY

Line Drawings *JOHN HOSTE*

Interlink Books
An imprint of Interlink Publishing Group, Inc.
New York • Northampton

First American edition published in 2001 by
INTERLINK BOOKS
An imprint of Interlink Publishing Group, Inc.
99 Seventh Avenue • Brooklyn, New York 11215 and
46 Crosby Street • Northampton, Massachusetts 01060

The front cover shows *Study for Jersey Homestead* by Ben Shahn c. 1936, tempera
on paper on masonite. Collection: Merrill C. Berman. Reproduced by kind
permission.

Library of Congress Cataloging-in-Publication Data

McInerney, Daniel John, 1951–
    A traveller's history of the U.S.A./by Dan McInerney.
      p.   cm. – (The traveller's history series)
    Includes bibliographical references and index.
    ISBN 1-56656-283-X
    1. United States–History.   2. United States–Description and travel.
I. Title.   II. Traveller's history.
E178 .M48   2001
973–dc21
                          99-056028
                           CIP

Printed and bound in Great Britain

To order or request our complete catalog,
please call us at **1-800-238-LINK** or write to:
Interlink Publishing
46 Crosby Street, Northampton, MA 01060
e-mail: info@interlinkbooks.com • website: www.interlinkbooks.com

Table of Contents

CHAPTER ONE

The Native Land, the Native Peoples, and the New Arrivals

The story this book tells ends with a diverse America, made up of a patchwork of peoples, living in a vast, rich terrain. The story begins the same way, with a varied America, formed from multiple cultures, inhabiting an extraordinarily large and abundant land.

The Land

The United States covers an area that is both immense and wide-ranging. Its 3.5 million square miles of land covers 6 percent of the earth. The nation is roughly the size of Europe. Virginia and North Carolina, just two of the original 13 English colonies, are bigger than the United Kingdom; Japan could squeeze into California; all of Ireland could fit into South Carolina (which is the 40th largest of the 50 states). Even the largest *county* in the 'lower 48' states, San Bernardino in California, is nearly twice the size of Belgium.

The continental United States spans 3,000 miles from Atlantic to Pacific coasts. It has over 12,000 miles of coastline. Its Mississippi River system is the third longest in the world, after the Nile and the Amazon. Its 'Great Lakes' form the world's largest fresh water body; Lake Superior, jointly controlled with Canada, is second only to the land-locked Caspian Sea in size. Waterfalls in Yosemite National Park in California are among the ten highest on the planet.

Inhabiting that space are 270 million people, less than 5 per cent of the world's total but still the third most populous nation after China and India. All those Americans tend to be clustered; nearly a third of the nation's population lives in only ten metropolitan areas. Almost 80 per cent of Americans are 'urban'. That leaves a lot of open room. The country's population density is 74 people per square mile, more than that of Australia or Brazil, but about half the density of Mexico, a quarter that of France, a fifth that of China, and an eighth that of the United Kingdom.

The variations contained within the United States are remarkable. The nation contains some of the oldest living things on earth: the 3,000 year-old giant sequoia trees found in California's Sequoia National Park. The United States also contains a comparatively young geological feature, the Hawaiian Islands, formed by volcanic eruptions some 50 million years ago. The northernmost tip of the United States, at Point Barrow, Alaska, is 6,000 miles away from its southernmost point, at Ka Lae, Hawaii. Its easternmost point, in Maine, is separated from its westernmost point, in Hawaii, by 5,400 miles, across seven time zones and more than a fifth of the earth's circumference. The nation contains North America's highest and lowest points: Mt. McKinley (Denali) in Alaska at 20,320 feet above sea level and Death Valley in California at 282 feet below sea level. The second highest recorded temperature in the world was in Death Valley at 134°F (57°C) in 1913; the fifth lowest recorded temperature was in Prospect Creek, Alaska, at −80°F (−62°C) in 1971. Even the greatest one minute rainfall and one month snowfall occurred in the United States.[1]

Such weather extremes are not unusual for a nation that contains so many varieties of climate and topography. The United States contains arctic tundra, tropical jungles, and almost everything in between: marine West Coast, Mediterranean, mountain, and temperate climates, arid and semi-arid regions, coastal plains, grasslands, woodlands, desert lands, and wetlands.

If one could stand below Texas and look at a profile of the entire continental United States from sea level, the line formed would look like a cable draped on top of the twin towers of a suspension bridge: starting at sea level along the Pacific Coast, swiftly climbing along western mountain ranges, dipping low across the vast central plain, rising again with eastern mountains, and leveling off to the sea along the Atlantic coastal plain.

The terrain of the West Coast ascends quickly from the ocean's surface to mountain peaks. The rugged coast provides only a few favorable harbors such as Seattle, San Francisco, Los Angeles, and San Diego. The Cascade and Sierra Nevada Mountains – along with the Coast Range – rise up from the coastline, extend some 200 miles inland, and reach heights of 14,000 feet. Three major valleys lay within the ranges: the Willamette Valley in Oregon, the Imperial Valley in southern California, and the Central Valley in the middle of California. West Coast climates vary strikingly, from the Pacific Northwest's wet and moderate conditions to California's dry and warm 'Mediterranean' zone. Rainfall decreases in Southern California, creating a semi-arid climate that turns into a blistering desert further inland. Eastern Washington and Oregon, on the leeward side of the Cascades, also form semi-arid zones. And just 50 to 150 miles from the coastline, one enters a long north–south line of mountain climates.

To the east of the Cascades and Sierra Nevada, to the west of the Rockies, and to the south of the Columbia Plateau sits the Great Basin. The region is actually a combination of three basins separated by north–south mountain ranges. The easternmost basin, covering much of Utah, was once filled by the prehistoric Lake Bonneville, a huge 'terminal' lake with no outlet to the sea. Its remains are visible today in the Great Salt Lake, which is about one-tenth the size of its ancestor. The lands of the Great Basin sit on high ground, averaging 3,000–4,000 feet above sea level. The region is arid and scarred by erosion, sizzling on summer days and cooling quickly at night. The stark, primitive qualities of the landscape lend the area a dramatic and severe character. The Colorado Plateau and desert lands of Arizona and New Mexico that sit south of the Basin have their own intense and forbidding climate. But the region also contains breathtaking landscapes. The level desert can burst with magnificent and rich colors from flowers that have adapted to limited rainfall. The peaks of Monument Valley are familiar to generations of filmgoers as icons of the American West, especially as they were captured in director John Ford's *Stagecoach*, *My Darling Clementine*, and *The Searchers*. The depths of the Grand Canyon, formed by the furious carving of the Colorado River, follow a path a mile deep, 4–18 miles wide, and more than 200 miles long.

The Rocky Mountains rise east of the Basin. Part of the 'Cordillera'

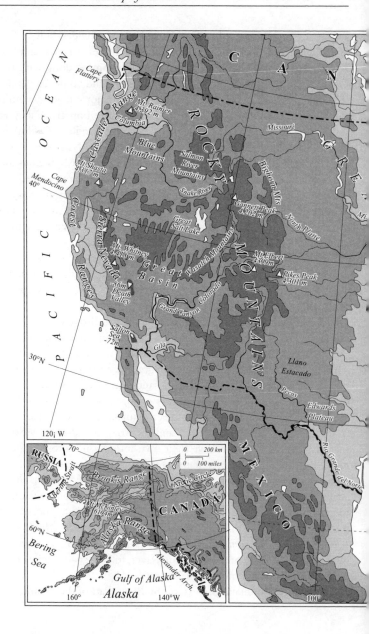

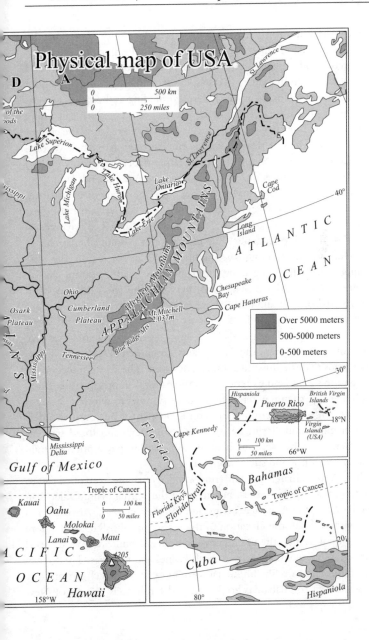

Physical map of USA

D   A

| | 0 | 500 km |
| 0 | 250 miles | |

of the
ods

Lake Superior

ssissippi

Lake Michigan

Lake Huron

Lake Erie

Lake Ontario

St. Lawrence

St. Lawrence

Cape
Cod

40°

Long
Island

ATLANTIC

OCEAN

Ohio

Cumberland
Plateau

Osark
Plateau

Allegheny Mountains

APPALACHIAN MOUNTAINS

Mt. Mitchell
2,037m

Blue Ridge Mts.

Chesapeake
Bay

Cape Hatteras

Tennessee

Mississippi

30°

Over 5000 meters

500-5000 meters

0-500 meters

Florida

Cape Kennedy

Mississippi
Delta

Gulf of Mexico

Hispaniola

Puerto Rico

British Virgin
Islands

18°N

Virgin
Islands
(USA)

| 0 | 100 km |
| 0 | 50 miles |

66°W

Bahamas

Tropic of Cancer

Tropic of Cancer

Florida Keys

Florida Strait

20°

Kauai

Oahu

Molokai

Lanai   Maui

4205

ACIFIC

OCEAN   Hawaii

158°W

Cuba

80°

Hispaniola

system running from Alaska down through South America, the Rockies are rich in minerals (such as copper and lead), climates (such as sub-arctic and alpine), and national parks (such as Glacier and Yellowstone). In the lower 48 states, the Rockies reach a high point of 14,400 feet in Colorado at Mt. Elbert. Forbidding as the range appears, a number of passes have allowed wagon-bound settlers, rail-riding travelers, and interstate-cruising drivers to cross west. Along the crest of the Rockies, the Continental Divide runs through Montana, Wyoming, Colorado, and New Mexico, separating rivers that drain west into the Pacific from rivers that drain east into the Atlantic and Arctic.

The eastward-moving waters flow into the immense, v-shaped, central plain or lowlands that sit between America's two great mountain chains. The Missouri, Platte, Arkansas, and Red Rivers carry water from the Rockies; the Ohio carries water from the Appalachians. All five, in turn, flow into the mightiest river in the nation, the Mississippi, which has long transported minerals, grains, cotton, *and* silt down to New Orleans. The lands between the Missouri and Ohio Rivers are both flat and fertile. Forests once covered northeast sections of the region. From Indiana west to the Missouri River and south down to northern Texas, a vast thick-grass, treeless prairie once existed. West of the Missouri sit the Great Plains, composed of semi-arid, short-grass lands that rise upward as one travels west. The western sections of the nation's heartland experience erratic patterns in precipitation along with dramatic swings in temperature from summer to winter. Northern and eastern sections enjoy more consistent rainfall but must also deal with a more humid climate, scorching summers, and frigid winters. Southern sections avoid the blasts of arctic air but pay a price for mild winters with hot and sticky summers.

The Appalachian Mountains run on a diagonal line from northeast to southwest along the eastern boundary of the central plain. Older than the Rockies, the Appalachians are also rounder, gentler, narrower, and lower, about half the elevation of the western peaks. Rich in folklore and natural beauty, the mountains also hold an abundance of coal used since the nineteenth century in both homes and factories. The foot of the mountains, or 'Piedmont', is a rolling plateau which, from New Jersey down to Alabama, holds rich and fertile soils. North of New

Jersey, the land is rockier, the soil thinner, and the farming hard enough to 'build character'. Dealt a bad hand by glaciers, New York at least got the Hudson River with Manhattan Island at its mouth; New England wound up with good harbors like Boston. The Northeast's inhabitants could turn to the sea and commerce when they got frustrated with the land and agriculture.

The edge of the Atlantic contains a natural feature largely missing along the Pacific: a coastal plain wrapping from New Jersey around to Texas. The rich soils of the plain have provided abundant yields on farms and plantations. Goods moved to markets along waterways that opened to the Atlantic from the Appalachians: the Delaware and Chesapeake Bays in the upper regions; the James, York, Cooper, Ashley, Savannah, and Alabama Rivers further south. The cities of Philadelphia, Baltimore, Norfolk, Charleston, Savannah, and Mobile grew up at the heads of these bays and at the mouths of the rivers. The plain boasts another feature that took on greater importance in the twentieth century: the lovely beaches that have made the Atlantic Coast a popular vacation destination. Ocean front accommodations provide scenic beauty as well as an escape from the sizzling, muggy summers along the coastal plain. Winters that are damp, chilly, and nasty in the northern stretches of the plain are milder in the southern zones. As a refuge from wintry discomfort, Florida offers just what the ads have long promised: a tropical paradise.

From the 'plain' Atlantic, across the verdant Appalachians, the central breadbasket, the dramatic Rockies, and the stern Basin to the rugged Pacific, the different regions of the United States provide an environmental diversity that complements the country's social diversity. A land made up of many lands, the nation also springs from many cultures.

The Native Peoples

The story of America is the story of immigrants. At the start of the 21st century, nearly 10 per cent of Americans were foreign born. Most new arrivals came from the Western Hemisphere. The second largest group came from Asia, the likely home of the first American immigrants.

In the late 1990s, debate stirred about the origins and routes of the first people to inhabit the land. On the basis of excavations in Chile and the Eastern USA, some concluded that the earliest migrants (from Asia or perhaps from Europe) came by sea, moving along the western or eastern coasts of the Americas over 16,000 years ago. The prevailing theory, in sharp contrast, has held that hunters from eastern Siberia came by land, crossing the wide plain of Beringia (which once connected Asia and North America) over 12,000 years ago. As glaciers melted, a corridor opened from northern Alaska through northwestern Canada to the present-day Dakotas. Groups moved throughout North America and, by 8000 BC, ventured down to the tip of South America. The population north of the Rio Grande River reached a peak of 4–12 million while the number living in North and South America combined reached 40–110 million.

Nomadic 'Paleo-Indian' hunters moved throughout the hemisphere from 10,000–9000 BC. Their descendants, 'Archaic Indians', were pre-agricultural hunter-gatherers in the period from 8000–1500 BC. Archaic peoples had more diverse diets and greater populations. Most migrated, but some societies created large settlements. Agricultural practices that began in the Western Hemisphere 7,000 years ago spread to North America by 3500 BC, reached the southwestern areas of the present United States by 1500 BC, and extended into southeastern regions by AD 200. Early cultivators produced maize (corn), potatoes, beans, squash, and tomatoes. Where food production became more predictable, populations rose, settlement became more permanent, trade expanded, and cultures grew more complex. One other consequence was that the status of women often grew more diverse. In many groups, women tended fields; in some societies they even controlled the land and owned tools. Matrilineal social structures and women's participation in political decisions marked some later tribes.

Complex cultures developed after 1500 BC, especially in Central and South America. The Olmecs of Gulf coastal Mexico, the Mayans of the Yucatan Peninsula, the Toltecs of central Mexico, the Aztecs (or Mexica) of central and southern Mexico, and the Incans of Peru developed writing, mathematical and astronomical calculations, urban societies, and elaborate religious ceremonies. The Aztec capital of

Tenochtitlán, with a population of 100,000 to 200,000, was one of the world's largest cities, occupying the site of present-day Mexico City.

A few Indian cultures that lived in the present-day United States also created societies and communities of a striking scale. Some of the largest, located in the Illinois, Ohio, and Mississippi River valleys, were 'mound-builders' who created earthwork constructions ranging from 20 to 70 feet high, covering acres and, in some instances, several square miles of ground. The geometric and natural shapes they formed served a variety of religious purposes. Some 3,500 years ago, one such culture flourished at a site known today as Poverty Point in northeastern Louisiana, creating elaborate semicircular, conical, and bird-like mounds and embankments in an urban center that served as a hub for trade in quartz, copper, and crystal. A later group, the Adena-Hopewell culture, dispersed over a wide area of the Ohio and Illinois valleys from 500 BC to AD 400. A well-preserved, quarter-mile long 'Serpent Mound' of the Adena culture sits on a plateau in southern Ohio some

The Great Serpent Mound

60 miles east of Cincinnati. The 'Mississippian' culture built the large city of Cahokia in Illinois (east of modern St. Louis), which, at its height in the twelfth century, served as a six-square-mile trading center and home for 20,000–40,000 people.

At roughly the same time, the Anasazi people of the Southwest created a remarkable group of social, religious, and commercial centers. Their culture emerged in the 'Four Corners' region of Utah, Arizona, New Mexico, and Colorado as early as the first century AD. But from the 900s through the 1200s, the Anasazi created their most striking constructions whose ruins may be viewed today. At Mesa Verde, in southwestern Colorado, the 'Ancient Ones' lived for more than seven centuries, from the 500s to the 1200s, dwelling in caves or simple structures. In the twelfth and thirteenth centuries, however, the Anasazi built large, multi-story, apartment-like complexes called *pueblos* in the overhangs and ledges of the canyon walls. The largest of these, the Cliff Place, contained over 150 rooms and more than 20 *kivas* or ceremonial spaces. At Canyon de Chelly in northeastern Arizona, where Indians had lived since the fourth century, the Anasazi created another group of stunning cliff dwellings in the 1100s and 1200s. Chaco Canyon, in northwestern New Mexico, holds dozens of masonry structures built by the Anasazi, each containing scores of rooms. The largest construction was Pueblo Bonito, composed of four stories and 600 rooms. One other remarkable feature of the site is the complex, carefully built roadway system that connected Chaco to 75 other communities in the region, some located more than 60 miles away. For reasons that remain unclear, the Anasazi left their massive and elaborate centers by the later thirteenth century, perhaps because of drought, perhaps because of war.

Though the mound-building and Anasazi cultures built large urban centers and created remarkable engineering projects, most tribes inhabiting the lands of the modern United States lived on a more modest scale. Their societies were smaller in size; many migrated in the search for food; kin-based systems commonly defined the organization of their communities; regional trade networks kept groups in contact with one another. Throughout the continent, natives created patterns of life and cycles of activity shaped in large measure by the environment

The Cliff Palace, Mesa Verde National Park

in which they found themselves. Indian groups were not, as some modern legends have it, 'nature lovers' who existed in passive harmony with the landscape. Rather, they (like all societies) actively shaped, developed, and at times, depleted the resources around them.

At the time of European contact, 'Woodlands' tribes formed one major region of native life in the northeast and southeast. Their languages were varied (Algonquian and Iroquoian in the Northeast, Muskogean in the Southeast). They relied on diverse natural resources from fields, forests, rivers, and the ocean. They usually inhabited villages built along the many waterways of the region. The tribes' economies revolved around a number of tasks including fishing, farming, hunting, and gathering. Many Northeastern groups migrated seasonally. Southeastern areas were home to larger and more permanent settlements with more complex social and political systems.

The Great Plains formed the more sparsely settled home of nomadic societies. The lives of the Cheyenne, Comanche, Teton Sioux, and others revolved around the hunt for large game, especially the buffalo of the area. They pursued game on foot; it was not until Spanish colonization that native peoples were introduced to horses. Plains tribes such as the Mandans and Pawnees, often living along the region's rivers, engaged in agriculture.

Great Basin tribes concentrated on medium to small game while also depending on the nutrition from seeds and nuts. Six to seven hundred years ago, Ute, Paiute, and Shoshone tribes entered the area, roamed the hard, arid, and varying environment in small, mobile bands, and took on the ways of the region's ancient hunter-gatherers.

The arid Southwest was home to a number of tribes. The Hopi and Zuni were descendants of the Anasazi; the Pima and Papago traced their lineage to the Hohokam culture that developed in southern Arizona in the third century BC. Their farming communities controlled valuable water supplies by constructing dams, canals, and irrigation systems. In the 1200s, Athapascan tribes from the north entered the region, skilled more in hunting, gathering, and warfare than agriculture. Their descendants became known as the Apaches and Navajos.

Along the Pacific coast, tribes from the Northwest down to California lived in a rich environment. The abundance of the ocean and, in many areas, the wealth of resources in rivers, streams, and forests provided more stable food supplies than in regions such as the Great Basin. Larger and more concentrated populations grew. Permanent to semi-permanent villages were found along the coast. Because the sea and land provided so many of their needs, tribes of the area did not rely as much on agriculture but remained tied mainly to a hunter-gatherer existence.

Inuit (Eskimo) and Aleut peoples in the Arctic and Subarctic hunted sea mammals such as seals and whales. Further east and south, in the upper regions of present-day Canada, Inuits, Crees, and others pursued land animals such as caribou and moose. In Hawaii, settlement did not begin until the 300s when travelers from the Marquesas Islands reached the area.

THE CULTURES OF NATIVE PEOPLES

Generalizations about the rich and varied cultures of native groups at the time of contact with Europeans are difficult to make. However, two sets of ideas were of particular significance in the societies that inhabited the present United States before 1492.

One of the central principles of Indian life involved the importance of the community. Native peoples commonly based their notions of identity not on the isolated self but on the wider society. Extended family networks of kin and clan grounded a person both to the present world and to the past while also serving as the basis of social and political organization for all. The distinctive patterns of 'reciprocity' that most cultures displayed reinforced a sense of connection and interdependence within the group. Methods of discipline that focused on 'shaming' also emphasized the responsibilities and expectations that individuals owed to the larger society. Ideals of order and equilibrium revealed a commitment to preserve balance among the different elements of the group. And concepts about the communal 'ownership' of land pointed to a belief that nature's resources were meant to serve many, not just the few.

A second informing principle of native life was the importance of religion. Indians held that the world was alive with spirit. Spiritual powers were, in part, external, contained in creative, directive, ancestral, and guardian forces outside the tribe. Spiritual powers were also, in part, internal, developed by a person's reflection and vision and enhanced by their balance with the world. But such powers were also, in part, mutual, composed of the *collective* spirituality of a people. Because spirit suffused the world, even the most mundane features of experience could take on extraordinary meaning. Native folk often associated the different directions of the landscape with particular values; the form of the circle commonly assumed special spiritual significance; for the Hopi, the colors of corn kernels expressed guiding principles of life.

The universe of native peoples was filled with many gods rather than one god. The gods that a tribe honored were tied in a unique way to the particular group. As a result, a tribe did not see its particular religion as 'universal', applying to all peoples, at all times, in all places. Instead, their religious understanding applied to one people, in one place, at one time.

Indians north of the Rio Grande did not have written languages;

they did not study 'scripture'; they did not invoke sacred texts. Instead, they preserved their traditions through an oral culture. The spoken word rather than the written word conveyed the core of a tribe's beliefs. In such a world, the elders of a society usually received exceptional respect and deference on religious matters. Their age, experience, and memory kept a people's truths and traditions alive.

Religious life also revolved around a wide variety of rituals. The stages of life, the seasons of the year, or the cycles of economic activity were all appropriate occasions for spiritually significant ceremonies. *Shamans*, the spiritually endowed members of a society, commonly led such events. Through its rites and observances, a tribe might invoke aid, offer thanks, placate gods, seek counsel, eliminate evil, repair relationships, or restore equilibrium. Its rituals might include prayers, songs, dances, stories, and costumes. In all of these forms, religious life was largely a matter of enactment and performance, witnessed or realized by the group, as part of the regular rounds of daily life.

Although rich, evocative, and meaningful for native societies, most Europeans viewed Indian spirituality as anything but 'religious'. The animistic, polytheistic character of native beliefs only demonstrated the natives' 'pagan' qualities. The absence of God's *written* word testified to the 'backward' character of Indian religion. But matters of faith formed only one of many areas of conflict that would emerge when native and European cultures confronted one another.

European Voyages of Discovery

The land and peoples of North and South America remained unknown to Europeans. Around AD 1000, Scandinavian explorers under Leif Ericsson established 'Vinland', a settlement on modern-day New-foundland. But the outpost did not last long, and news of the discovery spread to only a handful of communities. For five centuries, Europeans continued to speculate on what lay west of their homelands across the sea.

After 1450, Europeans inspired by the pursuit of profits and piety began to explore and colonize a world that was 'new' to them. A rising commercial fever set off a search for new, fast, and efficient trading routes to Asia. Missionary zeal within the Church of Rome – and, after 1517, its competition for all souls with dissenting, Protestant churches – led the faithful to seek a greater spiritual glory in the Western Hemisphere. Several other trends heightened worldly and other-worldly desires: the rise of nation-states that enjoyed centralized authority, military might, and capital; their expanding populations in a healthier Europe a century after the Black Death; their quest for wealth and power (to accumulate for themselves and to deny to others); and their willingness to tap into new humanist studies and the latest navigational technologies.

Commercially, all the buzz in Europe involved trade routes to Asia – people really seemed to like those silks, spices, and precious stones from the East. But there were some problems concerning the movement of goods. The trade was mainly overland; the travel was long and expensive; Arabic Muslims controlled the routes; and, in 1453, a key link in the trade, Constantinople, fell to the Ottomans. The challenge facing Europeans in the fifteenth century was one that shoppers still mull over today: how to keep prices down by cutting out the middleman.

The Portuguese came up with one answer. Instead of heading east across land, Prince Henry the Navigator thought it made more sense to go south, *then* east – and travel across water. Having already created contacts in West Africa dealing in the trade of natural and human resources, the Portuguese moved further down the coast. By the late 1480s, Bartholomew Diaz reached the southern tip of Africa. By the turn of the century, Vasco Da Gama led traders across to India. Later, the Portuguese established trade centers in Indonesia, Japan, and China.

SPANISH EXPLORATION AND COLONIZATION

The Spanish, on the other hand, looked west, taking a chance on the theories of a sailor from Genoa, Christopher Columbus. By his reckoning, a 4,200 mile voyage west from Spain would take him to the Indies. Backed by Spain's monarchs, Ferdinand and Isabella, Columbus's three vessels set sail in August 1492. In two months, he landed on a Bahamian island, named it San Salvador, and called the inhabitants 'Indians'. Columbus explored other Caribbean islands, packed up gold objects, and returned to Spain to report on his findings. Three more voyages took him back to a region that, he insisted up to his dying day, was simply eastern Asia. He guessed wrong about that. A German geographer in the early sixteenth century also guessed wrong about which European first set foot on western territories. In a 1507 book, he identified another Italian explorer, Amerigo Vespucci, as the discoverer and named the new land 'America' in his honor.

Spanish monarchs, however, guessed right. Columbus's Caribbean discoveries opened the door to a hemisphere which, except for Portuguese claims in Brazil, Spain kept all to itself up to the start of the seventeenth century. The Spanish claimed lands in Central and South America and, later, in North America. They brought with them the armed power of the military, the spiritual power of missionaries, and the bureaucratic power of the state. In the early 1520s, forces commanded by Hernando Cortés conquered the Aztecs. Moving to the southeast, Spanish troops defeated the Mayans. By the early 1530s, Francisco Pizarro had advanced to South America and subjugated the Incan peoples. To supplement their labor force, the Spanish (and Portuguese) brought over 100,000 African slaves to the New World colonies by the end of the century.

Spain's victories in the Americas did not come from the size of its military forces. Of greater importance were the weapons soldiers bore, the horses they rode, the unity they displayed, and – most destructive of all – the diseases they carried. Smallpox, influenza, and measles decimated native peoples who had not built up immunities to the deadly microbes carried by Europeans. Estimates vary widely, but many historians believe that 50 per cent to 90 per cent of the natives who came in contact with European diseases died as a result of their exposure. Roughly 20 million people lived in Central America in 1519 on the eve of the invasion by Cortés; by 1650, the native population stood at only 2–3 million. The most powerful weapon European colonizers wielded was one they did not even know they possessed.

Spanish interest focused on lands south of the Rio Grande River, although explorers drawn by legends of immortality and wealth also ventured into other North American areas. At the time, the land that would become the United States showed little promise. Ponce de Léon

Interior of slave ship

explored Florida in 1515 and 1521 searching for a fountain of youth. From 1539–1542, Hernando de Soto wandered through the southeast from Tampa Bay to North Carolina to Arkansas looking for another Aztec empire. In 1565, the military post at St. Augustine in Florida became the first permanent settlement in the future United States. But Spanish interest remained focused on the West. In the early 1540s, Francisco Vásquez de Coronado explored Arizona, New Mexico, Colorado, and the edges of the Great Plains looking for a fabled city of gold. Missionaries accompanied military forces under Juan de Oñate into New Mexico in 1598 in a search for gold, silver, and souls. The city of Santa Fe became the center of government in the royal province in 1610. In the last two decades of the seventeenth century, Pueblo peoples of the region rose in rebellion against Spanish rule; colonial forces finally subdued their resistance in 1696. In the last third of the eighteenth century, Spanish military and religious power expanded along California's Pacific coast. Authorities constructed a series of military outposts starting in San Diego. Under the direction of a friar, Junipero Serra, Franciscans built 21 missions in places such as San Gabriel, Santa Barbara, Santa Cruz, and San Francisco. The largest settlement was a town named Los Angeles, founded in 1781, which boasted a few hundred inhabitants by 1800.

The natural riches that conquerors extracted through the labor of Central and South American peoples made Spain the wealthiest nation in Europe in the sixteenth century and the leader of the largest empire since Rome. The good fortune eventually turned bad, however. The influx of precious metals into Europe created an inflationary 'price revolution'. Spain's economy did not continue to grow and diversify. And political and military leaders engaged in an expensive series of wars against Protestant heretics in northern Europe that ate up much of the empire's revenue. Competition for colonies in North America heated up by the early seventeenth century.

FRENCH AND DUTCH VENTURES

Making their own attempt to find that elusive shortcut to Asia, the French commissioned a voyage of exploration in 1524 under the direction of Giovanni da Verrazano. The captain's travels took him along the Atlantic coast from the Carolinas up to Maine. Jacques Cartier's voyages in the 1530s and 1540s went further north to the Gulf of St. Lawrence. From there, Cartier ventured up the St. Lawrence River to Montréal. But it was not until 1608 that Samuel de Champlain founded his nation's first permanent North American settlement, Québec. Another 65 years passed before a Jesuit (Jacques Marquette) and a trader (Louis Joliet) pushed west from Québec and traveled down the Mississippi in 1673. Robert Cavelier, Sieur de La Salle, arrived at the river's mouth in 1682 and claimed the region of 'Louisiana' for France. In 1718, the French founded the city of New Orleans.

The French based their economic pursuits on the fur trade. For that purpose, trappers and traders penetrated deep into the interior of North America instead of remaining along the coasts. Since their numbers were small and state support remained limited, it made sense to stay on good terms with native peoples. Besides, the French were not grabbing land to build agricultural settlements. They were after pelts and needed the help of Indian tribes to gather furs from the area. Jesuit priests who accompanied traders also sought souls. Unlike Spanish Franciscans, the Jesuits tended to show greater respect toward the spirituality of the region's inhabitants and tried to discover common ground between Catholic doctrine and native practice.

Unencumbered by theological debate, Dutch colonization in the seventeenth century was a simpler matter of worldly pursuits revolving around the fur trade. An employee of the Dutch East India Company, Henry Hudson, sailed up the river that now bears his name in 1609 in yet another effort to find a passage to Asia. The Dutch built trading posts and by 1624, established the first permanent settlement at the mouth of the river, where New York City stands today. Two years later, Peter Minuit bought Manhattan Island from local Indians and christened the settlement 'New Amsterdam'. The village quickly attracted a diverse group of nationalities, religions, and races, most of whom were on the make for quick riches, a proud tradition that continued after the English took control of the settlement in 1664 and renamed it 'New York'.

ENGLISH EXPLORATION AND COLONIZATION

Like his monarch neighbors to the south in Spain, King Henry VII also turned to a Genoan navigator, Giovanni Caboto (John Cabot), to find a faster western route to the markets of the Far East. Like Columbus, Caboto was convinced that his 1497 voyage to Newfoundland and Nova Scotia placed him on the eastern fringes of Asia. Unlike Columbus, Caboto's luck ran out on a subsequent excursion; he was never heard from again. And unlike Spain, England did not follow up on the discovery and claims.

Political and religious divisions stalled England's ventures in the New World for over eight decades. Queen Elizabeth came to recognize that America provided a land from which the crown might extract great wealth, to which merchants might sell their goods, and on which the nation might project its Protestant aspirations against Catholic rivals. After 1565, the English also had the lessons of Irish 'plantations' to go on in developing new lands. The experience taught that colonizers should subdue native 'savages', appropriate their land, separate English settlements from the local populations, and suppress any resistance movements. Veterans of the Irish conquests led Sir Walter Raleigh's colonial venture off the Carolina coast on Roanoke Island in 1585. Friction with Indians and failure with mining caused the effort to fail in 1586. Raleigh tried again in 1587. When the crew of a supply ship returned in 1590, they found that the Roanoke settlement had been deserted; its more than 100 colonists were never seen again.

After a series of failures in the last quarter of the sixteenth century, the English finally gained a foothold in North America early in the seventeenth century. The project did not result from government intervention, state supervision, or military domination; the first colony to succeed relied on that principle of progress revered in American lore: private enterprise. The agency that launched the first permanent English colony was a joint stock company, created by businessmen who sold shares to investors hoping to cash in on the next great growth market, the New World. In 1606, King James I granted a charter to the Virginia Company. Its London division oversaw colonies in the southern reaches of North America; the Plymouth division took care of northern territories.

The promoters in Plymouth had little luck in getting a venture going in the new lands. But the London group managed to organize a project in the southern Chesapeake Bay, on a waterway named the James River, in a community called Jamestown, in the year 1607. Year after year, the settlement looked as if it would fail. Colonists found neither precious metals nor a northwest passage to the Indies nor instant wealth for the profit-hungry investors back in England. Food supplies remained low and spirits sagged as malaria spread and conflicts with native tribes grew. In the period 1610–1620, settlers hit on tobacco as a promising cash crop, secured the right to own land in the settlement, and even gained self-government through a representative assembly named the House of Burgesses. But workers remained in short supply, and colonists turned increasingly to indentured servants and even small numbers of slaves to expand the workforce. After a decade and a half of tinkering, the Virginia Company had still failed to make a profit, the business collapsed, and in 1624 the 'corporate' colony became a 'royal' colony.

Just to the north, the crown created a 'proprietary' colony in 1632. King Charles I granted a charter to the first Lord Baltimore, Sir George Calvert, whose family took personal possession of 'Maryland'. The colony offered a refuge for Calvert's fellow Catholics and provided a model of a medieval, manorial society built around large estates worked by tenant farmers. As in Virginia, however, almost nothing worked as planned. The Protestant population soared, and Catholics found themselves once again in the minority. And in a world of limited labor and unlimited land, a manorial system proved hard to duplicate. Hardly the stable haven its founders intended, Maryland became an economically and politically competitive center of settlement in the Chesapeake, drawing in thousands of servants and, later, African slaves.

Another group of religious outsiders from England landed in America in 1620. This time, the settlers were not Catholics but Protestants, a group of 'Pilgrim' dissenters who chose to separate from the Church of England rather than stay within a faith whose doctrines, rituals, and hierarchy smacked too much of that of Rome. Although intending 'to plant the first colony in the northern Parts of Virginia', their ship, the *Mayflower*, took them 200 miles off course, landing in Massachusetts Bay in a place named Plymouth. Because they were outside the area controlled by the Virginia Company, the settlers created their own rules for life in English America. In the 'Mayflower

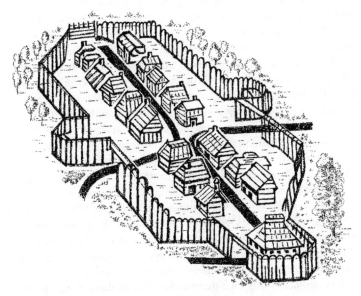

The 1627 Pilgrim village

Compact', the adult males in the community agreed to 'covenant and combine ourselves together into a civil Body Politick, for our better Ordering and Protection', promising 'all due Submission and Obedience'. Good order was all the more important because, as their political leader William Bradford explained, the Pilgrims lived in 'a hideous and desolate wilderness, full of wild beasts and wild men'. Besides, the settlers saw themselves as part of a divine project to purify religion; nothing less than perfection would do.

The Pilgrims were soon joined in Massachusetts by another, more ambitious group of church reformers who came up with their own design for living. These 'Puritans' were mainly Congregationalists who had not yet given up on the Church of England and planned to cleanse it from within – though at a distance of 3,000 miles. More worldly-wise than the Pilgrims, the new arrivals organized themselves into the Massachusetts Bay Company in 1629 and began arriving in America the following year. Their corporate charter gradually evolved into their structure of government, suggesting the importance of economic calculation even in spiritual ventures. The Puritans were not averse to success; after all, whether one was a farmer or a financier, it was important for individuals to pursue the 'calling' into which God had placed them. Besides, the settlers in Massachusetts Bay not only had a calling; they also saw themselves as 'covenanted', on special terms with a God who wanted them to change the course of earthly *and* redemptive history. They were to establish a harmonious, Christian community for themselves, resist Satan's wiles, and restore the church to its original state of 'primitive' purity. Theirs was no ordinary colony but a 'holy commonwealth'. While recognizing individual differences, social ranks, private property, and local autonomy, leaders urged settlers to remember their communal existence, their common commitments, and their collective interests. Nothing pleased their God more than unity. He wanted his covenantees to avoid contention, resist division, and live as one. Governor John Winthrop declared that they stood 'as a Citty upon a Hill', convinced that 'the eyes of all people are uppon us'. Massachusetts Bay's colonists thus became the first Americans to proclaim their special sense of mission and to identify themselves as part of a redeemer nation that would serve as a model for the whole world.

That meant the 'contrary-minded' need not apply. Puritans wanted religious freedom for themselves to do as their God presumably saw fit – but not religious freedom for everyone. The world was filled with all kinds of cock-eyed doctrines. If false prophets gained a foothold in Massachusetts Bay, the most important spiritual cause since the Reformation would go down to defeat. In 1635, officials banished Roger Williams, who dissented from the dissenters by insisting on a complete separation of church and state (in order to protect pure congregations from the impurities of politics). In 1637, Anne Hutchinson went on trial, technically for claiming that she was in personal union with the Holy Spirit, practically for claiming that a woman could defy male religious authorities. And in the 1680s and early 1690s, hysteria over witchcraft spread in Puritan communities, reaching a peak in Salem, Massachusetts, where tribunals accused over 100 people (mostly older women) and executed 20.

Puritans fanned out from Massachusetts Bay to other areas of the region called 'New England'. Some traveled to Connecticut, others to New Hampshire and Maine. Williams helped create Rhode Island which, for a time, was the only colony that granted religious toleration to all faiths. The most radical of the 'purifying' groups, the Quakers, left England to take up residence in another proprietary settlement in the Middle Atlantic region. In 1681, King Charles II granted over 45,000 square miles of land to William Penn, a leading English Quaker. The King's grant helped satisfy a debt to Penn's father and also helped rid the realm of a troublesome sect. The Quakers' challenges to social deference and hierarchical authority – along with their bizarre talk of the believer's 'inner light' and the spiritual equality of women – made them a clear and present danger to the stability of English life. Better, King Charles felt, to let them carry on an ocean away. Penn's 'holy experiment' sought to apply Quaker principles to everyday life, creating a world that shielded people from the arbitrary power of government, served their varied needs, and even tried to create peaceful relations with Indians. In the end, the colony of Pennsylvania was more of an economic than a theological success, attracting a wide diversity of settlers who, by 1701, created a form of government that even checked the power of the Penn family itself.

Charles II's generous land grants also extended to Carolina. Founded in 1663, its proprietors concocted an ambitious design for the colony in 1669. Anthony Ashley Cooper and his talented assistant, John Locke, wrote up the 'Fundamental Constitutions of Carolina'. As in Maryland, the Carolina proprietors wanted the New World to look a lot like the Old by creating landed estates, titled noblemen, fixed ranks, and a deferential society. But, again like Maryland, the experiment in neo-feudalism fell apart in the turbulence of a competitive commercial world. By 1729, Carolina had split into two parts.

In 1664, Charles II treated his brother James, the Duke of York, to a grant of American land. In the midst of a war with the Dutch, a small English fleet seized New Netherlands and made the colony part of a larger piece of real estate renamed New York. The new owner encouraged Dutch settlers to stay, sponsored emigration from England, and, by the end of the seventeenth century, rewarded political supporters in New York with huge estates that would serve as the basis of yet another manorial society. James eventually lopped off two portions of his property, giving New Jersey to a pair of proprietors in 1664 and Delaware to William Penn in 1682.

One other colony on the Atlantic coast, Georgia, founded in 1733, had a history unlike that of other English settlements. Rather than responding to the political designs of the crown, the personal ambitions of nobles, the financial dreams of investors, or the spiritual hopes of religious outsiders, Georgia was to provide for the economic needs of the poor. General James Oglethorpe and the other trustees who held George II's charter intended to create a refuge for debtors. They planned a settlement based on relatively small land holdings, worked by free labor and indentured servants. The population would be kept sober by limits on alcohol, kept diligent by a ban on slavery, kept peaceful by excluding blacks and Catholics, and kept useful by serving as a buffer against Spanish Florida. The experiment in social reform failed, however. Few debtors showed up in Georgia. Those who did settle in the colony would not agree to restrictions on landholding, slaveholding, and rum drinking, so by the middle of the eighteenth century, the whole project reverted to royal control.

Social and Economic Conditions in the English Colonies

The population of the English settlements in America grew slowly but steadily, from 2,000 colonists in 1625, to 50,000 by 1650, to a quarter of a million by 1700. By that time, Virginia and Massachusetts were the largest of the English colonies, accounting for nearly half the population. Another third of the colonists lived in Maryland, Connecticut, New York, and Pennsylvania. Compact towns served as the basic unit of settlement in New England, dispersed counties in the South; Mid-Atlantic colonies combined concentrated and scattered populations.

The basic material conditions that settlers faced were simple enough to understand. Land was cheap and plentiful. Labor was in short supply. And capital was scarce. So much soil to cultivate; so few workers available; so little money to cover costs. It all posed quite a set of dilemmas. New Englanders had to deal with comparatively thin and rocky soils whose fertility gave out fairly soon under the colonists' exhaustive land practices. Large-scale agriculture was not the norm in the area; smaller farms were far more common, most often worked by the labor of the large families typical of the region. Fishing, lumbering, furs, and naval stores provided other types of livelihood in New England's diverse economy along with shipping, ship-building, milling, crafts, and commerce. The region's trading system connected New England not only to the home country, but also to important English customers in the Caribbean sugar islands.

At first, Maryland, Virginia, Carolina, and Georgia were unhealthy and downright dangerous places for Europeans. The hard work, stern conditions, and shorter life expectancy initially kept the South's population both limited and predominantly male. The area's land and climate were suited, however, to large-scale agriculture, particularly in the production of tobacco and rice. Taken together, environmental and economic conditions led to another set of choices that would have far-reaching effects both for the colonies and for the future nation.

Unable to attract sufficient numbers of free laborers, the first colonies in the South around the Chesapeake Bay quickly became dependent on unfree labor. The chief source of the workers was England, which provided 'indentured servants' for the region. Under this system, young men (and, to a lesser degree, women) between 15 and 25 with limited opportunities in their home country gained passage to America by agreeing to sell their labor for a period of four to seven years. Their contract, or indenture, was held by a master who put them to work, provided some basic necessities, and, at the end of the contract period, often provided an ex-servant with a small piece of land, a farm animal, tools, or some other form of 'freedom dues'. Servitude was difficult, rigorous, and demanding; but it was a choice many young people decided to make to better their condition or simply to change the circumstances of their lives. Three-quarters to four-fifths of those who came to the Chesapeake arrived as indentured servants. All told, half of the European immigrants to American colonies were bound laborers.

By the last quarter of the seventeenth century, however, several trends reshaped the face of labor in the Chesapeake – and eventually reordered American society for all time. First, property owners in Southern colonies increasingly consolidated their lands into larger estates requiring more workers. Secondly, prices for their key cash crop, tobacco, dropped in the 1660s and stayed low, encouraging cost-cutting measures. Thirdly, the pool of indentured servants declined as the rate of population increase in England slowed and economic opportunities improved. Fourthly, the laws of Virginia and other colonies began to undermine the status of blacks and to institutionalize the system of chattel slavery. Free blacks started to find their civil, legal, and property rights constrained; whites could extend the period of 'service' they might exact from black servants; longer service soon became unlimited service; and the offspring of black female slaves began to inherit their mother's status. Fifthly, the Royal African Company's monopoly on the slave trade came to an end in 1697, expanding the supply of slaves (and the number of slave-trading businesses) in the marketplace. Sixthly, racist assumptions about the inferiority of dark-skinned people reinforced the readiness (and willingness) of whites to enslave blacks.

Looking in cold, hard, economic terms at the choices available to them, more whites began to prefer slaves to servants as the long-term answer to their labor needs. Slaves cost more to begin with, but over time the expense of a slave labor force was low. As health conditions in Southern colonies improved, the number of years a master could get out of a slave increased. Rather than dealing with temporary workers, masters could now have a permanent work force. Slaves were also controllable, subject to the rule (and punishment) of white owners. And slaves formed a self-reproducing labor force since masters owned the children of slave mothers.

At first, the Portuguese and Spanish dominated the slave trade in the New World. Later, the Dutch entered the system along with the English and the French. In the grisly game of human commerce, Africans supplied the traders with other Africans in exchange for goods produced in Europe. Most of the captives came from the west coast of Africa, out of a wide range of cultures, political units, religions, languages, and family systems from Angola up to Senegambia.

Ships carried their shackled cargo across 5,000 miles of the 'Middle Passage' from Africa to the Americas. Captains packed 100, 200, or more slaves into horribly small, cramped spaces for the voyages. Up to a fifth of the slaves died *en route* to buyers in the West. From the early 1500s to the mid 1800s, European traders forcibly removed 10–12 million Africans from their homelands. By the later eighteenth century, the largest group to arrive in the colonies of North and South America were Africans, not Europeans.

Of those transported to the Western Hemisphere, 80 per cent were taken to the West Indies and Brazil. A small fraction (4–5 per cent of the total) entered what would become the United States. Most of those slaves were sold to Southern masters who generally put them to work in tobacco or rice fields. The Chesapeake's tobacco-producing areas were comparatively healthier by the later 1600s and the labor less excruciating than rice production. Masters often purchased females and created more of a gender balance in the slave population, providing a measure of solace for blacks who could *try* to recreate some semblance of the family life from which they had been torn. There was something in it for whites as well: the offspring of sexual unions with female slaves (whether the father was black *or* white) added to the master's 'property holdings'. In Carolina rice fields, both the labor and the environment were harsher, life expectancy was shorter, and female slaves were less common. Plantations in the deep South were deadlier and more brutal than those in the upper South.

The total number of slaves in the American colonies was approximately 7,000 in 1680; 3,000 were held in Virginia alone. By 1700, the number more than tripled to 25,000, or 20 per cent of the population of the South. The general figures, however, mask the large concentrations of slaves in some areas. For example, in 1720, blacks formed 70 per cent of the population in South Carolina. Blacks also formed the majority of the population in the river settlements of Virginia where Europeans had first settled 100 years earlier.

Slavery existed in all the English colonies of America. The highest demand for slave labor was in the South, the lowest in New England. Middle Atlantic colonies, with soils and growing conditions that favored larger-scale grain production than the Northeast, had nearly twice as many slaves as New England (and, earlier, more indentured servants). But New York, Pennsylvania, New Jersey, and Delaware had more diverse economies than the South with greater levels of commerce and small-scale manufacturing. Their slave populations were small compared to colonies from Maryland down to Georgia.

The Middle Atlantic region stood apart in other ways. It was home to the thriving urban centers of Philadelphia and New York which, by the later 1700s, surpassed Boston as the largest cities in America. The middle colonies also attracted the most diverse ethnic mix from Europe with English, Irish, Scots, Scots-Irish, Welsh, German, Dutch, French, Swiss, Norwegian, Swedish, and Finnish settlers. And one middle colony, Pennsylvania, even followed what, for the time, was a remarkable policy towards Indians: William Penn assumed that the land was theirs.

During Penn's leadership of the colony, Pennsylvanians and native peoples did not war with one another. Some Indians, such as the Tuscarora and Shawnees, even came to Pennsylvania to avoid confrontations with more belligerent settlers in other colonies. Penn held that native groups had to receive compensation for the fields and forests whites wanted to claim. His government supervised other relations between settlers and Indians, including regulations on trade with native peoples. Unfortunately, once Penn left power, the European immigrants attracted to his colony proved much more willing to resort to coercive measures against Indians.

The conflicts that erupted later in Pennsylvania's history generally occurred earlier in the settlement of other colonies. Some of the most brutal struggles between whites and Indians took place in 1675 and 1676. In New England, Wampanoag Indians led by Metacom (named 'King Philip' by Europeans) struck in mid-1675 at colonists who had deprived them of tribal lands. During 'King Philip's War', Metacom's forces attacked more than half of the Puritan towns. Four thousand died in fighting that lasted until Metacom's death in the late summer of 1676.

At the same time in Virginia, frontiersmen led by Nathaniel Bacon pressed for control of more land by launching attacks on Indians. The governor of the colony, William Berkeley, tried to prevent widespread warfare with native tribes, especially those with whom the government had come to terms. Bacon's supporters had no sympathy with colonial authorities who seemed unresponsive to the needs of people on the frontier. His forces continued their assaults on local tribes. 'Bacon's Rebellion' even led to an attack by frontiersmen on Jamestown. But following Bacon's death in the fall of 1676, the uprising came to an end.

Four decades later, in Carolina, another struggle broke out over issues tied to trade. Yamasee, Creek, and Choctaw tribes infuriated with the fraud, deceit, and brutality of white traders, organized attacks that drove Carolinians from inland settlements back to the Atlantic coast. The 'Yamasee War' ended after colonists entered into an alliance with the Cherokee, long-standing rivals of the Creeks. Playing Indians against Indians, whites managed to end another challenge by native peoples.

By the later 1600s, the English had learned that the real profits in the Western Hemisphere came from their holdings in the Caribbean which produced sugar for an increasingly sweet-toothed world. Areas further north along the Atlantic coast of North America paled in comparison. It would take some time before their importance to the empire became clear.

For the moment, the English had to make do with colonies on the mainland that were unlike those established by imperial rivals. English

America did not provide rich deposits of mineral wealth. Rather than a small population of *conquistadores* and traders, the colonies filled with settlers who made a permanent home in the New World. Taking to farming, they often fought with native peoples over the control of land. Settlers who already had families or who found other white companions usually did not mix sexually or socially with Indians. Colonists generally saw tribal members as savages to be subdued and obstacles to be removed.

Geographically, most settlers remained along the coast rather than moving far into the interior. Religiously, many not only remained apart from the established church of the home country but were downright hostile towards it. Politically, the government in London intervened little in local affairs since the colonies were generally decentralized ventures rather than carefully coordinated state projects. Economically, while many settlers enjoyed the freedom of lax government control, most colonists came to America bound to the service of others.

Some colonial projects, such as those in Maryland and Carolina, began as efforts to recreate the conditions of the Old World in the New. Other ventures, such as Rhode Island, Pennsylvania, and Georgia, began as efforts to build a new order in a new land. Everywhere, initial designs failed and colonies eventually took unexpected forms. Many settlers retained a strong sense of the mythic, epic quality of their lives. They believed that their history in America was exceptional and that their experience would hold meaning for all people.

CHAPTER TWO

Colonial America,
1700–1775

For the first three-quarters of the eighteenth century, colonists were loyal subjects of crown and Parliament, although they were rarely subject to the government's close scrutiny. They were ever more important to the Empire's prosperity, but they were never more cavalier about their commercial obligations. The colonists' basic traditions were formed largely by their nominal home country, yet their ways of life were changed steadily by their actual homeland. The colonial settlements were solidly 'British', converging with the expectations of leaders in London, but at the same time increasingly 'American', diverging from the paths and programs established 3,000 miles away.

Colonial life from 1700 to 1775 had a distinctly dual character. In society, politics, and the market, colonists blended British principles with American practice. The combination was subtle, sometimes scarcely obvious, and far from deliberate, resulting from haphazard twists of experience. The mixture hardly warranted anything as extreme as separation from the Empire. When the break did occur in 1775, it came only after a dramatic change in imperial policy that the British deemed essential and the Americans found unbearable. Up to that point, the colonies proved stable and successful, contributing what Britain wanted most: imperial wealth and power.

Colonial Society in the Eighteenth Century

Officials assumed that the American colonies would produce an expanding society modeled on British lines. They turned out to be half right. While the numbers of colonists increased dramatically, the character of American society departed from British expectations.

Perhaps the most striking feature of American life in the eighteenth century was the rapid rise of its population. From 250,000 people in 1700, colonial society grew to 2.5 million by 1775. The absolute numbers were lower than England's seven million, but the rate of growth was far higher: every generation, the American population doubled. Natural increase, continued immigration, and steadily lower mortality rates all contributed to the rise. Over time, the American environment had become more hospitable and healthy – for white settlers. For blacks, free and enslaved, mortality rates remained higher. For Indians, a native land increasingly occupied by Europeans only became more threatening, both in territorial and epidemiological terms. Their population, perhaps as high as 12 million before contact, shrank to under one million by the end of the eighteenth century.

In terms of settlement, the population that expanded along the Atlantic coast was overwhelmingly rural rather than urban. In terms of age, it was unusually young, and in terms of background, it was, indeed, English – but only barely. At the start of the century, most colonists were transplanted Englishmen; by mid-century, a slim majority traced their origins to that land. Most of those who arrived in America between 1700 and 1775 were African, Scots-Irish, German, Irish, and Scottish. The profile of the colonial population differed significantly from English society. By the end of the century, less than one out of every two Americans had English roots; one out of every five was of African heritage. The colonies were home to a multi-ethnic and multi-racial society quite unlike that of England.

Another difference lay in the basic codes that organized social life. Patterns of deference, rank, and subordination were difficult to duplicate in the colonies. Americans today might think it absurd that anyone could even imagine such a social order emerging in their land, but to colonists accustomed to servitude, obedience to masters, and submission to superiors, the possibility was not entirely off the mark in the eighteenth century. In addition, the disparity of income between rich and poor grew sharper in colonial cities. Yet a rigid, titled class system did not develop throughout the colonies. Exceptional wealth and exceptional poverty certainly existed but not to the same degree as in England. Most Americans fell in between the two extremes. Nearly three-quarters of the colonists were part of a vast 'middling' order, compared to a third of Englishmen. Per capita income in America kept growing even as the population expanded, land remained affordable and available, and colonists enjoyed a higher standard of living than most European societies of the time. In other words, many factors worked against the type of hierarchies common in Europe. Commentators were repeatedly struck not by stark social divisions but by the general equality they saw around them in the colonies.

Of course, the 'equality' they noted was relative, not absolute. Compared to Europe, America seemed a level field, but examined on its own terms, the colonies' social terrain was rough, jagged, and uneven. One in five human beings was a slave. Half of all immigrants came to the colonies in some state of labor bondage. Half the population occupied a permanently subordinate status based on gender with few legal, property, or political rights. In New England, a rising proportion of the population became landless by the 1700s. And a homegrown aristocracy evolved in Southern colonies, fashioning itself on a 'cavalier' tradition. Yet, while the region's planter elite may have come closest to traditional social models, its power and prestige derived more from the control of labor than the ownership of land. Speculation in real estate remained a lively sport, and the families that occupied its ranks moved in and out of their elevated position in a fairly steady stream.

Colonial Politics in the Eighteenth Century

Just as colonial society borrowed and departed from British norms, so did their political system. Outwardly, the shape of colonial politics seemed to be the mirror image of that of Britain, but on closer inspection, the *practice* of colonial politics was a world apart.

British leaders assumed that the colonies' political system would be a scaled-down reproduction of the system in the home country. That meant that a 'mixed' or 'balanced' model of government would operate in the colonies. And that meant that the colonies would create a political system incorporating all social orders and combining different forms of governance. As in Britain, colonists would presumably build little replicas of monarchic, aristocratic, and democratic power. Again, to modern ears, the idea may sound odd, but in fact that is what happened. Most colonial governments were composed of three basic institutions: a governor, usually appointed, who theoretically stood at the top of the heap as a kind of quasi-king; an upper house or advisory council, usually appointed, which acted as an American equivalent to the House of Lords; and a lower house or representative assembly, popularly elected, which served as the local version of the democratic House of Commons, making law and levying taxes.

Of course, the British viewed all of this as a rough analogy; colonists, they assumed, could easily work out that their neighborhood legislature did not have the same standing as Parliament. The colonists merely *copied* (rather than shared in) the power arrangements based in London. Sovereignty, or ultimate authority, only resided in that impressive palace in Westminster, not in some small building in Boston or

A view of Fort George with the city of New York
(After an engraving by Carwithan *c.* 1730)

Philadelphia. With that understanding in mind (at least, in the British mind), officials confidently left day-to-day decision making in the hands of colonial governments. King and Parliament had more important things to do than micro-manage the relatively insignificant American colonies. A policy of benign neglect 'governed' the settlements for much of the 1700s. Colonists enjoyed a large measure of self-rule, London interfered as little as possible, and the Empire reaped the economic rewards of its stable and expanding possessions.

Colonists obliged leaders in London to a great degree. Americans cherished their English political heritage, valued the traditional rights they held, and admired the magnificent operation of a mixed constitution. They took pride in their ties to the Western world's mightiest imperial order, knowing first hand how that helped to keep French and Spanish rivals at bay. And they loudly proclaimed loyalty to the king, raised toasts to his name, and defended his royal interests.

Unfortunately, political realities had a way of undercutting political professions. The institutions of colonial government may have looked like lovingly crafted miniatures of King and Parliament, but they did not operate the same way. The offices could hardly reflect separate social orders since a rigidly structured hierarchy did not exist. Colonial governors were weak political figures who seldom had a base of popular support. They usually fought alone against provincial legislatures and rarely controlled the patronage rewards that could buy reliable political allies. Elected assemblies, on the other hand, were powerful and power-hungry, taking on legislative tasks with great gusto, dabbling in executive and judicial work whenever they could, and carrying on as if they did have a legitimate share in imperial sovereignty. All of these institutions sat atop a body politic that barely resembled that of the home country. Perhaps a quarter of English men could vote; but half to three-quarters of adult white males in the colonies exercised the franchise. Political participants were often non-English. And large numbers of voters traced their personal roots to a 'dissenter' heritage, linking them to groups that had long been power-conscious and suspicious of authority. With a wide, diverse, and wary electorate, colonial politics tended to be more competitive and turbulent than their English counterpart.

American politics were far from 'democratic'. The colonies may have had the broadest electorate in the world, but most people in the colonies were not eligible to vote. Almost all women and blacks were excluded from participation. High property requirements for office-holding even limited the access of most adult white males to the reins of political power. As a result, political leadership tended to be concentrated in the hands of a small elite. Colonists assumed early on that access to power was limited, but they also learned other lessons from their political experience. They took self-government as a given; they remained suspicious of distant, centralized authority, and they trusted more in local, representative power. Colonists inhabited a political world that was British in form and American in function.

Colonial Economics in the Eighteenth Century

Britain interfered little with the operation of government in America because it had another way to manage the colonies: trade. Regulation of commerce, rather than the domination of politics, served as the glue of empire. Britain was confident that colonists could perform their small but necessary political chores competently and faithfully. Meanwhile, the Empire could focus its attention on a larger goal: building riches and power.

Like its rivals, Britain created a 'mercantilist' system in which government managed the marketplace in order to generate wealth and strengthen the state. Colonies were a vital part of the system, serving specific interests of the home country. They provided raw materials that could not be produced at home, lessening Britain's dependence on other nations for important commodities. They acted as a market for British processed goods, helping to maintain employment (and political peace) in England. The colonies' supply and demand functions allowed the home country to enjoy a favorable balance of trade. As long as the value of exports exceeded imports, Britain continued to accumulate more capital. More capital meant more power. And more power meant a growing Empire. To achieve all of this, an elaborate set of regulations operated from the 1650s to the 1750s, restricting commerce to British vessels, specifying the route of valuable raw materials leaving the colonies, defining the flow of goods into the colonies, and placing duties on many transactions in order to channel trade. The whole arrangement was complicated but ultimately advantageous, from London's perspective, if it managed to keep most trade and wealth within the boundaries of the Empire and out of the hands of foreign competitors.

The American possessions lived up to British expectations. Colonists traded primarily with Britain. Americans sent most of their products to the home country, nearly doubling their exports from 1700 to 1770. They received almost all their processed goods from Britain, more than quadrupling the value of imports over the same seven decades. While most colonists were self-sufficient farmers, many sold commodities that could not be grown in the British Isles. Southern colonies supplied tobacco, rice, indigo, and naval stores. New England and Mid-Atlantic colonies offered lumber, fish, furs, and shipbuilding services to Britain and grains and livestock to the South and the West Indies. Mercantile policies offered advantages to the colonists, providing access to lucrative markets, guaranteed buyers for their products, a steady supply of finished goods, and the protection of the Royal Navy on the high seas. Perhaps the greatest benefit was that Britain did not rigidly enforce navigation laws. The home country directed its administrative attention where it paid off the most: in the lucrative sugar islands of the Caribbean. In comparison, Southern colonies were not as critical, and Northern colonies even less so.

Unfortunately, the fit was not perfect. The North's agricultural products were hardly exotic and often duplicated, rather than supplemented, production in the British Isles. New Englanders who turned from poor soils to try their hand at manufactures also ran the risk of competing with the home country. Parliament responded by restricting the manufacture or export of colonial iron, hats, and woolens. Tobacco planters in the Chesapeake faced a roller coaster ride of erratic pricing in the 1700s, a situation made worse by marketing that was almost entirely in the hands of Europeans. Planters responded by bringing more land into production, buying more slaves, and producing more tobacco, all of which tended to destabilize prices even further.

North or South, colonists faced a larger, and intractable, problem tied to mercantilism: as subordinates in the system, they got the short end of the stick. Money drained out of colonies that produced mainly raw materials and imported most finished goods. While Britain enjoyed a favorable balance of trade, the colonists' commercial scales tipped unfavorably. Gold and silver flowed to Britain, currency remained in short supply in America, and the colonists' bills continued to mount. To ease the problem, Americans made a spirited effort to evade even the most loosely enforced mercantile laws. They traded with other empires, purchased illegal goods, and avoided duties and imposts. The legacy of mercantilism was far from ennobling: it helped bolster proud, American economic traditions of indebtedness and smuggling.

Crèvecoeur's Question

The correspondence and contrast between British and American life was played out in the wider culture as well. Whether in the lofty realm of literature, architecture, and the law or the everyday world of language, place names, and consumer goods, connections to the home country permeated provincial life. Britain set the tone and established the standard for both elite and popular tastes in the colonies. Yet here, too, colonists began wandering along different paths, slowly, awkwardly, imperceptibly defining an alternative, American way.

Consider the religious experiences of colonists. With the exception of small numbers of Catholics and Jews in the colonies, Americans and Britons held a common spiritual heritage. Both expressed faith in a divine father, fear of damnation, and hope for saving grace. Both shared a Protestant tradition that defied rigid, ecclesiastical hierarchies and embraced Luther's principle of the priesthood of all believers. Both took guidance from the King James version of the Bible as the authoritative record of God's will. And both witnessed a rise of religious revivalism in the second quarter of the eighteenth century.

Despite these similarities, America was a very different religious world from Britain, starting with the Church of England itself. Anglicanism may have been the officially 'established' faith throughout the South and in many Northern counties, but it embraced only a minority of church members. Its operations were undermined in great part by Anglican authorities themselves who offered the church little administrative support in the colonies. If any churches were the 'norm' in America, they were those that broke from the Church of England; Presbyterians, Congregationalists, Baptists, and Quakers, were far more representative of the American church-going public. Their 'dogma' was dissent, or at least the dissenting tradition, which was long on protest and purification and short on submission and conformity. Even the fires of revivalism burned with a slightly different glow in America during the 1730s and 1740s. While inspired by such clerical celebrities as the English minister, George Whitfield, the long-term message of the colonists' Great Awakening was one that exalted challenges to religious convention and authority in the name of truth and purity. As some historians have argued, the intense spiritual debates of the Awakening may have accustomed Americans even more to a culture of confrontation, one which could easily spill over from religious to political questions. The colonists' conception of 'liberty' had taken on both a secular and an otherworldly cast.

Rev. George Whitfield (1769)

Whether in the lofty realm of the spirit or the mundane rhythms of daily life, there was something about the colonies that recalled – and recoiled from – the home country. One person who tried to define those qualities was a transplanted Frenchman named Michel-Guillaume-Jean de Crèvecoeur. In the 1770s, he began writing a series of papers on the character of American life. Published in 1782 as *Letters from an American Farmer*, one essay posed a straightforward but complex question: 'What then is the American, this new man?' Crèvecoeur answered:

> He is either a European, or a descendant of a European, hence that strange mixture of blood, which you will find in no other country ... *He* is an American, who, leaving behind him all his ancient prejudices and manners, receives new ones from the new mode of life he has embraced ... Americans are the western pilgrims, who are carrying along with them that great mass of arts, sciences, vigor, and industry which began long since in the east; they will finish the great circle.[1]

Americans shared in and departed from the patterns of European life. Not fully defined by an older world, not quite distinct in a new world, they blended the habits and values of the two. Crèvecoeur saw around him colonists in a curious relation to their home country.

Strains in the Bonds of Empire

Despite their puzzling character, it is difficult to discern any major problem or predicament faced by white American colonists in the middle of the 1700s. Yet by the third quarter of the century, they were in revolt. What could possibly have happened to make conditions that were so favorable become so galling? How could anyone fashion a revolution out of such good fortune?

The answer, in simplest terms, was that conditions did not remain the same: Britain altered the rules of colonial life and Americans could not abide the changes. In place of loose administration, Britain tightened the enforcement of colonial policies. Rather than holding the colonies together through commercial regulation, officials relied more on extensions of political authority. And instead of footing the bill for colonial operations, the Empire thought it was time for prosperous Americans to pay their own way.

To those in charge of colonial affairs, the changes seemed reasonable, fair, and necessary. To those on the receiving end, the changes appeared ill-conceived, malicious, and tyrannical. The British insisted they were not ruthless despots but responsible managers trying to bring order out of imperial chaos. The Americans insisted they were not fanatical hotheads but sincere conservatives preserving the traditional rights of Englishmen against government encroachment. Each party assumed an identity their opponent could not comprehend. Each side increasingly spoke non-sense to the other. After a decade of squabbling, patience and unity collapsed. Britain's reorganization of empire met first with American resistance and then open rebellion.

The Roots of Colonial Reorganization

Britain changed the rules of the imperial game for what it considered sound reasons: the Empire faced the sudden, unfamiliar, and confusing outbreak of peace. For more than 70 years, from 1689 to 1763, Britain had fought four major wars against its chief imperial rivals, France and Spain, demonstrating what fierce market competition can really be like. The last of these struggles, the French and Indian War, spanned nine years and four continents. It began, inauspiciously enough, on 4 July 1754, when an inexperienced militia officer from Virginia named George Washington surrendered to the French forces whose Ohio Valley expansion he had tried to stop. It ended, remarkably enough, with a 1763 peace treaty that dismantled France's empire, leaving it with only a few islands off Canada and in the Caribbean.

Britain may have enjoyed uncontested power in North America, but it was also saddled with a vast new territory to control, a large non-English population to govern, and a pile of debts to pay. The Empire now encompassed Canada and land west of the Appalachians. The French and Indian peoples who inhabited this territory had little experience – or sympathy – with British rule. The costs of running an enlarged imperial enterprise were high: a standing army of 10,000 men in the region soon ran to £400,000 annually. Unfortunately, the funds required for such projects were scarce. Britain's debt had nearly doubled during the war, standing at well over £130 million by 1763. The interest alone came to £4.5 million per year, almost half the peacetime budget. Residents of the British Isles were already overburdened with taxes and protested efforts to exact even more revenues from their pockets. Officials in London recognized that victory in North America came with a high price tag and a bundle of new political and financial problems.

Who better to turn to for a solution than the colonists themselves? The war was fought, in great part, to protect their lives and property. The removal of French power enhanced their security. The enlarged peacetime army safeguarded their interests. It was only fair that they should pay a share of imperial costs – especially in the light of their purported behavior during the war. British military officers complained that American soldiers were ineffective and undependable, that American legislators were tightwads reluctant to fund the fighting, and that American merchants were traitors who kept up a lively commerce with the enemy during the war. The laxity and haphazardness of past colonial policy had only jeopardized imperial interests. It was time for Britain to steer a more rigorous course.

Colonists, of course, had a much higher opinion of themselves and of their contributions to the military effort. Americans saw themselves as loyal subjects who made considerable sacrifices during the war. Having helped to defeat a common enemy, they felt deserving of Britain's deep gratitude, not its critical scrutiny. At the very least, colonists believed, the Empire ought to show compassion for the economic downturn that had hit America since 1760. An enlarged standing army in their midst hardly seemed like an appropriate response. With the French gone, what imperial threat would such a force suppress? Britain's defense policy appeared quite strange in the light of the Allies' great victory.

As if the divergent assumptions of the British and Americans were not difficult enough to handle, one other factor complicated colonial affairs: the rule of George III. Ascending the throne in 1760 at the age of 22, King George intended to lift British politics out of a morass of factionalism and corruption by taking a more active role in policy making. The result was not only greater initiative on the part of the crown but greater instability in government and leadership. Ministries changed frequently as individuals and policies fell out of favor with the king. At a time when the Empire hoped to reorganize its operations, colonial policy shifted course repeatedly.

Although imperial reform proceeded awkwardly, it proceeded nonetheless. Ministries wasted little time in implementing changes in settlement, trade, revenue, and law enforcement. With each move, colonial dissatisfaction – and British impatience – grew.

The New Imperial System, 1763–1772

Britain first addressed land settlement. Colonists may have wanted to swarm into territories taken from France in the 1763 treaty, but a massive and sudden migration would be likely to spark conflicts with tribes living west of the Appalachians. Native groups in the area had long protected their interests by playing European rivals off against one another. With the French gone, Indians in the region now had to deal with one, large, ambitious, and unified white power. To keep peace with anxious native peoples, the British drew up the Proclamation of 1763, which temporarily halted white colonial settlement at the fall line of the Appalachian Mountains. Frontier settlers, land speculators, and displaced Eastern farmers all grew irritated at the new policy.

After ordering settlement, the British turned their attention to the colonial economy. The king's chief minister, George Grenville, promoted two laws in 1764 to regulate colonial trade. The Sugar Act tightened navigation laws in order to stop smuggling and corruption and also placed customs duties on sugar, coffee, wine, and foreign textiles. Discerning colonists expressed concern because Grenville imposed the duties primarily to raise revenue rather than to channel trade. In other words, they were taxes masquerading as duties. A Currency Act passed later in the year raised more worries because it prohibited colonial governments from issuing paper money as legal tender. In place of a freewheeling economy where rules were as commonly ignored as obeyed, Americans suddenly found themselves constrained and burdened by British administrators.

To offset the costs of the North American military force, in 1765

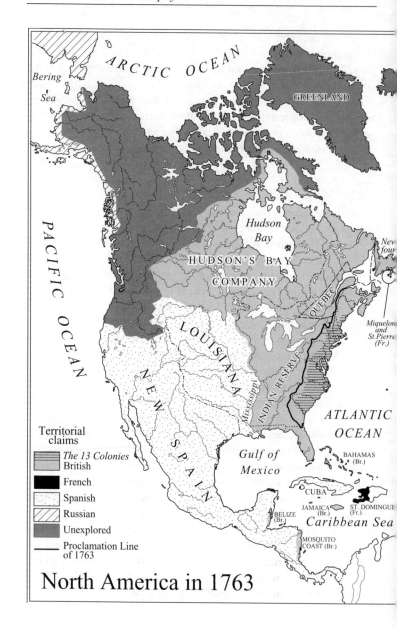

North America in 1763

Grenville imposed a tax on printed materials in the colonies. Unlike the Sugar Act, the new Stamp Act affected most Americans, not just New Englanders, and this time, the revenue came from a direct tax, which the Empire had never imposed on colonists. The measure made bureaucratic sense, but it quickly raised a political firestorm. 'Patriot' protestors condemned the measure both for its financial burdens and for its threats to constitutional principle. Organized mobs led by the 'Sons of Liberty' harassed stamp agents, local groups led boycotts of British goods, and nine colonies sent representatives to a Stamp Act Congress that petitioned Parliament to repeal the law.

Delegates maintained their loyalty to the king and recognized Parliament's right to make laws for the colonies, even laws regulating trade, but they drew the line on taxes. Appealing to the traditional rights of Englishmen, Congress argued that there could be 'no taxation without representation'. A people could not be taxed without their consent, and consent could only be granted through representative assemblies. The British insisted that Americans were 'virtually' represented in Parliament, a body which theoretically upheld the interests of all members of the Empire. Colonists replied that the only legislative system worth its salt was one based on 'actual' representation in which a broad electorate placed legislators in power, lawmakers lived in the districts from which they were elected, and the people instructed representatives on how to vote.

The protestors' message was simple: Parliament's powers were not absolute. Colonists wanted to preserve local autonomy and actual representation. Britain rejected both claims. After all, few in the Empire, even people in England itself, enjoyed 'actual' representation. And colonial notions of 'sovereignty' were too preposterous for words. Supreme power was not something to cut up and divide within the Empire. Parliament either held ultimate authority or no authority; it could make any law or no law; it either governed or it did not.

However principled their stand, British officials could not get around the fact that the Stamp Act backfired. Revenue collection collapsed, exports to America fell, and day-to-day disorder in the colonies mounted. The new ministry of the Marquis of Rockingham cut British losses and repealed the law in March 1766. At the same time, Parliament passed the Declaratory Act, reasserting its power to legislate for the colonies 'in all cases whatsoever'. The British believed they had saved face, although that required putting aside their stamp collection. The Americans believed they had won the argument, although that required ignoring the Declaratory Act. The crisis was thereby defused, but hardly resolved.

Tensions escalated again the next year with a new ministry and a new colonial program. Charles Townshend, Chancellor of the Exchequer, assumed that if colonists conceded Parliament's right to regulate commerce and impose trade levies, then duties could provide a legitimate source of money for the Empire. The Revenue Act of 1767 slapped duties on paper, glass, paint, lead, and tea imported from Britain. The money raised would pay the salaries of royal officials in America. To keep the system running smoothly, Townshend secured legislation to enforce commercial laws more strictly. And to keep the colonies in line, he urged Parliament to suspend New York's assembly after the colony failed to provide funds for quartering British troops.

Colonists now had even more reason to complain. Hated taxes reappeared in a new guise; royal officers won financial independence from colonial legislatures; officials could try violators of commercial laws in vice-admiralty courts; and the British could dissolve American assemblies at will. In response, another round of protests, petitions, boycotts, and civil disorder flared up in the colonies. Trade declined and tensions mounted for nearly two years. Then, on 5 March 1770, the conflict moved to another level when a Boston crowd taunted soldiers stationed in their city. British troops opened fire, killing five and wounding six. News of the 'Boston Massacre' spread quickly and aroused even greater hostility to imperial policy.

Earlier that very day, 3,000 miles away, Parliament had already acted to contain the colonial crisis. Concerned by a 40 per cent decline in exports to America and alarmed by escalating protests, the new prime minister, Lord North, urged repeal of the Townshend duties. Parliament complied but retained the duty on tea as a sign of its rightful authority over the colonists. The British once again believed they had held their ground; Americans once again believed their opponent had retreated. However skewed their readings of events, the continued misunderstanding at least helped to restore calm (and healthy commerce) for another two years.

From Resistance to Rebellion, 1773–1775

The relative calm that lasted from 1770 into 1772 masked several lingering problems. Despite two heralded repeals, most imperial reforms remained in place: 'taxes' undermined constitutional principles; vice-admiralty courts jeopardized basic legal rights; royal officials compromised self-rule; currency rules hampered the economy; and a standing army threatened fundamental liberties. 'Committees of Correspondence', formed in the fall of 1772, spread patriotic news, opinion, and warnings throughout the colonies, keeping lines of communication – and agitation – open among Americans. It was not long before the correspondents had something big to write home about.

In order to save the faltering East India Company, Parliament passed the Tea Act of 1773. The firm received a virtual monopoly over the tea trade to America and, through customs waivers, managed to undersell the popular but illegally smuggled Dutch tea favored by most colonists. While the beverage's price was low, Townshend's duty on tea remained in place. The Tea Act's economic favoritism and constitutional challenge were too much for patriots who condemned the measure and blocked crews from unloading the cargo. On 16 December 1773, Bostonians took matters further by dumping the city's £10,000 consignment into the harbor. Britain responded by closing Boston harbor, reorganizing Massachusetts's government, naming a military governor, moving trials of royal offenders to England, and quartering troops in private homes. Britain intended the 'Intolerable Acts' of 1774 to strike fear in the hearts of Americans. Instead, the laws united patriots as never before and intensified challenges to British authority.

Most importantly, the coercive laws convinced more Americans that Britain had plotted to destroy their remaining liberties, confirming long-held assumptions about politics and history that had fueled colonial protests. For a decade, patriots had done more than just

The Boston Tea Party

observe and condemn imperial reforms; they had also tried to make sense of them. Borrowing heavily from Greek, Roman, and Enlightenment political theory as well as the writings of English oppositionists such as John Trenchard and Thomas Gordon, patriots came to believe that British actions resulted not from mismanagement but from a deliberate effort to destroy freedom. All of history appeared to confirm that political power was dangerous, that it tended to grow uncontrollable, and that it inevitably corrupted those in authority. When power expanded, it took liberty as its victim. A people's rights were never secure; they could protect their freedom only through constant and vigilant oversight. It was their inherent right to defy tyranny, to stop despots in their tracks whenever government served special interest over the public good. A string of abuses by rulers would reveal that oppression was afoot and popular resistance was necessary.

It took only the slightest stretch of the patriot imagination to believe that recent events conformed to this ominous pattern. British officials had amassed wider authority; increasing corruption had accompanied the Empire's increasing power; colonists' liberties had gradually declined; the rights of local governments had steadily eroded; and an alarming series of imperial acts since 1763 pointed to a deliberate British conspiracy to destroy American freedom.

Fitting the pieces of the imperial puzzle together was only part of the problem. If power everywhere was dangerous and corruptive, how could Americans escape its curse? Patriots believed the answer lay in the character of the people and the constitution of their government. To remain free, a people had to embody the classical qualities of 'civic virtue', sacrificing personal interests for the common good. Fortunately, patriots argued, protests against Britain revealed the American capacity for self-discipline, simplicity, and industry. The colonists' character was well suited to the difficult political challenge ahead. And when trusted with self-rule, colonists avoided the forms of government most prone to tyranny and corruption. Americans chose to govern without kings, without inherited power, without centralized authority. They created simple, representative, and responsive political institutions. In their habits, conduct, and governance, Americans were a peculiarly republican people who could resist the temptations of power.

The patriots' republican ideology helped colonists understand their predicament and express their beliefs. Its principles also guided the work of the Continental Congress, an assembly of 55 delegates from all colonies except Georgia, who gathered in Philadelphia in September 1774 to discuss the growing imperial threat. The Congress responded in three ways. First, it recommended resistance, condemning the Intolerable Acts and encouraging Massachusetts to defend itself against possible British attack. Secondly, delegates affirmed self-rule, conceding Parliament's limited commercial powers while asserting their individual rights as Englishmen and their assemblies' exclusive authority to legislate and tax. Thirdly, Congress urged retaliation, establishing the Continental Association to ban all commerce with Britain.

Within a short time, the local committees of the Continental Association did more than oversee an economic boycott. They also began to supervise courts, raise militias, and form assemblies. From 1774 to 1775, the daily operation of government slowly shifted from official royal hands to a variety of extra-legal, patriot organizations. Armed supporters of these *de facto* governments prepared to stop any imperial effort to reverse the trend.

The first encounter between patriot militias and British forces came on 19 April 1775. Redcoats in Boston received orders to seize patriot arms and supplies stockpiled in Concord, some 20 miles away. Before reaching their destination, British troops exchanged fire with American 'minutemen' on the Lexington village green. Soldiers proceeded to Concord, fought again with patriot forces, and then withdrew back to Boston facing militia attacks along the way. In the end, the British suffered 273 casualties, the Americans 95. Two months later, a second and bloodier clash occurred at Breed's Hill and Bunker Hill near Boston, claiming over 1,000 British casualties and some 400 American dead and wounded. On that single June day, the Empire endured the worst losses it would face in the struggle with colonists.

The Second Continental Congress created a Continental Army in June 1775 and appointed George Washington as its commander. Still, the assembly affirmed its loyalty to George III in early July, extending an 'Olive Branch Petition' that asked the monarch to rein in his wicked ministers. Delegates also denied any intention of separating from the Empire, although they were determined to resist tyranny. A struggle that began with scattered protests and escalated to organized resistance and civil disobedience had now become an armed conflict, albeit one meant to redress grievances. Americans had still not yet proclaimed themselves independent. It would take another year to reach that point.

One influential document that made the case for separation was *Common Sense*, written by a recent immigrant from England, Thomas Paine. In brash, lively, and vulgar terms, Paine pressed two points. First, he asked readers to acknowledge they were not 'English' but a separate and distinct people, drawn from many regions, innocent in their manner, and free from the corruptions of European life. Secondly, these independent and virtuous people had to form their own political order, one that rejected monarchic, hereditary, and deferential rule, one that favored liberty, equality, broad political participation, and simple, lean, limited republican government. Americans could construct not only a new political system but also a new age. 'We have it in our power to begin the world over again', Paine wrote. 'The birth-day of a new world is at hand.'[2]

The middle ground of compromise and petition evaporated that spring. On 7 June 1776, the Second Continental Congress finally caught up with popular sentiment and battlefield events: delegates began discussing a formal call for independence. On 2 July, members passed the resolution. On 4 July, they approved the Declaration of Independence, written largely by Thomas Jefferson, which proclaimed and justified America's separation from Britain.

The Declaration moved from the universal to the particular, opening with statements on human equality, the rights human beings hold by their very nature, the power that government derives from the consent of the governed, and the right of a people to 'alter or abolish' a political order that becomes destructive to their interests. Most of the document, however, focused on a specific problem: the ways in which the British monarch had failed his people. Ignoring Parliament, whose authority patriots had by now completely rejected, the Declaration indicted the king on 18 counts, asserting George III's responsibility for a series of 'injuries and usurpations' all of which exposed him as a tyrant unfit to rule. With the link to the crown broken, the bonds between America and Britain were dissolved.

Conflict between the American colonies and the British Empire developed in a land of prosperity, not impoverishment. It began in the aftermath of victory, not the chaos of defeat. It arose in response to subtle changes in land, trade, and tax policies, not to some sudden and brutal exercise of force. And it grew into a crusade to preserve traditional constitutional principles, not to reject them. In other words, the Revolution was hardly predictable, imminent, or inevitable. Despite its curious origins, however, the struggle made a lasting impression on the nation's political imagination. Over the next two centuries, Americans would continue to distrust government power, venerate individual liberty, monitor conspiratorial threats, and portray themselves as a model society. In these core beliefs, the legacy of their Revolution lives on.

CHAPTER THREE

The American Revolution and the Creation of New Governments, 1775–1789

Over the course of a decade and a half, Americans found themselves caught up in two long, protracted (and, for a time, simultaneous) struggles. One involved the armed conflict against Britain. The other was the attempt to construct their own political system. Both efforts proved difficult, considering the impressive military might of the Empire and the considerable political differences among Americans. And both efforts led in unexpected directions. Battles with the British began in 1775 among a people who, for the most part, wanted a redress of grievances; the war *became* a struggle for independence. Battles over self-rule began in 1776 among a people who, for the most part, wanted to rid themselves of powerful, centralized rule; they wound up creating a strong, extensive national government.

Legend has it that, as the troops of Lord Charles Cornwallis surrendered at Yorktown in 1781, a British band played 'The World Turned Upside Down'. It was a fitting anthem, both for that remarkable military moment and for a topsy-turvy political era.

The Revolutionary War Begins

The Sons and Daughters of Liberty who launched widespread protests against British policy in 1765 had no idea their actions would lead to separation from the Empire. So, too, the militias that fought British forces in April 1775 at Lexington and Concord had no sense that their combat marked the beginning of the American Revolution. Patriots may eventually have agreed on a clear-cut declaration of independence, but they did not issue as blunt a declaration of war.

However fuzzy the military state of affairs in the spring of 1775, one thing was clear: Britain seemed to have all the advantages. Its population was over four times the size of that of the colonies, its economy far more diverse, its army large, professional, and well trained, and its navy the finest in the world. By comparison, the Americans had fewer men and far less wealth to draw upon. Their military force was composed of a small Continental Army (that quickly grew desperate for manpower and supplies) and various state militias (that were long on comradery and short on discipline). No strong central government directed the military effort or held the population together. In fact, a fifth of Americans were 'Loyalists' dedicated to the king and home country, opposed to independence, and appalled at the dangerous behavior of rebels.

As in many conflicts, however, the balance sheet was not as lopsided as it first appeared. Britain faced a conflict 3,000 miles from home, in coastal colonies stretching 1,500 miles along the Atlantic, against a predominantly rural, scattered population with few cities, a decentralized government, and no vital nerve center. The British conducted a war despite political division at home, strategic differences among its leaders, and shifting international pressures from imperial rivals. Americans, on the other hand, grew increasingly hostile to Britain and increasingly committed to independence. They fought on familiar ground, in a largely defensive effort, *for* a common cause rather than *against* a nebulous 'enemy.' International rivalries helped rather than hindered their effort. Their national army, although composed of society's lowest and poorest ranks, proved persistent, resilient, and unconventional in its fighting ability. In seven years of conflict, from 1775–1781, in three theaters of war, they won by outlasting – and exasperating – their opponent.

The Conflict in New England, 1775–1776

From the spring of 1775 to the spring of 1776, British attention focused on New England, convinced that disturbances were chiefly the work of agitators centered in Boston. The British tried to quell the resistance movement by force rather than through negotiation or regulation. The faster the Empire acted the better, before the infection of rebellion spread to other places. Having crushed the insurrectionaries, Britain would resume its peaceful, stable rule of the colonies.

There was good reason to pursue such a policy because, while most colonists were still neutral in the controversy, the most belligerent were centered in Boston. Still, signs pointed in a more ominous direction. British forces in Boston suffered heavy losses in their 'limited' police action. The Congress that honored monarchic sovereignty had also formed a Continental Army in June 1775. From 1775 to 1776, Continental forces made an ambitious (though futile) attempt to invade Canada. Colonial opinion could easily tilt to the patriot cause when Americans were forced by circumstance to choose sides. The operation of government in one colony after another passed from British to patriot control. All told, the situation was far more volatile than imperial officials first thought. When rebels around Boston secured artillery from Fort Ticonderoga and aimed their cannons down on British troops, the Empire's commanders realized a reassessment was in order. Sir William Howe, the new head of British forces, evacuated troops from Boston in March 1776 and repositioned then in Halifax. The second phase of the struggle was about to begin.

The Conflict in the Middle Colonies, 1776–1778

By the late spring of 1776, the British decided on a different approach to the troubles in America. Rather than trying to subdue bands of insurgents, the Empire's forces would engage in a more thorough, conventional war. Rather than concentrating on the instability in Boston, the military would capture other large cities in the colonies. Rather than facing intense opposition in New England head on, the British would bypass the region, cut it off from other colonies, and isolate its rebels. And rather than depending on the military to do all the work, imperial officials counted on loyalists to join in the effort to restore order.

On 2 July 1776, as the Continental Congress voted in Philadelphia to make America independent, British forces landed near New York

Mobilizing for war   (after a 1779 woodcut)

City to keep America subordinate. General William Howe and his brother Admiral Richard, Lord Howe, gathered 32,000 troops to do battle with a 19,000-man Continental force. The British planned to take New York City, defeat General Washington, and use local loyalists to restore legitimate authority. In the late summer and early autumn, the British enjoyed a string of victories in Brooklyn, Manhattan, and White Plains, pushing the Continental Army north into upper New York. The patriots fled south to New Jersey and then retreated again, crossing the Delaware River into Pennsylvania. The high hopes of July faded quickly. Even the enthusiastic Tom Paine lamented that these were 'the times that try men's souls'. Washington, however, kept his beleaguered troops on the move rather than settling them into winter quarters. His forces seized enemy posts in Trenton and Princeton and pushed the British out of New Jersey. The small victories lifted patriot morale and unnerved local loyalists.

The episodes also revealed a serious flaw in Howe's strategy. Rather than polishing off Washington's troops, the British commander preferred a more cautious and diplomatic approach. Militarily, Howe hoped to conserve resources, save lives, and eventually outmaneuver his opponents. Politically, he hoped to convince the Americans of Britain's superiority, pacify occupied areas, and extend irresistible peace terms to rebels. The plan was complex, reasonable, even tactful; but it offered the Continental Army opportunities to retreat and regroup at times and places of their choosing. In the end, it is likely that Howe's strategy extended the length of the war. That turned out to be a mistake for, as events in 1777 would demonstrate, time was on America's side.

Britain's long-term problems with the war became evident just as its forces achieved a seemingly impressive victory. Howe, still based in New York, had set his sights on Philadelphia. He planned to draw Washington's army into one more large battle, this time for the home of the Continental Congress. Howe moved his troops out of New York harbor, down the Atlantic, and up the Chesapeake Bay. Washington met Howe's forces at Brandywine and Germantown, lost both encounters, and saw the British take Philadelphia in September 1777.

By the military standards of the eighteenth century, Howe achieved a resounding success. By the practical standards of American life, he had little to show for his efforts. The loss of the 'capital' made little practical difference to patriots who lived under a weak central government. With power widely dispersed, and Congress able to meet in other locations, the business of government, such as it was, continued. The British commander also ate up valuable time in the spring and summer organizing his flotilla out of New York harbor. Even worse, his foray into Philadelphia kept him from meeting a more important appointment in central New York.

Britain's master strategy for 1777 called for a three-pronged offensive: one force to move south from Quebec under General John Burgoyne; a second to move east across upper New York under Lieutenant Colonel Barry St. Leger; a third to move north from Manhattan under Howe. Advancing in their appropriate directions, the three armies would defeat Continental troops, slice the colonies in two, and seal off the troublemakers in New England. What actually happened was quite different. Patriots stopped St. Leger at Fort Stanwix in August and forced him to retreat; the occupation of Philadelphia tied up Howe in the late summer and early autumn; and Continentals under General Horatio Gates defeated Burgoyne at Saratoga on 17 October. Three weeks after the triumph in Philadelphia, the British were humiliated with the surrender of Burgoyne's forces.

The British defeat at Saratoga gave the patriots something to applaud, and the French something to appraise. As a monarchic, colonial nation, the French were wary of republican revolution, but they believed that the American conflict could weaken the British and pave the way for a renewed French presence in North America. For two years, France, along with Spain, helped the Continental Congress pay mounting war bills with a series of loans. An American delegation in Paris headed by Benjamin Franklin also pressed for a formal alliance. The French held out, waiting for proof that the Americans could make good on their claim of independence. Saratoga gave the French solid evidence. Word of British interest in a negotiated settlement to the Revolution made the French move even faster. In February 1778, French and American diplomats concluded a Treaty of Alliance; by June, France and Britain were officially at war. Spain allied itself with France the following year, and the Dutch later severed relations with Britain. The three allies provided patriots with money and supplies; French and Spanish naval forces challenged the British fleet; and the French committed troops to the American conflict. Leaders in London saw themselves increasingly isolated in Europe. What had begun for the British as a local police action in New England widened into an armed struggle across America and a war around the world.

The Conflict in the South, 1778–1781

Victory at Saratoga did not change the course of the war immediately for the Americans. Continental forces outside Philadelphia endured an agonizing winter in 1777–1778 at Valley Forge. Short on pay, food, and clothing, over 2,500 troops died, as many as had perished in battle up to that time. Discord and bitterness ran high. A foreign volunteer, Prussian-born Friedrich von Steuben, helped stem the disorder and turn the soldiers into a better-disciplined fighting force. Drilling troops in the spring of 1778, von Steuben brought back a measure of order and confidence to the Continental Army. As the new British commander-in-chief, Sir Henry Clinton, moved his troops out of Philadelphia in May to resume positions in New York, Washington's forces followed, pursuing the redcoats up to White Plains. Anticipating word from French naval forces about joint military actions, Washington kept on eye on British troops. The wait was a long one, running through 1778 and 1779. The war in the North had turned into a frustrating stalemate.

Although Washington grew impatient with the French, the standoff had more to do with a change in British thinking. In June 1778, as warfare expanded across the globe, the Empire re-evaluated its general strategy and focused its attention on the most valuable and strategically important colonies. In North America, that meant concentrating on the West Indies sugar islands and the South's rich lands and key ports. The war effort would proceed with less conciliation and more force, isolating and subduing patriots, enlisting the aid of supposedly sizable loyalist groups, securing the South, and then slowly reclaiming areas further north.

At first, the strategy seemed to work. The British scored victories in Savannah, Georgia, in December 1778, Charleston in May 1780, and Camden, South Carolina in August 1780. But once again success was met with miscalculations and surprises. The very determination of the British military effort alienated Southerners and drove more into the patriot camp. Loyalists proved to have less breadth (and staying power) than first expected. An ugly and brutal civil war erupted from mid-1780 into 1782 between bands of patriot and Loyalist militias. And Continental forces under the command of Nathanael Greene led Lord Charles Cornwallis's troops on a wild, costly, and frustrating chase through the Carolina countryside. The British commander moved his men back to the Atlantic coast and up to the Chesapeake in the spring of 1781.

Cornwallis planned to concentrate his military operation in Virginia where he hoped to knock out local patriots and move his troops northward. The strategy might have worked except for one small complication. After years of delay, American and French forces finally agreed on a joint military venture – and chose Cornwallis as their target. Admiral de Grasse positioned his French fleet to challenge British naval power; von Steuben and the Marquis de Lafayette led Continental forces in Virginia; troops under Washington and the Comte de Rochambeau moved down from New York. They converged at Yorktown, located on a coastal peninsula between the James and York Rivers, where Cornwallis had positioned, and isolated, his army. By the late summer of 1781, a Franco-American force of 17,000 confronted Cornwallis's 8,000 troops. The allies laid siege to Yorktown and finally forced Cornwallis to surrender on 19 October 1781. Hearing of the loss, Lord North moaned, 'Oh God, it's all over'. For once, his assessment of conditions in America was right on target. The war continued sporadically for months, but the debacle at Yorktown spelled defeat for Britain and independence for America.

The Treaty of Paris, 1783

By early March 1782, Parliament voted to end the war and make peace. Talks began in June with American negotiators Benjamin Franklin, John Jay, and John Adams. Congress gave the team instructions that complied with the 1778 treaty: co-operate with France in hammering out a peace treaty. But the French were also committed to working with Spain in settling its differences with Britain, and neither France nor Spain had any desire to see a strong, anti-monarchical, anti-colonial, republican power in North America. US negotiators feared that the interests of their nation might be lost in the bewildering machinations of European diplomacy. Rather than risk an unfavorable settlement, they proceeded to talk with the British on their own.

The negotiating team cleverly maneuvered the discussions: the imperial rivalries that worked to America's advantage in the war effort were now used to the republic's advantage in the peace effort. To gain

Independence declared

leverage with Britain, the Americans suggested that their alliance with France could, under the right circumstances, be weakened. To pacify the French, irritated over a separate agreement, the Americans warned that a dispute between the two nations could easily drive the United States into Britain's arms. The end result was a treaty quite favorable for America. Britain formally recognized US independence and agreed that the new nation would extend north to Canada, south to Florida, and west to the Mississippi. In varying degrees of clarity, the treaty also addressed fishing rights, compensation to Loyalists, debt repayment, and British evacuation of American territory – though all of these issues continued to rankle with the two nations in the coming decades. Whatever problems remained, newly independent Americans believed they had secured some impressive bragging rights, first in battle and then in bargains.

The United States might have won the war and the peace, but it still faced the challenge of self-rule.

Forming State Governments

When the Second Continental Congress called for the formation of new state governments in May 1776, the response was swift and fervent. The project galvanized America's greatest political minds because they and their contemporaries conceived of their political identity in local, rather than continental, terms. For most Americans, their state was their 'nation'. Even as cosmopolitan a figure as Thomas Jefferson insisted that 'Virginia, Sir, is my country'.

Though the states constituted themselves in different ways, several common themes tied them together. The constitutions formed in 1776 and 1777 created republican forms of government with political structures that represented the popular will. All were *written* constitutions that defined the authority (and limits) of public officials. The states saw themselves as sovereign and independent republics, reflecting the belief that republican governments worked best when they were kept small and compact, extending their control over a narrow area rather than an unlimited space. Most constitutions tightly controlled the executive branch, restricting the power of governors. Most enlarged legislative authority, trusting legislators as the true and responsible representatives of the people. Most also reduced property qualifications for the vote and for office holding. And all of the constitutions protected citizens through bills of rights that specifically stated the freedoms government could not infringe.

One other point tied the states together: their internal political conflicts grew so intense that, by the early 1780s, most constitutions had to be revised. Americans had learned their revolutionary lessons well and applied them diligently, but the republican systems they created turned in unexpected directions. Legislatures grew ambitious and often assumed executive and judicial powers. The people's will proved to be divided and unpredictable, sparking fears of popular 'passions' and narrow interests. And the weakness of executives left states at times with ineffective leadership and direction. The revised documents of the 1780s addressed the problems in two ways. First, states 'balanced' their governments by enhancing the powers of the executive and judicial branches. Secondly, states made certain that legislatures did not have the last word on constitution making. Beginning with Massachusetts, the 'fundamental law' of states was put to a final vote before constitutional conventions, special single-purpose gatherings of delegates whose only task was to approve or disapprove a proposed constitution.

The political principles that cut across state lines offered one indication of the revolutionary thinking of Americans. Those shared convictions also contributed a common political ground that eventually fashioned a national constitution.

The Articles of Confederation

As the Revolution began, the *de facto* government of the United States was the Continental Congress. Most recognized that the hurriedly arranged convention was no substitute for a formalized and legitimate political system. In 1776, Congress created a committee to draw up a plan of government. The panel came back with a proposal for 'Articles of Confederation and Perpetual Union'. A year passed as Congress debated the recommendations. The body finally sent a revised plan to the states in November 1777 and awaited their unanimous approval, but it was not until March 1781 that the Articles of Confederation officially went into effect.

Although largely forgotten by present-day Americans, the Articles were a significant if short-lived achievement. Its authors were audacious enough to believe that people should get the kind of government they were fighting for. Revolutionaries wanted to end the tyranny posed by executive power. Under the Articles, the national government had no executive branch; what better way to solve the problem than to eliminate it? Patriots trusted the power exercised by their representatives, by legislators. Under the terms of the Articles, the national government was composed *only* of a legislature, a one-house Congress. No courts, no president, no other office or wing or agency would exist. The Revolution sought to contain the power of government, no matter who held it. The Articles determined that the national Congress's powers were limited and well-defined. It could conduct foreign affairs and Indian affairs, standardize coins, weights, and measure, run a postal service, and mediate in the disputes of states. Additional powers required amendments to the Articles, something unlikely to occur because all states had to agree to such measures. The Revolution was fought to keep power decentralized, to defend divisible sovereignty, and to demonstrate the benefits of compact republics. The Articles outlined a 'confederation' rather than a single, consolidated political order, an alliance of states, each of which held ultimate authority, each of which was independent. The result was more a 'League of American Republics', joined together 'for their common defense, the security of their liberties, and their mutual and general welfare'.

If such loose arrangements sound odd today, they were true to the Spirit of 1776. The Articles thwarted executive tyranny, protected local autonomy, and removed the threat of a menacing central government. The success of the Articles went beyond ideological fidelity, however. The government under the Articles successfully conducted a war against the British Empire, negotiated a favorable peace treaty, and set up procedures for admitting territories as states (ensuring that new states would enter as equals rather than as subordinates).

Unfortunately, the Articles also created a weak and ineffective government. Congress did not have the authority to regulate trade. It could not require states to obey the treaties formed with foreign nations. It could not draft men into military service. It had no independent source of income. It relied on requisitions from the states for its operating revenue, and states jealous of their own authority would not likely approve amendments to expand Congress's powers. Most significantly, the government under the Articles could not enforce its will on states or citizens. It could plead but not compel. It held powers of persuasion but not powers of coercion. The old adage about being careful what you wish for held true. Revolutionaries got exactly the kind of government they all wanted. Unfortunately, it was a system that hardly governed at all.

The problems of the national government grew in the 1780s. Britain and Spain refused to comply with the terms of treaties. Settlers feared European intrigues with Indian tribes in the Old Northwest and Southwest. Depression hit in 1784; ineffective monetary policies only

The Great Seal of the United States, adopted by Congress 1782

compounded economic problems. Civil disorder broke out in western Massachusetts in 1786 during 'Shay's Rebellion' as debt-ridden farmers sought relief from taxes and foreclosures. By 1786, barely five years after launching the Confederation, a call went out for a convention to discuss ways of making the national government 'adequate to the exigencies of the Union'.

The Constitution

The convention, approved by Congress, met in Philadelphia in 1787 in Independence Hall, where almost 11 years earlier patriots had declared independence. Some would have nothing to do with the proceedings. Rhode Island refused to send any delegates. The revolutionary patriot, Patrick Henry, cast a wary eye, claiming he 'smelt a rat'. The 55 individuals who did gather formed, in Jefferson's eyes, 'an assembly of demi-gods'. Although heroes such as George Washington and Benja-min Franklin may have been present, demi-demi-gods such as James Madison, George Mason, James Wilson, and Gouverneur Morris took the lead.

Early on, nationalists dominated the debate. They wanted to scrap, not modify, the Articles and replace them with a strong national government, composed of three branches, empowered to regulate trade and levy taxes, and able to enforce its will on states and citizens. Their 'Virginia Plan' even gave the new Congress the power to veto state laws. Delegates from smaller states feared their interests would be swallowed up in a consolidated government. The opposition devel-oped an alternative 'New Jersey Plan' to reform rather than discard the Articles by granting greater authority to the existing, one-house national Congress. A month into its proceedings, the convention ori-ginally called to revise the Articles voted instead to construct a brand new government. Several factors explained the shift. Constitutional changes in the states provided a precedent; sentiment among delegates ran toward greater national authority; a few firm opponents simply walked out rather than trying to stem the tide; and the meetings were closed, allowing delegates to speak their minds freely without being disturbed by public scrutiny.

Having agreed to start from scratch, debate over details of the new political system began. One contentious issue involved representation. Nationalists supported proportional representation in the two-house legislature: the larger a state's population, the more representatives in the lower house; and lower house members would elect members of the upper house, chosen from nominees provided by the states. Opponents feared that small states would have too few representatives in one body and perhaps none at all in the other. They called for equal representation. The 'Great Compromise' settled the matter by applying proportional representation to the House (based on a state's population) and equal representation to the Senate (granting two senators for each state).

At the same time, delegates squabbled over what constituted a state's 'population'. It was in this context that the question of slavery arose, not as a moral issue but as a political and economic one. Firmly committed to revolutionary republican principles, the delegates, for the most part, firmly resisted any discussion of abolition. The questions of power and liberty that they debated had to do with whites – or, more accurately, white men. In other words, they talked about the chattel system as it affected free whites, not enslaved blacks. Southerners wanted slaves counted as part of the population for purposes of representation: the more slaves, the more political power for the region in the national government (although, of course, slaves never exercised any political choice). Northerners wanted slaves counted as part of the population for purposes of taxation: the more slaves, the more 'wealth', and the more wealth, the higher the tax bill for the South. The solution came in a formula used under the Confederation Congress: three-fifths of slaves would be counted for purposes of representation *and* taxation. As it turned out, there were no direct federal taxes over the next seven decades, so the South ended up as the big winner in the bargain.

The delegates then disposed of two other questions related to slavery: Congress would not interfere with the foreign slave trade until 1808; but it *would* interfere by recapturing fugitive slaves. Remarkably, while the proposed Constitution dealt so clearly with slavery, its authors managed to avoid completely using the words 'slave' or 'slavery' in the text. Instead, they chose phrases such as 'person held to service or labor in one State' or 'all other persons'. The Founders could 'settle' the problem of slavery without naming it. Whatever literary conceits they employed, the Constitution both recognized and protected the interests of slaveholders.

Having indirectly set the limits of liberty by race and gender, delegates then directly defined the new government's powers. By comparison, those discussions went rather smoothly. In September, the document was ready for ratification. Special conventions in each state would vote the proposal up or down. Only nine of the thirteen conventions had to approve for the document to take effect. The ground rules made ratification more likely, but not certain.

Consider how odd and alarming the proposed government looked to those who adhered to revolutionary republican principles. The document created a coercive, centralized government that wielded unprecedented authority. It could force its will on citizens, tax them, regulate their commerce, raise armies, and deploy the military to execute its laws and quell insurrections. It created a strong executive that concentrated power in the hands of one individual and even allowed a veto over the legislature. It outlined all sorts of controls exercised by government but provided no corresponding list of rights guaranteed to citizens. A person might legitimately ask how any of this was different from the oppressive rule that the Revolution had challenged. Consider, as well, all of the government's bewildering branches and institutions and posts and terms of office and election procedures. The framers seemed to forget Paine's call for simplicity in government and, instead, reproduced all the Byzantine political complexity that Old World regimes used to wield force and hide corruption. And consider, finally, that the whole project hinged on the new nation's success as an *extended* republic, in the belief that one government could rule over a large country and a diverse people and still retain its republican principles. The very idea was absurd, standing hundreds of years of republican theory on its head. Everyone knew that successful republics existed only in relatively small areas with a homogenous population. What could have possessed those fellows in Philadelphia? Why would they take such a gamble, ignore the lessons of the past, and betray the spirit of the Revolution?

Because, the fellows in Philadelphia responded, their proposal would save, not sacrifice, the republican Revolution. Proponents of the Constitution argued that the new government was the logical extension of 1776, not a dangerous departure. They took on the name 'Federalists', a clever ploy since the term more accurately described the position of their opponents who favored dispersed, state authority and opposed a strong national government. The truly federalist-minded group was a bit slow on the public-relations uptake and promptly found themselves saddled with the label 'Anti-Federalist', with all the negativity and obstructionism the name implied.

Having muddied the political waters by claiming a false identity, the Federalists redeemed themselves through their illuminating political commentary. James Madison, Alexander Hamilton, and John Jay penned a series of 85 anonymous essays, known later as *The Federalist Papers*. They explained the failures of the Confederation, the benefits of their new system, and the proper goals of a republican government. Their analysis remains the best introduction to the Constitution.

The essayists uncovered flaws in the origins, premises, and arrangements of government under the Articles. The very creation of the Confederation raised one set of concerns. A committee of the Second Continental Congress had drafted the Articles; the whole Congress tidied it up; state legislatures ratified it. In other words, standing governments wrote and approved the Confederation. Government made government. How could anyone feel secure in their liberties under such a system? Secondly, the Confederation located sovereignty in the states themselves. Ultimate authority, quite simply, rested with those in power. The idea seemed a sure way to undermine freedom. Thirdly, the Articles placed all national power in *one* body, the Confederation Congress. This totally ignored the lessons of the Revolution. Was it not certain that concentrated power would turn tyrannical, even if the center of power was a legislature?

Federalists insisted that a form of government so badly conceived was not only unworkable but inimical to basic liberties. Reforms would only make things worse, *especially* the Anti-Federalist suggestion that Congress, the sole power center, should receive more power. Confederationists seemed oblivious to recent history: legislators had proved themselves perfectly capable of becoming both bungling and abusive. The problem was particularly severe within each compact republic (or 'state'). With the relatively similar political interests of citizens, it was easy to form large and permanent political majorities that dominated office every election and paid little heed to minority interests. The end result was a political order where large groups held power unchallenged, where the rights of small groups remained vulnerable, where each state went off in its own direction, and where common national interests were largely ignored.

Step by step, *The Federalist Papers* showed how the Constitution solved these dilemmas. First, existing government had no hand in its creation. Instead, delegates gathered just to write the Constitution; then they went home. Specially elected delegates in special ratification conventions voted on the proposal; then they left rather than remaining in power. In other words, delegates of the citizenry wrote the Constitution, not agencies of the ruling order. The document's first three words made the point: it was created by 'We the People', *not* 'We the States'.

Secondly, the framers of the document recognized that ultimate authority must not sit in state government – nor in national or local government. Ultimate authority had to rest *outside* government entirely. Sovereignty must rest in the hands of citizens, and the people's fundamental law, the Constitution itself, stood as 'the supreme law of the land'.

Thirdly, Federalists argued that their proposal carefully contained power – by sticking with revolutionary principles and following recent republican experience. They recognized that power was corruptive, no matter where it was located, no matter who held it: in national government, state governments, among executives, judges, legislators, even the people themselves. Since all power was suspect, it might appear best to keep power to a minimum; but the last national government had tried that approach and failed. Government obviously needed some 'energy'.

The Constitution had a better answer: grant power, but trust no one. 'If men were angels', *Federalist 51* stated, 'no government would be necessary. If angels were to govern men, neither external nor internal controls on government would be necessary'. Clearly, there was a bit of the devil in both the rulers and the ruled. The solution was to design a government that took these suspicions seriously, that institutionalized its skepticism of human nature.

One way was to place the government's enhanced powers in different hands, through a separation of powers. Instead of one body running the nation, have three, each 'representative' of the people, each with its own function: making law, executing law, interpreting law. A second way was to place checks and balances on the different branches. Instead of merely hoping they would stay out of each other's business, give them ways to defend their position: Congress could create laws; presidents could veto them; and Congress could override the veto with a two-thirds vote. A third approach was to vary the ways in which government officials received and held their posts. Instead of putting everyone into power at one time through one election held in one way, mix up the procedures: select House members through popular vote; have state legislatures (originally) pick senators; choose presidents through an 'electoral college' (whose members were – and still are – elected by the states); allow presidents to nominate Supreme Court justices; let senators vote on the nominations. And instead of taking everyone out of office at one moment, stagger the terms so that the government never changed at once: House members serve two years, presidents four years, senators six years, judges for life. A single election could, at best, remove a president, the entire House, and a third of the Senate. A fourth way to keep government in line was through a division of power. Instead of creating an all-powerful, consolidated national government (which Hamilton had in mind at first), a 'federal' system emerged: the national government had significant powers, but states retained the authority to control education, local business, most criminal procedures, marriage laws, and the like.

A fifth safeguard against tyranny was the Constitution's endorsement of an extended republic. Instead of assuming that small republics protected freedom, the Federalists charged that compact units undermined the rights of the few and jeopardized the harmony of the whole. Localism was a problem, not a solution. Those narrow little concerns of narrow little individuals in narrow little communities had already damaged the nation's general welfare. But selfish interests of petty people in isolated areas would always be present. Forget about eliminating the difficulty. Instead, live with it, and use it to the nation's advantage. A lively, continuous competition of interests would keep one group from becoming too dominant for too long. 'Take in a greater variety of parties and interests', Madison wrote in *Federalist 10*, and 'you make it less probable that a majority of the whole will have a common motive to invade the rights of other citizens'. A group of wise, judicious, cosmopolitan leaders would rise to the top of this kinetic and highly-charged political mass, filtering out the people's rantings, discerning the citizenry's true interests, and demonstrating the importance of thinking 'continentally'. Geographic expansion meant more security. The bigger the better, because variety was the spice of republican life.

A final way to monitor power was to amend the whole apparatus when it broke down. Instead of relying on a process that required complete agreement of the states (or one that allowed changes willy-nilly), the Constitution offered a strict but realistic set of procedures for proposing and ratifying amendments. The possibility of change did not undermine the Constitutional system; the amendment process simply acknowledged that even the framers were not angels.

The Federalists' arguments were long and complicated. That was part of their message: it was not easy to protect liberty. Paine may have argued that the best government was lean and uncomplicated, but unfortunately, that spirit of 1776 was thrown into doubt by recent events. Simple designs in government only made the work of tyrants less difficult. Federalists insisted that the times called for un-common sense. However odd their appeals to enlarged powers, vigorous executives, legislative checks, popular follies, and an extended political order, the Federalists believed their Constitution offered republican answers to republican problems.

What was not certain was whether the document would win

Thomas Paine, English radical

approval. Conventions in five states ratified the document in December 1787 and January 1788. In February, the Anti-Federalist majority in Massachusetts relented and agreed to the proposal by a vote of 187 to 168. In the spring, more conventions accepted. Ratification by the nine required states came by June 1788. Nine months after conception, the new republic was born. Officially, that is. Practically speaking, the new political order had little hope of succeeding without ratification from Virginia and New York. The brilliant analyses of *The Federalist Papers* swayed some votes, but pledges to amend the new Constitution helped garner more support. Key Federalists promised that they would work to add a 'bill of rights' to the document, outlining the individual rights that the new government could not violate. In June, Virginia approved by a vote of 89 to 79; New York assented one month later, by a slim 30 to 27 vote. North Carolina and Rhode Island did not join in until the new federal government was already in operation, the former waiting half a year, the latter staying out until May 1790 (and, even then, voting only 34 to 32 in favor of the Constitution).

In the space of 14 years, Americans fought a war for independence, organized state governments, reorganized most of them, lived under a temporary national 'government', formed another, threw that model out of the window, and started a third. George Washington guessed that the new Constitution would probably unravel within a couple of decades. In the context of his times, what stands out about his comment was not its pessimism, but its optimism.

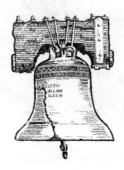

CHAPTER FOUR

The Political 'Revolutions' of the Early Republic, 1789–1840

One might think that after nearly a quarter century of political struggle, virtuous republicans would long to lay down their verbal arms and take a break from intense disputes over power and liberty. One might think so. It is a measure of the deep politicization of American culture that arguments about the nature of government and the fortunes of freedom took off again with renewed vigor in the 1790s. Many signs of good will, agreement, and co-operation were in evidence during the first years of the new republic. Yet the ship of state had barely been launched before it was tossed about by fierce political storms which, to a great extent, still swirl today.

By the turn of the century, some began voicing the argument that the nation badly needed a make over. Either the experiment had gone wrong or it had not gone far enough. A nation ostensibly so new had apparently fallen badly short of expectations. Fortunately, many were eager to offer handy tips for republican rejuvenation. Thomas Jefferson congratulated himself on creating yet another revolution in American politics in the election of 1800. Andrew Jackson reclaimed the Jeffersonian mantle and continued the work of political resuscitation by the mid-1820s. In the process, one political world died and another took its place.

Sources of Political Harmony

All was not contentious as the 1780s closed. The presidency of George Washington provided perhaps the greatest base of unity in the new nation. Chosen unanimously by the Electoral College and sworn into office in April 1789 in New York City, temporary capital of the nation, Washington imparted dignity, respect, and confidence on the new government. He was a cautious and deliberate individual, conscious of popular fears and aware of political differences, keen to avoid any unnecessary public alarm and eager to reconcile competing interests.

Above all, Washington recognized that Americans were apprehensive over the whole business of having a president. The office smacked of monarchy and held the potential for wicked abuses of power. Fittingly, he had long identified himself with the Roman republican hero, Cincinnatus: Washington served when his country called but remained uneasy over translating military renown into political power. He rejected John Adams's silly suggestion that Americans address the chief executive as 'His Highness'. He balked at serving a second term and retired from office rather than serving a third. When he stepped down from power, he stepped out of government service completely, returning to private life at his Mount Vernon home in Virginia.

Washington held back from exercising too much power, calculating that his duties revolved around two main tasks: serving as the national 'executive' to administer laws; and serving as the 'commander in chief' to direct military and diplomatic affairs. The rest was the business of others. He interfered little with Congress and cast only two vetoes. He consulted frequently with his appointed secretaries of state, war, and treasury as well as the attorney general. These 'cabinet' members came from the North and South, representing a range of political opinions. Washington demonstrated caution, allowed open debate, and tried to remain above the political fray.

Washington had a high opinion of himself and helped craft his own mythology. But he was also a sincere patriot. He believed revolutionary warnings about power; he respected his countrymen's fears of the new federal order; he took seriously notions of duty; he avoided inordinate displays of authority; and he attempted to make the presidency an office of trust rather than an agency of tyranny. His republican heroism derived as much from refraining as attainment. His sense of balance, caution, and deliberation was well suited to the moment. Washington was, in many ways, the right person at the right time.

George Washington, after a chalk drawing on paper *c.* 1800 by Sr. Memin

Like Washington's controlled presidency, a second source of unity came from controls placed on the entire federal government. In ratification debates, Constitutional opponents had called for amendments that would protect popular liberties from the expanded authority of the new government. The key framer, James Madison, originally challenged such arguments, contending that a bill of rights was unnecessary and that the real threat to freedom arose from state powers. But later, as leader of the House, Representative Madison realized he had to reckon with widespread fears of the Constitution and the new republic's new powers.

Madison directed the amendment process. Beginning in June 1789, he took more than 200 proposals and whittled them down to 17. Only one provided assurances for state authority; most protected *individuals* against the power of the federal government, guaranteeing freedoms of speech, the press, religion, assembly, and petition, the right to bear arms, protections against unreasonable search and seizure, and safeguards in legal procedures. In other words, the proposed amendments had more to do with civil rights than with states rights. That was not what proponents originally wanted; but that is what the nation eventually got.

Congress sent 12 proposals to the states for approval. Ten were ratified and became part of the Constitution in December 1791, forming the 'Bill of Rights'. As it turned out, the amendments did not dismantle any of Congress's key powers. But by outlining fundamental personal liberties and deterring the government from interference with the thoughts, opinions, and consciences of citizens, the amendments represented something notable and remarkable: one of the first acts of the new national government was to limit its own authority.

The ratification of the Bill of Rights helped end years of debate about America's form of national government. Along with Washington's presidency, it provided a sense of legitimacy that the government badly needed and made the new, enlarged, and unprecedented experiment in republicanism acceptable to most Americans.

Sources of Political Division

Despite these grounds for unity, major questions remained about the purposes and scope of the new government. Washington, while an admired national hero, was hardly an executive 'activist'. The Bill of Rights, while of great importance, focused on what the government could *not* do. What would happen when the federal government actually made a decision and tried to implement it, when it tried to accomplish something? As it turned out, political hell broke loose.

The sparks started flying with, of all things, a series of economic reports drawn up by Washington's Treasury Secretary, Alexander Hamilton. A man who was literally an ambitious bastard, Hamilton had earned Washington's trust and admiration during the Revolution. Hamilton viewed his secretarial post as the equivalent of a 'prime minister', giving him access to the President and influence over other federal agencies. And, indeed, Washington so admired his secretary's judgment that, to a considerable extent, he entrusted Hamilton with the development of domestic policy. The Secretary laid out his agenda in reports written between 1790 and 1791 on such tantalizing subjects as public credit, a national bank, and manufactures. The topics appear dull and mundane, but Hamilton's suggestions raised a storm of controversy because of the questions he raised about the new government's power and purposes.

One proposal dealt with the way the new nation should handle the money it owed. Rather than viewing debts as a burden that an honorable government should settle quickly, Hamilton saw them as an opportunity, a way to place the new nation on a more secure financial and political footing. The *last* thing he wanted was to pay off debts. Instead, 'a national debt, if it is not excessive, will be to us a national blessing'. Note holders would have a stake in the new government; if it failed, they would lose their principal. The debt would help build a base of support for the national government, especially among the republic's wealthier citizens.

Hamilton suggested 'funding' the national debt, calling in old IOUs and replacing them with new, interest-bearing bonds. He also called for the federal government to 'assume' state debts. *All* public creditors, therefore, would 'receive their dues from one source, and having the same interests, they will unite in support of the fiscal arrangements of the government'.

Hamilton may have had a keen sense of political economy but not of public relations. The 'funding' proposal seemed to many an outrageous scheme that benefited paper profiteers over loyal patriots. The 'assumption' plan also ran into opposition from representatives of states that had paid off most of their obligations. In their eyes, Hamilton's proposal penalized states that acted responsibly and rewarded those that remained derelict in their financial duty.

The funding measure passed, but the assumption proposal ran into opposition. Key critics such as Virginia's Representative Madison and Secretary of State Jefferson backed the bill only after entering into a political deal that would influence the lives of politicians – and tourists – for years to come. Jefferson and Madison supported assumption when they got Hamilton to support something in their interest: the Secretary pledged to locate the new national capital farther south than originally planned. The city would be built right in the heart of the Chesapeake region, in Virginia's (and Maryland's) back yard. To win passage of his murky economic proposal, Hamilton promised to place the 'District of Columbia' on some swampy real estate along the Potomac – where the federal government still deals with the effects of its permanent national debt.

If Hamilton's other economic reports did not produce as shrewd a political deal, they did generate as rancorous a political debate. One report called on Congress to create a national bank to store funds, issue money, make loans, monitor state banks, and stabilize the economy. Hamilton believed the proposal was modest and responsible; critics felt it was reckless and dangerous. Opponents saw the project as doubly cursed: not only had Hamilton modeled the institution on the corrupt Bank of England, but the Constitution did not grant Congress power to create a bank. There might be any number of sensible tasks Congress could undertake; but should its authority extend to anything and everything? Then Congress and the whole federal apparatus could become as all-powerful as skeptics in the late 1780s had feared.

Jefferson, Madison, and others argued that the Constitution meant what it said: Congress could only exercise certain specific powers. Those not 'enumerated' were not lawful. 'To take a single step beyond the boundaries,' Jefferson warned, '... is to take possession of a boundless field of power, no longer susceptible of any definition.' A narrow interpretation of the document was the best way to limit government power and protect popular liberties.

Hamilton disagreed, pointing to the part of the Constitution that spelled out the authority of Congress. The last sentence of Article I, Section 8 stated that Congress could 'make all laws which shall be necessary and proper' for carrying out its legitimate powers. Congress had the power to collect taxes and regulate trade; the bank was simply necessary and proper for carrying out those tasks. It was constitutional. Some of the document's ambiguous statements *implied* federal authority; those powers 'ought to be construed liberally in advancement of the public good'. Such a reading promoted a responsible government that served changing national needs.

In a close vote, Congress passed Hamilton's bill and chartered the first Bank of the United States. When the charter came up for renewal 20 years later, political leaders again debated the merits of the institution. And again, the bank stirred fundamental political passions. Jeffersonian 'strict constructionists' once more engaged Hamiltonian 'broad constructionists'. Debate over the meaning of the Constitution has continued to occupy Americans ever since.

Debate about the proper economic course for the republic also became a semi-permanent national obsession and, again, Alexander Hamilton enlivened the discussion. His 1791 'Report on Manufactures' outlined a route toward prosperity that did not follow traditional agricultural paths. He sensed that while individual farmers enjoyed modest success, America was still subordinate to more diversified nations that provided the valuable finished goods and commercial services the new republic lacked. Politically independent, the United States remained an economic colony.

Hamilton reasoned that the nation had to broaden its economic horizons by building factories as productive as its fields, but such a change would come about only if government lit a fire under Americans to rouse them from their wistful agrarian reveries. Tossing *laissez-faire* thinking aside, Hamilton proposed a new mercantilism: the federal government should incite a market revolution. He asked for protective tariffs to assist manufacturers, excise taxes to raise revenues, bounties to encourage commercial agriculture, subsidies to help fishermen and whalers, and transportation improvements to move goods and services. The government, he believed, should be an active player in the economy, building the wealth and power of the nation.

Jefferson, however, took the view that *agriculture* best served the needs of citizens and their republic. Economically and politically, he argued, title to the soil provided individuals with a source of wealth, a stake in society, a voice in politics, and a refuge from market storms. The land 'grounded' ideas of liberty and freedom. Morally, Jefferson viewed farmers as 'the chosen people of God, if ever he had a chosen people, whose breasts he has made his peculiar deposit for substantial and genuine virtue'. Farming was not only a worthy occupation for individuals but a worthwhile preoccupation for all republicans interested in the stability of their society. A manufacturing society, on the other hand, tore people away from the land, crowded them in dirty cities, and subjected them to the will of unpredictable employers and capricious markets. Instead of promoting freedom and virtue, industrialization produced dependence and vice. No sensible republican government should pursue such a goal. Fortunately, Jefferson concluded, small-scale, decentralized manufacturing, based in republican households, could meet the nation's needs.

Opposition to Hamilton's program proved formidable. Congress granted a small increase in tariffs on imports, modest excise taxes on items such as whiskey, and little else. Perhaps it was just as well, for what did pass caused considerable controversy. Southwestern Pennsylvania farmers in particular resented the whiskey tax. Far removed from markets, they routinely distilled their crops into spirits instead of paying high prices to transport bags of grain overland. The tax not only cramped their style but also ate into their profits. By 1794, the locals had disrupted tax collection, retaliated against those who complied, and threatened federal agents. An angry Hamilton called for a show of force against the insurgents. Washington complied and an army of 13,000 marched west to put down the 'Whiskey Rebellion'. By the time they arrived, there was no insurrection left. Troops rounded up a small group of agitators, two of whom were convicted of treasonable offenses and later pardoned. Tussles between federal 'revenuers' and cantankerous 'moonshiners' continued over the years and became a staple of American folklore. The Whiskey Rebellion itself was hardly a laughing matter, however. By choosing to quell civil unrest, the federal government had made a simple but profound point: it would enforce the laws it enacted.

Of course, that was just what Hamilton wanted, although it would take time to get his point across. Localist-minded Americans came to understand the hard way what it meant to live under a strong central government. Hamilton's cherished economic vision also eventually took hold, although the rise of new market relations began, ironically enough, under the leadership of Jeffersonians. By then, Hamilton was no longer there to savor the victory, having met his end in an 1804 duel with an unscrupulous political foe, Aaron Burr, Jefferson's vice president.

Hamilton's economic and political nationalism promoted an active government and a diverse economy, all brought into being by an elite cadre of wise leaders. If nothing else, he has as fitting a memorial as any American hero. Hamilton's face does not adorn a public temple or a cherished seal but one side of the ten-dollar bill; turn the sawbuck over and there one finds a picture of the Treasury Building. His grave does not sit in some rural churchyard or ethereal setting but in the cemetery of Trinity Church near Wall Street where Hamilton rests in eternal peace, enjoying the pleasant company of stockjobbers and speculators.

The Birth of Political Parties

Before taking a bullet, however, Hamilton's controversial programs helped to spark the rise of two, opposing political camps. Both supported republican government, constitutional principles, and revolutionary patriotism. Each charged the other with subversive intent; neither saw itself as a permanent party. On these matters, at least, they sounded alike, but much divided them. The opponents disagreed not on the threat of power but on the locus of power, not on the glory of the Constitution but on its interpretation, not on the necessity of a central government but on its extent, and not on the growth of America but on the proper route to its expansion.

One group, led by Hamilton, John Adams, Thomas Pinckney, and others, placed its trust in vigorous and energetic federal leadership. Identified as 'Federalists', they believed that the best government actively served the public good. Their opponents, led by Jefferson, Madison, George Clinton, and others, insisted that the new federal government should limit the exercise of its power and defer to the authority of local institutions. Identified as 'Democratic-Republicans', they believed that the best government governed least.

Taking coherent shape by 1794, the rivals went at it hammer and tong, each believing that the future of the young republic lay in jeopardy. To a considerable extent, the arguments they waged in the last decade of the eighteenth century remain important issues at the opening of the twenty-first. When does power become excessive?

How are rights best preserved? Does the republic's strength rest in unity or in the protection of liberty?

Hamilton, Jefferson, and their allies were worlds apart in their political thinking because they held very different visions of the good society and human nature. Hamilton believed the nation was working with a desirable but untested political system. The problem lay not with government itself but with the governed. He viewed his countrymen as unstable and narrow in their political tendencies, driven by wild passions, and limited by petty localism. Given the choice, average folk would remain in their fields, identify with their small communities, and view distant power with suspicion, neglecting the larger concerns that affected all Americans. It was far better, Hamilton assumed, for a talented and cosmopolitan few to take charge of a vigorous national government and guide the people through the complexities of national life.

Jefferson also believed that the nation was working with a desirable yet untested form of government. But what made the new republican order precarious was not the governed but those who did the governing. The greatest danger came from small groups of ambitious and cunning leaders who presumed to define national interests and sought to monopolize national power. Fortunately, Jefferson argued, most citizens remained committed to Revolutionary principles. They understood how the new Constitutional order should operate and recognized that they would 'preserve the liberty we have obtained only by unremitting labors and perils'. The national political system could remain limited in its operations because the competence, wisdom, and vigilance of local governments (and informed citizens) would leave it little to do.

Out of such differences, the first political parties emerged. None of the principals meant to create permanent parties because all feared 'factions' in a republic. Still, political leaders saw their spontaneous and ragged organizations change over time into fixed institutions. Never mentioned in the Constitution, never intended by the Founders, and never honored in republican tradition, parties went on to become prominent players in American politics. And, to a remarkable extent, their debates over two centuries have continually centered on the choice posed in the 1790s between a strong and a limited federal government.

The Political Storms of the 1790s

Hamilton's domestic programs may have raised the heat and volume of political debate, but it was the course of foreign events in the 1790s that sparked an all-out partisan struggle for the republican soul of the United States. The Treasury Secretary's economic reports compelled Americans to consider the proper response to power exercised by their own government; the French Revolution and European warfare compelled Americans to consider the proper response to power exercised by other governments. The question was how the newly formed nation could survive and carry on with its principles intact in the face of titanic imperial rivalries.

The contest that engulfed Europe stood at the center of party disputes in America. On one side stood the Jeffersonians: their sympathies lay with the French struggle for republican ideals. France was a friend that supported the American revolutionary cause, an ally to whom the United States was tied by a 1778 treaty, and a sister republic that fought to throw off the chains of monarchy and aristocracy. Together, France and America stood against Britain's royal, hierarchical, and corrupt empire. On the other side stood the Hamiltonians: their sympathies lay with the British struggle for world stability and order. Great Britain was a key economic partner that helped secure prosperity and a key political partner that helped secure established rule. Together, Britain and the United States stood against France's bogus and anarchic 'republican' revolution.

Each side claimed that the United States faced a clear-cut choice, but each side had mixed motives. Jeffersonians on the frontier knew that a pro-French policy conveniently served their interests: if French military adventures made life miserable for Britain and Spain, the latter pair might focus their attention on Europe, loosen their grip in the West, and unintentionally open up new lands for settlers. Hamiltonian merchants and shippers knew that a pro-British policy suited their needs: since Britain was the major customer for American products and the major supplier of manufactured items, good relations with the Empire promised trade, employment, and profits.

Each side also attempted to overlook their European allies' worst excesses. Democratic-Republicans tried to play down the violence and mayhem of the French Revolution: the Jacobins' radical turn; the imprisonment and execution of the king and queen; the Reign of Terror in 1792–1794; and the wars with Great Britain, Spain, Austria, and Prussia. Things became more uncomfortable – and hit closer to home – with a 1793 visit to the United States by French diplomat Edmond Genêt, who reminded the nation of its 1778 treaty obligations to France and called on American support for the new war effort against Britain and Spain. Cheered by 'Democratic Societies' that hailed the French Revolution and derided the Federalists, Genêt kept up his popular appeals even after President Washington officially proclaimed that the United States would steer a 'friendly and impartial' course. In the end, 'Citizen' Genêt helped set American privateers loose on British vessels, failed to launch successful military expeditions from the United States, and embarrassed supporters such as Jefferson by launching 'indecent' political attacks on the administration.

Meanwhile, Federalists had their hands full dealing with the heavy-handed tactics of the British. On land and sea, the Empire's policies ignited anti-British sentiment in the United States. The British maintained posts in the Old Northwest, inflamed tensions between Indians and settlers, closed off the republic's trade with the West Indies, intercepted US shipping, and engaged in the impressment of American sailors. In response, President Washington launched a diplomatic offensive, trying to settle by negotiation what the United States knew it could not secure by force.

The tactic paid off in Jay's Treaty of 1795. While British notions of 'neutrality' prevailed in the agreement, the treaty arranged for the evacuation of western posts and reparations for intercepted cargo. Jeffersonians saw the settlement as a defeat for America's interests at home and liberty's interests around the world, but Senate Federalists secured passage of the accord. The treaty was probably the best that the young republic could manage and helped spark an expansion of trade in the latter part of the decade. Two other agreements in 1795 also helped

US ambitions on the frontier. The Treaty of Grenville forced Indian tribes to make large land cessions in the Old Northwest. And the Treaty of San Lorenzo (with Spain) granted the United States navigation rights to the Mississippi River. For a government caught in the squeeze of European conflict and domestic political debate, the Washington administration managed to pull off some fairly respectable diplomatic accomplishments as it also strengthened American sovereignty in the West.

The gains came at a high political price, however. Democratic Societies hounded the administration about its foreign and domestic agenda. Federalists accused their opponents of demagoguery, radicalism, and various forms of villainy. Secretary of State Jefferson had had enough a few years earlier and left the cabinet in 1793. Washington himself came in for quite a drubbing, especially during his last year in office, amid inflammatory debates over foreign policy, treaties, taxes, and whiskey. Even Tom Paine called the president an unprincipled hypocrite.

Drained by partisan struggles and longing for quiet times at his Mount Vernon home, Washington announced he would not accept a third term. He bade farewell to the nation in an address that both Madison and Hamilton helped draft. Washington warned of the dangers posed by sectionalism, party politics, and European entanglements. The divisiveness of regional ties could break apart the union that was so necessary for liberty. The narrow loyalties endorsed by permanent factions and the fiendish traps produced by 'permanent alliances' would also unravel the interests of the republic. Washington argued that, at home, Americans should define common ground and put aside petty differences; abroad, Americans should extend commercial contacts and withdraw from political controversies. Most applauded the outgoing president's sentiments, but before long the nation was plunged right back into the thick of domestic and overseas disputes.

The Last Federalist Hurrah

Partly because of Washington's absence from the scene, the 1796 election became the first overtly partisan contest for the presidency.

With no single heroic figure to rally around, caucuses of Federalists and (as they were now known) Republicans nominated candidates loyal to particular party principles. John Adams, Washington's vice-president, carried the Federalist banner while Jefferson was the Republican's standard-bearer. Adams squeaked out a victory in the Electoral College only to find himself thrust into an unruly and contentious single term in office.

From the start, nothing seemed to go right for Adams, even among his supposed allies. Many members of his cabinet turned for political guidance to Hamilton, who had favored Federalist Thomas Pinckney over Adams. Even more divisive was the person who served directly under Adams. Under the original rules of the Constitution, the candidate with the second highest number of electoral votes became vice-president. In 1796, that turned out to be Jefferson!

Adams also had to contend with the hostile actions of the French. That nation's raids against American shipping had increased since the United States and Britain settled their differences with Jay's Treaty. Negotiators sent to Paris in 1797 met with three Frenchmen (later named in a report as Messieurs 'X', 'Y', and 'Z'). The trio agreed to negotiate only if the Americans arranged both a loan to the French government and a bribe to get talks underway. The commissioners refused, news of the 'XYZ Affair' spread, and Americans stood aghast at France's deplorable diplomatic affront. Adams pushed for an expansion of American defenses, the 1778 treaty with France was repealed, Congress created a naval department, Washington assumed command of the army, and, by 1798, an undeclared 'Quasi-War' had broken out with the French.

War turned out to be one of Adams's better political moves. By stirring the martial spirit, Federalists rallied public support and picked up more House seats in the 1798 election. But then the party demonstrated how skillfully it could snatch defeat from the jaws of victory. Armed with greater political clout and eager to thrash their opponents, the Federalists passed a series of acts in 1798 designed to quell domestic dissent and break Republican influence. Convinced that foreign subversives had infiltrated the United States, Congress passed the Alien Act, giving the president greater power to imprison or deport dangerous aliens. Convinced that immigrants had swelled Republican ranks, Congress passed the Naturalization Act, imposing more stringent requirements on those who sought citizenship. Convinced that irresponsible political criticism had undermined the nation's interests, Federalists passed the Sedition Act, making it a crime to write, utter, or publish 'false, scandalous and malicious' statements directed against the government.

Hoping to silence their political opponents, Federalists used the law to secure 25 arrests, 15 indictments, and 10 convictions, most directed against Republicans. In response, Jefferson and Madison drafted the 'Virginia and Kentucky Resolutions', arguing two key points: that the federal government was formed out of a compact or contract among the states to serve specific purposes; and that when the federal government violated those purposes, a state could 'interpose' itself in the dispute and nullify the law in question.

Other legislatures, however, chose not to 'interpose' themselves in support of the resolutions' 'states' rights' principles, though the argument surfaced again in United States history. Foes of the Federalists remained fearful of attacks on free speech and press and became even more alarmed in 1799 when federal forces once again ventured into Pennsylvania to put down another tax revolt. 'Fries Rebellion' challenged the higher levies Federalists had imposed to pay for military spending. As in 1794, the insurrection fizzled by the time the cavalry arrived.

While peacemakers prevailed among Pennsylvania German farmers, peace feelers flowed from French officials. Sensing the public's desire to end hostilities, Adams agreed to negotiate – in opposition to other Federalists who had discovered the politically rejuvenating properties of war. By 1801, through a settlement with the new government under First Consul Napoleon Bonaparte, the United States released itself from the 1778 treaty with France.

Having freed the nation from a small-scale war, an entangling alliance, and a domestic rebellion, Adams ran for a second term. His own party was troubled and divided; the opposition Republicans were efficient and well-organized, running Virginia's Jefferson as their candidate for president and New York's Burr for vice-president.

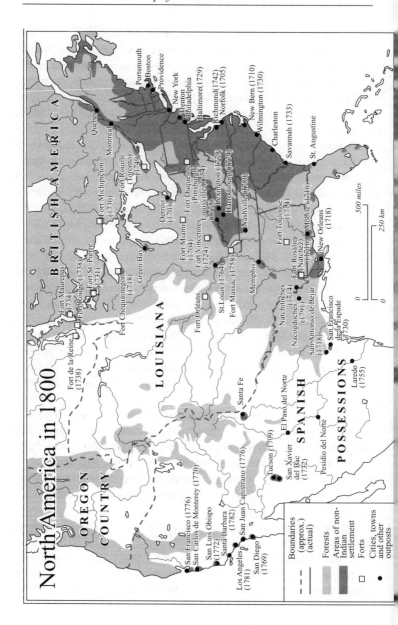

North America in 1800

OREGON COUNTRY

BRITISH AMERICA

LOUISIANA

SPANISH POSSESSIONS

Portsmouth
Boston
Providence
New York
Trenton
Philadelphia
Baltimore (1729)
Richmond (1742)
Norfolk (1705)
New Bern (1710)
Wilmington (1730)
Charleston
Savannah (1733)
St. Augustine

Quebec
Montreal
Fort Michipicton (1730)
Fort Rouillé (Toronto) (1749)
Detroit (1701)
Fort Duquesne (Pittsburgh) (1754)
Louisville (1758)
Lexington (1779)
Harrodsburg (1774)
Nashville (1780)
Fort Toulouse (1714)
Mobile (1710)
New Orleans (1718)

Fort Maurepas (1734)
Fort Rouge (1738)
Fort St. Pierre (1731)
Fort Chequamegon (1718)
Green Bay
Fort Miami (1704)
Fort Vincennes (1724)
Fort Orléans
St. Louis (1764)
Fort Massac (1758)
Memphis
Natchitoches
Nacogdoches (1791)
Fort Rosalie (Natchez) (1716)

Fort de la Reine (1738)

San Antonio de Béjar (1718)
San Francisco de la Espade (1730)

Santa Fe
El Paso del Norte (1709)
Presidio del Norte
Laredo (1755)

Tucson
San Xavier del Bac (1732)

San Francisco (1776)
San Carlos de Monterey (1770)
San Luis Obispo (1772)
Santa Barbara (1782)
San Juan Capistrano (1776)
Los Angeles (1781)
San Diego (1769)

500 miles
250 km
0

Boundaries (approx.) (actual)
Forests
Areas of non-Indian settlement
Forts
Cities, towns and other outposts

As in 1796, the election created yet another odd result. Jefferson and Burr each ended up with 73 electoral votes, more than the Federalist candidates but not a majority of the electoral votes. The election was thrown into the Federalist-controlled House which selected two highest vote getters. Thirty-six ballots later, Federalists decided a repugnant Jefferson was better than a repulsive Burr, and the Virginian became president. An 1804 amendment altered such clumsy arrangements by allowing electors to vote *separately* for president and vice-president.

Federalists lost the presidency in 1800 and never won the post again. They also lost their majorities in the House and Senate and never regained control of Congress. But before leaving office, Federalists passed a Judiciary Act allowing the lame duck, Adams, to fill up the courts with party appointees. The third branch of government remained in Federalist hands for years. Despite the shady maneuver, the nation witnessed at least one major triumph: authority passed from one political center to another in a calm, orderly, and peaceful fashion.

The Jeffersonians' Political 'Revolution'

Long after leaving office, Jefferson described his electoral victory as 'the Revolution of 1800 ... as real a revolution in the principles of our government as that of 1776 was in its form'. He believed in a limited central government, one that dealt only with the mutual and external relations of the states and deferred to their decisions on all other matters. Yet, as time passed, his party came act to like Federalists in many of the policies they adopted, expanding the range of federal power and helping lay the groundwork for a modern market economy.

Through purposeful design, Jefferson managed to reduce the power of the central government. At home, the Republicans cut the national debt, slashed military spending, repealed all internal taxes, and allowed the dreaded Bank of the United States and the Alien and Sedition Acts to expire. For the most part, the federal government was left to deliver the mail, administer public lands, and handle Indian affairs. In foreign policy, Jeffersonians announced their support for liberty, their opposition to despotism, and their belief that republican societies were naturally pacific, depending less on force and more on forms of 'peaceable coercion'.

Through good fortune, Jefferson benefited from the mis-fortunes of another ruler. In 1803, the cash-strapped Emperor Napoleon offered the Louisiana Territory for sale, a parcel which Spain had transferred to French control in 1800. The land stretched from the Mississippi across to the Rockies, from the northern plains down to New Orleans. Jefferson jumped at the offer, and for fifteen million dollars he doubled the size of the republic, providing 'an empire of liberty' for all future generations of Americans. There was one tiny problem for the strict constructionist: the President had no Constitutional authority to make the purchase. However, by turning to a clause on treaties, the administration made the deal legitimate. Jefferson regretted the precedent he might have set for expanding executive authority but remained 'confident that the good sense of our country will correct the evil of loose construction when it shall produce ill effects'.

It was not the only time that Jeffersonians appeared strangely Hamiltonian. Tariffs, federal transportation improvements, a national

Monticello

debt, the Bank of the United States, and Hamilton's funding and assumption schemes all remained in place. Jefferson could also turn up the partisan heat with the best of them. And when the nation found itself caught in the middle of Continental warfare, Jefferson took the audacious step of stopping all commerce overseas, intervening 'energetically' enough in the free market to stun most Federalists.

Commerce, Settlement, and Foreign Policy

Jefferson took drastic foreign trade measures because the republic was caught in an international struggle that seemed to present nothing less than a second war for independence. Conflict between Britain and France flared up again in 1803. Americans remained aloof from the struggle militarily but got into the thick of things commercially, expanding their international shipping while the belligerents battled one another. The United States may have taken a stand for 'neutral rights' – and a quick buck – but Britain and France saw things differently. They believed the United States profited from their misfortune while giving aid and comfort (and supplies) to each other's enemy. From 1805 to 1807, the warring parties placed severe restrictions on US shipping. Both sides stopped and seized American vessels. The British even hauled away (or 'impressed') members of American crews whom they suspected of having deserted the Royal Navy. Jefferson found his nation bullied on the high seas by France and Britain, one 'a den of robbers and the other of pirates'. He responded not through military means but by a 'peaceable' form of coercion: his 1807 Embargo Act stopped American ships from departing for foreign ports.

For a year and a quarter, the Embargo inflicted serious damage on shipping interests, merchants, and farmers – not in Britain and France, but in America. Federalists, not surprisingly, had a field day with the domestic turmoil. Frustrated with the economic and political costs of his embargo, Jefferson repealed the measure as one of the last acts of his presidency. His successor, James Madison, reopened foreign trade in 1809 with all nations except Britain and France, reopened trade with the belligerents in 1810, and then closed trade with Britain after France agreed to stop interfering with American shipping, a pledge that Napoleon soon ignored.

While Easterners denounced British threats on the seas, Westerners fumed over British challenges on the frontier. Settlers and their political allies complained that the Empire purposely stirred up Indian tribes in order to halt American settlement. In the Old Northwest, whites were particularly upset over the activities of Shawnee leaders Tecumseh and his brother Tenskwatawa who had the audacity to defend tribal lands and culture and unify their people. The Shawnee effort met defeat at the Battle of Tippecanoe in northern Indiana Territory in the fall of 1811. Congressional 'war hawks' such as Henry Clay of Kentucky and John C. Calhoun of South Carolina called for armed hostilities with Great Britain as a way to stop Indian threats, defend American honor, and gain more territory for the republic in Canada and Florida.

The War of 1812

Responding to war fever on 1 June 1812, President Madison expressed outrage over British assaults on sea and land. Although Britain rescinded its commercial interference on 16 June, the change came too late. Before word reached the United States, Congress had declared war on 18 June. The neutral rights dispute that precipitated fighting was settled before the conflict began – just one of many ironies in the War of 1812.

A second paradox was that an administration so eager for war was so ill prepared to fight. Fearful of a large standing army, Republicans left the nation defended by only 7,000 soldiers and fewer than 20 naval vessels. Spooked by the power of concentrated money, the party left the nation without a central financial institution by allowing the Bank of the United States to expire. Suspicious of excessive government revenues, Jeffersonians had little cash on hand to pay for the conflict. The nation had no internal taxes; Congress balked at raising taxes to finance the war; and tariff receipts fell as combat interrupted trade. Relying on loans to pay for most of the fighting, the party opposed to debt went into hock to pay for its second war of republican independence.

A third odd twist in the war involved strategy: a war supposedly sparked by violations of American rights on the seas opened up with conflicts on the land. Since American vessels were no match for the British navy, it seemed more prudent to take on enemy forces ashore rather than afloat, and by doing so, satisfy the territorial cravings of war hawks. The United States launched its initial campaign against British forces in Canada. Yankee leaders planned three assaults. Two failed; one never got started. As it turned out, America's greatest triumphs in the first phase of the war were in naval encounters, highlighted by the success of 'Old Ironsides' (the frigate, *Constitution*) and Captain Oliver Perry's victory over British forces on Lake Erie in 1813.

A fourth twist was that a conflict intended to reassert America's independence marked the only war in the republic's history in which its national capital was severely damaged. British forces launched the second phase of the war in 1814 with a three-pronged offensive. The first drive, in New York, failed. The second, in the Chesapeake, resulted in the burning of the White House, the Capitol, and other buildings in August of 1814. The British then continued their drive north to Baltimore, where their approach inspired Francis Scott Key to write the audibly-stirring and vocally-straining 'Star-Spangled Banner', later adopted as the republic's national anthem.

Britain's final offensive effort focused on New Orleans, a campaign which eventually led to a fifth irony in the conflict: America's most notable military success came *after* the war had ended. Sir Edward Pakenham's troops met Andrew Jackson's army at New Orleans on 8 January 1815. The battle claimed fewer than 60 American deaths and injuries; the British suffered over 2,000 casualties. While the republic hailed Jackson's triumph, negotiators in Ghent had already accomplished something far more significant two weeks earlier: they signed a peace treaty on Christmas Eve of 1814, bringing the war to a conclusion.

The Treaty of Ghent marked a sixth irony in the war: it settled nothing. The agreement asserted the *status quo ante bellum*, skirting disputes about impressment, territories, and indemnities. Americans, however, joyously linked the news of New Orleans and Ghent and assumed that the forces of republicanism had once again turned back the tide of monarchism.

CONSEQUENCES OF THE WAR OF 1812

The conclusion of the war may have produced a dubious triumph over a foreign foe, but it led the Republican majority to a certain victory over its domestic 'enemy'. The war broke the back of the Federalists who were stung both by trade disruptions and by charges of 'disloyalty'. The party criticized Madison's war policy at a convention in Hartford, Connecticut. Rallying behind arguments reminiscent of Republican 'states' rights' principles, Federalists challenged the power of the federal government and proposed Constitutional amendments to protect the interests of their main power base, New England. Unfortunately, the conference suffered from a terrible sense of timing: word of its war protests broke as news of America's 'victory' spread. The Federalists never recovered from their apparent treachery; by 1820, the party did not even run a presidential candidate. From 1817 to 1820, heated partisan debate came to an end; a cynic might describe the years as a time of 'one-party rule'. A Boston newspaper hit on a more upbeat tag, hailing the period as an 'Era of Good Feelings'. The label stuck.

The War of 1812 also led to a significant change in the position of native peoples. One of the key strategies for survival used by American Indians for over two centuries was to play whites off against one another, keeping expansionist settlers in check by creating shifting alliances with imperial European forces. The intention was to control white behavior by making Americans and Europeans fear reprisal – from Americans and Europeans. Native people hoped that any levers they could pull in the balance of power might help contain the spread of white settlement. But by 1815, French and Spanish power had been eroded and, with the conclusion of the War of 1812, US–British tensions eased considerably. It became increasingly difficult for native people to build defensive alliances that could hold back the tide of white American expansion.

The now-unbridled Republicans took a curious turn with the political dominance they enjoyed. War taught Jefferson's heirs the benefit, rather than the danger, of extending national power. Republicans re-chartered the Bank of the United States (to provide the sound financial footing desperately lacking during the war), tripled the size of the standing, peacetime army (to ensure military preparedness), passed the nation's first protective tariff (to assist the industries that had developed in the lean economic days of embargo and war), and pushed for transportation improvements (to avoid the traffic snarls faced by troops and to move people and goods more efficiently). With such an energetic set of national programs in the works, one critic charged that the Republicans had 'out-Federalized the Federalists'.

While extending national power, the Republicans also expanded the size of the national domain. In 1818, General Andrew Jackson launched a military campaign in western Florida to subdue Seminole Indians. By 1819, the United States had hammered out a Transcontinental Treaty with Spain through which the republic acquired all of Florida, fixed the western boundary of the Louisiana Purchase, and gladly accepted Spain's abandonment of its land claims in Oregon Territory. With northwest lands above the 42nd parallel jointly occupied by the United States and Britain (under an 1818 convention), America's territorial claims literally extended from sea to sea.

Having reasserted its political independence, the United States also moved to affirm its diplomatic independence. President James Monroe expressed concern over Western hemisphere nations that, since 1811, had broken away from imperial control in wars of national liberation. Would reactionary forces in Europe try to reassert their influence over these countries? Rejecting London's suggestion that the United States and Britain should jointly prevent such a calamity, the President and Secretary of State John Quincy Adams developed their own statement on international conduct. Announced in late 1823, the 'Monroe Doctrine' declared that the United States had no desire to intervene in European affairs, no desire to interfere in European colonies, *and* no desire to see further European colonization in the Western hemisphere. Any meddling by Europeans with independent governments in North and South America would be taken as an unfriendly act towards the United States. Americans cheered the doctrine as the proud, defiant proclamation of a sovereign republic defending its home turf. Europeans basically ignored it. That the doctrine's principles were upheld had little to do with US influence on world behavior. It mattered more that Britain looked favorably on the policy – and backed up its preferences with the Royal Navy.

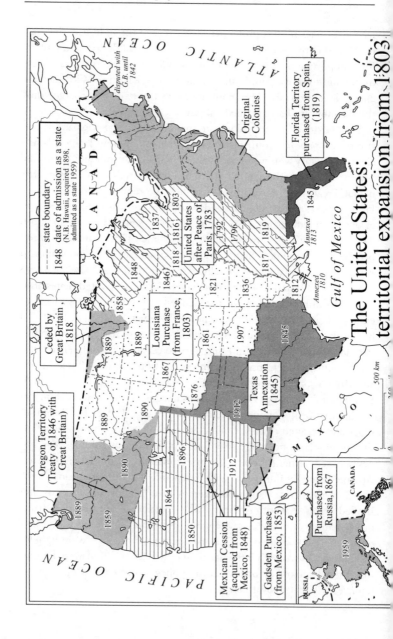

The United States: territorial expansion from 1803

state boundary

1848 date of admission as a state
(N.B. Hawaii, acquired 1898, admitted as a state 1959)

Original Colonies

Florida Territory purchased from Spain, (1819)

United States after Peace of Paris, 1783

Ceded by Great Britain, 1818

Louisiana Purchase (from France, 1803)

Oregon Territory (Treaty of 1846 with Great Britain)

Texas Annexation (1845)

Mexican Cession (acquired from Mexico, 1848)

Gadsden Purchase (from Mexico, 1853)

Purchased from Russia, 1867

disputed with G.B. until 1842

Annexed 1845

Annexed 1813

Annexed 1810

ATLANTIC OCEAN

PACIFIC OCEAN

CANADA

MEXICO

Gulf of Mexico

RUSSIA

CANADA

500 km

The Republicans' Legacy

For the first quarter of the nineteenth century, the Jeffersonians dominated national government. Some historians contend that the party did spark a revolution in the principles of American government. Its leaders maintained confidence in the common people, trusted their grasp of political realities, and acknowledged their capacity for self-government. The national government reflected rather than refashioned the public will. There was no reason to do more; citizens and states would fill in the gaps. Jeffersonians left government purposely weak.

But other historians argue that Republicans expressed the minimalist talk while making maximum use of Constitutional authority. Jefferson expanded executive power, serving as a forceful party leader, real estate developer, and economic manipulator. His followers forced the nation to learn some hard lessons about military and market un-preparedness and then shifted Constitutional gears to correct their errors. Republicans of the early 1820s acted more and more like Federalists of the 1790s. Federalists of the 1820s – what was left of them – grumbled more and more like their opponents in the republic's first decade. The two sides thus helped forge a proud tradition of ideological somersaults in American politics.

They also helped establish – and then kill off – the first party system. For all their insight and expertise, the Federalists proved dull-witted about public opinion, elitist about political leadership, and ill-timed in their war protests. But if Federalists defiantly marched down a path of self-destruction, Republicans proved even more clever: their *success* led to their failure. By 1820, nearly everyone was a Republican; and yet, after decades of heated debate, the 'good feelings' quickly turned sour. The old bogeyman of the Federalist Party had helped quarreling Republicans maintain a united front. By 1820, with the Federalists gone and with many Republicans moving in a Federalist direction, factions quickly formed within party ranks. The presidential election of 1820 turned out to be the Republicans' most – and last – harmonious campaign.

An era came to an end. By the early 1820s, the first political group to lead the republic faded away: a Constitutional order that did not call for any parties found itself initially with two organizations and then just one. By the mid-1820s, the political leadership of the Revolutionary generation had also passed away: on 4 July 1826 – the fiftieth anniversary of the Declaration of Independence – Thomas Jefferson and John Adams both died. By the end of the decade, a new political order began operating. While echoing Jeffersonian principles of limited government, the new, 'democratic' order operated by a different set of rules and a new style of politics.

The New Face of American Politics

Four key changes occurred in American politics by the late 1820s. First, the number of states expanded from 16 to 24. That meant more Congressmen, more electoral votes, and more distinctive regions hoping to satisfy their particular interests. Secondly, suffrage broadened. New states dropped property requirements for the vote; older states lowered or eliminated their property requirements. Nine out of ten adult white males were eligible to vote by 1840 – although Northern state legislators had cut back even further the voting rights of free African American males and eliminated the vote for women (with the end of female suffrage in New Jersey in 1807). Thirdly, voting procedures changed. More offices were opened to popular vote, including the direct election of state governors, judges, and even presidential electors. Those with the vote had more reason to turn out at the polls, leading to a fourth change in the political world: higher rates of voter participation. The percentage of eligible voters who took part in presidential elections increased from 27 per cent in 1824 to over 80 per cent in 1840.

All of these changes created a new political world. The rapidly expanding nation contained an enlarged, mass electorate that was more diverse (because it reflected new combinations of interest groups), more disorganized (because of the amorphous state of the Republican Party), and more active (because of the greater number of political contests up for grabs). To some, the political world appeared to sit on the brink of confusion. Americans had unleashed their enormous political energy but had not channeled that force in any orderly or purposeful direction.

John Quincy Adams won the election of 1824 in the House of Representatives
even though Andrew Jackson received the most popular votes

In 1820, the nation witnessed the uncontested election of James
Monroe. Four years later, different regional groups promoted different
regional candidates, and the nation faced a four-way race. William H.
Crawford, John Quincy Adams, Henry Clay, and Andrew Jackson all
ran for president. The election of 1824 was deeply divided *and* bitterly
fought. Jackson received most of the popular votes but less than a
majority of the electoral votes. The election was thrown into the
House. Clay, with the fewest electoral votes, was out of the running,
but he endorsed Adams for president. Adams won the race, and then
named Clay as his Secretary of State. Supporters of Jackson were
enraged; their candidate was the popular choice but lost out because of
a 'corrupt bargain'. Their bitterness lingered throughout Adams's ill-
fated single term of office. Jacksonians charged that the wide-open
world of American politics closed itself to the people's will.

RE-INVENTING THE POLITICAL PARTY

In New York, a political operative named Martin Van Buren worked
out a way to make sense of America's new political forces and contain
its bitter political disputes. Van Buren developed a new type of party,
one that was less ideologically motivated than organizationally driven.
Its goal was to tie together large, varied (and potentially conflicting)
groups of voters rather than to enact a precise and coherent set of

political principles. The party was principally a binding force rather than a philosophical force, one that joined disparate elements under one banner, rallied them behind appealing candidates, promoted cooperation, and asked only for loyalty to the will of its organization. Van Buren believed such a party would lead to a responsive government in which majority will ruled and national unity prevailed. Parties would act as a glue holding a fragmented nation together, helping overcome the splintering divisions of class, region, market, race, and ethnicity. Van Buren saw the party as an agency of political reform, bringing order out of chaos.

Van Buren's political savvy combined with Jackson's political fury in the mid-1820s to create the new 'Democratic-Republican' Party. Well-organized by the 1828 election, the Democrats, as they called themselves, launched a presidential campaign unlike any the nation had seen. The party mobilized voters through the hoopla of conventions, newspapers, rallies, parades, posters, buttons, and banners. Their platform, however, said next to nothing. Its candidate supported a 'just' tariff, favored Western expansion, and wanted to keep the power of the national government limited. But that was as specific as Democrats cared to be. Far more important was the party's central personality, Andrew Jackson. Supporters hailed him as a man who climbed to the top of national life from humble roots. Speeches, broadsides, and songs celebrated Jackson's triumphs: as a poor, 14-year-old frontier boy left without a family; as a scrappy, self-reliant Revolutionary patriot who faced the British; and as a determined adult who rose in the military, in farming, in law, and in politics.

At the opposite end of the spectrum stood the incumbent, John Quincy Adams, a person of breeding, schooling, gentility, and refinement who was more accustomed to power than deserving of it. Proud, aristocratic, and haughty, Adams led the people but was not one of them. Worst of all, he and his cronies betrayed the people in the chicanery of the 1824 election. It was time, Democrats insisted, to take back the popular mandate denied four years earlier by the forces of special privilege.

Jackson won with 56 per cent of the popular vote and nearly 70 per cent of the electoral vote, drawing heavily on all areas of the country except the Northeast, and building the kind of broad-based coalition Van Buren had in mind. After a rowdy and indecorous inauguration bash at the executive mansion, where an unruly crowd trampled on the mansion's furnishings and was finally lured outside with a large tub of alcoholic refreshment, the administration went to work.

JACKSONIAN 'DEMOCRACY'

Since the campaign showed how far a candidate could get on evasion and imprecision, one might think that the President had little incentive to hold true to 'principle'. Yet, as biographer Robert V. Remini has argued, Jackson's 'Democracy' actually stood for something: the people were the ultimate authority. Government officials served merely as agents of the sovereign power; the *majority* must rule; and several political reforms would make that happen. First, the people should vote for all officers in the national government, casting direct ballots not just for the House but for the president, senators, and even federal judges. Secondly, the people should instruct all office holders, forcing leaders to listen to the people's voice at all times, not just at election time. Thirdly, officials should rotate in and out of office, acknowledging that their posts were a public trust, not a private interest, suited for any competent person and not just a bureaucratic cadre. Fourthly, government should be responsive to the people at large, limiting its authority and, when it acted at all, serving popular needs rather than special interests.

Finally, one particular office in the national government held a special relation to the people. Jackson argued that only one federal figure came to office by a nationwide election; one leader represented the whole country; one official reflected popular will; one post was truly 'democratic': the president. The chief executive was the chief representative of the people, who translated their sentiment into policy and who monitored the actions of other branches. In such a role, Jackson argued, the president could not do enough to protect the public interest, even if that meant going over the heads of legislators and judges and taking controversial questions directly to the people. In his version of a democratic order – and as the present occupant of the executive office – Jackson genuinely believed he was 'a man of the people'.[1]

JACKSONIAN POLICIES

'Democratic' might be the *last* term one would use today to describe the President's policies. From a modern perspective, much of what Jackson did only strengthened his own hand, weakened public interests, or oppressed entire peoples. What 'democratic' elements existed derived from a set of specific, early nineteenth-century meanings Jackson connected to the term.

Consider President Jackson's stance toward Native Americans. Officially, the federal government accorded native peoples the status of sovereign nations during the republic's first eight decades; diplomatic decorum and propriety surrounded the ceremonies of policy. Practically, however, the government finessed notions of 'sovereignty'. In this area of diplomacy, *in*formal premises prevailed. Most whites viewed Indians as less than fully human and portrayed native people as nobly savage, entirely savage, or essentially childlike. Indians were not held in the same regard as other nations but seen as inherently unequal to whites.

In response, 'gradualists', such as Jefferson, defined native peoples as wards of the state unable to manage their own affairs. As the Supreme Court ruled in 1831, they formed 'domestic dependent nations'. Teachers and missionaries could help Indians shed native habits, assimilate with whites, and become 'civilized'. White expansion posed no problem because Indians held their lands by prior occupancy, not full title; their claims were tentative, not permanent. Anyway, Indians could eventually find another 'place' for themselves by accepting (rather than resisting) white ways. An 'agency' system that monopolized trade with native people would also keep them on the straight and narrow. And imposed treaties (or occasional battles) would help nudge tribes along in the right direction if they happened to tarry in their unenlightened state.

'Separationists', such as Jackson, planned to solve the Indian 'problem' by creating space between whites and natives, forcibly distancing the latter from the former. Native peoples might eventually give up their primitive and wasteful habits, but in the meantime they could not stand in the path of white progress. Society had to remove such obstacles, not negotiate with them. Jackson believed his tough policies were *natural*: whites simply watched 'the extinction of one race to make room for another'. The policies were also 'democratic': a stubbornly backward group that improperly used its resources could not hold back the potential prosperity of a rising people. The special interest of a few could not limit the economic opportunity of the many. 'True philanthropy', Jackson stated in 1830, 'reconciles the mind to these vicissitudes'.[2]

Jackson applied his democratic philanthropy to the Cherokees, Choctaws, Chickasaws, Creeks, and Seminoles, tribes that adopted, in varying degrees, economic, political, and judicial systems resembling those of white society. They picked up one other habit from their neighbors: the vigorous defense of property. The five tribes inhabited Southeastern lands, and they intended to keep what they had. Whites coveted the rich soils, and the President was eager to fulfill their dreams. Jackson pulled out federal troops that had protected the tribes and backed the Removal Act of 1830, forcing Southern tribes to resettle west of the Mississippi. He supported Georgia's efforts to wrest control over Indian affairs from the federal government, and when the Supreme Court balked, he supposedly said 'John Marshall has made his decision; now let him enforce it'.

Under pressure from white authorities, Choctaw, Chickasaw, and Creek leaders negotiated, giving up their lands for territory in present-day Oklahoma. The Seminoles fought, conducting guerrilla warfare into the 1840s. The Cherokees resisted, using the courts and refusing to leave. In 1838, federal officials rounded up over 15,000 resistors and marched them to Indian Territory in the west. On the 'Trail of Tears', one-quarter of the native peoples died. By 1840, nearly all Eastern tribes were removed from their homelands. From over 100 million acres of land east of the Mississippi, they were left with about 32 million acres in the west.

Jackson also applied his 'democratic' principles to federal-state relations. While the President feared that an enlarged central government threatened the rights and opportunities of the common (white) man, he was no friend of state sovereignty. The people, he insisted, not the states, formed the ultimate authority in the republic. States had some legitimate rights, but not the final say. They could not harm the integrity of the Union or the powers of the federal government. The 1798 Virginia and Kentucky Resolutions and the 1814 Hartford Convention had already challenged national authority. The next great test would come over tariffs. And the chief instigator of the quarrel was not some disgruntled opposition figure on the outs but a major political player from within: Jackson's vice president, John C. Calhoun.

Calhoun's arguments on federal and state power grew out of a series of calamities he felt had brought the South to near ruin by the late 1820s. The region suffered from the lingering effects of market panic in 1819, low cotton prices, indebted farmers, and damaging protective tariffs in 1824 and 1828. Back in South Carolina, Calhoun watched as soils grew depleted, residents moved to the west, and blacks outnumbered whites. When authorities uncovered plans for an 1822 slave insurrection in Charleston led by a free black, Denmark Vesey, whites grew more fearful. Calhoun pinpointed the root cause of the problems: it was that damn tariff. He took aim at the duties in order to focus the anger of South Carolinians – and Southerners in general – against the federal government's power. He would strike a blow in favor of state authority on the bland issue of tariffs – and make the point stick on a hot button question like slavery where the principle of local control was even more critical.

Calhoun's secretly-authored *Exposition and Protest* in 1828 explained that states could repeal harmful federal laws because they were sovereign. Their ratification conventions had approved the Constitution; they had formed the Union. States that determined the legitimacy of the Constitution could now determine the constitutionality of Congressional actions. A special state convention could declare federal laws null and void. The federal government could rescind the law or pass an amendment to make it legal. A state could then freely secede from the Union it had once freely joined. Calhoun's home state put his theory to the test after Congress passed yet another onerous tariff in 1832. A special convention nullified that law *and* the tariff of 1828.

Jackson favored tariff reduction but not Calhoun's argument, because states might then resist *any* law. The Constitution was the 'supreme law of the land', created in the people's name and authority, designed to form 'a *government* not a league'. States were not sovereign powers, and when they tried to act as such, the President was duty-bound to uphold the laws of the United States. To that end, Jackson strengthened federal forts in South Carolina, requested military enforcement of the tariff, and privately discussed his hopes to have Calhoun hanged for treason.

In the end, no rope was used in the resolution of the controversy. Other Southern states did not come to South Carolina's aid. Calhoun resigned as vice-president, won a Senate seat, and worked with Henry Clay to create a compromise reducing the tariff in 1833. Another South Carolina convention then rescinded the nullification. The Union was preserved. By upholding the people's compact and by resisting the 'revolutionary' acts of 'a small minority of the voters of a single State', Jackson was convinced that he had secured 'democratic' ends.

If the special interests of a single state posed a threat to democratic principles, so, too, did the special privilege of a single institution. The Bank of the United States, that satanic spawn of Alexander Hamilton, had, in Jackson's eyes, grown into an even more dangerous center of monetary power since it was rechartered in 1816. Bank officials (and anti-Jackson politicians) requested a new charter earlier than needed in 1832. Supporters felt certain that the President's interest in both votes and continued prosperity would make him agreeable to the measure. Congress promptly passed a bill rechartering the Bank; the President promptly vetoed it.

The Bank, Jackson charged, was an unauthorized, subversive, and unfair monopoly that rewarded fat cats and foreigners while leaving 'humble members of our society' subservient to its policies on money and credit. When Congress failed to override Jackson's veto, the President took the offensive in his 'bank war'. He pulled federal revenues out of the BUS in 1833 and redistributed the funds to state banks. In 1836, he divided surplus federal revenues among the states and pursued 'hard' money policies to restrain the evils of fluctuating paper currency. Jackson hoped to check the special economic interests of the few and restore openness, fairness, and opportunity to the many, creating a free, competitive, 'democratic' market.

First Bank of the United States, Philadelphia

As it turned out, the nation's economic fortunes started spinning topsy-turvy, in part because of Jackson's policies, in greater part because of international events. The BUS contracted credit in 1833; a recession hit. State banks widened loans; a boom occurred. The Bank of England tightened credit in 1837; the United States plunged into a seven-year recession, the worst in its history. There was plenty of blame to go around for the economic mess, but Jackson's bank war left the nation with one less stabilizing institution to cushion the blows. His campaign to protect popular economic interests helped usher in a period of widespread economic misery.

Jackson's contentious presidency also helped usher in a new opposition party. By 1834, Henry Clay, Daniel Webster, John Quincy Adams, and others helped form the 'Whig' party, identifying themselves in Revolutionary terms as opponents of the concentrated, tyrannical, and un-democratic power of 'King Andrew'. Challenging Jacksonian (and Jeffersonian) principles of limited government, the

Whigs stood as the party of nationalism, government interventionism, and social reform. Copying Jacksonian campaign techniques, they won the presidency in 1840 with a candidate who was, curiously enough, a military hero, unencumbered with a specific platform, supplied with slogans and images, aided by a strong organization, and identified as one of the common folk: William Henry Harrison. The 'second party system' had begun – on a decidedly popular, rowdy, and manufactured note. But in its lingering debates over government power, the preservation of liberty, and the republican legacy of the 'founders', American politics remained decidedly 'Revolutionary'.

CHAPTER FIVE

The Economic and Social Changes of the Early Republic, 1789–1860

Alexis de Tocqueville witnessed a 'strange unrest' as he toured the republic in 1831 and 1832. He wrote in *Democracy in America*:

> In the United States, a man builds a home to spend his latter years in it, and he sells it before the roof is on; he plants a garden, and lets it just as the trees are coming into bearing; he brings a field into tillage, and leaves other men to gather the crops; he embraces a profession, and gives it up; he settles in a place, which he soon afterward leaves, to carry his changeable longings elsewhere.

The breathless, frantic, restless swirl Tocqueville noted is still, in the eyes of some, one of the distinguishing marks of American life. 'Pick up the pace, go with the flow, head 'em on out; build it up, tear it down, start from scratch; got no time, feeling burned out, give me a break'. The everyday language expresses the fast, frenzied rhythm of everyday existence in the United States. There is much to justify the stereotypical hustle and bustle, but the story also holds some surprises. The high-speed chase of American life is not all that new, as Tocqueville's observations from the early nineteenth century indicate. And the trend has not been entirely welcome by those left dismayed at its ceaseless changes or defiant towards its demands and consequences. Their protests, and their alternative views of society, have a long history as well.

The New Economic Order

The 'feverish ardor' Tocqueville observed came, in large part, from a major change in the nation's economy during the early nineteenth century, an alteration that affected the North far more than the South, and a shift that both fulfilled and challenged cherished national values. Historians refer to the change as the emergence of a 'market economy', one in which Americans produced more goods (beyond their families' own needs), depended more on mechanized production (rather than hand labor alone), relied more on money as a medium of exchange (over practices such as barter), sold more in distant markets (not just local communities), and traded more with other Americans (instead of relying heavily on foreign commerce).

The shift is easily overstated. In 1789, most Americans were farmers, most lived in rural areas, and most occupied themselves in a pre-industrial economy. In 1860, all three patterns still held sway, but the trend clearly pointed toward more diverse activities, a more urban society, and a more industrial economy, especially in the North. Perhaps more important, the pace of change toward these new trends was fast and often disconcerting.

A cluster of changes, occurring at roughly the same time, contributed to this new order. America's new market economy came about through wider land settlement, transportation improvements, the rise of manufacturing, a wave of immigration, and a burst of urbanization.

Western Land and Western Settlement

One reason for the great transformation of America is tied to one of the great myths of America: the settlement of the West. In 1800, less than ten per cent of the population resided west of the Appalachians; by 1860, over half the population lived west of the mountain chain. Legend speaks of the heroic movement of rugged settlers longing to be free, unfettered, and independent. Attracted by open spaces, they presumably tamed a wild terrain through personal courage and fortitude. In many ways, the myth rings true; it took a hardy soul to leave coastal settlements and launch a journey that held few guarantees. There was natural abundance to tap, in the rich soils and on the plentiful rivers of the new lands, but there is much that the legends ignore or distort.

Rather than occupying far-removed territories around the Rockies or the Pacific Coast, the 'West' that most settled in the early nineteenth century was located between the Appalachians and the Mississippi. Rather than moving out on their own and separating from others, pioneers generally came west as families and often settled in areas inhabited by folks from their home area. Rather than abandoning community life, they recreated it. And rather than establishing only small, rural villages, they quickly built large cities such as Cincinnati, St Louis, and Chicago.

Settlers moved west not to flee the modern world but to plunge into it. They headed out not simply to provide for themselves but also to produce surpluses for others. Western lands cost as little as a tenth of the price of Eastern lands and could produce twice the yield. Farmers tried to settle near rivers to enjoy the fastest access to booming markets. In the West, they could grow much, deal much, and make much. They were oriented towards markets, not isolation. They focused on the sale, not the solitude. They were people of enterprise, not escape.

The 'opening' of the West came about through deliberate policy rather than fortunate happenstance. Four examples stand out. First, the federal government created standard procedures for surveying, selling, and administering western territories. Ordinances in the 1780s created townships measuring six miles by six miles, composed of 36 sections, each one mile square, further subdivided into halves, quarters, and eighths. These units formed the regular building blocks of settlement. Revenues from the sale of one section in a township supported public education. Once the population of a territory grew to 60,000, it could seek admission to statehood. The ordinances' right angles, simple proportions, and exact formulas spread freedom and opportunity throughout the region with mathematical precision and predictability. The ordinances also had an interesting aesthetic effect, which is visible today to airborne travelers: uneven, irregular terrain ended up divided into neat, uniform squares, imposing a rectangular grid over millions of acres. The lay of the land was no match for the law of the land; legislation ensured that geometry dominated over topography. The ordinances opened the 'wild' West of the imagination through an orderly and rational system of management.

Secondly, the federal government purposely enlarged the national domain through agreements with states, negotiations with European empires, and military pressure on native peoples. In a land deal struck with First Consul Bonaparte, a war fought to re-establish national independence, treaties signed with fading colonial powers, and organized efforts to open rich soils for agricultural interests, white Americans gained additional, fertile, and secure land, all thanks to the active efforts of their national government. What was good news for white Americans turned out to be bad news for native Americans. A cruel inverse ratio defined their relationship: as the former grew, consolidated, and succeeded, the latter were destroyed in large numbers, uprooted, and subjugated.

Thirdly, the federal government made public lands more affordable. The price per acre dropped 37 per cent between 1796 and 1820; the minimum acreage required for purchase fell 87 per cent. By the third decade of the nineteenth century, a farm sold for $100. Buyers snapped up the land. The federal government sold 68,000 acres of the public domain in 1800, 1.3 million acres in 1815, 3.5 million in 1818, and 20 million in 1836. Wittingly, the regulations brought landownership within the reach of many, filled space with settlers, launched commercial farming in the West, and spurred domestic economic development. Unwittingly, land sales often fed (and fed off) investment frenzies; as a result, speculators finished up with most of the acreage. In the end, individual farmers who bought from real estate agents acquired both rich soils and hefty debts.

Fourthly, the federal government sponsored efforts to move settlers and products more efficiently over the public lands it sold. In 1807, Congress approved a National Road linking the Potomac and Ohio Rivers. Construction began in 1811 at Cumberland, Maryland, and eventually stretched to Illinois. The highway opened an important path, but it did not launch the federal government on a road building spree: Constitutional concerns over national funding for local projects saw to that. A century passed before federally sponsored highway systems came into being, creating roadways such as US 40 and Interstate 70 that roughly parallel the route of the old National Road. The concrete ribbons that today's road warriors think of first for long-distance, overland travel were actually the last of the major transportation links to come into being.

Road Transportation, 1838

Whether organizing territory, expanding control, selling property, or clearing pathways, the national government was a key player in the opening of new lands. Settlers found themselves dispersed (and connected) in the frontier not only by individual determination but also through federal intervention. Still, whatever the historical record shows, popular culture remains critical of the government and its 'meddling' in the lives of pioneers. It is still more comforting to argue that passion, pluck, and providence – not policy – explain the opening of the West.

Transportation Improvements

The land abundance that offered so many economic advantages in the United States also posed a major economic problem: people and goods could not move rapidly, dependably, and cheaply over such a large area. Transportation across the land proved so difficult that most economic exchange took place over water and most of that among coastal cities or between the United States and Europe. In many ways, it was easier for Philadelphians to trade with New York or Boston or even London than with Pittsburgh. Dramatic changes had to take place if interior settlements were to contribute something more to the rising glory of America than a larger national map.

No single innovation solved America's transportation problems. Instead, a series of improvements changed the landscape of trade over five decades. Some of the earliest efforts focused on overland transportation in the form of highways, but road construction proved expensive because of the wooded, hilly terrain and high maintenance costs. Except for the National Road, highway building was left mainly to state governments and private entrepreneurs. Either way, the routes created turned out to be short – in length, profits, and life expectancy.

Up until the 1840s, Americans focused more on waterways than highways. Eastern rivers were numerous, but upstream travel was ten times the cost of downstream transportation. In 1807, Robert Fulton's steamboat, *Clermont*, demonstrated the potential for cheap transportation in both directions. By the 1820s, lighter, longer, and more cost-effective steamboats began to dominate transportation on Eastern rivers, the Mississippi and Ohio system, and the Great Lakes.

The real trick was to link all three water routes. In 1817, New York State began work on a solution: the Erie Canal. When completed in 1825, the 364 mile-long Erie was three times the length of any single canal in the United States. More importantly, it was a great economic success. With the canal in place, people and goods could flow north from Manhattan Island, up the Hudson River to Albany, west along the canal to Buffalo, and from there across Lake Erie and the other Great Lakes to points throughout the Old Northwest. Farmers and processors in the new western territories could send their products back to eastern markets along the same route. Canal freight rates fell to less than a tenth of the cost of wagon hauling. New York City, the starting point and end point of the trade route, became America's largest urban center and its commercial and financial capital. One state after another tried to copy the Erie's success; none proved as profitable. Some canals managed to operate successfully for a time. All were eventually affected by the next great transportation improvement, one which literally shook the ground over which it rolled.

Railroads proved to be the critical link in the new transportation system. Steam locomotive lines appeared as early as the 1820s. Rail transportation kept growing into the 1840s. A true network emerged in the 1850s as track systems expanded to 30,000 miles and became more uniform through the greater use of standard gauge. Backed by American and European investment capital – and enormous land grants from federal and state government (amounting, in the end, to an area the size of Texas) – railroads became the single most important transportation development of the era. Rail lines provided a *land*-based transportation improvement, one that offered fast, direct, reliable, year-round operations. The success of rail lines created one less reason for the construction of a sophisticated highway system. Railroad enterprises formed the first billion-dollar corporations in America and demonstrated the importance of such large economic organizations. Railroads drew more Americans into commercial production by offering a predictable way of getting goods to markets, and since most track was laid in Northern states, the rails forged strong economic and political links between the Northeast and Old Northwest.

While overseas trade remained high, its relative importance in the economy declined. With improved ways of moving people, goods, services, and money *within* the nation, internal trade boomed. Americans looked more and more to one another as the principal partners in commerce.

Manufacturing

The logic of expanded production applied outside agriculture as well. Just as it made sense to create greater supplies of corn, wheat, or other farm products, it followed that buyers would also gobble up larger surpluses of textiles, nails, or other manufactured goods. It took time for the argument to take hold, however: the Industrial Revolution came to America half a century after it hit Europe. US firms had trouble competing with the larger scale and lower costs of British and French industries. Businesses did not enjoy tariff protection against cheaper imports until 1824, and then saw those duties reduced in

1833. Labor and capital shortages, early transportation snags, and restrictions on the export of British technology also hampered US manufacturing.

Into the early 1800s, Americans produced most of their 'manufactured' goods in homes, mills, and small shops. Individuals or small groups of workers, relying on their skilled labor and hand tools, created goods for sale in local markets. It was not until the 1790s that a 'factory' system emerged in the United States, gathering large numbers of workers in one location, dividing production into several steps, assigning semi-skilled or unskilled laborers to specific tasks, relying on power-driven machinery, and producing greater amounts of goods for local and distant sale.

The first such factories appeared in 1790, in New England. The region's rivers offered abundant water power. Its cities yielded capital and entrepreneurial talent, and its thin, rocky soils inadvertently provided a labor force, since so many of the area's farm families fared so poorly against their competitors on fertile western lands. New England's ports also welcomed immigrants such as Samuel Slater who, through a variety of ingenious and nefarious ways, managed to steal the designs of European machines and copy them in America.

Technological thievery was one characteristic of American manufacturing. A second was the constant push to refine machinery. Since the number of available workers remained low, manufacturers kept trying to shave costs by making machines ever more 'labor-saving'. By the 1840s, American textile mills surpassed the efficiency of their British counterparts. Inventors such as Eli Whitney carried the process further by developing machines that could make interchangeable parts for products, creating the 'American system' of manufacturing.

That much-heralded American ingenuity also displayed itself in a third characteristic of US manufacturing: factory reorganization. In 1813, the Boston Manufacturing Company broke with precedent by consolidating operations at its Waltham textile plant, bringing spinning and weaving together in one factory. In its Lowell plant, the company experimented with a different kind of work force. Hoping to contain the costs (and turbulence) of labor while also respecting gender traditions, the factory relied mainly on the labor of young, unmarried women. The female 'operatives' lived in company houses, followed closely supervised activities, and formed a labor force that constantly turned over rather than remaining permanently in place.

The goods made in American factories suggested a fourth characteristic of US manufacturing: the 'popular' nature of its production. Factories typically churned out large quantities of standardized, inexpensive goods designed for the broadest possible market. Keeping prices low and appeal wide were more important than establishing the finest quality. In good old republican fashion, the high-end, luxury trade was generally left to those corrupt Europeans.

Factories spread rapidly in the 1820s and 1830s. Production levels rose as well. Between 1840 and 1860, manufacturing output doubled and by 1860, the total value of manufactured goods was nearly equal to the total value of agricultural goods. Most manufacturing plants and workers were located in the North. The manufacturing sector of the labor force grew quickly, from 3 per cent of workers in 1820 to 25 per cent by 1870, but during the same time, the percentage of agricultural workers dropped by a third. Despite the experiment at Lowell, factories increasingly depended on the labor of newly arrived immigrants for their work force.

Immigration

The phenomenal US birthrate – an average of seven children per woman in 1800 – slowly dropped after 1815 yet the population continued to soar. In each decade, from the 1820s through the 1850s, the figures climbed more than 30 per cent over the previous ten years. The key was European immigration. The arrival of new immigrants spurred the market economy even further, but also left many of the 'native-born' unsettled.

The pattern of European immigration to America from 1820–1860 was, in many ways, unprecedented. One difference was its sheer scale. In the 1820s, 106,000 European immigrants arrived in the United States; in the 1850s, the figure was 2.5 million. During the 1820s and 1830s, America took in an average of 37,500 immigrants per year, 1.5–4.5 percent of the total population. During the 1840s and 1850s, the average was over 200,000 per year, over 10 percent of the total population. By 1860, in a population of 31 million, one of every eight Americans was foreign-born.

A second difference lay in the origins of immigrants. Unlike earlier groups, the new waves of arrivals were overwhelmingly non-English. Nearly half were Irish, most of whom fled the famine of 1845–1849. Germans formed the second largest group. Differences in language, dress, diet, custom, and political experience set them apart, but in the case of nearly all the Irish and about half the Germans, religion was a far more important mark of distinction. The immigrants' Catholicism was both a point of contrast and a bone of contention for American Protestants, many of whom still feared that the Roman church twisted Scripture, corrupted Christianity, and enslaved believers. Raised in a tradition of authority and submission, Rome's followers presumably had few of the skills required for republican life. Yet their numbers rose so quickly that, by 1860, Catholics formed the largest single religious denomination in America.

Post-1820 immigrants also stood apart in economic terms; never before had so many poor and destitute immigrants arrived in America. The Irish were especially impoverished. Willing to accept menial jobs in homes, shops, and factories, Irish workers helped alleviate much of America's labor shortage while also accepting lower wages. The benefit that they provided employers fed resentment from other workers.

The new immigrants' patterns of residence were also distinctive. Nine out of ten settled in the North, avoiding what they saw as the more limited economic prospects in the slave South. By 1860, the foreign-born made up a fifth of the population in Northeastern states. Irish immigrants in particular, with little money to buy land and move west, tended to stay in the East Coast ports where they arrived. In Boston and New York, they formed over half the population.

In terms of numbers, background, status, and settlement, the United States had never witnessed such a surge of European immigrants. Along with Black, Indian, Spanish, and Chinese peoples, they changed America's social order, creating what Walt Whitman termed 'a nation of nations'.

Urbanization

One final factor contributed to the rise of a new market economy: the growth of cities. The pace of urbanization between 1820 and 1860 was the fastest of any 40-year period in US history. In 1820, fewer than 7 per cent of Americans lived in 'cities' (areas with over 2,500 people); in 1860, 20 per cent resided in urban areas. Of course, most Americans were still in rural communities, but Americans had never before witnessed such a remarkable rise in the rate of urban living.

City populations soared. Between 1830 and 1850, the number of people in Philadelphia and Baltimore more than doubled; New York's population grew more than two-and-a-half times; Cincinnati's population quintupled. Great Lakes cities like Cleveland, Detroit, and Chicago also grew rapidly.

As with transportation networks, manufacturing, and immigration, urbanization was, for the most part, a Northern phenomenon. By 1860, only 10 per cent of Southerners lived in cities compared to over 25 per cent of those in the North. In the Northeast, over a third of the people made their home in cities, and in Massachusetts and Rhode Island, more than half the populations were urban dwellers. The cities they lived in, serving as centers of labor, capital, demand, and transportation, were essential to the diversification of the economy and the expansion of markets.

Consequences of the New Market Economy

From 1820 to 1860, the new market economy led to the generation of more wealth, a rising standard of living, a doubling of per capita income, the availability of more land, swifter transportation and communication, productivity gains in agriculture and manufacturing, wider economic exchange within the nation, and a greater supply of desirable goods.

The same process also set in motion far more troubling changes. One problem was the economy's erratic performance. Recessions and depressions (or 'panics') hit the United States from 1819 to 1825, 1837 to 1843, and 1857 to 1858. Up to a third of all workers lost their jobs.

Prices tumbled, land values (and land sales) plummeted, debts mounted, and business failures climbed. A market that offered opportunity and growth did so in unpredictable and turbulent ways.

A second disturbing effect of the new market economy was growing economic disparity. In a period often considered an 'age of equality', wealth concentrated in the hands of fewer people. In 1800, the top 10 per cent of families held up to half of the nation's wealth. By 1860, the top tenth controlled two-thirds of America's wealth, and in cities, 85–90 per cent of the wealth. Few of the wealthy rose from 'rags-to-riches'; 'self-made men' were the exception rather than the rule.

A third effect of the new market was a growing problem of economic dependency. Poor and unskilled workers usually did not rise to a dramatically higher status during their lifetimes. Landless factory workers had little to fall back on during hard times. The home became less and less important as a center of production, and the economic destinies of individuals were increasingly determined by distant, impersonal market forces that defined prices, money, and credit. The hope of democratic power, social mobility, and boundless opportunity continued to burn in the popular imagination, yet the possibilities for personal control diminished. The lines between classes hardened, and the permanence of poverty became more evident.

Fourthly, the new market placed new demands on labor. As in Western Europe, the rise of manufacturing posed a challenge to people accustomed to the rhythms and routines of agrarian life. Farm labor was strenuous but irregular because of its seasonal changes, uneven pace, and mingling of work and sociality. Manufacturing required a new and stricter discipline that demanded steady, regular, punctual (and sober) labor habits. Manufacturing workers exercised less craftsmanship in the creation of goods, and the factory also required more labor. Historian William L. Barney points out that while a nineteenth-century farmer typically exerted 2,000 hours of labor per year, a factory worker had to provide 3,000 hours.[1]

Finally, the new marketplace that created stronger commercial and financial ties within the nation also left the United States sectionally divided. The economy of the South grew significantly (and profited handsomely) from the spread of cotton production, but the economies of the Northeast and Northwest witnessed growth *and* development. Their economic activities did not simply expand but also diversified, and they quickly outpaced the South in key economic categories. The Northern states produced over 90 per cent of all textiles, iron, coal, and firearms, contained 90 per cent of all factory workers, and generated over 75 per cent of America's total wealth.

Leadership in manufacturing, transportation, urbanization, and immigration came at a cost. Rapid changes in routines of work, patterns of residence, modes of travel, and the composition of society meant progress for some but disorder for others. As Northerners evaluated their new economic state, many called for a strict accounting of social, cultural, and spiritual values as well.

The Reform Impulse in the North

The new market may have ushered in a great age of 'expansion', 'modernization', and 'progress', terms that tend to have a favorable ring to our ears. For many who lived through these events, however, the outlook was quite different – and even quite bleak. Their familiar and traditional world was thrown upside down by a series of seismic social jolts. Of course, many other societies experienced the same sort of growth and change. But historian David Brion Davis notes that elsewhere, growth, industrialization, and social disruption all occurred 'in long-settled communities with traditions, customs, and class interests that served simultaneously as barriers to change and as stabilizers of society.'[2] In America, these social shock absorbers hardly existed. Few institutional or community agencies could contain the tensions caused by rapid alterations in everyday life. In this distinctive setting, hundreds of thousands of Americans responded to the upheaval in their lives by joining in a remarkable burst of reform activity between 1810 and 1860.

Reform groups had existed prior to this period, but never in such numbers, on such a scale, and with such enthusiasm. Unlike previous efforts, leadership generally came from the middle class rather than from social elites. The reforms usually demanded a total rather than a partial shift in behavior. The campaigns commonly called for the immediate rather than the gradual end of some social wrong. Reformers often linked their campaigns with other causes, and nearly all reform efforts were sectional rather than national, based overwhelmingly in Northern states rather than the South.

Although they addressed a wide range of issues, including drunkenness, enslavement, inequality, war, competitiveness, and godlessness, a recurring theme ran through the reformers' calls. Supporters did not usually think of their work as an innovation or novel experiment that welcomed and celebrated change. Instead, reform was a way to *contain* change, to create a more manageable community, to stop chaos in its tracks, to bring shape and sense and purpose back to society. Advocates took a world that had lost its order and literally tried to *re-*form it.

Perhaps this is the reason so few reform movements took root in the South: the region saw far fewer disruptive changes than the North. The agricultural slave states experienced less economic diversification, urbanization, and European immigration. Southerners who were self-sufficient, dependent on local exchange, or tied to foreign trading partners did not engage in as much internal commerce as Northerners. By comparison, the South was closed and static. There was less of a need to reform the South because its social order had become so firmly fixed.

The roots of reform efforts lay not only in anxiety about change but also in confidence that something could be done about it. In part, such trust stemmed from the secular principles of the Enlightenment, which affirmed the human ability to alter the conditions of the world by applying reason to the sources of social ills. In part, reform movements also rested on the religious appeals of the Second Great Awakening which held that men and women possessed the spiritual ability to perfect themselves and their world. Those who turned inward to renounce the disorder of sin within themselves also needed to turn outward and subdue the disorder at work in society, making the world a fit place for their Savior's second coming. Both secular and religious beliefs pointed to the possibilities of mankind, the malleability of the world, and the responsibility of social reform.

Those caught in the fervor of revivalism created a broad, nondenominational coalition of reform groups known as the 'Benevolent Empire'. In terms of principle, they perceived a breakdown of order and authority in American society. In terms of objectives, they distributed Bibles and tracts, organized Sunday schools and missionary work, and battled against prostitution and drinking. In terms of organization, American activists (like their British cousins) formed large, interlocking groups, staffed by professional reformers, supported by fund-raising campaigns, and promoted through the mass distribution of pamphlets, tracts, and newspapers. Participants in the Benevolent Empire applied their leadership experience and organizational skills to other reform campaigns in the 1820s and 1830s.

Temperance

The most significant movement to grow out of the Benevolent Empire was temperance reform. While advocates of the movement are easy to caricature as sour-faced party-poopers, they tackled a pressing crisis in American life. Per capita alcohol consumption in the United States in the early 1800s was triple the amount of the late twentieth century, and the avid use of distilled spirits bred problems of alcoholism, poverty, crime, domestic violence, and social instability. For those in the movement, alcohol was the emblem of American disorder.

By the mid-1830s, temperance gained over a million members (about 8 per cent of the population). Its supporters hailed from both the North and the South. And its appeals seemed to work: per capita alcohol consumption dropped from around 7 gallons in 1830 to under 2 gallons by 1844. Some reformers called for moderation in drinking, others for total abstinence; some relied on moral persuasion, others on political action. Despite the different appeals, over a dozen states had banned the manufacture and sale of intoxicants by the 1850s.

Like many *antebellum* reforms, temperance combined both 'conservative' and 'liberal' impulses. On the one hand, reformers imposed a firm moral code on society and directed the behavior of others. They believed their call for self-discipline would also yield economic benefits by producing more industrious and efficient workers. On the other hand, reformers attacked a serious problem and showed that drinking carried profound social consequences. Advocates were especially concerned about the interests of women who endured the effects of male drunkenness but who had few legal tools to defend themselves. In the end, the reformers' program was both constraining and compassionate, rigid and caring – a sort of early nineteenth century 'tough love'.

Public Institutions

The mix of humanitarianism and control also appeared in efforts to create new institutions for the dependent and the deviant. Americans commonly relied on crude and haphazard arrangements to educate youth, punish criminals, and assist the mentally ill. Publicly supported schools were the exception in a society that viewed education as a family and church responsibility. Prisons were harsh and severe places where violent criminals, non-violent offenders, and the insane were often thrown together for purposes of punishment rather than rehabilitation. The mentally incompetent usually ended up in homes or jails with no special or steady care for their needs. The condition of these facilities seemed as erratic, disorganized, and arbitrary as the state of the nation. The answer, reformers argued, was to bring form to this disorder by creating carefully designed environments that would change human behavior. Children, criminals, and the insane – however different their individual circumstances – all needed to be exposed to structured settings and systematic methods.

In schools, activists pressed for 'formal' education with public funding, a standard curriculum, fixed schedules, compulsory attendance, steadily advancing grades, trained teachers, and rote learning. In penal systems, advocates proposed state-supported institutions that removed law-breakers from the freedom (and mayhem) of the outside world, dressed them in 'uniform' attire, and exposed them to strict discipline and regular labor. In asylums, sponsors tried to fashion a world of regular, regimented, and repetitive activities that would bring order to the mental chaos of patients. In all three cases, reformers sought to remove 'at risk' groups from the instability and unpredictability of the day-to-day world and place them in environments that were structured, standardized, and supervised. The special settings would reshape unruly individuals, and perhaps even teach the outside world some valuable lessons in social order.

Abolition of Slavery

While school, prison, and asylum reformers believed that republican disorder stemmed from the absence of basic social services, two other movements insisted that the problem lay in the presence of a great social injustice: the dangerous, extensive, and corrupting exercise of power long permitted over two groups in America, slaves and women.

Turn-of-the-century opponents of slavery tended to focus on the deleterious effects that the labor system had on *whites*. The American Colonization Society, for example, emphasized gradual emancipation,

Garrison, 'The Liberator'

compensation to masters, and resettlement of ex-slaves outside the United States. Free blacks rejected the arguments, calling instead for immediate emancipation and equality within America. By the early 1830s, the abolition appeals of African Americans were echoed by white reformers, especially William Lloyd Garrison who, in 1831, launched a bold emancipation newspaper, the *Liberator*, and two years later organized the American Anti-Slavery Society.

Garrison, Lydia Maria Child, Frederick Douglass, Angelina Grimké, and others urged Americans to restore liberty to those denied its protections, end the absolute power wielded by masters, condemn the 'sin' of slavery, and guarantee the equality of freedmen. If the nation failed to act, it would only condone the inhumanity, tyranny, and corruption it so vigorously condemned in its struggle for independence. None of their arguments, abolitionists insisted, departed from past ideals but merely returned the nation to its proper foundations.

Upwards of a quarter of a million Northerners joined the abolition movement. Advocates spread their message through tracts, pamphlets, speakers, economic boycotts, and Congressional petitions. Their broad assault on slavery met with broad resistance. Anti-abolition mobs in the North, often led by 'gentlemen of property and standing', harassed and attacked reformers. Southerners banned the distribution of anti-slavery materials through the mails. The House of Representatives approved a 'gag rule' in 1836 that tabled all petitions from abolition groups.

Internal disputes also hampered the abolitionists. African American abolitionists saw evidence of racism among many white reformers. Women witnessed how male leaders neglected their contributions or dismissed their guidance. Garrisonians condemned the Constitution as a pact with slaveholders. A few groups tied abolition closely to pacifism, non-resistance, and disunion. Some advocates emphasized moral persuasion, others political action. However divided on strategies and tactics, those who called for immediate *abolition* pressed for a more thoroughgoing reform than more moderate '*anti-slavery*' forces – who focused mainly on containing (rather than eliminating) slavery in the Old South and preserving fresh Western lands for free, white labor.

The Rights of Women

The most divisive issue abolitionists faced involved the status of women. Should women participate fully in the campaign as both members and leaders? Should abolitionists demand an end to all forms of subjugation whether based on race or gender? On these questions, the organization split in 1840. The controversy encapsulated debates that swirled for decades in *antebellum* America over the roles, rights, and responsibilities of women in American society.

Advocates lined up behind one of several positions. Some contended that women occupied a separate sphere of activity, one centered on the care and nurture of home and family, where their presumably superior moral capabilities focused on refining human character. In her *Treatise on Domestic Economy* (1842), Catherine Beecher wrote that 'the success of democratic institutions ... depends upon the intellectual and moral character of the mass of the people'. The highest social task was to shape the conduct of the young, extend women's 'blessed influences' over 'degraded man, and "clothe all climes with beauty".' Proponents of the 'cult of domesticity' insisted that they honored women with the most important possible role in reforming society.

Others pushed the arguments behind 'separate spheres' to their logical conclusions and contended that women had critical *public* functions to perform. If women's moral and spiritual qualities were superior to those of men, then women also had a duty to apply their talents to the corrupt and chaotic world outside their homes. One organization built on such premises was the American Female Reform Society, which brought guidance, order, and moral reform to workers, servants, prostitutes, and other women living largely on their own. If such reformers were merely 'cleaning house', they were doing so on a grander social scale than Beecher anticipated.

A third group of proponents dispensed with the language of 'spheres' and 'moral superiority' and embraced a message of 'natural rights'. Rather than claiming distinctive female qualities, Sarah Grimké wrote in 1837 that 'men and women were *created equal*'. Since both were endowed with intelligence and responsibility and possibility, 'whatever is right for man to do, is right for woman'. Start with this simple fact,

Elizabeth Cady Stanton (1815–1902) *Left*   Lucretia Mott (1793–1880) *Right*

her sister Angelina wrote, and it was apparent that 'the present arrangements of society... are a violation of human rights, a rank usurpation of power, a violent seizure and confiscation of what is sacredly and inalienably hers'. The recognition of a woman's rights and equality relied on no special favors or novel experiments but only on the restoration of what was naturally and properly hers.

A decade after the Grimkés, Lucretia Mott and Elizabeth Cady Stanton sounded the argument of equality at the first American conference to discuss women's rights. Held in Seneca Falls, New York, in July 1848, the convention stated its platform in language modeled on the Declaration of Independence and Revolutionary creeds. The participants' 'Declaration of Sentiments' proclaimed the 'self-evident' truth of women's equality with men, condemned the 'long train of abuses and usurpations' that degraded women, and 'submitted to a candid world' examples of their subjugation. They argued that women 'have immediate admission to all the rights and privileges which belong to them as citizens of the United States'. Decades passed before those rights were acknowledged; it was not until 1920 that the Nineteenth Amendment granted women the vote. But those who assembled at Seneca Falls formally launched the project of reforming a republican order that denied freedom and independence to half of all Americans.

Utopian Communities

Utopian thinkers proposed some of the most ambitious social changes of the era. Not content to correct a moral flaw here or a behavioral failure there, communitarians tried to recreate the entire social order, re-forming all parts of human experience. During the nineteenth century, more than 100 utopian societies sprang up in America. Perhaps 100,000 men and women participated in these experiments at the height of utopian excitement from 1840–1860. Advocates questioned a culture of possessive individualism, feared the disruptive effects of competition, and criticized forms of toil that degraded workers. They tried to recover a sense of community, renew a spirit of equality, regain a sense of fulfillment from labor, and rekindle social cooperation. Communitarians sought to restore men and women to their pre-sumably true and intended state.

Religious groups inspired many communities. The most enduring experiments were created by the Shakers, a society of devout and enthusiastic Quakers who went to America in 1774, guided by a revelation given to their founder, 'Mother' Ann Lee. The Shakers built some 20 settlements across the Northeast and Old Northwest with as many as 6,000 members. Their carefully structured lives embodied the tenets of their faith. Worshipping a God who contained both male and female qualities, the Shakers overcame many gender distinctions and gave women considerable authority over the community. Devoted to a life that was spiritually rich and materially sparse, they cherished an ethic of simplicity, a plain style still evident today in restored settle-ments such as Pleasant Hill, Kentucky, with its austere, clean, and balanced architectural forms. Dedicated to principles of love and brotherhood, the settlements advocated pacifism and embraced a notion of family that extended over the entire community. Honoring their Creator through labor, members took tremendous care with the products they grew and the goods they crafted. And committing themselves to a deeply religious existence, they practiced celibacy,

Round Stone Barn, Hancock Shaker Village, Massachusetts, 1826

avoiding sexual activity as a way to refine the soul and intensify their engagement with the divine.

Many other communities were avowedly secular, forming the good society on foundations of reason rather than faith. Robert Owen, a Scottish industrialist, led one such experiment. Having reorganized cotton mills at New Lanark, Scotland, Owen turned next to reordering the whole of society. Convinced of the beneficent effect environment can have on human life, he set out to create a planned community committed to cooperation, equality, education, and economic diversity. Owen established his community in 1824 in 'New Harmony', Indiana. He launched the society with much fanfare, great enthusiasm, and strong participation. The effort lasted only a few years, however, as his model of social harmony soon turned into a cauldron of internal discord.

Other secular utopias tended to suffer the same fate. Scores of American communities followed the theories of Charles Fourier, a French philosopher popularized in America by Albert Brisbane. Fourierists tried to overcome what Brisbane saw as society's 'distrust, isolation, separation, conflict, and antagonism'. The key was to remove people from a large, artificial, and disjointed world and to reorganize them into precise social and economic units called 'phalanxes', mathematically measured for optimal size and scientifically calculated to offer members the 'attractive industry' that suited their passions and inclinations. Like Owen, Fourier hoped that a re-engineered society would restore the inner and outer balance destroyed by the modern world.

Other communitarians blended spiritual and secular principles. Transcendental speculation merged with physical labor near Boston in the 'Brook Farm' community, founded in 1841 by Unitarian minister George Ripley. Hoping to develop the full range of human capacities, Ripley tried to place diverse people in a cooperative setting that required the exercise of head, heart, and hand. Unfortunately, strong communal bonds never developed among individual members. The experiment lured few workers, farmers, or artisans, but it attracted literary notables such as Ralph Waldo Emerson, Margaret Fuller, Bronson Alcott, and Nathaniel Hawthorne. Emerson, however, feared that by joining he would simply 'remove from my present prison to a prison a little larger'. Hawthorne became disillusioned and satirized the whole experiment in *The Blithedale Romance*. By 1846, even after trying Fourierism, the experiment failed.

Another famous (or infamous) community combined perfectionism, socialism, and some eye-popping sexual theories. John Humphrey Noyes and his followers established the Oneida Community in 1848, near Syracuse, New York. Convinced that the millennial Kingdom of God was underway, Noyes believed that human beings could free themselves from sin. They could also free themselves from the corrupt power of civil government and selfish, exclusive institutions of 'ownership' such as private property and monogamous marriage. The latter was an especially touchy subject. Unlike those nice Shaker people down the road who believed the community should collectively give up sexual activity, Noyes thought that his society should collectively give in to it. He proposed a theory of 'complex marriage' whereby the community's men and women were all married to one another. To outsiders, the arrangement seemed suspiciously European, what with all the carousing and free love that must have been going on. Local authorities remained on guard but simply could not keep that Noyes down. Actually, the Oneidans had not liberated sexuality so much as systematized it: the community screened members, approved partners, required male continence, and chose only a select few for reproduction. Still, it was more than the neighbors could stand. Noyes left for Canada in 1879 and the society gave up its distinctive marriage arrangements, taking up the production of animal traps and silverware instead.

Whether enduring or short-lived, utopian societies promoted communal, cooperative principles in a nation apparently driven by individualism, competitiveness, and selfish ambition. They, like other Northern reformers, remained anxious about their region's economic and social discord – a view shared, ironically, by Southern critics as well.

The Slave South

Costume-epics and potboiler romances are right about one thing: slavery was at the core of the Old South's daily life. The institution determined the fates of most African Americans, defined the area's economy, crystallized racial attitudes, and established the region's routines. It is hard to imagine the pre-Civil War South without conjuring up images of the chattel system.

Yet, at the end of the eighteenth century, things looked quite different. Slavery's strength, growth, and endurance did not seem certain. Thomas Jefferson recognized the toll taken on Southern soils by tobacco, understood the geographical limits of rice and long-staple cotton production, saw the beginnings of abolition in Northern states, considered the conundrum of enslavement in a 'land of liberty', and conceived of a different order for Virginia – and America – in the coming decades. The republic's interests depended not on duplicating the world the planters had made but on releasing the energy of a different group, independent yeoman farmers, and allowing their labor, their freedom, and their presumed virtue to shape the United States. Jefferson's ideas took shape in the Ordinance of 1784 dealing with lands north of the Ohio River: he proposed that there should be no slavery. The clause was rejected, but three years later the prohibition did become part of the 'Northwest' Ordinance of 1787. Jefferson was not alone in this thinking. Prominent slaveholders such as George

Washington, Patrick Henry, and James Madison also expressed concern about the vitality and validity of the chattel system. The results of their soul-searching were limited, though. Concerned that the abolition of slavery would constrain the 'liberty' and property rights of whites – and release a presumably inferior people into white society – no Southern state did away with the chattel system. All except North Carolina, however, eased laws allowing masters to set free (or 'manumit') their slaves. And Southern leaders, for a period, reconsidered the course of their region. For the time being, Jefferson and his contemporaries would retain the institution of slavery as a 'necessary evil' and as a bulwark of racial 'order'. But the future did not seem to belong to the chattel system. The coming decades presumably would not look like the past.

The Land of Cotton

Slavery, of course, did not wither away. It only grew larger and more dominant. How did a system riddled with economic, moral, and political uncertainty endure and expand? How did an institution so problematic become so strong? The answer turned, to a considerable degree, on a simple mechanical device that transformed a humble plant into an economic monarch.

One of the most promising and potentially profitable crops that Southerners could raise was short-staple, or green-seed, cotton. Unlike the luxurious long-staple variety, short-staple cotton was suited to the soils and climate of the South as a whole. Southerners could grow it abundantly and consistently, but short-staple cotton posed one awkward little problem: the seeds took a very long time to remove from the fiber. One individual in one day could clean a grand total of one pound of cotton; this was hardly the mode of production that would generate fortunes.

In 1793, a Northerner named Eli Whitney, preparing to serve as a tutor in South Carolina, inadvertently taught Southerners one of the most important economic lessons of the era. Whitney, with the assistance of Catherine Greene, widow of Revolutionary War hero Nathaniel Greene, devised a contraption to remove seeds from the lint.

The cotton engine (or 'gin') allowed one worker in one day to clean over 50 pounds of short-staple cotton. With efficiencies in labor to gain (and a simple mechanical design to purloin), cotton gins popped up all over the South. Green-seed cotton soon became the crop of choice, and the basis of future wealth.

There were, of course, several other reasons why cotton became so important. World demand for cotton grew tremendously. Textile factories in Britain consumed huge quantities of the fiber. Growers received a good price for their cotton and the production of cotton fitted well with the demands of the slave labor system. Masters bought slaves in order to work them, work them hard, and work them steadily. Cotton gave masters just what they wanted. The crop took a full year to bring to market, keeping workers well-occupied preparing fields, planting, tending, thinning, cropping, harvesting, and cleaning. Since the demands placed on laborers varied during the year, masters could put crews to work on food production, buildings, and general maintenance, making plantations considerably, although not entirely, self-sufficient.

The production of short-staple cotton spread quickly, from the coastal southeast across to Alabama, Mississippi, Louisiana, Arkansas, and Texas. From 1790 to 1820, the number of bales produced grew eighteen-fold. Another eighteen-fold increase occurred from 1820 to 1840. The 1.3 million bales produced in 1840 nearly tripled to 3.8 million by 1860.

More significant than the amount of cotton produced was its importance to the economy: cotton became America's largest single product for shipment abroad. Before 1810, cotton represented less than 10 per cent of all US exports; by 1820, 33 per cent; by 1860, nearly 60 per cent. One item, produced in one region, dominated the export sector of the entire country and influenced America's balance of trade, available credit, and payment for imports. It would have been hard to miss the larger significance that cotton, and the slave labor that produced most of it, held for the entire nation. South Carolina Senator James H. Hammond understood the economic and political clout of the South. 'Without firing a gun, without drawing a sword, should they make war on us, we could bring the whole world to our feet', the senator declared in 1858. 'No, you dare not to make war on cotton. No power on earth dares to make war upon it. Cotton is king'.

The Expansion of Slavery

Cotton may have been monarchic in its dominion and influence, but ultimately its power was dependent on the labor provided by African-American slaves. The rise in cotton production occurred along with a rise in the slave population of the South. There were 700,000 slaves in the United States in 1790. The number more than doubled by 1820 to 1.5 million. By 1840, 2.5 million slaves toiled in the United States and by 1860, the figure increased to nearly four million slaves. Part of the total number derived from the transatlantic slave trade: masters bought 250,000 slaves from the time of the Revolution to 1808, the year slave importations officially ended. The rest of the increase came mostly from reproduction, something that masters touted as proof of the slaves' humane and beneficent treatment. Of course, masters were also willing to move slaves freely wherever the market action was found. A new, *internal* slave trade developed. From the birth of the new republic to the eve of the Civil War, upwards of one million slaves were moved by masters or 'sold down the river' to new owners setting up operations in the Lower South.

Three-quarters of all slaves were field workers; and nearly three-quarters of that number were engaged in cotton production. They did the long, difficult, and draining work most whites preferred to avoid. Little wonder. The cotton crop required nearly double the labor-hours of corn production and almost four times the labor-hours of wheat production.[3] It was the labor of African American slaves that produced the crop that generated the wealth that provided the economic success of the South in particular and the nation as a whole.

By the 1830s, Southerners had moved away from Jefferson's reluctant embrace of slavery as a necessary evil and developed, instead, a vigorous defense of the chattel system. Part of their argument was scriptural, noting the slaves held by God's chosen people in the Old Testament, Paul's call for servants to obey masters, and the absence of any condemnation of slavery by Jesus. A second argument was quasi-scientific, asserting the inequality found throughout nature, the inferiority of blacks, and the superiority of Caucasians. A third argument was historical, pointing to traditions of slaveholding in revered Grecian and Roman societies. A final argument was humanitarian. Southerners claimed to perform a generous service by enslaving a people who could not compete with a superior race and who would otherwise never learn valuable skills, proper behavior, and Christian truth. Masters envisioned themselves as beneficent, paternal figures who uplifted a group that would otherwise remain ignorant and backward. There could be no reason to question such a decent and honorable institution. Slavery was a positive good.

SLAVERY AND SOUTHERN LIFE

While the slave *system* was widespread in the antebellum South, slave *ownership* was not. In 1860, 12.25 million people lived in the South: eight million whites, 250,000 free blacks, and four million slaves. The slaves were owned by 400,000 masters, 5 per cent of the white population. If one changes the math and figures 'ownership' on a family rather than individual basis, about 25 per cent of Southern white families held slaves. Either way, a minority of Southern whites owned slaves and a minority of that minority owned large numbers of slaves: 'planters', with 20 or more slaves, made up less than 12 per cent of the slaveholding class and only 0.5 per cent of the South's white population.

What of the other 75 per cent of Southern whites with no slaves? Most were yeoman farmers. They worked modestly sized farms, held little cash, relied on family labor, and achieved a rough self-sufficiency by raising corn, potatoes, pigs, and chickens. They were tied to small, rural communities rather than far-flung markets; they valued local ways and local control and remained suspicious of distant, centralized authority. To judge by the basic facts of their condition and the simple statistics on slaveholding, one might think that the chattel system had little impact on their lives. But the numbers tell one story, historical experience quite another.

A minority of Southern whites owned slaves but the slave system was of central importance in Southern affairs. That is because slavery did not simply form an individual investment, a labor system, or a mode of production; it was a way of life. It shaped the basic contours of Southern existence for blacks, for white slaveholders, and for white non-slaveholders.

Slaveholding defined capital investment. In 1860, the region's four million slaves were worth $3–4 billion – and yielded handsome profits. Masters could expect a 10 per cent return on their slaves, better than many Northern industrialists could expect from their ventures. Slave prices rose by the 1850s, making the investment pay off even more. Profits went back into more slaves and more land; why tinker with a winning formula? Slaveholding also defined Southern wealth. The average slaveholder was ten times as wealthy as the average non-slaveholding Southerner. The quarter of Southern white families who owned slaves in 1860 controlled 90 per cent of the South's chief asset, its agricultural wealth. And in a region with less economic diversity than the North, slaveholding offered one of the few available paths to success.

Slavery also defined the region's social relations. The South was a caste society in which a permanent group of superiors dominated a permanent group of inferiors. Skin color defined one's rank; enslavement secured one's place. No black (free or enslaved) could rise above his or her base position; no white (rich or poor, smart or stupid, virtuous or criminal) could sink to the level assigned to blacks. All whites rose above the hardship and toil reserved only for the lowliest orders. Senator Hammond noted that 'in all social systems there must be a class to do the menial duties, to perform the drudgery of life ... It constitutes the very mud-sill of society ... Fortunately for the South, she found a race adapted to the purpose'. All whites in the Southern social order, whether slaveholders or non-slaveholders, benefited from the chattel system.

Those harmed by the expansion of the chattel system included *free* blacks as well as enslaved blacks. Before 1810, free African Americans formed the most rapidly growing segment of the Southern population. Some had purchased their freedom from enslavement, others earned freedom by virtue of military service. Still others were freed by masters. After 1810, as cotton production and the slave system widened, conditions changed. Whites increasingly viewed free African Americans as a dangerous influence on the discipline of enslaved blacks; free people of color muddied the otherwise sharp and stark divisions in Southern life between independent, 'superior' whites and servile, 'inferior' blacks. Southern states began to tighten laws that governed the freeing (or 'manumission') of slaves. At the same time, Southern legislatures passed tighter 'Black Codes' to regulate the lives, and restrict the rights, of free African Americans. By the end of the 1850s, Arkansas had even ordered all free blacks to leave the state.

Socially speaking, the least precarious group in the South was the planter elite who enjoyed wealth, prestige, and leadership in the region. In 1860, some 10,000 families owned 50 or more slaves. As people of considerable privilege, the wealthiest built lavish homes, practiced a highly conspicuous form of consumption, and fashioned themselves to be arbiters of taste and style as well as of investments and politics. The architectural results of their efforts still stand in places such as Natchez, Mississippi, which boasts antebellum palaces befitting the wealthiest county in America in 1850. The élite also presumed to display a model character. While accentuating traits of dignity, grace, and decorum in personal and public conduct, they adhered as well to aristocratic notions of obligation and guidance towards the lesser folk of the community.

Slaveholders who defined the marketplace and society also shaped the politics of the region. Slaveowners occupied 50–85 per cent of the seats in Southern state legislatures and a large percentage of Southern Congressional seats. For the most part, they determined the region's political policies, arguing forcefully for the protection, and expansion, of slave interests.

Slavery also defined what historian William J. Cooper calls the 'particular politics' of the region in which Southerners, ironically, tied their fundamental concepts of 'liberty' to enslavement. Southern whites understood perfectly well what happened to a people deprived of freedom: they could see the consequences in the degradation, oppression, and dependence of their slaves. That ever-present sight made whites all the more anxious and vigilant about any infringement of their own independence. Their central right, the one that served as a touchstone of their liberty, was the right to enslave blacks. If whites were not free to hold African Americans in bondage, if whites were not free to make that kind of 'local' choice, then whites were not free at all. The enslavement of blacks symbolized the freedom of whites.[4]

Slavery also shaped the culture of the South. One sign of this influence was the very phrase Southerners used when referring to slavery: it was their 'peculiar institution'. The words sound odd to modern ears: 'peculiar' connotes oddness or strangeness. Southerners meant something quite different: the phrase referred to the *distinctiveness* of slavery. The chattel system set the South apart from the rest of the nation. The region remained rural and non-industrial, agrarian and non-commercial; its society displayed deference, stability, and structure. Politicians, preachers, journalists, and essayists boasted of the South's singular balance and unique identity.

The chattel system produced a special world not only for the slave owner but for all Southern whites. Slavery generated wealth, defined leadership, structured society, and shaped policy. Its arrangements of people, resources, and production presumably reflected the order and harmony of nature. Each group had its proper place; every part contributed to the wealth, security, and stability of the whole. There was little need for change or alteration in such a society; the South had created the best of all possible worlds.

Of course, one had to overlook a few problems to reach such a conclusion. Morally, the South was increasingly isolated by its peculiar way of life: one of every three human beings in the region was a slave. Economically, slavery proved profitable for individuals but detrimental to the long-term development of the region. The steady production of cotton took its toll on Southern soils; the impressive profits from cotton tended to go into more slaves and more land. Meanwhile, the South lagged behind the North in manufacturing, transportation, and urbanization. Since the region focused heavily on the production of raw materials, the North and Britain wound up marketing the area's crops and creating the processed goods that Southerners consumed. The South, in other words, found itself in a condition of colonial dependence.

Politically, Southern leaders pressed for the territorial expansion of slavery in order to ease problems of soil depletion, to expand a valuable labor system, and to gain greater power (through more slave state admissions) in the House, Senate, and Electoral College. On this issue, however, the South faced considerable opposition. Northern politicians accepted slavery in the existing Southern states and even protected the institution through various Constitutional means. But when it came to new, unsettled territories in the West, the story was quite different: those lands were considered a reserve for free – white – laborers. In other words, the North was concerned about slavery where it might exist, not where it did exist. The competing interests of the two regions would, eventually and tragically, collide. While Southerners may have believed they created the best of all possible worlds through their peculiar institution, they had in fact only laid the groundwork for a horrible conflict that would leave their idealized vision in ruins.

THE SLAVES' WORLD

State codes throughout the South asserted that slaves were pieces of property held and controlled by masters. Slaves were things. As such, they had no inherent rights, no will, no humanity. In purely legal terms, slaves were creatures stripped of personhood, mere possessions directed by their owners. Whatever the legal fiction, all but the most ruthless masters knew they were dealing with human beings. Despite the stark division between 'mastery' and 'enslavement', slaves exercised considerable judgment and choice, and despite the concerted efforts of slaveholders, African Americans constructed communities among themselves. Slaves deemed passive in Southern theory were, in fact, active players in the life of the region.

The family was perhaps the most important social structure slaves created. In the eyes of the law, marriages between slaves were not recognized. In the eyes of one another, enslaved husbands and wives were permanent partners heading strong families. Slaveholders commonly allowed such unions, since marriage could produce a measure of peace and stability on the plantation, and offspring to add to the master's wealth. Slaves found something quite different in these unions: an identity for themselves, a sense of commitment to other slaves, and a

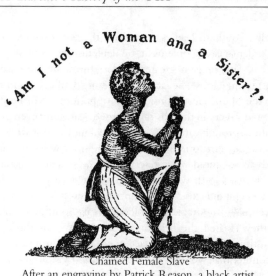

Chained Female Slave
After an engraving by Patrick Reason, a black artist,
in 1835

source of continuity with their heritage. The 'families' that slaves developed went beyond the core of woman, man, and children. Slaves usually built strong ties to a wider group that included 'relations' not tied by blood. Whether acknowledging elders as 'aunt' and 'uncle' or addressing peers as 'sister' and 'brother', the slaves' extended families broadened their ties of obligation and community. An extensive family network also provided one way of dealing with the instability that masters created by buying, selling, and trading slaves from one plantation to another. The slaves' family ties were precarious but invaluable, providing an important refuge in a hostile world.

A second source of comfort and identity sprang from the slaves' religious communities. By the late 1790s, masters stirred by evangelicalism felt an obligation to bring Christianity to slaves. Confident that they were not only saving souls but instilling a higher discipline in their work force, masters often brought slaves to Sunday services to hear the lessons imparted by white ministers. Slaves were not seated by the master's side, however. Instead, they listened from separate, segregated areas of churches. Returning to their homes after these sanctioned ceremonies, slaves often gathered again for another set of services that they conducted among themselves. Their meetings commonly took place away from the master's view, often at night, sometimes in wooded areas. Here, slaves voiced their spiritual thoughts. The beliefs of this 'invisible institution' (as Albert Raboteau terms it) were quite different from the tenets the masters taught. In a blend of Christian and African traditions, slaves danced and spoke and sang of a loving God who dispensed hope rather than wrath, a liberating Savior who befriended the poor and oppressed, and a coming Day of Jubilee when, like the ancient Israelites, they would be delivered from Pharaoh's lash. Far from acting as an opiate, the slaves' religion stimulated a strong sense of personal worth and collective endurance that countered the intentions of the masters.[5]

A third way African Americans shaped their world was by manipulating the labor routines of a farm or plantation. While whites assumed that masters simply commanded and slaves dutifully obeyed, the rhythms of work usually proceeded in quite a different manner. Masters did work their slaves from sunrise to sunset, 10 hours in winter, 14 hours in summer. Slaves who balked faced whippings and other severe punishments. Watched by masters and overseers, slaves had few opportunities to control such a system. Yet in covert and astute ways, slaves tried to construct a more reasonable pace and intensity of labor. A tool broken here, an illness feigned there, an animal spirited away, a piece of machinery misplaced, a building burned, an overseer played off against a master – strategies such as these could help in small ways to create more manageable work loads and to draw limits around a master's demands.

A related response to enslavement involved deliberate concealment, guile, and deception, presenting a false (but pleasing) front to the masters while recognizing the bitter truth of their condition. The ex-slave Frederick Douglass commented on this tactic in the *Narrative* of his life. Slaves who spoke frankly and honestly could often expect punishment rather than reward for their words, Douglass wrote. 'The frequency of this has had the effect to establish among the slaves the maxim, that a still tongue makes a wise head. They suppress the truth rather than take the consequences of telling it.' Slavery inverted the proper order of things and made deceit a virtue.

Another form of resistance was to run away from a master. Those who fled were mostly young men who ventured out on their own, often trying to avoid a punishment, reunite with loved ones, or simply taste freedom. They usually returned. Others sought a permanent escape, but perhaps only a thousand or so attempts per year succeeded. Most slaves, who lived in the lower South, had too far to travel to freedom. White patrols made the attempt even riskier. At times, fugitives received help along the way. Free African Americans in Southern cities offered important assistance. So, too, did a loose network of abolitionist allies who concealed, sheltered, and guided runaways to liberty through the so-called 'Underground Railroad'. Harriet Tubman of Maryland, for example, made 19 trips into the South, leading some 300 slaves to freedom.

Of the different ways to endure, control, or resist the chattel system, the one least chosen by slaves in the United States was overt rebellion. Rumors of insurrection swirled constantly among anxious whites, but only three major instances of rebellion occurred in the first part of the nineteenth century. In 1800, Gabriel Prosser drew as many as a thousand slaves into a plan to seize Richmond, Virginia, and attack whites. In 1822, whites charged that a free black, Denmark Vesey, had hatched a plot to lead slaves into Charleston, South Carolina, and there wreak havoc, seize weapons, and even board ships to take them out of the United States. In both cases, the plans leaked out, whites rounded up suspected African Americans, and jailed, expelled, or killed them. A bloody revolt did occur, however, in Southampton County, Virginia. A slave named Nat Turner was inspired by mystical visions to punish whites for the terror they had imposed on enslaved blacks. In August 1831, he led a band of followers to different houses in the county, killing 55 whites. White patrols and courts caught, punished, and executed some 100 blacks.

To many Southern whites, the dearth of insurrections proved that slaves were docile or content in their condition. In the end, however, the decision not to engage in rebellion reflected insight, not passivity. How could rebels succeed? They were outnumbered in most areas by whites. Slaves could not have weapons. State laws prohibited them from learning how to read and write. And even if successful, where would rebels flee? Their knowledge of the land was limited because of restrictions on their movement. They lived in the midst of an armed and hostile white police state. And if state governments could not contain slave threats, the federal government was constitutionally bound to quell insurrections. The odds were simply stacked against slaves.

While the conditions of enslavement were determined, the conduct of the enslaved was not. In technical terms, the law denied a slave's humanity; in practical terms, slaves quietly, skillfully asserted their self-worth and dignity. Their strategies combined adaptation, indirection, modest challenge, and subtle subversion. They exercised a *measure* of control over the conditions of their lives, a level of power that proved most advantageous when its presence was least apparent. The slave-holders' 'mastery' was incomplete, not absolute. The slaves' 'servility' was similarly partial, owing in great part to the basic humanity that 'chattels' preserved for themselves.

Even the 'peculiarity' of Southern society had its limits: in their language, religion, cultural background, and revolutionary heritage, Southerners were strong partners in the larger, American nation. Yet, as the century progressed, Southern states increasingly moved in a separate direction, attuned to a distinctive set of values and committed to a way of life that had less and less in common with the aspirations of the North. The two regions contained their differences for decades, but a collision between their competing orders proved, eventually, inescapable.

CHAPTER SIX

America's Cultural Revolution, 1800–1860

As the United States moved in new political, economic, and social directions, some worked to fashion another type of revolution appropriate to the new republic. Their efforts had less to do with modes of governance than with forms of expression. Having turned the world upside down by unleashing human freedom, many assumed the new American order would also generate a change in the state of arts, letters, and belief. Liberty threw familiar forms of rule into a turmoil; who was to say the same thing could not happen with the products of the imagination?

The Cultural Colony

Unfortunately, the great artistic transformation was a bit behind schedule. The nation might have cut itself loose from European traditions of state and society, but culturally the United States seemed as dependent and subordinate as ever. The nation still took its artistic cues from the Old World, imitating Europe's models of taste and refinement, bowing to its aesthetic standards, and paying homage to its creative dominance. Politically free, America remained a cultural colony. In artistic accounting books, the United States was a net importer of Truth and Beauty.

Europeans also noted an imbalance in the cultural trade. In 1770, the Abbé Raynal observed that 'America has not yet produced one good poet, one able mathematician, one man of genius in a single art or a single science'. Writing in the *Edinburgh Review* in 1820, Sydney Smith asked 'who reads an American book? or goes to an American play? or looks at an American picture or statue?' The people of America, another critic wrote, 'have no national literature'.

Even some Americans wondered if the nation had anything to contribute to the nourishment of the human imagination as it had to the state of the body politic. In 1783, educator Noah Webster noted that Americans believed 'the king, the constitution, the laws, the commerce, the fashions, the books and even the sentiments of Englishmen were implicitly supposed to be the *best* on earth'. Henry David Thoreau complained in 1836 that Americans 'have dissolved only the political bonds which connected us with Great Britain; though we have rejected her tea she still supplies us with food for the mind'. Ten years later, Margaret Fuller wrote that England was like a dominating cultural parent wielding 'excessive influence' over its American child: 'We use her language, and receive, in torrents, the influence of her thought, yet it is, in many respects, uncongenial and injurious to our constitution.' The extent of the injury was considerable: as late as 1830, most of the books published in America were written by non-Americans. Within two decades, however, native writers dominated the printing presses.

Raising a New Cultural Standard

The turnaround grew, in part, from the work of figures such as Ralph Waldo Emerson. Speaking to the Phi Beta Kappa Society at Harvard in 1837, he announced an end to America's artistic groveling. 'We have listened too long to the courtly muses of Europe', Emerson stated. America's 'sluggard intellect' would arise and 'fill the postponed expectation of the world with something better than the exertions of mechanical skill'. At last, he insisted, 'our day of dependence, our long apprenticeship to the learning of other lands, draws to a close'.

Emerson's 'American Scholar' oration presented a declaration of cultural independence, proclaiming that the nation was prepared to break free of the artistic and imaginative domination of Europe and launch a new cultural order in America, one that complemented the new political experiment already underway. The call had gone out to

Ralph Waldo Emerson   (1803–1882)

invent what historian Larzer Ziff called 'a distinct way of imagining the world'. The nation's thinkers and dreamers needed to create a unique, democratic perspective on human vision that would match America's singular way of addressing human governance. Emerson and others expected, in the words of historian Joseph J. Ellis, that 'America would become the cultural as well as the political capital of the world'.[1]

The project was a daunting one. The nation's artistic hall of fame had a great many vacancies; the republic still deferred to European tastes; and the United States seemed to lack local cultural materials to compete with the rich resources of the Continent. America was young and naïve, devoid of legend, monuments, myths, or mysteries. As James Fenimore Cooper observed in 1828, 'There are no annals for the historian; no follies (beyond the most vulgar and common place) for the satirist; no manners for the dramatist; no obscure fictions for the writer of romance; no gross and hardy offences against decorum for the moralist; nor any of the rich artificial auxiliaries of poetry.' America was simply too fresh, too primitive, too obvious, too artless to amount to much of anything according to the traditional standards of cultural achievement – unless, of course, those traditional standards did not amount to a hill of beans. Europe's political norms meant nothing on the other side of the Atlantic; why should its cultural norms? Having already flipped traditional political thinking upside down, why not stand cultural convention on its head as well?

There seemed to be good reasons for tossing out revered axioms and starting a republican cultural revolution. First, commentators argued that liberty changed all the rules in the cultural equation. Creative expression in republican America would not resemble that of monarchic, aristocratic, or despotic nations where, poet William Cullen Bryant wrote, 'laws chain men down' and 'contract and stint the intellectual faculties'. There, the mind remained open to new thoughts, capable of liberating political behavior *and* creative potential. Since their capacity for self-improvement and learning had no limits, Americans could create what no people before had even dreamed. Support for the arts would come from all of society, not just a privileged elite. Culture would reflect the wholesome, civic-minded spirit of the masses, not the self-indulgent, debauched passions of the few. Writing in the 1790s, dramatist William Dunlap argued that a free nation opened knowledge and opportunity for all; culture could not help but flourish. Even a skeptical Herman Melville noted in 1850 that Americans were 'bound to carry republican progressiveness into Literature, as well as into Life'.

A second reason for such confidence was that artistic greatness appeared bound for the United States. A familiar eighteenth-century concept held that 'culture' was not geographically fixed but mobile, following a westward course. The glory of ancient Greece passed to Rome; the next stop was Western Europe; cultural supremacy now aimed its sights on America. One could track the course of culture like the movement of the sun. America may have long sat in artistic darkness, but the light of creativity and imagination would soon shine bright on its shores. In 1785, poet Philip Freneau predicted that

> Far brighter scenes a future age,
> The muse predicts, these states will hail,
> Whose genius may the world engage,
> Whose deeds may over death prevail,
> And happier systems bring to view,
> Than all the eastern sages knew.

Fifty years later, Emerson echoed the same confident cultural forecast: 'Who can doubt that poetry will revive and lead in a new age, as the star in the constellation Harp ... shall one day be the pole-star for a thousand years?'[2]

A third reason for challenging the Old World's cultural values involved the New World's artistic possibilities. The United States lacked antiquity, refinement, cultivation, and opulence, everything that defined *traditional* cultural achievement; but it overflowed with raw, rough, and primitive materials. Those traits made America the perfect environment for *renewed* cultivation of the mind and spirit. There, one confronted the world head-on, in its original, unmediated form. The artist lived at first hand, in direct contact with experience, viewing the world without filters or pretense or presupposition. When culture found a new home in the new republic, it would turn its attention to new subjects, which America had in abundance and Europe lacked. The American artist would focus on unexplored materials found in the natural (rather than the civilized), the new (rather than the ancient), the ordinary (rather than the exceptional), and the authentic (rather than the derived). The basic stuff of American life would prove to be an artistic tonic. On a foundation of the concrete and commonplace, the new cultural order of the ages would arise.

Emerson asked 'not for the great, the remote, the romantic; what is doing in Italy or Arabia; ... I embrace the common, I explore and sit at the feet of the familiar, the low.' The artist of the new nation recognized that 'things near are not less beautiful and wondrous than things remote'. From the Constitutional era to the Civil War, scores of authors and artists recognized 'the worth of the vulgar' and tried to build a distinctly American body of cultural expression out of such native, natural resources.

Literature

Writers came up with diverse uses for indigenous and commonplace subjects. The 'Connecticut' or 'Hartford Wits', a group of nine writers from Yale University, celebrated the mundane splendors and political triumphs of republican life. Joel Barlow, composed a mock-heroic poem to 'Hasty Pudding', celebrating the glories of corn mush. Singing the praises of his 'virgin theme', Barlow recalled that 'simplicity of diet' ranked among the highest of virtues. Americans triumphed over corruption and vice, he argued, by consuming the right political arguments and the right victuals. Republican patriots knew that you are what you eat.

Playwright Royall Tyler put homegrown materials to work in his 1787 comedy, *The Contrast*. Tyler focused 'on native themes' and dismissed those who dwelled on foreign subjects: 'Why should our thoughts to distant countries roam/When each refinement may be found at home?' The play dealt with a romantic tussle for the hand of a fair maiden, fought between an affected Briton, Dimple, and a virtuous American, Colonel Manly, ably assisted by his doltish but dependable servant, Jonathan. In the silly proceedings, European pomposity proved no match for American simplicity. In the end, love came to the homely rather than the worldly.

Dramatist William Dunlap borrowed an episode from the Revolution for a play dealing with contrasts of a more complex order. *André*, written in 1798, dealt with the case of Major John André, a British officer convicted as a spy during the War for Independence and sentenced to die. Rather than pitting corrupt monarchists against heroic Yankees, Dunlap portrayed André as a noble figure, committed to cause and country but guilty of a terrible crime. The drama turned on the tension between the Revolution's high principles and war's cruelties.

For Noah Webster, the Revolution was not as culturally ambiguous: it offered a clear opportunity to correct both the political *and* linguistic errors of Britain. Having broken free of the King's rule, there was no reason for the nation to remain subject to the King's English; both were corrupt, outmoded, and inappropriate. If Americans rejected legal and political codes established by a distant, privileged elite, why should they submit to standards of spelling and punctuation created by the same, favored few? On matters of language, as in questions of governance, the voice of the people ought to prevail. In Webster's *American Spelling Book* and *American Dictionary of the English Language*, popular usage defined standards of grammatical correctness.

Ironically, the first American to make a living as a professional author harbored mixed feelings about an independent national literature. Washington Irving sensed that pretty landscapes were no substitute for 'the shadowy grandeurs of the past'. His popular *Sketch Book of Geoffrey Crayon, Gent.* (1819–1820) drew heavily on Continental motifs and subjects. Among the many sketches, two achieved instant fame: 'Rip Van Winkle' and 'The Legend of Sleepy Hollow'. Although drawing on Germanic legend, both tales managed to focus on distinctive American traits, describing evocative Catskill Mountain settings and the theme of rapid change in the United States.

James Fenimore Cooper also looked to Europe as a guide to literary greatness but, unlike Irving, remained more firmly grounded in native soil. The result was one of the great imaginative achievements of the period: a series of five novels about the American frontier, known collectively as *The Leather-Stocking Tales*. The stories, including *The Pioneer*, *The Last of the Mohicans,* and *The Deerslayer*, created a major character and a mythic theme that continue to resonate in American culture. Cooper portrayed his central character, Natty Bumppo, as an Adamic figure who emerged on his own, in a new land, without clear origins or social connections, and who remained self-taught and self-sufficient. The novels revolve around the tension between nature and culture. Bumppo lived on the cusp of the two worlds, as a frontiersman who helped create new communities while continually retreating from their grip. His story was wrapped up in the struggle between the civilized order of the settlement and the anarchic freedom of the wilderness.

Essayists such as the New England 'Transcendentalists' explored some of the larger, philosophical ideas behind these literary themes. A small, barely organized band whose work flourished from the 1830s through the 1850s, the Transcendentalists urged audiences to look beyond the present arrangement of their lives and adopt a 'wider view' of human possibilities. Their advice carried the same message as the project of cultural reform: challenge the errors of inherited wisdom and artificial constraint; establish 'an original relation to the universe'; and trust in one's innate ability to grasp truth and meaning.

Emerson, a key figure in the movement, challenged those who lived at second-hand, guided more by custom and convention than principle. He believed truth flowed from 'intuitions of the mind itself', not from outside authorities. A genuine life opened itself up to 'new lands, new men, new thoughts' and embraced 'our own works and laws and worship'. Individuals who recognized their genuine being and the harmonious currents of nature were perfectly capable of constructing for themselves higher truths and a more meaningful way of life.

Henry David Thoreau shared Emerson's hostility to the shackles of tradition that had produced 'lives of quiet desperation'. But he felt that 'new views' of this condition did not flow from abstract speculation alone. Thoreau relied more on sensory overload, immersing himself in the primitive and wild qualities of life. He could be found devouring a woodchuck, sitting in a swamp, listening to a loon, or climbing a peak. His most famous experiment, recorded in *Walden*, recounted his 'life in the woods' outside Concord, Massachusetts, a project he took up on 4 July 1845. Exploring 'the true necessaries and means of life', he tried 'to live deliberately, to front only the essential facts of life, and see if I could not learn what it had to teach'. His attempt to get back to basics grew from the conviction that 'it is never too late to give up our prejudices. No way of thinking or doing, however ancient, can be trusted without proof'.

One Transcendentalist took up Thoreau's challenge to test an old prejudice: the status imposed on women. Margaret Fuller applied Transcendental principles of self-development and wholeness to questions of gender in her 1845 work, *Woman in the Nineteenth Century*. She argued that 'the slavery of habit' prevented women from exploring the full range of their being and left them downgraded to a separate, distinct, and inferior condition in life. Nature intended no such hierarchy or ranking; male and female principles were co-equal, two parts of a larger whole. When the two forces stood in balance, when every 'arbitrary barrier' to women fell, 'the divine energy would pervade nature to a degree unknown in the history of former ages'. Although she presented a highly spiritualized argument, Fuller did not lose sight of at least one substantial demand: that women's freedom must be 'acknowledged as *a right*, not yielded as a concession'.

Among the voices of American poetry, four of the most intriguing figures rose from remarkably different sets of circumstances. Phillis Wheatley was born in Africa in 1753 and bound into slavery at the age of seven. Purchased by a Boston family and held as a slave for two decades, she was raised a Christian, granted an education, and penned *Poems on Various Subjects, Religious and Moral*. Printed in London in 1773, the volume was the first published by an African American. While her works owed much to the manner of Milton and Pope and dwelled at length on religious themes, Wheatley occasionally touched on the circumstances of blacks in America. 'On Being Brought from Africa to America' recognized that 'some view our sable race with scornful eye', but closed with a call to 'Remember, *Christians, Negros*, black as *Cain*/May be refin'd, and join th'angelic train.' Wheatley held that 'in every human breast God has implanted a principle, which we call love of freedom; it is impatient of oppression, and pants for deliverance'.

In contrast to Wheatley's Christian and social themes, the poems of William Cullen Bryant reflected on America's natural riches. Bryant urged American authors to give up their 'sickly and affected imitation' of English poets and discover the 'rich and varied field' of literary resources that lay before them. In their home land lay 'elements of beauty and grandeur' that would inspire images as lofty as those of Europe and spiritual insights as profound as any learned treatise. America's distinctive contribution to literary imagination sprang from its 'wilder image'.

The quiet, compact, elegant meditations of Emily Dickinson provided a strikingly different poetic voice. 'I see New Englandly,' Dickinson wrote, referring to works drawn from her small rounds of local, domestic experience in Amherst, Massachusetts. On that world, she trained her 'frugal eye', expressing herself in tight but elliptical verses. 'Tell all the Truth', she wrote, 'but tell it slant – /Success in

Emily Dickinson at seventeen

Circuit lies.' In precise, witty, and often anguished words, she gazed not at the vast exteriors of the physical world but peered microscopically into the recesses of interior space which she found filled with mystery and unfulfilled desire: 'One need not be a Chamber–to be Haunted–/ One need not be a House–/The Brain has Corridors–surpassing/ Material place – .'

The loud, exuberant works of Walt Whitman stood in sharp contrast to Dickinson's. Rather than creating intensely private and small-scale verses, Whitman identified himself with all experience and filled the page with the expansive world he encountered. The substance, technique, and style of his poems revealed his intoxicated fascination with the republic and his desire to express 'the jealous and passionate instinct of American standards'. Whitman's works overflowed with images of the country, bursting at the seams with the details and textures of commonplace life; he wrote as if creating catalogs of quotidian culture. He vigorously experimented with language in an effort to capture distinctive local sounds and rhythms. The poet Whitman wrote in

'Song of Myself', immersed himself in the abundant and bewildering mass of details he saw around him. Yet, as 'Brooklyn Ferry' and 'Passage to India' suggested, there was an overarching order and connective meaning that tied together this 'teeming nation of nations'.

Some authors, however, could not bring themselves to join in the affirmations of 'aye-sayers' like Emerson, Whitman, and others. They reflected on American life with a greater degree of caution, ambiguity, and even a touch of perversity, suggesting that quick, easy, and universal fixes for humanity's ills might be illusory at best and irresponsible at worst. One such writer was Nathaniel Hawthorne who, as Henry James noted, carried the 'heavy moral burden' of New England Puritanism into nineteenth-century American literature. Hawthorne's works revolved around two recurring themes: the inescapable evil that resided within the human heart; and the need to maintain one's sympathies with others despite that fallen condition. In works such as *The Scarlet Letter*, he examined the problems caused by those who pulled back from social affections through egotism, idealism, self-righteousness, suspicion, or guilt.

'[T]he grand truth about Nathaniel Hawthorne,' Herman Melville commented, was that 'he says NO! in thunder'. Melville was no slouch himself, saying, writing, and exuding NO! in thunder *and* lightning. In a body of work rich in adventure, symbol, and metaphysical speculation, Melville aimed his harshest rebukes at those who blithely dismissed the darker qualities of life, who naïvely felt themselves free from any form of constraint, and who confidently proclaimed their communion with the universe. 'This "all" feeling', Melville remarked, contained some truth; 'but what plays the mischief with the truth is that men will insist upon the universal application of a temporary feeling or opinion'. The greater wisdom Melville expressed – and narrators, such as Ishmael in *Moby Dick*, voiced – was to acknowledge the limits that fate placed upon freedom.

Edgar Allan Poe acknowledged one other dark theme: the limits of the mind in grasping the many layers of reality. Other peoples, he argued, gained knowledge by turning to the external world of society and custom, but in America, manners and traditions were in short supply. Understanding would come by turning inward rather than outward, probing the unexplored terrain of the human interior. His works were the psychological equivalents of the frontier, leading readers into 'the lone regions where hath trod no foot of man', where, as one of his narrators suggested, the 'wild ideas of the land of dreams' took center stage. Poe surveyed the 'virgin' territory of the human psyche.

Painting

American painters also turned to the nation's distinctive subjects and features. Scenes of republican life inspired one group; the scenery of American landscapes stirred another.

Painters of portraits and historical scenes found themselves attracted to American subjects, but they were equally drawn to Continental training. One prominent artist, Benjamin West, left Philadelphia in the 1760s to study in Europe – and never returned home. Others, such as John Singleton Copley, Gilbert Stuart, and Charles Willson Peale, also headed to Britain, sailing east to study with West. While they based their work on Yankee themes and became the first recognized group of American painters, the artists were commonly known as the 'London school'.

The artists infused their subjects with dignity, solemnity, and monumental status. West created neoclassical depictions of colonial history in *The Death of General Wolfe* (1770) and *Penn's Treaty with the Indians* (1771). Copley produced a range of portraits and scenes, from the contemplative *Boy with the Squirrel* (1765), to the straightforward, dignified *Samuel Adams* (1772), to the swirling, violent *Watson and the Shark* (1778). John Trumbull painted canvases commemorating the War of Independence, such as the *Battle of Bunker's Hill* (1786). Congress later commissioned him to fill the Capitol rotunda in Washington, DC, with four murals of the Revolution. Although the scenes were widely viewed, they paled by comparison with the many portraits of George Washington created by Gilbert Stuart. The most famous, the unfinished *Athenaeum Portrait of George Washington* (1796), served as the model for the image of Washington Americans see every day on the dollar bill.

Charles Willson Peale trained under West but returned home to serve the high ideals, and paying customers, of his native land. Peale believed in the uplifting potential of painting but also kept his eye trained on the market; as Joseph J. Ellis notes, he 'remained an artist-entrepreneur'.[3] Peale welcomed (and served in) the Revolution, using his canvases as political weapons in the struggle for liberty. With the War of Independence, he found engagement in a cause, fulfillment in his craft, and buyers for his wares. All of these interests came together in 'public art', which he deemed an appropriate and inspiring form of cultural expression for a republican society.

Other painters turned from the grand and heroic elements of republican life to the mundane and everyday. Rendering Emerson's celebration of the common in pictorial terms, artists such as William Sidney Mount, Richard Caton Woodville, and George Caleb Bingham drew inspiration from the folkways of American life rather than the triumphs of American history. Mount centered his sights on daily scenes of Long Island life with works such as *Bargaining for a Horse* (1835) and *Eel Spearing at Setauket* (1845). Woodville captured the intensity of popular political debate in *Politics in an Oyster Bar* (1848), a canvas depicting the strongly punctuated opinions of a newspaper-toting man and a distracted, somewhat weary, dining companion. Bingham's images caught glimpses of life on the American frontier, in the calm and clarity of *Fur Traders Descending the Missouri* (1844), the formal construction of *Jolly Flatboatmen* (1846), and the hurly-burly of election day in *Verdict of the People* (1855).

Mount, Woodville, and Bingham drew inspiration from Dutch genre painting. They focused on the explicitly ordinary, emphasizing elemental features of structure, light, color, and line rather than the depiction of mighty deeds, turbulent movement, or weighty symbols. They painted bucolic, amiable scenes and presented a peaceful, inclusive world of wide public participation where good feeling and camaraderie prevailed. All three artists represented the *social* rather than the individual American, depicting the relationships of republican citizens in their collective, rather than their isolated, lives.

While great deeds of the past and simple events of the present filled some painters with a sense of what was quintessentially American, other artists turned their attention to the ground upon which all of these actions took place. What more distinctively American subject to commit to canvas than the land itself? The abundance, variety, sublimity, and spirituality of nature in the new republic seemed the perfect material for artistic expression.

Whether sketching the brooding heart of the forest, the placid banks of a stream, or the quiet lane of a rural settlement, landscape artists pictured nature not as a passive backdrop but as the central force animating republican life and distinguishing its cultural expression. While 'the primitive features of scenery' had all but vanished in Europe, painter Thomas Cole wrote, 'nature is still predominant' in America. The economically and culturally untapped lands opened up a vast, new field for imaginative endeavors, but artists sensed that they needed to act quickly to capture the precious state of nature before the landscape lost its unique qualities.

The most renowned landscape painter was the British-born and American-raised Cole. After living on the Ohio frontier, Cole found his great passion in New York's Catskill and Adirondack ranges, whose peaks and valleys became the subject of canvases by the 'Hudson River' school of painting he helped found in the 1820s. Cole saw himself as a cultural 'pioneer'. He was a trailblazer who explored Northeastern woodlands on what he called 'perilous and difficult journeys' where he confronted 'the sublimity of untamed wildness'. Cole also broke ground in an imaginative sense, making some of the earliest *aesthetic* penetrations of the American landscape and demonstrating that the nation's natural scenes were fit subjects for artists. He observed 'virgin waters which the prow of the sketcher had never yet curled, ... the stern mountain peaks never beheld by Claude or Salvador'. As he noted in 1835, 'all nature here is new to art'. *The Oxbow* (1836) visualized the contrast he saw between nature and society. Cole split the canvas in two, its 'western' half portraying an unsettled, rough, and stormy wilderness, its 'eastern' half depicting the quiet, sunlit charm of an agricultural community. Cole pictured himself in the middle foreground, nestled in the woods with brush and easel, looking across at the settlement. He had become the artistic Natty Bumppo, a pioneer staking out the frontier in advance of civilization.

For Asher Durand, the landscape provided both a fitting subject for American canvases and the finest training for American artists. Formal instruction about old masters in stuffy academies was no way to learn about one's craft. 'Go first to Nature to learn to paint landscape,' he advised, 'and when you shall have learnt to imitate her, you may then study the pictures of great artists with benefit.' Durand honored his own heroes in *Kindred Spirits* (1848) which pictured Thomas Cole and William Cullen Bryant on a rocky outcrop in the Hudson River Valley, admiring the views they had opened up on canvas and paper.

Durand's gentle scenes showed one side of American landscape painting. Other artists favored the grand and spectacular, capturing the land's massive scale, awesome beauty, and primeval power. The 'Rocky Mountain' school brought the vastness of the West to American art, creating enormous canvases that overflowed with natural detail and dramatic perspectives. Albert Bierstadt's six-by-ten foot *Rocky Mountains* (1863) depicted the sublime home of American Indians, while his five-by-nine foot *Emigrants Crossing the Plains* (1867) showed the advance of white settlers onto the native people's lands. Thomas Moran's eight-by-fourteen foot *Grand Canyons of the Yellowstone* (1893-1901) focused on the sheer physical energy of the wilderness. Half the size of Moran's work, the horizontally sweeping curve of Frederic Edwin Church's *Niagara Falls* (1857) captured the drama of the watery natural wonder while his six-by-ten foot *Heart of the Andes* (1859) offered a taste of the exotic in the wilder world of South America.

In contrast to intimate or sublime landscapes, 'Luminist' paintings turned attention to the subtle play of light on the natural features of America. FitzHugh Lane's *Ships Stuck in Ice off Ten Pound Island, Gloucester* (1850-1860), John Frederick Kensett's *Paradise Rock, Newport* (1865), and Martin J. Heade's *Approaching Thunderstorm* (1859) focused on simple scenes made extraordinary by the dramatic light of sunrise, sunset, and storms. The works feature precise lines, atmospheric clarity, and an eerie, dreamlike stillness. Though they illuminated the land in a distinctive way, the Luminists were not alone in thinking that a special light shone on America.

Religion

A variety of nineteenth-century religious movements proclaimed that America would not only transform the imagination but also uplift the soul. While the nation occupied a special place in the history of the world, its role in the course of salvation was of even greater consequence. The United States was not simply a republican nation but a redeemer nation.

In the post-Revolutionary period, Americans became much more 'religious' – at least as measured by church affiliation. Revolutionaries themselves tended to be more dedicated to political causes than denominational creeds. In 1776, only 17 per cent of Americans were church members. By 1850, the figured doubled to 34 per cent and kept rising in later decades. The greatest growth occurred in Baptist and Methodist congregations, which, by 1830, formed the nation's largest denominations.

All of this occurred despite the gradual disestablishment of churches. Although the first amendment prohibited the establishment of religion by the *national* legislature, *state* legislatures were a different matter. Before 1776, nine of thirteen colonies had 'established' churches that received government endorsement and public funds. Slowly, state constitutions moved away from the practice by establishing multiple churches, granting tolerance to different groups, or stopping government support of religious organizations. Establishment lasted the longest in New England, where Massachusetts maintained the practice of public endorsement until 1833.

Even without the institutional and financial backing of the states, churches flourished in the decades following the Revolution. At the heart of republican religious rejuvenation was the confidence inspired by a bold shift in theological thinking that formed the 'Second Great Awakening'. Beginning in the 1790s, the fires of revivalism that had earlier broken out in Europe spread to the New Republic. Evangelical fervor swept all parts of the nation. By 1850, historian George M. Marsden, writes, 'virtually the whole United States was a Bible belt'.[4]

Evangelical Protestants carried a simple message: heaven was within everyone's reach. Forget orthodox warnings of human frailty and damnation; forget established churches with their lifeless observances, bookish clergy, and theological errors. Sin was a matter of choice, not destiny; all people were capable of choosing grace rather than evil. Human beings could become perfect, 'sanctified' in this life. The 'born again' would generate happiness for themselves and others, creating unity, progress, and social uplift in both the outer and inner worlds. Millennial expectation filled adherents with hope: the long-awaited thousand years of happiness could begin any moment now, preparing the way for the second coming of their Lord.

Ministers urged audiences to question established ways, cast off elitist leaders, trust their own natures, fall back on their own spiritual resources, and proclaim the word of their God in their own voices. The Second Great Awakening brought both a revived and a democratized Christianity to the New Republic, a faith which, historian Nathan O. Hatch notes, continues to 'distinguish the United States from other industrial democracies'.[5] America's alteration of religious belief complemented its revolution in political habit.

Most of the believers attracted to revivalism were women. They spoke up in ecstatic and joyful tones at tent meetings; they often dominated the rolls of new churches; they assumed more ministerial posts; they organized charitable and reform groups. Women found new voices and roles for themselves in evangelical causes. Working in public life, outside of the home, women developed a sense of collective purpose that would also come to serve their secular goals.

African Americans were also affected by the Awakening. Many free Northern blacks had grown weary of the degradation they regularly faced in white religious organizations with pro-slavery ministers, segregated seating, divided Sunday Schools, and separate communion services. In response, leaders such as Richard Allan and Absalom Jones and groups such as the Free African Society created independent African-American churches, institutions that often became the center of black community life. The Second Great Awakening also changed the lives of enslaved blacks in the South. For the first time in American history, large numbers of slaves were converted to Christianity. Ironically, African American slaves saw in that faith a message of defiance, liberation, and equality that their masters had not anticipated.

Richard Allen, a key founder and first bishop of the African Methodist Episcopal Church

In addition to the African Methodist Episcopal Church, the Awakening witnessed the rise of several other new religious organizations such as the Adventists, the Mormons, Christian Scientists, and various 'primitivist', 'fundamentalist', and 'spiritualist' groups. A religiously-varied nation grew even more diverse as the flames of revivalism moved across the land.

Post-revolutionary religions, like other forms of cultural expression, conveyed the belief that America would transform the human condition. Ministers spoke of God's special place for the nation in the plan of salvation. The discovery of America, after all, coincided with the rise of the Protestant Reformation; conveniently, just as churches purified themselves in Europe, they could export their saving message to a new continent. In a land distanced from corrupt ecclesiastical traditions, and in a society where spiritual conviction was a matter of individual choice rather than civic obligation, humanity's redemption would find fulfillment. The westward transit of salvation accompanied the westward course of the arts. America's manifest spiritual destiny would presumably lead all people towards freedom *and* salvation.

The Church of Jesus Christ of Latter-day Saints, founded in 1830 by Joseph Smith, offered one expression of American religious nationalism. 'Mormon' followers believed that the young Smith received revelations and spiritual visitations in the 1820s, after which he produced the *Book of Mormon*, purported to be a translation of ancient golden plates containing a long-lost part of Scripture. The book described America as a place like no other. According to Smith, America was the site of the Garden of Eden; a tribe of ancient Israelites had traveled to America; Christ visited the New World after his resurrection; in America, a new prophet would recover the full word of God, receive divine revelation, expose the falsehoods of other faiths, and restore God's true church. In this 'land of choice above all other lands', the faithful would establish the kingdom of God on earth. The creed Smith expressed was not simply an example of a religion *in* America; Mormonism was a faith *about* America.

That sense of conviction – about the rightness, the inevitability, and even the sanctity of the New Republic – captured something of the confidence and bombast of post-revolutionary America. Writers, artists, ministers, and congregants commonly assumed that independence would undoubtedly generate a cultural and spiritual rebirth for all people. Their nation would make a difference in the world. Whether others actually wanted to be swept up in the rising tide of Americanism was of minor concern. What worked there could not help but work elsewhere.

Of course, it remained to be seen if America itself could 'work' at all. The republic was still an experiment. And sometimes, things go haywire in the laboratory. While many nationalizing and unifying principles bound citizens together, elements of discord and division also played themselves out, with harrowing consequences, in nineteenth-century America.

CHAPTER SEVEN

The Gathering Storm, 1845–1861

In 1805, Jefferson spoke of an 'empire of liberty' with ample land for virtuous republican farmers. In 1845, newspaperman John O'Sullivan wrote of America's 'Manifest Destiny' to acquire more land and to bestow its blessings on other peoples. Later in the 1840s, the 'Young America' movement conceived of the United States as the model for a world renovated by republicanism. It was all heady stuff, premised on America's cultural, social, political, and racial superiority – and on national growth as necessary, proper, and preordained.

Sometimes dreams come true, and the results turn into nightmares. In the second half of the 1840s, the republic quickly expanded but failed to determine whose benefit and what interest the enlarged domain served. For 15 years, the nation endured a series of rapid, continuous, and increasingly volatile crises that polarized its people and paralyzed its government. The cause lay in an issue that appeared manageable but proved uncontrollable: the growth of slavery in a growing nation. Over time, expansion's bright promise resulted in catastrophic loss.

The contentious course that the nation traced began with apparent triumph in the Southwest. A new star in the national flag soon brought new scars to the national scene.

War with Mexico

Since 1824, Mexico had tried to develop its lands in Texas by encouraging American immigration. The young republic succeeded all too well. By 1835, 30,000 Americans – and their slaves – lived in Texas, far outnumbering the Mexican population. The Americans soon demanded autonomy. Settlers declared their independence in 1836, and fighting broke out with Mexico. The rebels suffered defeat early in the conflict, as in the disastrous March 1836 loss at the Alamo in San Antonio, but their forces under Sam Houston overcame Mexican troops at San Jacinto in April. A peace treaty (never formally ratified by Mexico) granted independence. For years, Texans tried to join the United States, but concerns about the sectional imbalance its admission would create prevented annexation. Finally, after Democratic Party maneuvering, Texas gained admission as a slave state in 1845. The expansionist-minded President, James K. Polk, set his sights on even more territory. He dispatched an emissary to Mexico City to gain recognition of the annexation and to bid for other Mexican lands. Mexico's government rejected the proposals.

Failing at negotiation, Polk turned to force. He ordered General Zachary Taylor's troops to cross the Nueces River into disputed territory, and to provoke a fight with Mexico. Skirmishes erupted. Polk accused Mexico of invading US territory, and Congress declared war in May 1846. Taylor crossed the Rio Grande, took Matamoros, attacked Monterrey, and defeated Mexican troops further south at Buena Vista. Colonel Stephen W. Kearney led forces from Kansas to Sante Fe where he secured the territory of New Mexico. Kearney then marched to the coast and, joining with the US Pacific squadron and a band of insurgents directed by John C. Frémont, took control of California by January 1847. General Winfield Scott's troops seized Vera Cruz in March and led forces westward to Mexico City, which fell in September 1847. Peace terms were outlined in the Treaty of Guadalupe Hidalgo as the war came to an end in early 1848.

The war opened an immense range of land for the United States. The treaty secured American claims to Texas and also transferred control of Mexico's northern provinces to the United States (an area including present-day California, Nevada, Utah, and portions of Wyoming, Arizona, New Mexico, Colorado, Oklahoma, and Kansas). The 'Mexican Cession' and Texas covered nearly a million square miles. Oregon Territory, obtained two years earlier in negotiations with the British, stretched across 285,000 square miles. In three years, from 1845 to 1848, the United States acquired more territory than in the previous 50 years. The new lands were larger than the Louisiana Purchase and larger than the original 13 states. Their acquisition 'produced a new American nation'.[1]

The territorial gains pleased many but alarmed some. Emerson predicted that the United States would defeat Mexico, but 'it will be as the man swallows the arsenic, which brings him down in turn. Mexico will poison us'.[2] The land Americans coveted as a golden elixir turned out to be that poison. Historian William Wiecek notes that the United States maintained internal peace on the slavery question by relying on sectional bargains created within fairly fixed borders. In 1820, Congress tried its hand at one such move with the Missouri Compromise, prohibiting slavery in all lands of the Louisiana Purchase north of 36°30'. Drawing a line across space presumably solved the issue of slavery because the space itself did not change – at least for a quarter of a century. What undercut the old formulas, what brought the national house down, was sudden and rapid growth. As Wiecek explains, 'the Civil War would probably not have occurred – and certainly not in 1861 – had the dispute over slavery been argued out in a stable, nonexpanding nation'.[3]

By 1848, the continental republic, poised for even further expansion, tried to determine how to deal with its new lands. Some suggested prohibiting slavery in the Mexican Cession. Others pushed for 'free soil' in all territories. Some considered extending the 36°30' line further west. Many Southerners insisted that citizens could bring their property (including human possessions) into all territories. Still others advocated a system of 'popular sovereignty' that allowed territorial legislatures (rather than the federal government) to decide the slavery question. One small group maintained that the only answer was to abolish slavery entirely. Over the next decade, the debate swirled and intensified. Ironically, as the ground of settlement in America grew, the ground of compromise narrowed.

The Compromise of 1850

The immense new lands posed problems of their own. Complicating matters further were large movements of people onto the territory. In

July 1847, Brigham Young led nearly 150 Mormons into the north-eastern edge of the Great Basin. By the shores of Salt Lake, he declared 'this is the place' where persecuted church members would find solace and security. Thousands of Mormon pioneers quickly followed. The nation watched anxiously as Utah Territory in the West filled with religious radicals deemed too menacing and subversive for the East.

A different community sprang up on the Pacific coast, inspired by dreams of earthly riches rather than heavenly rewards. In January 1848, gold was discovered in the foothills of the Sierra Nevada Mountains. Over a two-year period, settlers swept up in a 'Gold Rush' swelled California's population from 14,000 to 100,000. In only eight years, San Francisco grew from 200 to 50,000 residents. Economically, the territory boomed. Socially, the area grew more diverse with European, Mexican, Chinese, and native peoples. Politically, the numbers of Californians quickly reached the point where they could seek admission to the Union as a state.

Political leaders recognized that the balance of 15 free states and 15 slave states would tip with the admission of California, whose residents did not want to establish the chattel system. Oregon, Utah, and New Mexico Territories would also eventually join the Union and upset the balance further. Senators Henry Clay of Kentucky and Stephen A. Douglas of Illinois offered a package of solutions. Although their 'omnibus' bill went down to defeat in July 1850, five critical measures, voted on separately, were passed by September. First, California gained admission as a free state. Secondly, a bill organized Utah and New Mexico Territories under the principle of popular sovereignty, which allowed the people of the territory rather than Congress to decide the fate of the area (both territories eventually adopted slave codes). Thirdly, a measure fixed the borders of Texas. Fourthly, a law abolished the slave trade (but not slavery itself) in the District of Columbia. Fifthly, Congress granted greater federal protection to the property holdings of masters.

The last of the measures, the Fugitive Slave Act, sparked intense controversy. As Philip S. Foner has written, the act made the federal government a major player in the capture of runaway slaves. Federal commissioners supervised reclamations and named marshals to make arrests. Marshals could demand the assistance of bystanders to seize suspected runaways; citizens who refused to cooperate faced fines or jail. Masters merely had to supply oral or written proof of ownership in order to pursue a 'fugitive' and commissioners decided cases without a jury. Their fee doubled if they ruled in favor of the master rather than letting the suspect go free. Those arrested could not testify on their own behalf. Such was the nature of republican 'compromise' in 1850.[4]

Although sponsored by advocates of limited government power, the Fugitive Slave Act was one of the strongest federal laws in US history up to that time. The exercise of that authority raised a storm of protest. Federal officials seized 200 suspected runaways between 1850 and 1856. The enactment of the law was felt almost entirely in 'free' states, not slave states. Northern reformers, incensed at the law's legalized 'kidnapping', formed rescue committees to disrupt arrests and hearings. Several Northern legislatures passed 'personal liberty laws' to block enforcement of the act. Some African Americans urged emigration as the only safe way to escape oppression in the United States, and one Northern woman, deeply distressed at the misery and suffering caused by the law, responded with her pen to the new national crisis.

UNCLE TOM'S CABIN

Harriet Beecher Stowe was the daughter of Congregational minister Lyman Beecher. Brought up in a family committed to social service, Harriet was keenly aware of the pressing social and moral problems tied to slavery. Her father served as president of Lane Theological Seminary in Cincinnati, the site of debates over abolition. The city, across the Ohio River from Kentucky, was the scene of dramatic slave escapes. Harriet followed the controversy close at hand and through tracts written by reformers such as Lydia Maria Child and Frederick Douglass.

During a church service one Sunday, Stowe claimed she was over-taken by the vision of a pious, gentle slave. She began recording her thoughts in a work she entitled *Uncle Tom's Cabin*. The novel focuses on a man who stands at the center of a slave community until torn from his family and sold 'down river' to a vicious master. Tom finds redemption not through emancipation but through death. Other characters include a young woman who escapes to freedom, a passio-

Harriet Beecher Stowe (1811–1896)

nate man who envisions a black republic, and a mischievous girl who plays havoc with the conventions of white society. They inhabit a world dominated by whites, some of whom defend slavery, some of whom subvert it, and some of whom remain paralyzed by uncertainty.

The range of Stowe's characters gave the romance its sweep. The complexity of her message gave the work its power. Stowe did not simply pit immoral Southerners against virtuous Northerners: her most reprehensible character, the villainous master Simon Legree, was a New Englander. Her argument revolved around two themes: that slavery was a sin requiring immediate repentance; and that the whole nation shared in the guilt of the sin. Stowe's insistence on Northern complicity lent her work a cutting edge that left no side in the debate comfortable and secure. She urged all regions of the country to work for the abolition of slavery. And she assumed, in the end, that the impetus for change would come not from meeting halls or marketplaces controlled by men but from the domestic circle of love and faith maintained by women. The female power that defined home, hearth, and soul should, Stowe assumed, extend its influence to the world at large.

The work proved enormously popular. In its first year, 1852, the story sold over 300,000 copies. It was the first American novel to sell a million copies. The book also became a play that toured Northern states. The story of slavery's threats to family life, republican ideals, and Christian commitments left readers moved, fearful, and angered. One Chicago observer hoped the novel would 'exert a favorable influence for the rights of humanity and have a happy tendency towards the enfranchisement of the down trodden millions of our own land'.

In the South, the novel evoked shock and derision. Stowe seemed to be another wild-eyed radical who passed off lies as truths, who fed suspicion and hatred in her audience, and who recklessly condemned a region, its people, and their way of life. Southerners expressed alarm that a work allegedly so false could prove so popular in the North. The nation had reached such a fragile state that an author's book, not just a lawmaker's bill, drove a wedge between Americans. When President Abraham Lincoln met Harriet Beecher Stowe in 1863, he reportedly remarked, 'So you're the little woman who wrote the book that made this great war?'

Dreams of Expansion

American expansionism found an economic outlet in increased commerce with Asia. Between 1844 and 1858, agreements with China opened over a dozen ports to American trade. An 1858 treaty with Japan opened another five ports in another key Pacific market.

Expansionism intersected with transportation development in 1853 as Democratic President Franklin Pierce dispatched South Carolinian James Gadsden to Mexico. Gadsden had his eye on a quarter of a million square miles of northern Mexico that would provide land for American settlers (and their slave laborers) and a desirable route for a transcontinental rail line from New Orleans to San Diego. Mexican officials resisted Gadsden's demands; Northern politicians wary of Southern designs sparked a Senate debate. In the end, the 'Gadsden

Purchase' secured less than 30,000 square miles of land south of New Mexico territory for $10 million – while opening one more point of contention between Northerners and Southerners.

Expansionism's overtly imperial ambition revealed itself in a covertly fashioned scheme for the Caribbean in 1854. Since the Polk administration, the United States had set its sights on Cuba as a desirable piece of real estate with strategic significance, economic value, and political importance (as a slave society). Polk's purchase plans went nowhere; efforts to stir up revolution against Spanish control also failed; and Spain rebuffed President Pierce's renewed efforts to buy Cuba. Foreign ministers discussing the predicament issued a confidential memo outlining the approach the United States should adopt towards Cuba. Their 'Ostend Manifesto' revealed the extraordinary lengths to which some officials believed America should go in its future expansion.

The ministers wrote that 'Cuba is as necessary to the North American republic as any of its present members, and . . . belongs naturally to that great family of States of which the Union is the providential nursery'. Insisting that 'the Union can never enjoy repose, nor possess reliable security, as long as Cuba is not embraced within its boundaries', they recommended renewed efforts to purchase the island. If that failed and if continued Spanish possession endangered the 'internal peace and existence of our cherished Union', then the United States was justified by 'every law, human and divine' to take Cuba from Spain. America could not stand by idly and 'permit Cuba to be Africanized and become a second St Domingo, with all its attendant horrors to the white race'. Allow freedom for blacks 90 miles from US shores? Unthinkable. America's mission was to keep bondsmen enslaved and to take Cuba by any means possible.

Unfortunately for the administration, the dispatch leaked to the press, caused a storm of controversy, and forced Pierce to disavow the strategy. But where government undertakings failed, private enterprise stepped in to assist. During the 1850s, freebooting adventurers led numerous 'filibustering' expeditions into areas of Central America and the Caribbean. Some of the groups were satisfied with mere robbery and plunder; others added a dash of idealism to their raids and tried to seize lands, 'liberate' their peoples, create new nations, or augment the slave territories of the United States. One such visionary was a Tennessean, William Walker, who launched attacks into Mexico and Central America. One invasion proved successful: a victorious Walker named himself president of Nicaragua. His last incursion hit a bit of a snag: Walker was captured by Hondurans and executed by a firing squad. Backed by Southern supporters (and allies within the Pierce administration), the filibuster campaigns fueled more sectional antagonism. To Northern eyes, in particular, the raids revealed a manifestly corrupt destiny for the Republic.

Civil War in Kansas

With expansionist escapades underway outside America's borders, another divisive series of events took place in the nation's heartland. In 1854, Congress passed the Kansas-Nebraska Act, the brainchild of Senator Stephen Douglas. The bill broke a large territory into two parts, Kansas and Nebraska. The hope was that the admission of these lands as states would not upset a sectional balance. The establishment of slavery was a possibility even though both areas lay north of the 36°30′ line; the final measure simply voided the 1820 Missouri Compromise. The federal government would not decide the issue of slavery in these lands; instead, the act invoked popular sovereignty and granted territorial legislatures the authority to determine the status of slavery. Douglas anticipated vigorous settlement, which would be likely to spur a rail line to the Pacific, whose eastern terminus could be in, say, Chicago, a pleasing prospect for the Illinois senator.

   Settlement proceeded, but not in the orderly and peaceful fashion Douglas anticipated. From the start, both pro- and anti-slavery organizations sponsored settlers in Kansas. A series of hotly disputed elections followed, establishing *two* territorial governments, one protecting slavery, the other prohibiting it. Two sets of leaders, two sets of laws, two proposals for state constitutions: divisions ran so deep that, by the spring of 1856, fighting erupted between the factions. The struggle came to be called 'Bleeding Kansas'. During one episode in May, abolitionist John Brown led a retaliatory raid against a proslavery settlement, hacking five men to death. Brown's 'Pottawatomie Massacre' inflamed tensions even further, leading to months of guerrilla fighting that left nearly 200 dead and $2 million in property destroyed.

Violence made its way into the halls of Congress as well. Massachusetts Senator Charles Sumner rose in the chamber on 20 May to denounce pro-slavery colleagues, including Senator Andrew Butler of South Carolina. Two days later, Butler's nephew, Representative Preston Brooks, confronted Sumner about the insulting comments and beat the senator over the head with a cane. The severely injured Sumner did not return to the Senate for two and a half years. Brooks was censured by the House, resigned his seat, and returned to his South Carolina home, where supporters rewarded him with replacement canes and re-election.

Throughout the Kansas controversy, President Franklin Pierce and his successor, James Buchanan, sided with the pro-slavery territorial government, but elections in Kansas in 1858 revealed how firmly settlers rejected the slave system. Admission of the territory was delayed until 1861, after the start of the Civil War, when Kansas finally entered the Union as a free state.

Events in the territory polarized the nation. 'Popular sovereignty' fell into disrepute as presidents and Southern leaders tried to extend slavery into territories despite the will of settlers. The dispute devastated the Whig Party, already weakened by defections of anti-slavery members. The controversy divided the Democrats as a national political force: increasingly, Northerners saw the party as the lackey of a Southern 'Slave Power' that seemingly conspired to control fresh lands for the chattel system. As a result, a new Republican Party gained strength. The party favored government promotion of the economy. Its leaders defended 'free labor' by celebrating hard work, economic opportunity, and social mobility. And they called for 'free soil' by prohibiting the expansion of slavery into the territories. For the first time in American politics, a major party stood openly opposed to slavery interests.

To Southerners, the new political developments were ominous. Republicans appeared unconcerned about the sectional base of their support. The party's success in the North and its disregard of the South fed bitterness and division; the North's social quirks only compounded its political hostility to the South. Northerners seemed to live in a competitive, greedy, unsettled society, ripped from its moorings by extremist reformers, left without a coherent center, and dependent on ever-greater concentrations of power to solve its problems. Radical abolitionists presumably fed Northern disorder even further by continually carping about the awful sin of slavery, the inherent equality of blacks, and the contemptible nature of Southerners. And the abolitionists' violence in Kansas portended a wider race war in the South. If Northerners feared 'Slave Power', Southerners dreaded 'Black Republicanism'. The alarm felt on both sides left little ground for compromise.

The Dred Scott Decision

In the midst of the Kansas struggle, another branch of the federal government tried its hand at resolving the slavery debate. Up until the mid-1850s, the Supreme Court had not ruled on questions concerning slavery in the territories. The opportunity to issue a decision arose when

Dred Scott

the Court accepted a case first raised in a Missouri courtroom – by a slave, Dred Scott.

Scott's master had taken him from a slave state, Missouri, to Illinois, on to Wisconsin Territory, and then back to Missouri. Scott, assisted by white reformers, sued for his freedom on the grounds that his residence in a free state and a free territory made him a free man. A ruling in Scott's favor was later reversed by a higher court in Missouri. The case came before the Supreme Court in 1856, and in March 1857, the Court issued its rulings.

The Court declared that no black person, enslaved or free, could qualify as a citizen of the United States. Constitutionally, Chief Justice Roger B. Taney argued, blacks were 'beings of an inferior order [who] had no rights which white men were bound to respect'. Blacks, according to Justice Peter V. Daniel, formed a separate group of persons removed from 'the family of nations' and were never meant to be included among American citizens. Furthermore, the justices declared, slaves were property. By virtue of the Fifth Amendment, Congress could not violate the property rights of citizens (such as masters) without due process of law. The 1820 Missouri Compromise had already deprived citizens of their property in the territories. Congress had rendered the Compromise obsolete in the Kansas-Nebraska Act and now, the justices of the Supreme Court declared that it had been null and void all along.

If the *national* legislature had no authority to exclude slavery from the territories, did *territorial* legislatures possess such power? The answer, according to Taney, was no. Neither the federal government nor territorial governments could deny the property rights of masters. The concept of popular sovereignty was moot: territorial settlers could debate slavery but not ban it.

One other issue remained unclear. If national and territorial legislatures had no power to exclude slavery, could *state* governments? The legislatures of New York and Massachusetts, for example, had already abolished slavery within their borders. Had they exceeded their lawful authority by violating the Fifth Amendment? Were their laws abolishing slavery null and void? The justices said nothing, but the logic of their position seemed to indicate that *no* legislature could make laws conflicting with the Fifth Amendment. Slavery appeared to enjoy secure, national protection while freedom held only local, and tenuous, protection.

Southerners celebrated the rulings issued by the justices (the majority of whom were themselves Southern). Northerners questioned the Court's 'judiciousness' in defining questions of citizenship, property rights, and legislative power. Observers recognized that more cases about slavery would be likely to come before the Supreme Court, and the next time the Court spoke, it might clear up lingering issues concerning state legislatures. The South hoped for continuity in the Court's makeup and thinking. Northern Republicans hoped for something different. Their party needed to galvanize support, elect a Republican president and Senate, and let the new administration make appointments to the Court that would change the next decision.

John Brown's Raid

State governments had made their decisions about slavery. So, too, had Congresses, presidents, and the Supreme Court. To one man, John Brown, it appeared that established authorities all agreed that slavery enjoyed protection and assistance while liberty suffered restriction and decay. There seemed little reason to continue pressing the issue through legitimate channels; all such offices had become illegitimate through their collusion with the 'slave power'. The righteous had to act on their own to eradicate the sin of slavery and redeem the nation.

After fighting in Kansas, Brown returned East. He now intended to take the struggle into the heart of the beast, into the South itself. Financed by a group of northeastern abolitionists known as the 'Secret Six', assisted by 21 followers, and fired by a passionate commitment to liberty, Brown planned to spark a series of slave insurrections throughout the South. The process would begin at a mountain base along the Potomac River on the Virginia–Maryland border. Brown and his men would attack the US arsenal in Harpers Ferry, seize and distribute its arms to slaves, lead an uprising, retreat, and then launch more attacks against the slave system.

John Brown

On 16 October 1859, Brown's band struck. The group took the armory, held its arms, and waited to be joined by slaves from the surrounding area. Local residents gathered outside and began shooting at the occupants. US Marines, under the command of Colonel Robert E. Lee, soon arrived, killing some of the raiders and capturing others, including Brown. Authorities charged him with treason against the state of Virginia and conspiracy to incite slave insurrection. By early November, the state tried and convicted Brown, sentencing him to death. From his cell, he wrote, 'I John Brown am now quite certain that the crimes of this guilty land will never be purged away but with Blood'. On December 2, Brown was taken from his cell and hanged.

An unprecedented outpouring of sorrow and sympathy issued from the North. Groups marked the moment of his execution with solemn meetings, eloquent speeches, and quiet ceremonies. To participants, Brown's means may have been regrettably violent, but his purposes were exemplary. For some, Brown nobly tried to enact, rather than merely espouse, the highest ideals of humanity. For others, Brown heroically defied the slave power. For still others, Brown bravely sacrificed his own life for the redemption of four million slaves.

While the North grieved, the South shuddered. How, Southerners asked, could so many admire a man so mad? Brown was a killer, an insurrectionary, a threat to the nation's security, yet Bostonians, New Yorkers, and Philadelphians honored the man's principles and actions. Their grotesque mourning showed how chaos in the South brought cheer to the North. What sign more clearly demonstrated that the two sections of the country shared nothing in common? What further proof did anyone need to recognize that all Northerners – fiery abolitionists, 'moderate' Republicans, average citizens – had conspired to serve their own narrow interests by destroying the fabric of Southern life? Now was the time to close ranks, to ward off Northern violence, and to purge those who would weaken the South from within. As the Atlanta *Confederacy* stated, 'We regard every man in our midst an enemy to the institutions of the South who does not boldly declare that he believes African slavery to be a social, moral, and political blessing.'

The Election of 1860

In such a charged environment, Americans chose a chief executive. Not surprisingly, the presidential election of 1860 was as deeply divided as the nation. The contest revolved around four (rather than two) principal candidates. Essentially, Northerners and Southerners each chose from two candidates. Only one of the four office seekers campaigned in both regions. A national decision, in other words, was rendered through sectional means.

The Democratic Party was hopelessly torn within its own ranks over questions of slavery in the West. Senator Jefferson Davis of Mississippi insisted that the party had to protect slavery in the territories. Senator Stephen Douglas tried to salvage popular sovereignty. Deadlocked party members eventually held two separate conventions and nominated two presidential candidates. Southern Democrats chose John C. Breckenridge. Douglas held the party's banner for Northern Democrats, though he also took his campaign into Southern states. A third candidate, John Bell of Tennessee, represented moderate, border-state Southerners pledged to compromise on slavery.

Republicans believed that moderation was the key to victory. The candidate who best conveyed that image was Abraham Lincoln who had gained attention in the party during his unsuccessful senatorial bid in Illinois two years earlier. Lincoln was a man of humble origins who could appeal to farmers and workers. He was a Midwesterner who could carry the crucial states of Illinois and Indiana. He was cautious on slavery, opposing its extension into the territories of the West but affirming its right to exist in the states of the South. And he was a relative newcomer on the national scene who was not weighed down with political baggage.

The Republican platform echoed Lincoln's stance on slavery. To distance itself from radicals, the party condemned John Brown's raid as 'the gravest of crimes'. To revive an economy recovering from the 1857 depression, Republicans proposed vigorous federal intervention including protective tariffs, free homesteads, and transportation improvements. The party hoped it had concocted a recipe for success, at least in the Northeast and West.

The results of the contest were favorable for the Republicans but unsettling for the nation as a whole. Lincoln won nearly 60 per cent of the electoral votes with less than 40 per cent of the popular vote. He did not won a single electoral vote in the South, not surprising considering that Lincoln's name did not even appear on the ballot in ten Southern states. Lincoln was a minority president (in terms of popular vote) and a sectional president (in terms of electoral vote). His base of support was sufficient to win an election but inadequate to bind a nation.

The results were chilling for Southerners who saw further proof of the North's invincible political strength. Northerners could win whenever they ran and do whatever they wanted in national politics and never depend on Southerners for support. The slave states were politically dispensable. The South's residents now feared that victorious Northern Republicans would freely trample on Southern needs and well-being, and not have to pay a political price for their actions. What guarantees, what security could the South possibly preserve under such a regime?

The Disunion of the States

Hearing of Lincoln's victory, Southern political leaders met to discuss the threat to their region. A new president and party came to power owing absolutely nothing to Southern states. President-elect Lincoln would not allow slavery to expand onto fresh public lands and without that expansion, slavery would wither and collapse. The containment of slavery equaled the eradication of slavery. Southerners believed a long-standing fear had come to pass: 'abolitionists' controlled the federal government. As president, Lincoln would nominate like-minded men for Supreme Court openings. How would his justices decide the next test case on slavery? As chief executive, Lincoln enforced the laws of the land. How eagerly would he administer the Fugitive Slave Act? As commander in chief, Lincoln guided US military forces. How quickly would he respond to raids like that of John Brown? As party leader, Lincoln doled out offices. How many Republican-appointed post-masters would be likely to destroy incendiary abolitionist literature sent through the mails? Southerners saw themselves in jeopardy at all points.

For decades, extremists had urged one escape from sectional cata-strophe: secession. On 20 December 1860, South Carolina decided to make the break. The state repealed its ratification of the Constitution and declared its union with other states dissolved. By February 1861, six other Lower South states joined in secession. The seven adopted a provisional constitution for the Confederate States of America and elected a provisional president, Jefferson Davis.

Members of the Confederacy argued that, with Lincoln's election, they had to act before it was too late. Republicans would certainly dismantle federal protections of slavery. If the national government distanced itself from the chattel system, slave insurrections would soon sweep across the South. Supporters also argued that secession was a legitimate and lawful step. States that presumably had exercised their sovereignty in the 1780s by approving the Constitution only invoked their sovereignty again by repudiating the government and its Union. Furthermore, Southern leaders were convinced the North would do nothing to retaliate. The North was far too dependent economically on the South – and far too incompetent militarily – to force the issue.

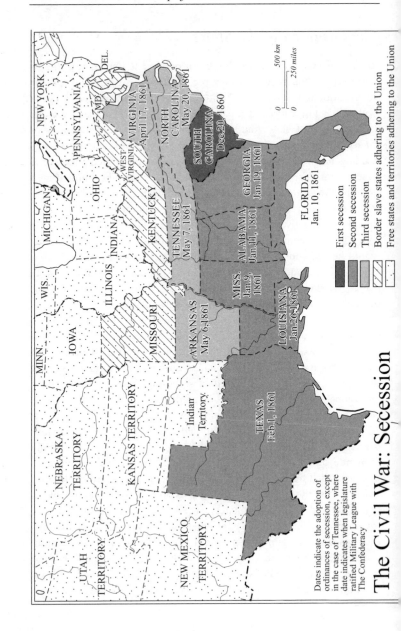

Dates indicate the adoption of
ordinances of secession, except
in the case of Tennessee, where
date indicates when legislature
ratified Military League with
The Confederacy

The Civil War: Secession

Finally, even if Northerners did provoke a struggle over secession, Southerners believed they could count on support from their loyal customers (and presumed political allies) in Britain and France.

While seven states had seceded by early 1861, eight other slave states stayed within the Union. The Upper South hoped to win federal concessions for slavery that would coax the Lower South back. Congress failed to achieve a compromise; the proposals appeared to reward the seceding states while punishing the victorious Republicans. Outgoing President Buchanan denounced secession as illegal but did not act decisively against the Confederate States. Incoming President Lincoln refused to discuss the controversy publicly. He remained convinced that secession was unconstitutional, that bargaining with seceders was pointless, and that Union sympathizers in the South would soon wrest control from an extremist minority.

Matters remained in limbo for a month. On 4 March 1861, Lincoln took the oath of office. His inaugural address expressed both firmness and conciliation. Lincoln declared secession illegal, vowed to preserve the Union, pledged to hold federal property in the Lower South, and insisted that slavery would not expand into the territories. At the same time he would not interfere with slavery in the states where it existed. Lincoln looked forward to the seceded states' return to the Union, and he appealed to the 'bonds of affection' that tied Americans together even in times of passionate conflict. In little more than a month, however, those bonds broke apart.

Fort Sumter

One of the pieces of federal property Lincoln vowed to protect was Fort Sumter. Sitting on a small island in the harbor of Charleston, South Carolina, the fort symbolized Union authority in the heart of secessionism. The fort's commander, Major Robert Anderson, notified federal officials that his men were low on provisions and needed fresh supplies as soon as possible. On 6 April, Lincoln informed the governor of South Carolina that a relief expedition would bring food to the installation – but not soldiers, weapons, or ammunition. Convinced that a confrontation would win over the Upper South to the Confederacy, President Jefferson Davis ordered General P. G. T. Beauregard to demand the fort's surrender and to take it by force if necessary. As relief ships neared the island on 12 April, Confederate batteries opened fire on Fort Sumter. On 14 April, Major Anderson surrendered. Soldiers lowered the stars and stripes of the US flag and raised the stars and bars of the Confederate banner. On 15 April, Lincoln called 75,000 state militiamen into federal service for 90 days. Their mission was to suppress an insurrection.

The states of the Upper South now had to take sides in the conflict. By May 1861, Virginia, Arkansas, Tennessee, and North Carolina cast their lots with the Confederacy. In four other slave states the story was different. In Delaware, with only 2 per cent of the population composed of slaves, the decision to remain in the Union came quickly. In Maryland, the arrests of pro-Confederate leaders, the imposition of martial law in Baltimore, and the suspension of writs of habeas corpus helped keep the deeply divided state in the Union (and, unfortunately, helped sacrifice basic civil rights in the name of urgent national security). In Kentucky, Confederate troops violated the state's proclaimed neutrality, occupied several cities, and pushed the government into the Union camp. In Missouri, fighting broke out between Unionists and pro-Confederate forces; a guerilla war continued for years, but Union supporters held sway.

Eleven Confederate states stood against Union forces by late spring 1861. Both sides expected a speedy resolution to the conflict. Neither anticipated the horror of coming events, what poet Walt Whitman called 'the red blood of civil war'.

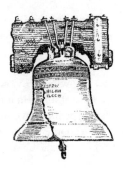

CHAPTER EIGHT

The Civil War and Reconstruction, 1861–1877

Southerners called it the 'War between the States', Northerners the 'War of the Rebellion'. Even *nominal* agreement escaped the two sides. Yet differences over designation were minor compared to the chasm that separated Americans on questions of nationhood and freedom. Nathaniel Hawthorne concluded that 'We never were one people, and never really had a country since the Constitution was formed'. The Civil War stood as a tragic, epic voyage of American rediscovery, exploring not the land but its principles. The struggle clarified the meaning of union and redefined the idea of liberty – but at a price that was unimaginable and agonizing.

Four years of conflict, a million casualties, and the devastation of a region brought both the Confederacy and slavery to an end. But the war did not define how to reunite the republic. And the struggle did not clarify how (or even if) ex-slaves could act on their newly won freedom. The course of reconstructing the nation after war proved almost as divisive as the events that led America into conflict. There were bitter disputes among those who presumably won, renewed strength for those who presumably lost, and a brief period of hope for those who became free.

The Causes of the Civil War

For the Lincoln Administration, the immediate cause of hostilities involved the need to preserve and protect the Union. The violent assault on federal property at Fort Sumter marked an insurrection against the legitimate government of the United States. Lincoln was moderate, at best, on questions of slavery: he would not allow the chattel system in the West but would not interfere with the peculiar institution in the Old South. Lincoln was also moderate, at best, on questions of race: he assumed that blacks held basic rights deserving protection, yet he also shared general white suspicions about the inferior nature of African Americans. But Lincoln was rigid on questions of Union: the principles of the Constitution, the rule of law, and the future greatness of America all depended on a perpetual and indissoluble Union. Compromise on matters of slavery or race was possible and preferred; compromise on matters of Union was unthinkable. The suppression of a rebellion against the Union was the immediate cause of the Civil War.

Slavery in and of itself had not brought the country to this state. The peculiar institution was part of the republic since its founding. But the prospect of slavery *outside* the Old South, the image of masters leading slaves to fresh Western lands, and the fear that opportunities for free white laborers might dwindle all raised serious political problems. Southerners insisted on their right to take slave property west into territories jointly held by the states. The Republican Party remained equally steadfast that slave interests should not gain more land for the chattel system. One after another, compromises on this question collapsed; year after year, politicians failed to find a stable middle ground in the controversy. The expansion of slavery led to the breakup of the Union.

A people with a seemingly rational, enlightened political system held profoundly different ideas about the meaning and purposes of their government. Quite simply, Americans had never reached consensus on the nature of their political union. They engaged in a war for independence; they created a written constitution to clarify the arrangements of power and the protection of freedom; they expanded rapidly under their Constitutional banner; and they created a popular identity for themselves as Americans. But they never clearly understood if their republic was one, central, unitary political order or a group of smaller, sovereign, and co-operating political units.

As historian David M. Potter pointed out, 'perhaps the United States is the only nation in history which for seven decades acted politically and culturally as a nation, and grew steadily stronger in its nationhood, before decisively answering the question of whether it was a nation at all'. Americans, in their basic political grammar, had not agreed on whether the 'United States of America' was a singular or plural noun. 'Thus,' Potter noted, 'the phrase '*E pluribus unum*' was a riddle as well as a motto.'[1] It took a civil war to answer the riddle. Over 600,000 men gave up their lives in order to end the debate over nationhood. A mass democracy suffered mass slaughter in order to understand what it was all about.

Strengths and Weaknesses of the Two Sides

Against a background of division and distrust, the two sides confronted one another in war. In ideological, cultural, and social terms they were certainly a match for one another. But in material terms, the contest appeared lopsided, pitting the large, urbanized, wealthy Union against the smaller, rural, and economically weaker Confederacy. In hindsight, one might wonder why Southern states would risk a fight with such a powerful opponent.

Northern states enjoyed far greater resources than Southern states. The North had two and a half times the population of the Confederacy. It produced 92 per cent of the nation's manufactured goods. The region held twice the railroad mileage of the South, four times the bank deposits, and most of the nation's shipping and mercantile firms. Surely, Southerners recognized the greater strength and size of the North? They had to have understood that the odds were against them. They must have realized the reckless nature of their actions.

As it turned out, Confederates viewed these circumstances quite differently; they remained confident about the outcome of hostilities. Their optimism revolved around the *duration* of the conflict. The North was an economic powerhouse, but it would take time to mobilize the region's resources into a disciplined, national war effort. In a brief war, the Confederacy might attain its objectives before the Union could mass its potential strength. And the South would prevail, so the argument went, because the CSA enjoyed several short-term advantages over the North.

The South held an initial military edge because of its well-trained officers and their feasible mission. America's most talented military leaders sided with the Confederate cause. Its officers had more formal and battlefield training than their Northern counterparts. The Confederacy's officers also faced a more limited military task. While a Union 'victory' required the invasion and conquest of the insurrectionary South, a Confederate 'victory' required only the defense of the South against an invading army. For the South, a stalemate meant triumph.

Geography provided another advantage. The CSA covered over half a million square miles, a huge area for the North to conquer and hold. The barrier of the Appalachians, the heavily wooded terrain of the region, and the poor roadways of the South would all hamper the movement of Union forces.

Diplomatic considerations also seemed to work against the North. Southerners believed that their control of cotton would pressure industrializing countries into close ties with the Confederacy. Southern leaders also felt that their commitment to stability and order in a fixed, hierarchical system matched the larger social goals of European regimes. And the war offered Britain and France an opportunity to hobble a potential rival, the Union government. Full diplomatic recognition from Europe – even full matériel assistance – would undoubtedly occur.

Finally, the South seemed to have the political upper hand on the North in terms of executive leadership. Jefferson Davis, the president of the Confederate States, had an exemplary military and political career. Having served as a war veteran, a representative, a senator, and a Secretary of War, Davis held a distinguished record that would command respect at home and abroad. Abraham Lincoln, the president of the United States, seemed, even to some in his own party, a bumbling incompetent who would be likely to jeopardize the war effort and create disarray in the North. Lincoln's résumé showed limited military experience and ample political failures. Voters expressed their disapproval of his leadership in the midst of the war in the Congressional elections of 1862. One Republican even complained that Lincoln was 'as near lunacy as anyone not a pronounced Bedlamite'! Confederates rested assured that a more stable, intelligent, and capable hand guided their ship of state through the tortuous waters of war.

The Union enjoyed material advantages, but its wealth would not come into play very quickly. The Confederacy enjoyed other types of advantage that it could draw on immediately. In a war lasting a few months, victory seemed assured for the CSA. As it turned out, several Union 'disadvantages' were only apparent, some never materialized, and others were readily overcome.

Militarily, Lincoln faced serious problems, especially in finding a general prepared to fight a brutal and ruthless brand of war. Still, the North drew on a larger pool of men: of the nearly three million who served in both armies, almost three-quarters were in the Union's forces. That translated into a considerable infantry advantage. The region's manufacturing leadership also gave the Union a clear artillery advantage. Northerners held the superior naval forces, owing to their long-standing maritime experience. The only military wing with a clear Southern advantage was the cavalry, although its military significance was in decline.

Geographically, the North enjoyed its own 'natural' advantages. Southern river systems provided a useful invasion route for Union forces. The Cumberland and Tennessee Rivers opened pathways into Kentucky, Tennessee, northern Mississippi and Alabama, and western Virginia; control of the Mississippi offered a way of dividing the western regions of the Confederacy from the east. In addition, the South itself turned out to be the major battlefield. The lands of the Confederacy, not the Union, suffered the devastation of warfare. And as time passed, that conflict only became more destructive to farms, fields, and communities.

Diplomatically, the North did not face the calamities anticipated by the South. The Union maintained diplomatic ties to Europe. The administration provided firm leadership in the State Department and in its British and French embassies. More important were the decisions that Europeans made for themselves. Great Britain and France had little to gain by casting their lot with either the North or the South; with no pressing self-interest at stake, they proclaimed neutrality. The Confederacy received some aid by virtue of its status as a 'belligerent'; the

Union quarreled with Britain over maritime and neutrality laws. Yet the North managed to create a naval blockade against the South, and direct European intervention on behalf of the CSA (and against the USA) did not occur.

Politically, Northern leaders demonstrated greater skill in directing internal conflict and the war effort than their Southern counterparts. Unlike Davis, Lincoln shared the burdens of leadership with talented and respected cabinet members. Rather than alienating strong-willed advisors, Lincoln managed to check their ambitions through his self-effacing, restrained, yet persuasive style. Because an opposition party remained strong in the North, Republicans interested in a united political front generally gave Lincoln at least grudging support. In contrast to Southern Democrats, Northern Republicans did not shy away from centralized power. Their willingness to grant greater authority to the national government was more in tune with the demands of modern warfare than the localism and decentralization of Southerners.

Most importantly, the Union's lead in human, natural, and industrial assets turned out to have increasing importance as the Civil War dragged on unexpectedly. The North could direct massive and relentless pressure against the South, and in the end, that mammoth, continual, ruthless force overwhelmed the resources and resolve of the Confederacy.

Shifting Strategies

At the beginning, however, both sides anticipated a different type of struggle. Traditional training held that war was limited, that offensive operations defined combat, and that strategic brilliance rather than battlefield brutality decided the outcome. Henri Jomini's writings were especially important in American military education. He argued that armies must conquer enemy territory and capture its capital by focusing professional, highly trained forces on the enemy's point of weakness. Armies conducted war on a well-defined field through perceptive maneuvers.

In July 1861, Northern and Southern commanders applied their textbook lessons at Manassas, Virginia, along a stream called Bull Run (the South named battles after nearby towns, the North by natural features). Union General Irvin McDowell led 35,000 troops against 22,000 Confederates under General P.G.T. Beauregard. It seemed self-evident that they would defeat the opponent's army and end the war with one battle. McDowell at first prevailed, but his assault stopped when Confederate reinforcements hit the North's right flank. Union forces retreated chaotically back to Washington and Southern troops, exhausted from battle, did not pursue them. The fighting was indecisive yet still claimed nearly 900 soldiers dead and 2,600 wounded. Bull Run gave the first bitter taste of the war's course: fighting would take a heavy toll; battles often proved inconclusive; the struggle would grind on; and traditional approaches to warfare betrayed serious flaws.

As time passed, commanders discarded old lessons and applied new ones. They did not lead armies consisting of professional soldiers. Instead, a wide range of men brought into service quickly (and held there with difficulty) required considerable training, not only for the rigors of battle but also for mundane tasks such as marches and retreats. Soldiers used weapons far more refined than the old smoothbore musket and bayonet of previous wars. Springfield and Enfield rifle-muskets and Minié bullets had greater accuracy, range, reloading speed, and killing power, hitting targets up to twice per minute at three to four times the distance of older arms. Because of the weapons' greater precision, well-armed, well-positioned defenders held a clear advantage over advancing attackers. The dream of soldiers simply marching forward, defeating an opponent, and taking the enemy's capital proved not only elusive but perilous, ensnaring tens of thousands in a fatal trap. The assumption that fighting would play itself out on well-demarcated fields of battle faded. Troops destroyed one another while also scavenging and ravaging surrounding areas, bringing their destructive force to bear on soldiers and civilians alike.

Rather than fitting traditional expectations, the struggle introduced Americans to modern warfare. The fighting taught that war was unlimited in time and space. The military had to engage in a protracted rather than a brief conflict; the advantage passed to the side that could hold out the longest. Commanders focused not only on opposing forces but also on an enemy's capacity and will to resist; those who occupied another's land also needed to destroy its resources and morale.

One Northern leader, General Winfield Scott, proposed a rough version of this strategy at the start of the war. Like many, he felt it necessary to secure Washington, DC, while keeping pressure on the opponent's capital in Richmond 100 miles away. Unlike others, Scott advised two other plans: creating a naval blockade around the South to stop supplies of foreign goods; and penetrating the Confederacy through its western river systems, slowly cutting, dividing, and subdividing Southern regions from one another. Critics scoffed at the idea of encircling and squeezing the South, labeling it the 'Anaconda' strategy. Lincoln, who also yearned for a climactic battle to start and finish the war quickly, harbored doubts about the scheme. After the disaster at Bull Run, however, the president came to recognize the wisdom of a gradual strategy, one that would chip away at Southern resources and stamina and incrementally defeat the enemy.

Over time, the Union settled on a multi-pronged strategy. First, federal forces guarded their own capital while coveting their opponent's. Secondly, the North tried to maintain its hold on the border states of Maryland, Kentucky, and Missouri. Thirdly, by moving along the Tennessee, Cumberland, and Mississippi Rivers, the Union hoped to cut the Confederacy in two and gain control of its western regions. Fourthly, by moving troops through the South later in the war and seizing local resources, the Federals intended to exhaust the Confederacy. Fifthly, in eastern, western, and trans-Mississippi confrontations, the North sought to annihilate Southern armies.

Committed to subduing a breakaway region and reuniting the republic, the North had no choice but to pursue an offensive strategy. Committed to its independence, repelling an invasion, and avoiding defeat, the South had no reason to pursue anything but a defensive mission. If the Confederacy could hold off the North, the enemy's determination might fade, support for the war might collapse, and the Union might seek a negotiated settlement.

Yet the appeal of decisive offensive action also had a hold on the Southern imagination. Militarily, a move against Northern targets could draw Union forces away from other battle zones where rebel forces needed relief. Confederate forces marching into the North could re-supply themselves with the Union's vast resources, break the morale of federal troops, and bring the war's destruction to *Northern* communities. The North might quickly choose the bargaining table over the battlefield. Diplomatically, a devastating blow against the North could also earn the CSA the respect, recognition, and support of major European powers. Politically, Confederate leaders knew that defensive action alone would not generate tremendous enthusiasm for the war effort; Southerners wanted to inflict damage and pain on the Union. The logic behind these arguments may have been sound, but the results were disastrous. The Confederacy's great offensive operations all met with strategic failure and considerable human suffering.

The Course of Battle

1861

Over the Civil War's four years, the fighting that took place between Richmond and Washington attracted considerable fame and renown. In the Chesapeake area, large armies gathered, capital cities stood fortified, troops fought extended battles, and the war came to a dramatic and savage climax. Yet despite widespread attention, combat in the area was frequently inconclusive. Victors were often too weak or disorganized to pursue retreating forces; the 'winners' in battle occasionally suffered greater casualties than the 'losers'. Considering the eventual direction and outcome of the war, some of the most significant events took place elsewhere: on the lands west of the Appalachians and on the rivers and coasts of the South.

Stalemate dominated the Eastern Theater in the months following the First Battle of Bull Run. But to the west, Union commanders achieved two modest objectives. Northern forces checked a secessionist effort in Missouri, maintaining a hold on the state, and late in the summer of 1861, George B. McClellan moved troops into western Virginia, gave support to its Unionist-minded population, and won back the area for the North.

Another major project at the start of the war involved the Union's naval blockade of the South. With 3,500 miles of coastline and nearly 200 ports to cover, the 40 or so ships available to the North faced a daunting task. At first, Union vessels stopped only one in ten ships that tried to run the blockade. The navy's grip gradually tightened as the United States expanded its fleet. By 1865, the North had stopped half of all blockade runners; in the meantime, key coastal areas came under Union control. In November 1861, Northern forces seized Port Royal and nearby sea islands off South Carolina, and the following year, the Union secured river outlets along the North Carolina coast.

1862

Union forces made a number of gains in the Trans-Mississippi and Western Theaters during the second year of the war. Colorado volunteers halted a Confederate advance in New Mexico by late March at the Battle of Glorieta Pass. California units helped secure the territories of Utah and Arizona, and a Northern victory at Pea Ridge in Arkansas strengthened control in Missouri. The Union was able to maintain its hold of lands west of the Mississippi.

East of the area, General Ulysses S. Grant used the Tennessee and Cumberland Rivers as pathways into the Confederacy. His forces took Forts Henry and Donelson in February and then pushed farther south through western Tennessee. On 6 April, at Shiloh Church, a surprise Southern attack by Generals Albert Sidney Johnston and P. G. T. Beauregard almost destroyed Grant's army. Pushed back, Grant regrouped his forces, secured reinforcements, and defeated the Confederates the following day. The fighting claimed 13,000 Northern casualties and 10,000 for the South. The Confederates' rail hub at Corinth, Mississippi, fell to Union troops shortly thereafter. At year's end, during the Battle of Murfreesboro, Northern forces also turned back Braxton Bragg's effort to push his Confederate army through Tennessee and Kentucky.

A potential threat to Union naval power in 1862 proved short-lived. Confederates clad the USS *Merrimac* with iron plate, renamed it the CSS *Virginia*, and sent it out to destroy Union warships. On 9 March,

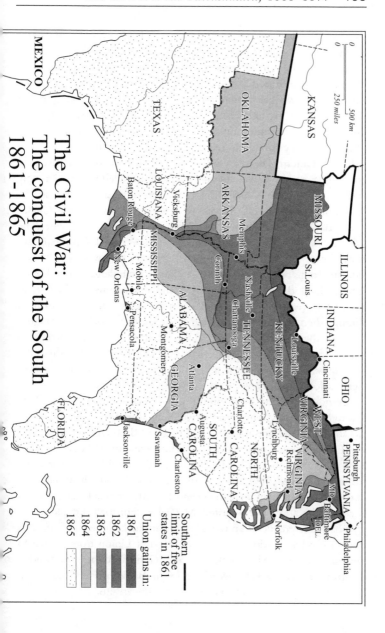

The Civil War:
The conquest of the South
1861-1865

Southern
limit of free
states in 1861

Union gains in:

1861
1862
1863
1864
1865

the vessel faced off against the Union ironclad, *Monitor*. The encounter was a draw and the *Virginia* withdrew – only to be destroyed two months later when Confederates evacuated Norfolk. In late April, Union forces captured the port of New Orleans. Admiral David G. Farragut followed that triumph by moving upriver, taking Baton Rouge in May. By late spring, Union forces moved down the Mississippi from Illinois and captured Memphis on 6 June. Control of the great river valley passed more and more into Union hands.

In the Eastern Theater, both sides launched ambitious advances, both failed, and by year's end stalemate still prevailed. After seemingly endless preparation, McClellan began an offensive drive against Richmond in the spring. He chose a circuitous route down Chesapeake Bay to the mouths of the York and James Rivers where he believed he would encounter less resistance. As McClellan moved his army down to Richmond, Thomas J. 'Stonewall' Jackson led Confederate troops up the Shenandoah Valley. Jackson defeated two Union armies along the way and diverted the reinforcements McClellan desperately requested. General Robert E. Lee's Army of Northern Virginia then launched attacks on McClellan from 25 June through 1 July. At the end of the Seven Days' Battles, Southern forces had repulsed but not defeated McClellan. He failed to renew his drive and, by August, Lincoln ordered him to return north to join forces with General John Pope.

Lee now launched an invasion north, directing forces against Pope before McClellan's army could arrive. Southern troops under Lee and Jackson defeated Pope at the Second Battle of Bull Run in late August, and Lee continued pressing his drive into western Maryland. On 17 September, at Antietam Creek, his forces confronted McClellan's in a battle of unprecedented ferocity. Antietam was the bloodiest single day of the war: 4,800 men were killed and 18,500 wounded. Having lost a quarter of his army, Lee retreated. McClellan, horrified at the losses his men had suffered, did not pursue. His forces blocked the Confederacy's first great offensive drive into the North, but Union troops failed to capitalize on the situation, especially after General Ambrose Burnside's disastrous defeat at the hands of Lee in the Battle of Fredricksburg in December.

General Robert E. Lee

EMANCIPATION

Antietam's carnage stood out in American military history, but the battle also marked a turning point in American social, political, and racial history. When the fighting subsided, Lincoln issued the Preliminary Emancipation Proclamation. As of 1 January, slaves living in areas under rebel control were 'thenceforward and forever free'. Up to September 1862, the North fought a war to reunite the states; after Antietam, the North fought a war for both union and liberty.

Lincoln recognized that slavery was central to the war's origins, but he did not make its elimination central to the war's purpose. Politically, Republicans wanted to contain rather than abolish slavery; opposition Democrats would have denounced anything more. Constitutionally, Lincoln believed he did not have the authority to break up the slave system; he hoped states would take the initiative. Socially, the president sensed that any move to end slavery might meet with intense Northern white hostility. Strategically, he feared that a call for emancipation would alarm border state residents and push them into the arms of the Confederacy.

Meanwhile, other events moved the issue more decisively. Slaves who labored for rebel armies or who worked in fields at home provided the Confederacy with steady supplies while also freeing more whites for military service. Leaving slavery intact only sustained the South. In increasing numbers, however, slaves made their way to, or found themselves behind, Union lines. By late spring 1861, Northern officers began treating escaped or captured slaves as 'contraband of war', putting them to work for Union forces. A few commanders went further and actually liberated slaves. Congressional Republicans passed 'confiscation acts' to clarify the procedures, first authorizing seizures and then freeing slaves held by the Northern military.

Guided by military necessity, presidential war powers, and higher ideals, Lincoln decided to support emancipation by the summer of 1862. He waited for a significant military achievement before making the announcement. Union 'victory' at Antietam gave Lincoln what he wanted, and he issued the preliminary proclamation. On 1 January 1863, he signed the Final Emancipation Proclamation. In practice, the proclamation emancipated no slaves that day; it only affected slaves in areas still controlled by the CSA. But the proclamation clarified that, in coming days, a victory over the South's rebellion would also mean the end of the region's peculiar institution.

What started as opposition to slavery's expansion widened into an attack on slavery's very existence in the Confederacy. As the war went on, several border states and occupied states chose to end slavery within their jurisdictions. In 1865, Congress passed and sent to the states an amendment abolishing slavery entirely. On 18 December 1865, the Thirteenth Amendment became part of the Constitution. A forced labor system based on race, which had been in place for over 200 years and controlled the lives of most African-Americans, came to an end.

Many who gained freedom acted on it quickly. Nearly 200,000 African Americans, mostly from the South, served in the US military.

Unidentified young African-American corporal

The troops were underpaid, poorly housed, assigned menial tasks, and segregated in black units led by white commanders, but their regiments saw significant battlefield action. The First Carolina Volunteers staged successful in raids in Florida and elsewhere. Half of the Fifty-Fourth Massachusetts Infantry commanded by Colonel Robert Gould Shaw died in an attack on Fort Wagner near Charleston, South Carolina. The Second US Colored Light Infantry fought in the battle of Nashville. The One Hundred Seventh Colored Infantry helped seize Fort Fisher in North Carolina. Confederate troops killed several dozen black soldiers who surrendered to Rebel forces at Fort Pillow, Tennessee. African American units made a significant contribution to the Union cause, but at a high price. Suffering a higher mortality rate than whites, 20 per cent of African-American soldiers died in the war.

1863

As the war entered its third year, the Confederacy enjoyed several advantages. Northern anti-war sentiment ran high, especially in the

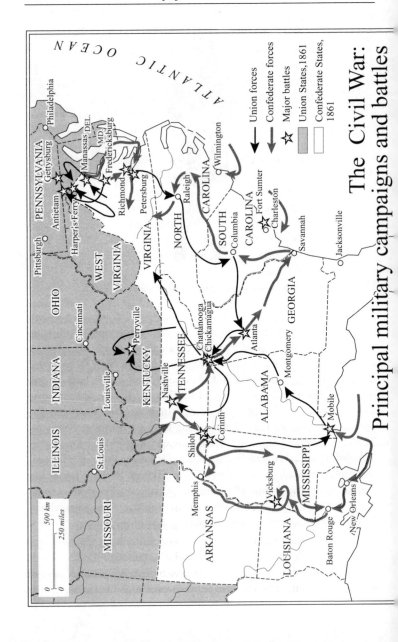

The Civil War:
Principal military campaigns and battles

Legend:
→ Union forces
→ Confederate forces
★ Major battles
Union States, 1861
Confederate States, 1861

face of urban riots led by mobs angered at conscription laws, Republican officials, and African Americans. Union advances on the Mississippi slowed as Northern troops tried to control the remaining stretch of river from Vicksburg, Mississippi, to Port Hudson, Louisiana. And in early May, midway between Richmond and Washington at a place called Chancellorsville, General Joseph Hooker's 130,000-man Union army was defeated by a Southern force half its size led by Lee and Jackson.

Although he lost a fifth of his men at Chancellorsville – along with his comrade, Stonewall Jackson – Lee launched yet another offensive drive. His army traveled up to a village in southern Pennsylvania where they confronted Union forces under General George C. Meade. On 1 July, the first day of the Battle of Gettysburg, Lee pushed Meade's line back but left Union forces in high, strong positions. The following day, Confederate assaults on Meade's left and right flanks failed. In one final effort, on 3 July, Lee launched a 15,000-man infantry assault on the Union center. Two-thirds of the troops in 'Pickett's Charge' were cut down during their advance. Having lost a third of his army, Lee retreated. The battlefield was covered with casualties: 23,000 of Meade's forces, 28,000 of Lee's. Gettysburg turned out to be the last Confederate offensive of the war.

As Lee pulled south on 4 July, a vital Confederate position in the West also fell. Grant had slowly moved his troops towards Vicksburg, circling in a counter-clockwise direction, first into Louisiana, then east, and finally, in mid-May, west. Union forces began a siege of the city. After six weeks, on the 4th of July, the Southern garrison surrendered. On 9 July, Port Hudson fell to Union forces. Federal troops now controlled the entire length of the Mississippi.

A third defeat for the Confederacy came in late November. The armies of Grant and William Tecumseh Sherman pushed into Chattanooga and broke a siege on the Union-held city. As a result, the Union gained control of eastern Tennessee and stood poised to launch an assault south towards Atlanta; but the Confederacy still had large armies intact and still controlled a vast area from Virginia down through the Lower South. The war was far from over.

1864

Grant was brought east to serve as general in chief of Union forces, and to take on Lee's army. Sherman stayed in the West to move against General Joseph E. Johnston. The two Union commanders shared the same aggressive, ruthless conception of war. They would attack, defeat, and ceaselessly pursue their opponents; they would wage total war against the South's society as well as its armies. And they would accomplish their objectives through simultaneous, co-ordinated drives by all Union forces, relying on the North's superior numbers, confining Confederate armies, and preventing the enemy from deploying troops to points of weakness.

Grant drove south towards Richmond, leading his Army of the Potomac against a Confederate force less than two-thirds its size. In early May, Grant fought Lee at the Battle of the Wilderness west of Fredricksburg. Grant then moved to his left and south, engaging Lee at Spotsylvania Court House. In one week, the two armies suffered

General Ulysses S. Grant

50,000 casualties. Although Northern losses exceeded those of the South, Grant kept moving to his left and south, battling Lee's forces in early June at Cold Harbor. The Union endured 7,000 casualties in less than an hour. During a month of sustained and bloody fighting, Lee's casualties totaled 31,000 and Grant's 55,000. Again, Grant moved left and south, towards the railroad junction at Petersburg, 25 miles below Richmond. His troops laid siege to the city from June 1864 to April 1865. Grant also dispatched a force to the Shenandoah Valley. Their mission was to stop Confederate raiding parties and to control the valley by destroying its resources through a scorched earth campaign.

From Chattanooga, Sherman led 90,000 men against an opposing force that was also two-thirds its size. Joseph Johnston showed himself to be a capable Confederate defender, but his maneuvers failed to impress Jefferson Davis, who replaced him with John B. Hood. The latter's attacks failed to stop Sherman who captured Atlanta on 2 September. While Hood moved west and north on a desperate (and futile) move into Tennessee, Sherman moved southwest. Destroying much of Atlanta, his forces began a 300-mile march to the sea, severing supply lines, living off the land, and cutting a swath of devastation up to 60 miles wide across Georgia. Sherman reached the Atlantic coast in mid-December and occupied Savannah on 22 December.

Union forces divided the CSA, contained rebel troops in well-defined areas, pressed enemy forces relentlessly, and brought the war home to civilians in an astounding and terrible way. The North now prepared for the final acts of the war.

The Soldiers' World

Nearly three million men served in the armies of the North and the South during the four-year conflict. One out of every five soldiers died. The fighting in the field was horrible enough, but more than twice as many men died from disease as from battle wounds. To put the statistics another way, fully 2 per cent of the US population perished in the war, the equivalent of five million today. It was not the war soldiers had expected: extended, not brief; dominated more by accurate firepower than cunning brainpower; advantageous to defensive strategies over offensive ambitions; increasingly geared to trench warfare over open warfare; boundless in its targets rather than limited in its aim; and marked by gore over glory, violence over valor.

Considering the length of the conflict, its daily hardships, its political complexity, and its high casualty rates, historians have tried to understand what motivated soldiers. Some studies point to the loyalty servicemen felt toward other soldiers, friends, or one's unit, an important point to consider in a struggle where so many men fought alongside their neighbors and acquaintances. Some historians suggest that Confederate and Union soldiers saw the war as a test of courage or masculinity. Others argue that troops had little on their minds beyond survival, finding themselves in the middle of a terrifying conflict they could only hope to endure.

Historian James M. McPherson points to the importance that troops placed on principle. Their letters and diaries reveal serious reflections on the war's ideological and moral meaning. Soldiers on both sides declared allegiance to principles of liberty and republicanism. They believed that the future of freedom lay in the balance. The war would determine if human beings would continue to enjoy fundamental rights, if self-government would work, if the spirit of the Revolution would hold. Troops saw themselves as the sons of liberty, a generation called upon to validate and defend the forefathers' ideals of 1776. At stake was not merely an individual's survival but the Republic's survival.[2]

Troops remained divided over the meaning of liberty and revolutionary republicanism. For Confederate soldiers, the greatest threat to liberty rested in the tyranny of the national government and its efforts to subjugate the South to the will of the North. They fought to rescue local control from a despotic political order. Like the 'rebels' of the Revolution, they defended a newly independent land against a larger, oppressive, and corrupt regime. To Union troops, the greatest threat to liberty lay not in the supposed tyranny of the national government but in the actual treason of a vocal minority. The South plotted to destroy the Union. No greater betrayal of American ideals was possible because all republican hopes rested on the union of the states in a single nation. Northern soldiers saw themselves as defenders of that political order, carrying out the guiding purpose of the Revolutionary forefathers: to create a lasting basis for liberty.[3]

Troops on each side believed they alone understood the true meaning of freedom, the true form of republicanism, and the true memory of the fathers. Soldiers reflected on their roles in the war and believed strongly in the values for which they fought. They were not thought-less in their actions. The political ideas debated by leaders behind podiums and pulpits also had meaning for troops in camps and trenches.

1865: The War's Conclusion

The policy of total war worked on Southern battlefields and on Southern minds. A crisis of confidence and commitment existed throughout the Confederacy. Supplies ran desperately low. Few Southern whites were available for military service and those within rebel ranks deserted in record numbers. In March 1865, Confederate leaders took an unprecedented step: they authorized the arming of slaves to assist in the war effort and promised freedom to bondsmen who volunteered. The war came to an end, however, before any black regiments saw action.

Sherman continued his devastating march, moving north from Savannah. By April, he reached Raleigh, North Carolina. Grant extended his grip on Petersburg and by 2 April, Lee's forces could hold out no longer. They abandoned Richmond and Petersburg and moved west, with Grant close behind. The chase ended on 9 April at Appomattox, some 70 miles west of Richmond, where Lee and his 25,000-man force surrendered to Grant. By late May, all other Confederate armies had surrendered, and the war ended.

The Union was saved, its indivisibility assured, and its principles of liberty expanded. But the sacrifice of human life had not yet ended. On 14 April, a Confederate sympathizer pulled one more trigger against one more Northern target. At Ford's Theater in Washington, John Wilkes Booth shot Abraham Lincoln in the head. The president died the next day. Lincoln and 620,000 others had given their lives in the republic's most catastrophic struggle.

Abraham Lincoln

The Complexity of Reconstruction

After a long and costly war, it might appear a comparatively simple matter to reinstate peace. Surely a prolonged struggle left energies sapped and animosity vented? Yet the years after 1865, much like post-war periods in the twentieth century, demonstrated that as conflicts ended on battlefields, new struggles arose in different arenas. Many obstacles worked against a smooth and harmonious reconstruction of the nation.

One problem was the very depth of post-war bitterness. Southerners saw their lands destroyed, a way of life upended, and their share of national wealth cut in half. Atlanta, Charleston, and Richmond lay in ruins; key railways were damaged; emancipation wiped out $3–4 billion of investments in slaves; Confederate currency was worthless; and land values collapsed. Two decades passed before cotton and tobacco production regained prewar levels, three decades before sugar production recovered. A proud military was defeated. Over a quarter of a million Southern men lay dead, and an arrogant, reckless, and dishonorable society to the north now held unchecked national power. At the same time, Northerners mourned those who perished in the conflict, 40 per cent more than the number of Southern war dead. The blame rested not on any ambitious or aggressive designs by the North. The treasonable actions of a Slave Power conspiracy had destroyed lives and plunged an entire nation into tumult. It was difficult to feel sympathy for the vanquished; the war left compassion, good will, and trust in short supply.

A second problem was technical in nature: there were no Constitutional guidelines for reconstructing the republic. One would hardly expect the document to say much about its own undoing. Nevertheless, urgent questions remained unanswered. What was the status of Southern states that had renounced the Union? Were they a foreign nation or perhaps conquered territories? If secession was not constitutionally possible, had they ever 'left' the Union? Which federal agency took responsibility for reconstruction? Was it an executive, legislative, or judicial task? In the absence of clear guidelines on these matters, a struggle over authority and leadership emerged.

A third problem involved political questions about the uses of power. War led both sides to create stronger and more centralized national governments that drafted men, raised revenues, channeled resources, and suspended legal guarantees. The aftermath of war seemed to require an even greater expansion of authority; but alarms went off in a political culture long suspicious of concentrated authority and protective of fragile liberties. If some asked how much power was necessary to realize the goals of the war, others wondered how much power was sufficient to defeat the principles of the republic.

A fourth complication was that Reconstruction began *during* the Civil War. The process started as Northern troops occupied and administered Confederate territory. Lincoln believed such sensitive circumstances called for policies that encouraged rather than alienated Unionist sentiment. He called for a speedy and lenient plan, one that would reassure Southerners, shorten the war, promote emancipation, and quickly re-establish a single nation. More radical members of Congress viewed things differently, especially *after* the war. Southern whites found new ways to degrade African Americans and new honors to bestow on ex-Confederates. In the face of such intransigence, Congress insisted on more stringent measures and pushed for a program to make fundamental changes in Southern life. Shifting federal strategies generated further resentment in the South – and considerable division in Washington, DC.

A fifth complication was the assassination of Lincoln. Congress contested Lincoln's generous terms for Reconstruction; they cared little for his efforts to circumvent the legislative branch; and some believed that the new executive, Andrew Johnson, would fight harder to impose strict conditions on the South. In the end, Lincoln's political skill, measured command, and party leadership were sorely missed. Johnson displayed little tact and considerable ineptitude with Congress; he appeared more accommodating to the South than to legislators. A nation already torn by sectional battles would also endure a showdown between Congress and the president.

Perhaps the most serious problem facing Reconstruction was racism. As historian William Gillette notes, 'most white Americans believed unquestioningly in white supremacy'.[4] Racism hampered any sustained effort to guarantee the rights of blacks. Whites generally viewed African Americans as inferiors who were, at best, unprepared and, at worst, unfit for full participation in American life. Northern whites were reluctant to accept the Civil War as a struggle for the liberty of slaves; they had less patience with post-war efforts to secure the equality of blacks. Southern whites viewed the extension of equal rights to African Americans as a further affront to their region, a threat to social order, and an ominous experiment in *black* supremacy. When their political challenges to black equality failed, Southern whites applied terrorist tactics. Groups like the Ku Klux Klan, organized in 1866, buttressed efforts to undermine Reconstruction.

THE FEDERAL GOVERNMENT AND RECONSTRUCTION

Both the executive and legislative branches formulated plans for Reconstruction. The former, announced by Lincoln in 1863 and

Ku Klux Klan: Two Alabama Klansmen   (After a 1868 photograph)

revised by Johnson in 1865, was conciliatory, designed primarily to re-admit seceded states as quickly as possible and only secondarily to address African American rights. The latter, outlined by Congress from 1866–1870, set more demanding tests for re-admission to the Union, established military supervision of Southern states, and required the vote for adult black males. Presidential plans sought to get on with the business of governing a reunified republic. Congressional plans aimed at both political unity and social transformation.

Lincoln announced his proposals in December 1863. Acting under powers of presidential pardon, he called for a swift and mild approach towards rebuilding the nation. Lincoln offered amnesty to all South-erners (except high officials of the Confederacy) who swore allegiance to the United States and accepted emancipation. When 10 per cent of a state's 1860 voters took the oath, they could form new state govern-ments. The president recommended but did not require extending the vote to blacks. Tennessee, Arkansas, Louisiana, and Virginia followed Lincoln's plan, but an indignant Congress refused to recognize their representatives. Legislators drew up stricter standards for re-admission, raising Lincoln's 10 per cent figure to a majority of white male citizens and requiring that only those loyal to the Union in the past could help establish state constitutional conventions. Lincoln 'pocket' vetoed the proposal by refusing to sign the bill after Congress adjourned. The president remained open to discussion about reconstruction and suggested the possibilities of broader voting rights and federal supervision. But his death in mid-April 1865 left matters unresolved.

The new president, Andrew Johnson, seemed in many respects the person least likely to succeed in Reconstruction debates. Teamed with Lincoln in 1864 in order to broaden the ticket's 'appeal', Johnson was a Southerner, a former slaveholder, a racist, and a Democrat. But he also supported yeoman farmers against the planter elite. He was a Unionist who denounced Confederate treason. And he portrayed his Reconstruction program as a continuation of Lincoln's.

President Andrew Johnson

A month after Lincoln's assassination, Johnson announced his plan for 'Restoration'. With Congress out of session, Johnson tried to wrap up loose ends and move the nation on to other business. He pardoned Southerners taking an oath of allegiance and allowed them to set up state conventions that would renounce secession, ratify the Thirteenth Amendment, and establish new governments. He excluded leading Confederate officials and wealthy Southerners; but they could petition their cases to the president. By year's end, the former Confederate states had new governments up and running – and Congress refused to recognize any of them.

Legislators were upset that Johnson circumvented Congress, dispensed special pardons, curried favor with Democrats, and spoke in favor of black suffrage (chiefly as a way of silencing radicals in Congress). More alarming were the actions of Southern whites who dawdled on renouncing slavery and secession, rejected black suffrage, established 'black codes' to restrict the rights of freed people, and elected prominent ex-Confederate leaders to state office. A combination of presidential blunders and Southern defiance led Congress to wipe the slate clean and start Reconstruction all over again.

Congress began in 1866 by enlarging federal protection and assistance to freed people. Both houses extended the Freedman's Bureau, an agency first established in 1865 to administer abandoned Southern lands and provide food, clothing, and fuel to former slaves and the destitute. The Bureau's activities expanded to include educational and legal services for freed people. In an effort to overturn black codes, Congress also passed a civil rights bill granting citizenship to African Americans. Johnson vetoed both measures – and Congress overrode the vetoes.

Congress then drew up its first Reconstruction plan to protect freed people, extend suffrage, and remove ex-Confederates from power. Both houses approved and sent to the states the Fourteenth Amendment. The measure provided a Constitutional definition of citizenship, included African Americans as citizens, and guaranteed 'the equal protection of the laws' to all. States that denied the vote to adult males (white or black) faced a reduction in their Congressional delegation. The amendment also barred officeholders who supported the CSA from holding state or national office in the future. Denouncing the amendment, Johnson recommended that Southern states reject it. All followed the president's advice except Tennessee which accepted the measure and rejoined the Union. Rebuffed in his home state, Johnson suffered more setbacks in the elections in 1866 which gave Republicans comfortable majorities in both houses of Congress.

Legislators then outlined another plan for Reconstruction in 1867. Congress grouped the ten remaining states into five districts, each commanded by a military officer. Every state would call a convention elected by universal manhood suffrage and create a constitution that granted the vote to blacks. After ratifying the Fourteenth Amendment, a state could rejoin the Union.

After turning up the heat on hold-out states, Congress made certain the other two federal branches would not derail Reconstruction. Legislators narrowed the Supreme Court's jurisdiction in cases related to Reconstruction and restricted the president's powers over military orders and civil appointments. Johnson had to deliver his military orders through the general of the army – who just happened to be a Republican favorite, U.S. Grant. And Johnson needed Senate approval before removing civil officials whose appointment had been made with the Senate's consent – thereby protecting the cooperative secretary of war, Edwin M. Stanton.

Ever the prudent politician, Johnson tried to oust Stanton from office without the Senate's approval. Accusing Johnson of violating federal law, the House, in February 1868, impeached the president on eleven charges, most covering the Stanton affair, others dealing with his attacks on Congress and his efforts to block Reconstruction. Nearly three-quarters of the House voted for impeachment, but the subsequent Senate trial failed by one vote to convict. The proceedings set a general precedent: presidents would not be impeached for policy disputes or political offenses but only for high crimes and misdemeanors. Radical Republicans were chastened by the episode; Johnson became less obstructionist and actually began to execute laws passed by Congress.

Although six more Southern states soon re-entered the Union, the work of Reconstruction had not ended. Four states remained outside

The First Vote
From a lithograph which appeared in *Harper's* of November 1867

and questions about suffrage remained unanswered. Southern blacks still did not enjoy firm protection of voting rights: the Fourteenth Amendment penalized states that denied the franchise to blacks but did not positively grant the vote; and Southern states that guaranteed black suffrage in their constitutions could someday rescind such provisions. As a matter of self-interest, Republicans hoped black voters would provide strong, dependable support for their candidates: already in the South, enfranchised black men accounted for 80 per cent of the votes Republicans received.

   In response, Congress proposed the Fifteenth Amendment in 1869 prohibiting states from denying the vote to its citizens 'on account of race, color, or previous condition of servitude'. The measure prohibited *certain* restrictions on voting but not all. If a person could not be denied the vote because he was black, he might, in the nineteenth century, still be denied the vote for not meeting literacy or property requirements – or *she* could be denied the vote for not meeting gender requirements. Such loopholes pleased both Southerners and Northerners. The Northern states had a sorry record on African American suffrage: only five Northern states granted full voting rights to blacks in 1865; and from 1865 to 1868, six Northern states rejected attempts to extend the franchise to African Americans. When the amendment went out for ratification, several Northern and border states refused to approve it. The measure finally passed, in part, because the four remaining Southern states had to ratify it in order to gain readmission.

By 1870, with the Fifteenth Amendment ratified, all ex-Confederate states were once again part of the Union, and a two-party system operated again throughout the United States. The nation seemed to be back to normal. Also by 1870, African Americans had been granted citizenship, the vote, and equality under the law: blacks seemed to be on an equal footing with whites. Having made the political world whole again and having brought blacks to the point where they presumably could fend for themselves, most Republicans felt confident that they had accomplished Reconstruction's major goals. The momentum behind reform slowed.

THE FREED PEOPLE AND RECONSTRUCTION

Emancipation did not simply end a system of restraint but also opened a process of autonomy. The freed people of the South were key players in reconstruction. African Americans carved out new lives to match their new freedom. Because of their actions, the post-war South was not merely a world defined by the absence of black enslavement; it was also a world defined by the presence of African-American empowerment.

For most slaves, freedom did not come with the Emancipation Proclamation; the decree only covered slavery in areas outside Union control. Actual release from bondage usually came with an advancing Northern army, with word from an agent of the Freedman's Bureau, or by an announcement from one's master. Freed people greeted the news in various ways. For some the announcement was expected; for others it came as a surprise. Some gathered together; others reflected alone.

Some reacted with anticipation and joy, others with confusion and concern. Noticeably absent were acts of retaliation or vengeance against former masters.[5]

Freedom brought more than choice to former slaves. Historian Leon Litwack argues that emancipation also brought 'a leap of confidence in the ability to effect changes in their own lives without deferring to whites'.[6] For thousands of male ex-slaves, service in the Union military provided a way to fulfill one's own freedom. Seventy per cent of the African Americans in Northern forces came from liberated areas of the South. Even more freed people made another decision: to be mobile. Most did not travel far or continuously; few merely roamed. Some wanted to try economic opportunities in different areas; others sought a larger black community in towns and cities; most hoped to reunite family members separated by the slave trade and war. Whether joining the service or rejoining loved ones, the movement of African Americans was remarkable in a region where their movements were once so constrained.[7]

Freedom also provided a chance to clarify one's identity and reaffirm one's dignity. Ex-slaves took on surnames or selected names for themselves. Husbands and wives sought to have their marriages recognized. Men frequently asserted their role as head of household, sometimes beneficially to protect family members from exploitation, sometimes restrictively in order to confine wives to domestic activities. Outside the home, African Americans challenged deferential social codes. Whether keeping one's place on busy sidewalks or refusing to doff one's hat at the approach of whites, freed people redefined basic conventions of conduct.[8]

Southern blacks also tried to create decent economic circumstances for themselves. Freed people knew that land ownership provided the security and autonomy they desired, and hopes ran high that they would gain title to the soils they had worked as slaves. Their anticipation of '40 acres and a mule' was fed by popular discussion, Congressional debate, the actions of a few Union military commanders, and scattered federal experiments that leased sections of plantations to former slaves. But the North had no intention of confiscating and redistributing Confederate land; the sanctity of private property outweighed appeals for economic justice. Most freed people had to make do as landless agricultural workers.

In their limited circumstances, blacks tried to secure fair rewards, a reasonable work day, control over the pace of labor, and a measure of leisure time. At first, however, they found themselves tied to labor contracts with planters who wanted to re-create large, permanent work forces. Blacks resisted the gang labor, harsh supervision, and unfair compensation that too closely resembled enslavement. They forced a change in these arrangements. What emerged was the 'sharecropping' system under which plantations were divided into small farms rented to workers for a portion of the crop they produced. Planters owned the land, annual leases provided them with labor through harvest time, and their limited supplies of cash could go to other purposes. Blacks, although frequently caught in a cycle of debt both to landlords and merchants, still held some autonomy. They were freed from white oversight; they controlled their daily labor; they had part ownership of the crop they produced; and they often lived on the individual plot they worked rather than in the old, clustered slave quarters. Share-cropping was flawed and constraining, but as historian William L. Barney points out, it was 'in place by the end of the 1860s because blacks wanted it'. The system offered one limited way in which freed people could define labor conditions fit for human beings rather than chattels.[9]

Emancipation also led to a wave of institution building by African Americans. Some of the organizations were fraternal or mutual aid societies designed to aid and protect the community. Blacks also supported educational institutions to acquire the literacy and skills their masters had long denied them. Starting with meager facilities staffed by missionaries, reformers, and Northern blacks, the freed people sparked campaigns for more extensive, tax-supported schools, which helped to establish the first public education systems in Southern communities. Southern African Americans also created their own churches. The congregations, usually of Baptist or African Methodist Episcopal affiliation, formed the center of black life, providing spiritual guidance, social contact, emergency support, and community organization. The churches' ministers were commonly the most respected figures in black society, and their prestige carried from the pulpit to public affairs. The black clergy took a lead both in political advocacy and political office.

Freed people pursued an active role in politics. As early as 1865, black conventions met to discuss collective needs and to define political goals. As suffrage widened under Congressional Reconstruction, African-American men voted, served as delegates to state constitutional conventions, allied themselves with Republicans, and ran for political office. Within Southern governments, blacks held 15–20 per cent of offices; within Congress, 14 blacks served in the House and two in the Senate. Top state posts, however, went to whites, and the number of black officeholders did not correspond to the size of the black electorate.

The Republicans who controlled Southern state governments for a brief period were composed of three groups: African Americans, including ex-slaves and free blacks; Northerners who came South after the war in search of a livelihood (and earned the derisive nickname 'carpetbaggers'); and Southern whites with little attraction to the Democratic Party or planter interests (tagged as 'scalawags'). The Republicans pushed ambitious programs to protect political and civil rights, promote public works, and establish public institutions.

They faced several problems. First, their public projects were expensive, and the taxes needed to pay for improvements alienated many supporters. Secondly, their activities were occasionally questionable, especially with railroad programs that encouraged waste and corruption. Still, the fraud and extravagance paled in comparison to the high-stakes swindles of *Northern* politicians during the same period. Thirdly, Southern Republicans constantly tried to keep their fragile coalition of supporters together. And fourthly, they faced racial as well as political challenges from Southern whites who bitterly denounced the 'Black Republican' regimes that exercised power in the region. Beginning in 1869, control of Southern governments began changing to Democratic hands and the reforms of Reconstruction gradually broke down.

THE END OF RECONSTRUCTION

By 1872, amnesty programs left most whites eligible to vote, and the relative electoral strength of African Americans declined. Planters and merchants turned powerful economic screws to dissuade blacks from voting. The Ku Klux Klan used fear, intimidation, and violence to keep both blacks and whites on the straight and narrow path. Resurgent Democrats relied on persuasive and blatantly racist sets of appeals to voters. They painted a terrifying portrait of 'black rule' that threatened the region (even though whites held four-fifths of all political offices and African Americans enjoyed a legislative majority only in South Carolina). They branded as 'unrepublican' the military rule and centralized control imposed on Southerners by Congress. Party members expressed outrage over the corruption of state governments (keeping quiet about Democrats who were on the take) and they championed traditional values of local control and states' rights.

Above all, Democrats promised a return to 'home rule' and the 'redemption' of Southern governments. Whites would regain control, quash the influence of African Americans and the national government, and revoke Reconstruction reforms. By 1871, Democrats dominated Virginia, Tennessee, North Carolina, and Georgia. South Carolina, Florida, and Louisiana, all with large African American populations, also passed to Democratic control by 1877.

As the influence of Democrats in the South rose, the zeal for reform in Congress fell. To some Congressional Republicans, blacks who had achieved freedom, the vote, and legal rights were now on an even playing field; no further assistance from the national government was necessary. Other Republicans grew uneasy with the charges of 'organized robbery' pinned on Southern governments, and grew more concerned about the bribe, kickback, fraud, and corruption scandals that swirled around the Republican presidency of Ulysses S. Grant. The General's military brilliance helped win him the election in 1868; his political dimwittedness cost him the support of many party regulars when he ran for re-election in 1872. Those who bolted, including the radical advocate Charles Sumner, encouraged the party to cut its losses in the South, end federal intervention, limit government power, and allow a free, open, and competitive market to reign once more. The retreat from reform was well under way.

Other events also helped derail Reconstruction. Beginning in 1873, the American economy plunged into a half-decade of depression, and political attention turned from social equity to economic recovery. Democrats made hay with the collapse in the 1874 election, winning a majority of seats in the House and racking up gains in the Senate. In addition to market jitters and opposition victories, the Supreme Court began to chip away at Reconstruction measures. In 1873, the Court held that the Fourteenth Amendment protected only those rights tied to national citizenship rather than state citizenship. An 1876 ruling declared that the amendment covered discrimination by states but not by individuals or groups. Another 1876 decision maintained that the Fifteenth Amendment did not provide a blanket 'right' to vote but only prohibited specific limitations on suffrage. An 1883 case declared unconstitutional the 1875 Civil Rights Act that prohibited discrimination in public places. The Court's decisions opened the door to new forms of voting restriction, continued racial discrimination, and wider segregation.

By the mid-1870s, Reconstruction had become dispensable. The opportunity to abolish it came in the disputed presidential election of 1876. Democrat Samuel J. Tilden held 51 per cent of the popular vote, but both he and Republican Rutherford B. Hayes claimed victory in the electoral college. At stake were 20 contested electoral votes from four states. Party leaders met to settle the election. Democrats recognized Hayes as the winner after receiving assurances that his administration would remove all remaining federal troops from the South, sponsor economic development in the region, and allow 'home rule' on social and racial issues. By placing the fate of Southern blacks in the hands of Southern whites, the 'compromise' of 1877 brought Reconstruction to an end. The withdrawal of forces was one promise Hayes kept. But the troops would eventually return, in 1957, to back up federal policy at a school in Little Rock, Arkansas. Historian C. Vann Woodward pointed out that 'eighty years set a record for durability among the sectional compromises of American history. This compromise set no records in justice and statesmanship, but justice and statesmanship rarely make much history anyway.'[10]

In the end, local control, laissez-faire principles, and white superiority triumphed. Still, a significant set of transformations had occurred in the nation. The agents of Reconstruction had abolished slavery, repudiated secession, amended the Constitution (by *expanding* federal power), reaffirmed the unitary nature of the republic, and granted freedmen both the vote and public office. In comparison to emancipation elsewhere in the West, Eric Foner notes, America 'was the only society where the freed slaves, within a few years of emancipation, enjoyed full political rights and a real measure of political power'.[11] Freedom made a difference – but not in all cases and not for a time. Nearly a century would pass before its possibilities would be taken up again.

CHAPTER NINE

Politics, Industry, Society, and Reform,
1877–1917

The collapse of Reconstruction demonstrated the limits of federal power. A host of political factors also checked the ability (or even the desire) of authorities in Washington to mold day-to-day life. In the decades following the Civil War, the key forces shaping the republic did not spring principally from the halls of national government. To a greater extent, the factories of industrial giants, the crowded streets of expanding cities, and the diverse communities of new immigrants all redefined life in the United States. Politically united, turn-of-the-century America was not politically 'propelled'. Economic and social changes outlined a new direction for the nation.

Party Balance

Oddly, one reason why political events took a back seat to other factors influencing American life involved the remarkable health of the two-party system. Republicans and Democrats balanced one another so well that they ended up containing one another quite effectively. It was hard to get much accomplished in such a poised political world.

From one point of view, partisan competition of the era seemed uneven: from 1877 to 1917, Republicans controlled both the Presidency and the Senate. Over four decades, the party lost the chief executive office to only two Democrats, Grover Cleveland and Woodrow Wilson. But Republican 'domination' still had its limits, in part because most presidential elections were close contests. Only four chief executives of the period won office with a majority of the popular vote. All others were 'minority' presidents, elected with less than half the popular vote. In two elections, the candidate with the most popular votes actually ended up losing the contest (because of a deal in 1876 and because of the peculiarities of the electoral college in 1888).

Not only did 'minority' presidents dominate the period; it was also an era of one-term presidents. The exceptions were Cleveland, William McKinley, and Wilson. However, Cleveland's two terms were non-consecutive; McKinley was assassinated in the ninth month of his second term; and Wilson suffered from the effects of a stroke in the second half of his second term. Chief executives usually did not stay around long enough to leave their mark on the nation.

Then again, few turn-of-the-century presidents had the charisma, commitment, or cooperation to make the office energetic and influential. Theodore Roosevelt and Woodrow Wilson made the greatest changes, but their peers tended to be fairly lackluster. Most did not intend to expand the office. Most understood that Congress directed policymaking while Senators and party machines dominated political influence. Presidents were supposed to be pleasant and non-controversial, operating in the background of American politics. In such a world, having a hold on the presidency did not necessarily translate into political supremacy.

On Capitol Hill, Republicans held a Senate majority 80 per cent of the time from 1877 to 1917, but power in the House changed: Democrats controlled 11 Congresses, Republicans nine. For about half the period, one party (most often the Republicans) controlled the House, Senate, and presidency. For the other half, the parties split control of the three strongholds. Considering the practical limits on Republican power over the presidency and Congress, the two major parties were evenly matched. In such a balanced political world, it was hard to push for bold initiatives because the opposition was usually strong enough to put an end to any ambitious plans.

The Limits of Government

The two major parties never intended to do much at the federal level. Jeffersonian traditions of governance prevailed at the turn of the century. Party leaders, and the general public, wanted to minimize the federal government's activities, keep its hands off the marketplace, and leave most control at the local level. The Civil War demonstrated to many the dangers of centralized power; some feared that government efforts to manipulate the economy would lead to ruin; and Americans were confident that a national harmony of interests would heal any social conflicts. As President Grover Cleveland declared in 1893, 'The lessons of paternalism ought to be unlearned and the better lesson taught that while the people should patriotically and cheerfully support their government, its functions do not include the support of the people.' Parties kept their agendas vague and limited, all the better to keep their varied coalitions together. Party leaders pressed for votes rather than principles. They proved more adept at keeping regional political alliances together than imposing strict, national discipline on party members.

Combining the minimalist, localist, *laissez-faire* views of politicians with the 'divided government' that often split control between Democrats and Republicans, it is hardly surprising that the federal government was so inactive. Yet voter turn-out stayed high. Towards the close of the nineteenth century, 75 per cent of eligible voters usually showed up for presidential contests. One reason was the closeness of the competition: in most of the period's presidential elections, fewer than half a million votes separated the winner and loser. A second reason for high participation involved the spectacle and entertainment of party politics, with its parades, rallies, pomp, pomposity, and cheap beer. A third reason was that parties successfully linked their goals to the ethnic, religious, and regional identities of voters. Support of the party was not just a matter of formality but also of intense group loyalty. In the North and Midwest, evangelical Protestants commonly tied themselves to Republican calls for morality; Catholic immigrants of the Northeast and whites of the South usually supported Democratic appeals for liberty.

THE LIMITED ACTIONS OF GOVERNMENT

While singing the praises of government restraint, federal officials still addressed a variety of public issues. Their actions, however, rarely provided sufficient answers to national problems.

Verbal commitments to passivity did little to halt the growth of the national government at the turn of the century. From 1880 to 1910, federal spending more than doubled. Between 1871 and 1901, the number of federal employees quadrupled. Considering the rhetoric of minimalism, it is hard to imagine where all the money went – and what all of those people did. Some of the growth resulted from the need to serve a larger population and more states. The Post Office, Department of the Interior, and Department of Agriculture all expanded quickly. The federal government even administered a large social welfare program through annual pensions to Union veterans. By the start of the twentieth century, the program ate up a third of all federal dollars.

The combination of new and expanding services led to a burst of federal hiring, a trend that parties had little trouble accepting. Political victors commonly doled out government posts to their supporters, regardless of qualifications. Jobholders gave political loyalty, and part of their salaries, to the party responsible for their employment. As federal jobs expanded, so did the 'spoils' system. The management of patronage positions (about half of all federal jobs) became one of the main activities of political leaders. Calls for reform floundered until 1881 when a frustrated office seeker shot President James A. Garfield. Two years later, Congress passed the Pendleton Civil Service Act, creating merit examinations for government jobs and prohibiting 'contributions' by job holders. The law covered only a tenth of federal employees, however, and when 'donations' from appointees dried up, corporate 'support' of political parties expanded.

Political leaders also focused attention on issues of foreign trade, money, and big business. Republicans supported strong protective tariffs to raise the price of imports, to encourage consumers to buy American, and to keep the nation's workers employed. Democrats objected, insisting that tariffs raised prices, not wages, and imposed a 'tax' on the many for the benefit of the few. But party members tended to be indiscriminate when they voted on tariffs, commonly supporting their constituents' interests rather than the party line.

Party differences were even less clear on questions of money. Currency debates were conducted against four major economic trends. First, the money supply dropped after the Civil War and remained low for over three decades. Secondly, the backing for money kept changing: during the war, the government's word propped up the dollar; later, 'bimetallic' and gold standards supported the dollar. Thirdly, production expanded, creating large surpluses of manufactured goods and foodstuffs. Fourthly, prices tended to fall in almost all categories, especially in commodities.

Two general 'monetary' positions emerged out of all of this. 'Hard' money advocates (usually creditors, financiers, and businessmen) tried to limit the supply of money in circulation and back it with gold, hoping to raise the cost of borrowing, curb speculation, contain prices, and create a more orderly market. 'Soft' money advocates (usually debtors and farmers) tried to expand the supply of money in circulation and back it with a gold *and* silver, hoping to lower the cost of borrowing, spur investment, boost producer prices, and create a more equitable market. The former group believed it had integrity on its side: a dollar had to be worth a dollar, not a plug nickel. The latter group believed they had justice on their side: hard-hearted hard monetarists must not, Democrat William Jennings Bryan warned in 1896, 'crucify mankind upon a cross of gold'. By the beginning of the new century, Republicans who rallied 'round the gold standard and a tight money policy had won the debate – or so it seemed. With new gold discoveries in Africa and North America, both the supply of money and the prices of farm goods began to rise in the early 1900s. The Republican's 'victory' gave Democratic 'losers' just what they wanted.

Appearances were also deceiving regarding federal responses to big business. Reacting to abusive corporate practices, Congress did the unthinkable and actually asserted its Constitutional authority over economic activity that crossed state lines. One key law regulated the actions of a particular industry. The Interstate Commerce Act of 1887 attempted nationally what states had tried for years: to control the discriminatory, secretive, and unreasonable rates railroad companies charged to move goods. For the first time, the federal government regulated a business's practices, doing so through an independent agency staffed by technical experts. A second key law regulated the competitive behavior of all industry. The Sherman Anti-Trust Act of 1890 challenged businesses that reduced or eliminated competition and left one firm in control of a market. Such predatory behavior was now a federal crime subject to federal penalties.

The laws seemed vigorous, but neither proved effective. Enforcement remained uneven, the bills' language was vague, and the Supreme Court took a dim view of market meddling. The justices held that corporations, like individuals, were guaranteed 'equal protection' under the Fourteenth Amendment. Consequently, some of the greatest 'successes' of the Sherman Act came not against corporate combinations but against labor combinations – unions – that were ruled 'in restraint of trade'. One banker hailed the Supreme Court in 1905 as 'guardian of the dollar, defender of private property, enemy of spoilation, sheet anchor of the republic'.

A balance of party strength and a consensus on government minimalism left politicians unwilling or unable to take strong action against problems of the day. What partisanship and ideology could not contain, judicial review did. Federal authorities were largely ineffective and unresponsive in dealing with the economic, urban, and social changes reshaping American life.

Over time, many realized that Jeffersonian traditions were inadequate. The kind of republic suited to a limited and unengaged government no longer existed. The United States had become increasingly industrial rather than agricultural, urban rather than rural, and ethnically mixed rather than culturally homogenous. Critics charged that the nation needed a renovation in its political thinking to match the transformation of its social order.

The Rise of Big Business

In the 1850s, the American economy focused on the production of foodstuffs and raw materials; processed and finished goods usually came from somewhere else. By the early 1900s, the United States led the world in manufacturing, controlling a third of all production. The rise of railroads and small-scale industry before the Civil War laid the foundation for growth. The mechanization of farming generated food surpluses. The expansion of mining yielded greater amounts of natural resources. Technological innovations shifted manufacturing from water power to steam power to electrical power; and a rising population provided the necessary labor power. Domestic and foreign capital supplied the monetary power. Companies created goods not only for consumers but for producers as well, launching the phenomenal rise of heavy industry in the United States.

From 1870 to 1900, annual coal production grew tenfold, annual copper output increased twentyfold, and annual steel production climbed a hundred and fortyfold. The value of US-made industrial machinery tripled as did the number of workers in mining, manufacturing, construction, and transportation. The amount of railroad track increased five times. Investments in manufacturing expanded sixfold and the value of manufactured goods increased by 300 per cent. Much of the growth came in new industries like oil, steel, electricity, and, later, cars. By the start of World War I, US manufacturers were producing as much as Britain, France, and Germany combined.

Pittsburgh in the 1890s – from a contemporary photograph

Incorporation, innovation, administration, and consolidation spurred America's industrial growth. At the heart of big business lay big money. Large pools of capital grew out of liberalized incorporation laws that granted 'limited liability' to stock purchasers and confined their risk to the amount they invested. Financiers such as John Pierpont Morgan marketed stocks to their clients as promising investment vehicles. Morgan and Company, along with other investment banks, helped channel revenue into enormous corporate projects.

With huge amounts of money, big businesses built huge production plants. Massive factories churned out greater quantities of goods at lower per unit cost, achieving 'economies of scale', but manufacturers faced enormous fixed costs. The challenge was to keep output high, and innovations in mass production provided one answer. Frederick Winslow Taylor performed 'time-motion' studies, increasing worker productivity by decreasing unnecessary and wasteful movement. Henry Ford sped up production through the use of standardized interchangeable parts and the moving assembly line, reducing the time it took to build a car from 12 hours to 90 minutes. As production rose, prices fell; as prices declined, purchases increased; as purchases grew, production expanded. Ford responded with the highly integrated, two-square-mile River Rouge plant near Detroit where workers poured coal in one end and a car came out the other.

Improvements in finance and production solved some business problems; new approaches to administration answered others. An emerging science of business 'management' broke the operations of corporations into distinct components and created hierarchical chains of command. One energetic, entrepreneurial individual simply could not run the whole show. Instead, professionally trained experts guided the different operations, coordinating tasks, establishing lines of authority, and achieving the control, organization, and efficiency that companies needed. Strange as it may sound to modern ears, corporations considered bureaucracy their friend.

One other trend put the 'big' in big business: consolidation. Popular culture may have celebrated competition, but those at the top knew a dirty little secret: too many cooks spoiled the broth. Businessmen brought together unprecedented levels of capital, machinery, labor, and productive capacity in their new plants. The last thing they wanted – or could afford – was instability in their operations. Fluctuations in supply and demand were difficult enough to forecast. Wide-open, cut-throat competition made calculations of sales, prices, profits, and market share even more uncertain. The successful firm did not fight with competitors; it eliminated them.

One approach involved 'vertical' integration, in which a firm controlled all stages in the production of an item. Andrew Carnegie got to the top of the slag heap by owning the sources of iron, coal, and coke, the railroads that transported those resources, and the factories that converted them into steel. John D. Rockefeller tried a second approach, 'horizontal' integration, in which a firm bought up or absorbed its competitors. Standard Oil acquired one competing refinery after another until, by the early 1880s, it controlled 90 per cent of the nation's refining capacity. The House of Morgan calculated that if one approach was good, the two together were even better. In 1901, J. Pierpont took Carnegie's vertically integrated company and horizontally integrated it with other producers to form US Steel. Controlling two-thirds of the nation's steel production, the firm was capitalized at $1.4 billion, a handsome sum during a period when total federal spending came to only half a billion dollars a year.

The popular term for a large-scale business combination was a 'trust'. Conglomerations formed in sugar refining, tobacco, rubber, electrical, copper, meatpacking and other industries. By the start of the twentieth century, consolidated economic giants with monopolistic or oligopolistic control of the market became commonplace. In 1904, 1 per cent of all American businesses controlled 40 per cent of the nation's industrial manufacturing. 'The day of individual competition', Rockefeller declared, 'is past and gone'. The day of concentrated wealth and power had arrived.

Unfortunately, giants, whether individual or industrial, tend to have a high center of gravity; they topple easily. To keep them on their feet, the ground below must be firm. Consolidated businesses needed a steady market in order to contain risk and allow predictable returns, but stability was just what the economy did *not* provide. Hoping for a smooth ride, corporate America found itself strapped to

a market roller-coaster. Exuberant expansion alternated with catastrophic contraction. Panics hit the economy like clockwork, first in
1873, again in 1884, then in 1893, and once more in 1907. Business
activity rose and fell 15–20 per cent from one decade to another.
The depression of 1893 was the worst of all: levels of business activity tumbled by 30 per cent; 200 railroads went bankrupt; farm prices
collapsed by 20 per cent; and one-fifth to one-quarter of all workers
found themselves out of work. Rather than enjoying steady production, steady prices, steady supply, and steady demand, big business
confronted gyrations, swings, and unpredictability in the marketplace. Large firms may have gained the upper hand on small competitors, but they failed to gain control of the larger forces driving the
market.

Urbanization

The rise of concentrated cities paralled the rise of concentrated businesses. Between 1860 and 1910, the number of 'urban places' in
America jumped from 400 to 2,200. Many cities doubled their
population every decade. In 1860, only two cities had 500,000 residents; by 1910, there were eight. The rural population of the United
States doubled between 1860 and 1910, but its urban population
increased sevenfold. At the start of the Civil War, 20 percent of all
Americans resided in cities; by 1890, 33 percent were urban dwellers;
by 1910, nearly half lived in cities. When the twentieth century
began, New York City alone accounted for 4.6 percent of the entire
US population.

One reason for the spectacular growth of cities had to do with a
technological rather than a social change. After the Civil War, manufacturers turned increasingly to steam power rather than water power,
so instead of having to locate factories along rivers, they could build
them anywhere. What better place than in centers of transportation,
finance, commerce, and labor? Cities offered large-scale economic
resources to serve large-scale production. The centralization and
urbanization of factories proceeded alongside the centralization and
urbanization of people.[1]

The Flatiron Building, New York

The rise of modern cities generated problems everywhere in the Western world, but the process was particularly difficult in the United States: leaders simply did not anticipate the rapid growth of urban centers. The cluttered, congested, commercial look of American cities testified to a lack of long-range thinking about their design and appearance. 'Urban planning' was a dream, and private development commonly overrode public interest. Government officials neither expected nor prepared for the waves of people and enterprises that crowded into compact spaces. Tragically, cities with limited facilities became centers of immense hardship.

Housing was often shoddy, expensive, and congested. City dwellers lived in single-family residences, homes divided into apartments, or terrace houses. In Manhattan's Lower East Side, with one of the world's highest population densities, residents crammed into 'tenements', 4–8 story buildings with four apartments per floor, all of which had limited sunlight and fresh air, none of which had private bathrooms. Urban water supplies were generally inadequate until the end of the nine-teenth century. Sewage and drainage systems were so limited that, up to the early 1900s, most simply overflowed into the streets after heavy rains. Roads were narrow and poorly maintained, crammed with people, wagons, and animal waste. Homes and factories burning soft coal fouled city air. Burglary, gangs, prostitution, and urban rioting (against minorities) all contributed to rising crime. For their poorest residents, cities were hardly fit places to live.

The sad conditions resulted not just from a lack of planning but also from a lack of power. Cities usually did not have the political resources necessary to solve their problems. State governments traditionally chartered municipal governments, and the rural interests that domi-nated most state governments had little interest in sharing their power with emerging cities. To keep a political lid on urban centers, states left municipal governments weak.

Politicians abhor a power vacuum. They filled the void in America's expanding, jumbled, opportunistic, and mechanized cities by creating informal organizations appropriately called political 'machines'. Con-trolled by both Republicans and Democrats, machines sprang up throughout the urban United States. In the hierarchical world of machine politics, a 'boss' sat at the top, pulling the strings in municipal hiring, firing, spending, legislating, and bribing. Under a boss's direc-tion, city contracts appeared or vanished, regulations passed or failed, and judges ruled or winked. Representatives in city neighborhoods made sure of the vote from local residents, lubricating the machine by offering food, fuel, rent, jobs, or other forms of assistance to the party faithful. In a world where the poor and powerless were usually left to fend for themselves, political machines provided a crude system of social welfare, albeit one based on corruption, political loyalty, and personal favoritism. In turn-of-the-century cities, even disreputable service made a difference.

Immigration

Among the groups most threatened by city disorder – and most helped by party machines – were those who most changed the nation's urban history. The main source of population growth in American cities at the turn of the century came not from rural areas nor from natural increase but from the waves of immigrants who arrived in the United States between 1870 and 1920. Within those 50 years, 25 million people came to America. Eighty per cent entered through one gate: Ellis Island, in New York harbor, within sight of the Statue of Liberty.

Immigration was the oldest story in America. After tens of thousands of years, one might think that the arrival of new groups held no surprises. Turn-of-the-century immigration, however, stood in sharp contrast to earlier patterns. The new arrivals came largely from Southern and Eastern Europe rather than Northern and Western regions of the continent. They were mainly Catholic and Jewish rather than Protestant, complicating the religious 'norms' of the United States. Most spoke a foreign language. Most came from countries with different political systems from those of republican America. They entered the United States in the millions rather than the thousands. Their settlement was largely urban and concentrated rather than rural and scattered; they drifted more towards industrial than agricultural labor. And they were generally poorer than earlier immigrants.

The immigrants were both 'pushed' and 'pulled' to America. In part, they moved *from* a worsening set of economic, political, and social circumstances in Europe. Some left communities burdened by over-population, dwindling resources, mechanization, and the loss of jobs. Others left poor, less developed regions dominated by new power centers. For others, high taxes, military obligations, or natural disasters made life miserable. For East European Jews in particular, systematic, state-organized persecution made life perilous.

In part, immigrants also moved *to* America's economic and political possibilities. Growing industries needed cheap, unskilled workers and actively recruited European laborers. Steamship lines needed to fill berths and widely advertised their inexpensive and frequent sailings to US ports. Once in those harbors, immigrants lived under a relatively passive government that had little interest in restricting the arrival of new laborers and little authority to interfere in their daily lives.

Attracted to the United States and repelled by Europe, the new immigrants often, but not always, came to America to stay. European Jews were most likely to make the United States their permanent home, having no desire to return to a world where violent pogroms could destroy a community's security or an individual's life. But Italian immigrants, who fled economic paralysis rather than organized terror, often traveled as 'birds of passage', working hard, saving what they could, and moving back and forth between the United States and their home country before settling permanently.

Whether fixed or 'mobile', immigrants most often lived in communities of familiar faces. Large Italian, Jewish, and Slavic neighborhoods sprang up in US cities. The districts teemed with newcomers who ate customary foods, prayed in traditional houses of worship, played familiar music, read newspapers in their native language, and supported one another through fraternal and benevolent societies. From New York to Detroit to Chicago, 80 per cent of urban residents were foreign born or the children of immigrants. America's largest cities were places where the native born stood out like a sore thumb. Down to the present, four out of every ten Americans trace their family history to the individuals who came to the United States at the turn of the twentieth century.

The Consequences

Economic, urban, and social changes at the turn of the twentieth century altered the character and structure of American life. The good news was that life got better in many ways. The United States took a position of industrial leadership and achieved higher standards of living. National wealth expanded: per capita income and per capita output grew at 2 per cent a year and 'luxury' items became more commonplace. Public education became more widespread; life span increased; improved transportation speeded movement and new forms of communication kept an expanding people in touch with one another. And new immigrants often realized their hopes: from generation to generation, the children of working families generally bettered the conditions of their parents.

The bad news was that life did not get better in many ways. Wealth concentrated in fewer hands and by 1890, the richest 10 per cent of Americans controlled 75 per cent of the nation's wealth. At the very top, aristocratic families not only consolidated wealth but also conspicuously consumed it. Meanwhile, the economy lurched and lunged between prosperity and depression. A tenth to a quarter of the labor force found itself out of work during slack times. During good times, workers ran increasing risks of industrial accidents. Laborers had few, if any, safety nets to cushion frightening economic blows and relied almost entirely on the sporadic assistance of private charity for emergency support. Those who could stay employed found that pay increases did not keep pace with the cost of living. Working six days a week, ten hours a day, at 20–30 cents per hour, most workers could not make ends meet. Outside of one's home, corruption in government, consolidation in business, and destruction of the environment aggravated economic calamity.

While power concentrated at the top, no one seemed capable of taming wild market forces. Urban poverty and distress suggested a future of mass misery rather than mass happiness. The bewildering new mix of cultures suggested to some a threat to social cohesion, and the passivity and unresponsiveness of political leaders raised fears that no one stood at the nation's helm. The old century closed amid signs of confusion, upheaval, and chaos. As one political dissenter, Ignatius Donnelly of Minnesota, told an audience in 1892, 'we meet in the midst of a nation brought on the verge of moral, political, and material ruin'. The new century opened with a search for order, control, and stability, led by activists determined to restructure American life.

Farmers and Workers

Farmers and laborers led some of the earliest challenges to economic control and political corruption. Both groups suffered from the turbulent economy; both sensed that individuals were relatively powerless against concentrated market forces; and both determined that *organized* movements offered a better chance for protection and prosperity.

Farmers organized against catastrophes rooted in nature and business. Droughts, hard winters, and invasions of insects formed much of the natural background of farm life; indebtedness for land and machinery operated in the foreground. To pay off creditors, farmers grew more and as production increased, commodity prices declined. Discriminatory rates by rail lines and competition from abroad cut even further into profits.

In the Great Plains, the 'Grange' addressed farmers' common problems. Organized in 1867, the group began as a social and educational movement, teaching farmers how to deal with natural disasters and market calamities. With 1.5 million members by the 1870s, the Grange supported cooperative economic ventures and legislation to regulate rail rates. In the South and Midwest, a 'Farmers Alliance' movement gained strength in the late 1880s. The organization also addressed questions of debt, prices, production, corporate interests, and natural disasters. In addition, the Alliance focused on two other goals: supporting specific law-makers as well as specific laws; and organizing African-American farmers as well as whites. The latter effort led to the Colored Farmers Alliance, a group kept separate from white alliances but which, nonetheless, supported blacks locked into a world of tenancy, sharecropping, and white racism.

Non-farm laborers struggled with depressions, layoffs, wage cuts, and poor working conditions. They also faced obstacles to labor's organization. Much of the opposition came from businesses that used the law, and muscle, to weaken labor movements. Violent strikes fed corporate hostility. The Great Railroad Strike of 1877, Chicago's Haymarket Square riots in 1886, and the Pullman Palace Car Company strike in 1894 all resulted in death, injury, property destruction – and damage to the popular reputation of workers. But laborers also had to deal with divisions from within. Splits between the skilled and unskilled, the native-born and immigrants, Protestants, Catholics, and Jews, whites and people of color, and men and women all hampered organization, and workers who absorbed a culture of individualism often spurned efforts at collective change.

The National Labor Union (1866–1873) and the Knights of Labor (prominent in the 1870s and early 1880s) tried to bring diverse workers together under one, united banner. Their leaders agitated for the eight-hour day, workers' cooperatives, *and* immigration restriction. They also addressed the needs of women and blacks, but both focused more on social idealism and political engagement than hard-nosed bargaining. The American Federation of Labor took up the latter strategy. Founded in 1886 and headed for almost four decades by Samuel Gompers, the AFL took its a cue from consolidated industries: the union 'horizontally' integrated skilled workers into a national federation aimed at improving wages, working conditions, and benefits. Gompers' practical, non-idealistic labor leadership protected the day-to-day interests of a well-defined group of workers; he left the perfection of the world to others. One other reform-minded union for both the skilled and unskilled grew out of the International Workers of the World, launched in 1905. Unlike the NLU and the Knights, the so-called 'Wobblies' were born in the West among rugged groups of miners and lumberers. Like their predecessors, the IWW organized social and political visionaries who agitated for an end to class divisions and state corruption. But whatever their strategy, labor movements organized fewer than one in five non-farm workers by 1920.

In 1892, the People's (or 'Populist') Party offered another type of organization for workers. The party addressed the needs of farmers and laborers, whites and blacks, men and women. Its collaborative effort was extraordinary, as was its platform. Guided by Donnelly of Minnesota, Tom Watson of Georgia, and other leaders, the party advocated the direct election of senators, the eight-hour day, immigration restriction, monetary reform, tariff reduction, a graduated income tax, and *public* ownership of rail, telephone, and telegraph companies. Its 1892 presidential candidate won over a million popular votes, but the party took only four Western states and failed to make its mark on Southern farmers and Eastern laborers.

Another broad-based political coalition, the Socialist Party of America, enjoyed a measure of political success in the early twentieth century. Under its five-times presidential candidate, Eugene V. Debs, the party advocated a democratic approach to social and economic change that was neither passionate about revolution nor rigid in ideology. Its diverse members called for reforms ranging from a mixed-ownership economy to a nationalized system. Debs scored nearly a million votes in the 1912 election, and party candidates won over a thousand posts in state and local governments. But the party's fortunes faded as a result of its opposition to World War I and a crackdown on radical groups after the conflict. Farmers, laborers, and third parties had a difficult time challenging the power of consolidated capital and entrenched political interests.

Progressivism

Looking out on a world reshaped by big business, expanded cities, and new populations, reform-minded, largely middle-class activists re-examined traditional ideas about the self and society. They questioned popular assumptions about rugged individualism and the ability of any one, solitary person to master such a complex universe. They challenged notions of decentralized and passive government. They rejected suggestions that change in the outer world came about by self-reform from within. They disputed claims about the fixed, unalterable, 'nat-ural' order of things. In place of these conventional beliefs, critics emphasized the collective and continuing interest of citizens in con-trolling the conditions of their lives. In the words of journalist Walter Lippmann, they advocated 'mastery' over 'drift'. He and thousands of others formed a new, 'progressive' understanding of the world.

Progressive reformers emphasized the importance of *social* con-sciousness. They assumed that, by nature, women and men were creatures of community; their being took root in a collective, inter-dependent existence. No one was truly separate, independent, or self-sufficient. Life was neither possible nor desirable cut off from a web of connections with others. People shaped their identity by living as part of (rather than apart from) a larger social whole.

That larger collective life was filled with larger collective calamities. Economic panics endured for years; political machines controlled entire cities; monopolies dominated millions. 'Thus', journalist Henry George wrote, 'does the well-being of each become more and more dependent upon the well-being of all – the individual more and more subordinate to society.' Since the scope of social problems was vast, the scope of social solutions must be equally extensive. A volunteer here or a charity there was no match for the enormity of social threats. Americans had to form a large, beneficial *public* interest to counteract the influence of large, harmful private interests. Reform efforts had to be as linked and structured and coordinated as the dangerous combinations they fought, and the campaigns should be conducted not merely with the good intentions of amateur enthusiasts but with the skilled guidance of trained specialists who brought rational, scientific, systematic principles to bear on social problems.

Conditions demanded social activism and interventionism. *Laissez-faire* approaches would only perpetuate misery, surrendering to forces that appeared intractable but remained changeable. By applying both rational and moral force, the combined efforts of a united public could overcome obstacles to progress. Government should intervene continuously on behalf of the common good, serving the Constitutional goal to 'promote the general welfare'.

Progressives spoke of common, public interests; they stressed collective action; they built bureaucratic leadership; and they tried to end the divisive and ruinous competition of small, individual differences in society. Like farm and labor activists, they applied the organizational lessons of corporate America to society. That was one reason why Progressivism did not represent a 'revolution' in American life but only a 'reform'. Another reason was that most advocates simply wanted to correct the worst outrages of capitalism and republican government rather than to replace those systems entirely. They hoped to regulate (rather than overthrow) the abuses they saw around them. Progressives also embraced some of the most enduring values (and anxieties) in American culture: a suspicion of special privilege; a fear of concentrated economic authority; a belief that consolidated power bred widespread corruption; and a drive to put the common good above individual interest. They were strongly committed both to social justice and social control. While trying to eliminate blatant inequities, they also sought to eradicate behavior that did not fit their standard of the 'good society'.

TYPES OF PROGRESSIVE REFORM

One source of social protest came from 'muckraking' journalists and 'realistic' and 'naturalistic' authors who explored the seamy underbelly of American life. From Ida Tarbell's study of the Standard Oil trust to Lincoln Steffens's indictment of *The Shame of the Cities* (both in 1904), magazine exposés stirred public consciousness and moral outrage. Upton Sinclair churned anger (and stomachs) with his detailed look at meatpacking in *The Jungle* (1906). Novelists such as Frank Norris examined the conflict between farmers and corporations in *The Octopus* in 1901. Norris's *McTeague* (1899) and William Dean Howells's *A Hazard of New Fortunes* (1890) explored the corrupting power of the new marketplace. Stephen Crane's *Maggie: A Girl of the Streets* (1893) and Theodore Dreiser's *Sister Carrie* (1900) examined the innocence lost in the harsh conditions of urban life.

The shock and outrage provoked by such works helped inspire a broad range of reforms. Politically, Progressives tried to replace the corruption of machine politics with non-partisan commissions, administrative specialists, fair taxation, and public service regulation. To promote responsive government, reformers pushed for direct primary elections, the direct election of senators, the use of the 'initiative' and 'referendum' to give the public a greater voice, and the use of the 'recall' to give political scoundrels the boot.

Economically, Progressives supported legislation for minimum wages, maximum hours, old-age pensions, and the elimination of child labor. Reformers also called for tighter regulation of consumer goods through pure food and drug laws, tighter regulation of the workplace to ensure worker safety, tighter regulation of 'trusts' to avoid mono-polistic business practices, and tighter regulation of resources to con-serve the nation's natural wealth.

Socially, reformers attacked social disorder by promoting housing codes to prevent the spread of slums, public health programs to prevent the spread of infectious disease, anti-prostitution laws to prevent the spread of vice, and birth control campaigns to prevent the spread of unwanted pregnancies. Progressives stressed that reform should be led by professionals schooled in 'social' work. For example, the American 'settlement house' movement, led by Jane Addams, brought trained, middle-class women into the middle of immigrant neighborhoods. The workers set up community centers, taught American values, provided needed services, and protected immigrants from predatory economic and political practices.

Educationally, reformers such as John Dewey tried to expand *and* restructure learning. Dewey advocated 'instrumentalist' programs focused on inquiry rather than the dry memorizing of facts. He created democratic classrooms (as the preferable way to teach valuable life skills), nurtured students' social growth (rather than overemphasizing a focus on the self), and emphasized learning by doing (rather than passively learning about what someone else did).

Theologically, Progressives even altered notions of the divine. Turning attention from the way flawed individuals could find their way to heaven, urban ministers such as Washington Gladden and Walter Rauschenbusch re-examined the 'sequence' of salvation. Rather than trying to save the individual soul in order to build a better world, they argued that believers should first save the soul of society in order to build better individuals. God, they insisted, dealt with people as a group, not as separate beings. Humanity must be saved together or suffer the consequences together. The 'social gospel' movement urged the faithful to rid society of its 'sins' of poverty, corruption, and exploitation in order to fulfill God's Progressive will.

THE WOMEN'S SUFFRAGE MOVEMENT

One of the most important – and, in retrospect, most curious – of Progressive reforms involved women's political rights. Earlier advocates such as Elizabeth Cady Stanton had pressed for women's suffrage on the basis of equality and liberty. For Stanton, the vote was a natural right to which women were entitled. With the ballot, women could define their destiny free of male control. The bold arguments challenged long-held notions of women's presumably submissive and domestic character. However unconventional the appeals, ten Western states granted the vote to women between 1869 and 1914. By 1913, an Eastern state (Illinois), also joined the list.

The Progressive campaign for a Constitutional amendment on

women's suffrage drew strength, in part, from Western state precedents, in part from better reform organization, but also in part from
less radical forms of argument. Sponsors commonly stressed women's
distinctive 'character' as strong moral agents, arguing that female voters
would elevate political life and counterbalance the violent, passionate,
and blemished character of males. As a committee of the National
American Woman Suffrage Association argued in 1912, an amendment
would answer 'the need of Mother's influence in the State'. Playing up
common anxieties, the committee added that women formed 'the most
religious, the most moral and the most sober portion of the American
people. Why deny them a voice in public affairs when we give it for the
asking to every ignorant foreigner who comes to our shores?' The
Nineteenth Amendment, adopted in 1920, granted women the vote
based on appeals to social progress as well as to social fear.

While 'progressivism' connotes advancement, betterment, and forward thinking, the movement sponsored a number of campaigns that
appear reactionary and undemocratic today. Attention to social 'disruption' and 'disorder' prompted assaults on the powerful and privileged but also led to attacks on the weak and defenseless. Progressives
pushed for restrictions on immigration based on the 'scientific' claims of
eugenicists who warned of threats to the nation's racial stock. Reformers expanded temperance campaigns into agitation for prohibition,
leading, in 1919, to the Eighteenth Amendment that banned 'the
manufacture, sale, or transportation of intoxicating liquors' nationwide.
And Progressive whites, for the most part, turned a blind eye to the
legalized system of segregation that had marked national life since the
end of Reconstruction.

AFRICAN AMERICANS AND PROGRESSIVE REFORM

When federal troops pulled out of the South at the end of Reconstruction in 1877, African Americans found themselves in a region
'redeemed' by whites from the supposedly tyrannical grip of national
authority. Into the first four decades of the twentieth century, the area
remained overwhelming rural, agricultural, decentralized, and
impoverished. But two significant changes occurred. Political dominance returned to the Democratic Party, which would control the

'solid South' for the next 100 years. And whites formalized racial separation and white supremacy.

The consequences for African Americans were devastating. The door that briefly opened for black political participation quickly closed. Voting rights were soon denied to most African-American males. Those who tried to exercise the franchise faced new obstacles in the form of poll taxes and literacy tests plus blatant intimidation and violent threats. The number of black officeholders dropped precipitously. Lacking political leadership and clout, the limited economic autonomy of African Americans became more uncertain. Sharecropping might have answered some needs of black farmers who found themselves without money, tools, and other resources; a 'crop-lien' system might have allowed them to borrow from merchants against future harvests. But the combination of chronic indebtedness and political dispossession reduced the possibilities of Southern blacks even further. In addition, they faced new social and legal barriers. Whites systematized segregation, creating two different public worlds for themselves and blacks through 'Jim Crow' laws.[2] In education, recreation, transportation, and accommodation – even in cemeteries – whites inhabited one realm, blacks another. An 1896 Supreme Court case, *Plessy v. Ferguson*, upheld the institutionalization of 'separate but equal' facilities, although it was common knowledge that blacks inhabited a separate and inherently *un*equal world. Violence completed the work the law left unfinished. In the 1890s alone, nearly 2,000 lynchings of blacks took place. Most happened in the South – and continued well into the twentieth century.

One response to institutionalized segregation was gradualistic in nature. Booker T. Washington believed that blacks temporarily had to endure the limits whites imposed on them. The nation rested on principles of racial inequality. Recognizing that unjust, degrading, yet stubborn fact, African Americans should turn away from utopian dreams of social transformation. Instead, they should work strenuously at any task open to them, improve their material condition, and demonstrate that they were both essential to the nation's prosperity and the equals of anyone. Eventually, whites would no longer be able to justify and defend their racist beliefs. In *Up from Slavery* (1901),

Washington offered his own experience as a model for what blacks could achieve. His Tuskegee Institute in Alabama offered the training in agriculture, trades, and industrial labor that Washington hoped would improve the lives and prospects of African Americans.

A second approach was agitational in nature. W.E.B. DuBois insisted that African Americans had to resist the limits imposed on them by white society. A subordinate status in a caste society was simply intolerable; injustice had to end. DuBois did not pin his hopes primarily on the efforts of common African Americans to improve their condition, he also rejected the notion that vocational training would guide blacks out of their predicament. DuBois insisted that full academic opportunities must be opened for blacks. Those most capable of leading the struggle were trained, educated blacks, a Progressive 'elite' as it were, whom DuBois referred to as the 'talented tenth'. Relying on political action and legal challenges, African-American professionals would break down the walls of racial discrimination. In *The Souls of Black Folk* (1903), DuBois outlined his challenge to Washington's patient, accommodationist stance. With a small group of white reformers, DuBois helped form the National Association for the Advancement of Colored People (the NAACP) in 1909 to lead the fight for equality.

NATIONAL PROGRESSIVISM UNDER THEODORE ROOSEVELT

Eventually, local and state Progressive campaigns made their way to the federal level, changing the relation of the national government to its people as well as altering the role of the presidency. Theodore Roosevelt and Woodrow Wilson were key figures in the transformation.

The aggressive, energetic, and ebullient Roosevelt worked his way up through New York politics to serve as vice-president under William McKinley, unexpectedly rising to the presidency after McKinley's assassination in September 1901. Roosevelt brought a strong record of reform and a commitment to presidential activism. Like Andrew Jackson, Roosevelt viewed the chief executive as a national leader who could appeal directly to the people, bypassing special privilege and entrenched agencies to serve broad, national interests. Like Abraham

Lincoln, Teddy was willing to mobilize federal authority to counter threats to the republic. Roosevelt summoned the same energy in response to crises of an economic nature. He believed that changes were necessary in the nation in order to *prevent* a radical alteration of American life.

The key problem in the new economic order, according to Roosevelt, involved the issue of consolidation. He knew he could not turn back the clock to a world of small enterprises; anyway, big business had created too many big improvements in efficiency and productivity. The trick was to create order and fairness out of centralization, to form what he called in 1904 a 'Square Deal'. One way was to encourage the rise of competing power centers: for example, enabling big labor to challenge big business. A second way was to form a national, public interest that could balance private interest. A third approach, combining the other two, was to regulate large economic entities rather than to dismantle them.

Government regulation was the key. Roosevelt took regulation to new heights and applied it to new problems as a way to *avoid* extreme measures. For example, he threw himself into the middle of a coal miners strike in 1902, arbitrating an agreement that gave the United Mine Workers a large wage increase and a nine-hour day. But over the next two years, Roosevelt intervened on the side of corporations against 'excessive' labor demands. His point was not to serve one or the other group but to demonstrate the mediating and balancing role the federal government should play in major economic disputes.

Roosevelt steered a similar middle course through environmental regulation. An avid outdoorsman, the president feared that unrestricted growth could harm the natural world (just as unchecked economic power wreaked havoc on society). The wilderness was not just one company's interest or one state's interest but a national, public interest that needed to be defended through uniform federal policy. Roosevelt's approach was to *con*serve, rather than *pre*serve, nature's wealth. Instead of removing resources from commercial use, he intended to manage their exploitation. He deemed it prudent to limit, rather than halt, development.

Regulation also served as a path between extremes in relation to big business. Roosevelt may have gained fame as a 'trustbuster' when the Justice Department won a suit against a railroad conglomerate, the Northern Securities Company, but his strategy of choice was to *supervise* rather than shatter business combinations. He pushed for an expansion of the Interstate Commerce Commission's regulatory powers, proposed a Bureau of Corporations to investigate business practices, and fought for consumer protection through the Pure Food and Drug Act and the Meat Inspection Act. Federal regulation, guided by an interventionist president, would control the disorderly excesses of the new economic order.

Having pledged not to run for office again after his victory in 1904, Roosevelt left the White House in March 1909. He soon had a falling out with his successor, fellow Republican William Howard Taft. Their dispute over the future course of reform was so serious that Roosevelt threw his hat back in the ring at the end of Taft's first (and only) term. In 1912, Roosevelt campaigned for the executive office on the 'Progressive' (or 'Bull Moose') party ticket. His program of 'new nationalism' would shift the federal government's role from the defender of order and fairness to the champion of social justice and the public welfare. He gained more popular and electoral votes than Taft, but far fewer than the winner, Democrat Woodrow Wilson.

NATIONAL PROGRESSIVISM UNDER WOODROW WILSON

Wilson was a Southerner (from Virginia), a scholar (in political science), and a university president (at Princeton). His only political experience was to serve as governor of New Jersey where, in less than two years, he made his mark as a Progressive leader. Running against a divided Republican field in the election of 1912, he won a decisive victory in the Electoral College.

Like Roosevelt, Wilson advocated a powerful presidency. He viewed the chief executive as an American 'prime minister' who headed his party, kept it united, and guided its programs. In the federal government, the president was to shape and mold laws, not simply enforce them; and in the court of public opinion, the president rallied citizens behind critical national interests.

Wilson answered Roosevelt's 'New Nationalism' with his 'New Freedom' program, in some ways a plan to preserve traditional Jeffersonian Democratic ideals in an industrial age. To Wilson, 'bigness' was neither desirable nor inevitable – either in business or government. Both should be reduced to allow more of a free market and more local control. The solution to problems of consolidation required a temporary enlargement of federal activity, but only long enough to solve a pressing, immediate problem before gradually diminishing again.

In order to spur greater competition in the economy, Wilson pulled on the lever of tariffs. Lower rates, he reasoned, would increase the number of players in the marketplace. The Democratic Congress obliged with rate reductions through the Underwood-Simmons Tariff of 1913. To make up for the revenues lost in lower tariffs, Congress also passed a graduated income tax, providing a secure base of funding for national social programs.

Wilson then launched a full frontal assault on the so-called 'Money Trust' of Wall Street bankers and financiers. Rather than allowing a small cabal of firms to control the monetary fate of the nation, Wilson and Congress created the Federal Reserve System in 1913. The 'Fed' met national needs by stabilizing and ordering the entire economy. Its Federal Reserve notes provided a uniform currency. The agency monitored the funds member banks had in reserve, and its central board of supervisors (nominated by the president) kept an eye on the money supply and the costs of borrowing for the country as a whole. The system also met local needs by allowing for flexibility in an economically and geographically diverse society. The Federal Reserve created a dozen district banks that could respond quickly and precisely to local circumstances, raising or lowering the amount of money in circulation as conditions warranted.

Wilson then proceeded to his next project: dismantling the behemoths of American industry. Roosevelt tolerated business combinations as a fact of twentieth-century life; it was the federal government's responsibility to see that the worst of the lot did not get out of control. Wilson suspected monopolistic powers as a threat to liberty and justice; whether they were beneficial or detrimental, the federal government had to knock them down to size. In 1914, he won passage of the

Federal Trade Commission to scrutinize business activity. A companion bill, the Clayton Anti-trust Act, floundered, in part because Wilson did not enthusiastically press for the measure. Apparently, he had a change of heart and began, of all things, to approach the trust question in Rooseveltian terms: if you can't beat them, regulate them.

While the momentum of Progressivism slowed by 1914, electoral challenges from Republicans sent Wilson back on the path of reform. The president supported laws covering child labor, workmen's compensation, farm credits, and the eight-hour day for interstate railroad workers. He also appointed Progressive jurist Louis Brandeis to the Supreme Court.

Wilson's initial hopes for scaling back big business and big government faded. He never intended to usher in a new age of *laissez-faire*, and he did not accept conservative arguments about government passivity. In time, Wilson came to understand the functions of consolidation in the modern market and the desirable role of the federal government in regulating economic power. If he did not restore a more competitive and decentralized order, he could actively define and serve the greater, interconnected public good – and promote 'Progressive' reform.

In one other way, Wilson took Progressive principles further than any of his predecessors. Having applied the logic of Progressivism domestically, Wilson extended its reach to foreign concerns as well. The spread of liberal, activist, interventionist commitments nationally found a parallel in international events in the late nineteenth and early twentieth centuries.

CHAPTER TEN

Relations with Other Nations, 1850–1920

Some assume that US leaders came upon twentieth-century international relations with a blank slate. It may appear that the nation, up to the early 1900s, was essentially inward-looking, isolationist, and innocent in power politics. Try telling that to a Hawaiian, a Filipino, or an American Indian. While the United States steered clear of complex Western alliances, the nation dealt with many foreign peoples in the second half of the 1800s. The republic pursued territorial and commercial expansion and employed military means to secure its objectives. What the nation learned from such experiences may have misguided its officials as much as it assisted them. The simple point is that Americans carried quite a bit of foreign policy 'baggage' with them when they arrived on the scene of modern global warfare in the early twentieth century. All nations, including the United States had their illusions jolted in the wake of that horrifying event.

At Home: Changing Indian Policies

Relations with Native Americans provided one example of how the United States dealt with 'sovereign' nations in the nineteenth century. Indian policy revealed the approaches the United States adopted towards other societies, the military means of enforcing national goals, and the ideological arguments used to justify official actions.

As whites changed their thinking about the land, the fate of native peoples also changed. In the 1830s, white society 'solved' the Indian question by removing eastern nations to territory west of the Mississippi. Looking at a map today, one may wonder why the dominant group 'conceded' so much space to groups they so despised. The answer was simple. Land west of the 98th meridian was semi-arid, barren, and inhospitable, useless in the eyes of most whites. If the 'Great American Desert' served no market function, perhaps it could serve a political and social purpose: as an enclave where Indians remained separate from whites.

Whites established 'Indian Territory' and forced the Five Civilized Tribes to relocate to the area of present-day Oklahoma. The Great Plains was already home to other native peoples such as the Sioux, Blackfeet, Crow, Cheyenne, Comanche, Arapahoe, and Kiowa. These 'Plains Indians' were adept at horsemanship, skilled as fighters, and nomadic in their patterns, creating an economic, social, and religious way of life that revolved around the buffalo hunt.

By the mid-1800s, whites had a change of heart about the Great Plains. Settlers moved through on overland trails to the Pacific coast. Railroads hoped to clear the middle of the region as a corridor for transcontinental lines. Mining, cattle, and agricultural interests discovered the market potential of the area, and lands that had been presumed worthless suddenly took on great utility. Why let such valuable resources become, as Theodore Roosevelt said, 'a game reserve for squalid savages'? From 1851 to the early 1880s, federal

A Cheyenne Indian camp

Sitting Bull, Tatanka–Iyotanka (1831–1890)

officials launched a policy of 'concentration'. The plan restricted particular tribes to particular areas, moving some north and some south in order to open up the Central Plains. Treaties outlined federal subsidies for tribes that agreed to limit themselves to well-defined 'reservations', lands which native peoples would hold 'as long as the grass should grow and the rivers flow'.

The promises did not last long. As whites swindled and stole 'protected' lands, tribes defied federal policy and resisted the confinement of the reservation. Conflict erupted in a series of 'Plains Wars' from the 1860s through the 1870s. At Sand Creek, Colorado, in 1864, a militia force slaughtered over 100 Cheyenne and Arapahoe who gathered under what they thought was the protective cover of the army. In 1876 at Little Big Horn in Montana, Cheyenne and Sioux forces under Sitting Bull, Gall, and Crazy Horse annihilated Colonel George Armstrong Custer's Seventh Cavalry. Across the region, whites eliminated the buffalo around which Indian life revolved. Some 13 million bison roamed the plains at mid-century; by the 1880s, the animals were nearly extinct. Organized warfare and plunder, along with alcohol and disease, also took a heavy toll on Native Americans; *their* numbers declined to under 250,000.

For half a century, since Jackson, native peoples had had their military power broken and their lives confined to tribal reservations. Over the *next* half-century, federal officials seized on a new initiative: native peoples would become less Indian and more American. Rather than concentrating tribes on reservations, they would be assimilated into the dominant society.

One method of acculturation involved land. Under the 1887 Dawes Severalty Act, the federal government began to dismantle reservations, dividing up a tribe's collective holdings among its members. Land-owning Indians would be less communal-minded and more ruggedly individual, less inclined to identify with a tribe and more inclined to stand on their own, less dependent on federal assistance and more capable of fending for themselves. And the United States could conveniently take over 'excess' tribal claims. Through the Dawes 'allotment' policy, the landholdings of Indians declined by over two-thirds.

A second method of acculturation involved children. Rather than allowing Indian youth to grow up in their traditional- and backwardworld, policymakers expanded an educational program that separated children from their parents and sent them to 'boarding schools' for instruction in white ways. The motto of one school in Pennsylvania suggested the larger goal: 'Kill the Indian and save the man'. A government that once had deemed it best to remove Indian tribes from the white world now thought it best to remove Indian children from their own world.

From the 1830s to the 1930s, native peoples faced a government that wanted to strip them first of their home and then of their identity. Policies allowed a more 'efficient' society to bring order and bounty out of the land. Civilized whites hastened the evolutionary progress of inferior savages, guiding native peoples to a higher (and more uniform) level of cultural existence. If the formalities of negotiation, the influence of trade, and the benefits of cultural contact did not achieve the desired result, armed coercion would: the United States met resistance with a war of attrition. Indian policy revealed the capacity of the federal government to define the fate of other peoples, to control the conditions of their lives, and to reduce them to a state of dependency. With moral certainty and scientific confidence, officials who proved remarkably passive in most other projects secured one particular national interest aggressively and energetically.

What worked at home could also work abroad. The experience came in handy for a society that was about to learn that its own open spaces had closed. In 1893, historian Frederick Jackson Turner reminded an audience that the census just three years earlier had declared the frontier 'gone'. This was no mere statistical curiosity, Turner asserted: 'The existence of an area of free land, its continuous recession, and the advance of American settlement westward, explain American development.' The nation's democratic, individualistic, fluid character had grown out of its environment. Now, the frontier had passed but, as Turner noted, 'the American energy will continually demand a wider field for its exercise'. Some believed the nation needed new lands, new markets, and new opportunities to keep pressing its special destiny. The domestic frontier had already provided a training ground, complete with military drill, for that goal.

Overseas Interests

As officials clarified their intentions towards 'foreign' people at home, a scattered and unsystematic set of overseas objectives also coalesced in the minds of national leaders.

Economically, by the 1870s, industrial and agricultural interests came to recognize the advantage of opening more markets for America's surplus goods. Senator Albert T. Beveridge advised that 'we are making more than we can use ... Therefore, we must find new markets for our produce, new occupation for our capital, new work for our labor.' Otherwise, the nation faced rising inventories, collapsing prices, mounting unemployment, and continuing panics. Sales at home were the main source of consumption, but sales abroad could take up the slack. As Europeans increasingly protected their home economies, 'growth' markets south and west of the United States looked ever more appealing. While exports to the United Kingdom tripled between 1900 and 1920, exports to China increased almost ten times – and to Cuba nearly 20 times.

Politically, more consumers for American goods might just keep domestic radicalism under control. Laid-off laborers and indebted farmers got worked up every time the economy went into a decline: if they stayed busy behind their machines and plows, producing goods that somebody actually bought, perhaps the political climate of the nation would settle down in the same fashion as its economy. President Benjamin Harrison's Secretary of State, James G. Blaine, hoped that 'the reasons for and inducements to strikes with all their attendant evils would cease'. Commercial expansion abroad might mean greater harmony at home.

Strategically, the United States might be able to *control*, not just to enter, overseas markets. Naval Captain Alfred Thayer Mahan, developed a master plan for America mastery in his 1890 work, *The Influence of Sea Power upon History, 1660–1783*. According to Mahan, great powers gained control of international affairs through their command of the oceans. America's present nautical puniness inhibited its potential might. Mahan called for a larger navy, strategic bases around the globe, and the construction of a canal to facilitate movement between the Atlantic and Pacific. With sea power in place, the United States could acquire and exploit colonial possessions. By 1900, the nation's twelfth-rate navy grew to become the world's third strongest. Political and diplomatic leaders completed much of the work on Mahan's other goals by 1914.

Racially, appeals to Caucasian supremacy reinforced calls for a greater US presence in international affairs. Popular ideas about the superiority of all things white gained 'scientific' luster in the light of new research on evolution. As diplomat John Barrett observed, 'the rule of the survival of the fittest applies to nations as well as to the animal kingdom'. Relating principles of natural selection to human events, 'social' Darwinists forecast the triumph of strong, dominant whites over inferior people of color. The ignorant and indolent required the guidance of civilized peoples; Professor John W. Burgess declared there was 'no human right to the status of barbarism'. Who

Alfred T. Mahan

better to take the lead, Senator Beveridge argued, than Anglo-Saxons, whom God created as 'the master organizers of the world to establish system where chaos reigns'.

Religiously, the idea of national 'mission' also found expression in overseas evangelism. The number of Protestant foreign missions rose fivefold from 1870 to 1900. Those who served carried a saving message rooted in the gospel of Christianity and the civilization of the West. Reverend Josiah Strong combined appeals to America's racial and political superiority with arguments about the nation's providential destiny and spiritual obligation. In *Our Country* (1885), he argued that Anglo-Saxons led the world in their grasp of pure Christianity and civil liberty, ideas which were 'having a fuller development in the United States than in Great Britain'. Rising to the top of the racial pecking order, every American had to accept the evolutionary and divine call 'to be, in a peculiar sense, his brother's keeper'. The world was about to witness 'the final competition of races, for which the Anglo-Saxon is being schooled'. Strong believed the 'stock' of the United States would 'spread itself over the earth'.

Whether speaking in terms of sales or souls, stability or strategy, specie or species, a persuasive combination of interests led the United States to take a more engaged role in world events. Attention focused on Central America, the Pacific, and Asia. Some leaders envisioned territorial acquisition, political possession, and colonial control. The United States had worlds to conquer (and lost time to make up) before Europeans gained an even greater lead in the imperial race.

Others did not share the dream of international aggrandizement. Critics including Mark Twain, Jane Addams, Andrew Carnegie, Samuel Gompers, philosopher William James, and educator William Graham Sumner raised *anti*-imperialist arguments at the turn of the century. For some, the issue was one of practicality: why bother setting up elaborate bureaucracies for the colonial domination of foreigners when all the United States really wanted was a market for its goods and coaling stations for its fleet? For some, the issue was one of racial anxiety: why would the master race want to mingle with those lower orders and contaminate its precious stock? For others, the issue was one of integrity: how could a republican society that once condemned colonial subordination now support imperial conquest? As the American Anti-Imperialist League stated in 1899, 'The United States cannot act upon the ancient heresy that might makes right.'

In the end, expansionism proceeded by fits and starts from the mid-1800s to 1890 as the nation widened its interests in the Pacific and the Western Hemisphere. The United States signed a commercial treaty with China in 1844. Commodore Matthew Perry pried open trade with Japan a decade later. In 1867, the United States seized Midway Island in the Pacific and purchased Alaska from Russia. An 1875 Reciprocity Treaty with Hawaii granted islanders trading advantages (while limiting their options with other powers), and the United States secured a coaling station in the Samoan Islands in 1878 and naval rights at Pearl Harbor, Hawaii, in 1887. Secretary of State Blaine organized a Pan American Congress in 1889 to explore wider trade in Latin America.

National leaders, however, also displayed hesitancy. Congress stopped plans to annex Santo Domingo and to create naval bases in Haiti, Cuba, and Venezuela. France took the lead in constructing a canal through the Panamanian isthmus. President Grover Cleveland proved to be an opponent of expansionism. Spending on naval forces remained low for much of the post-Civil War era, and the United States foreign service remained both underfunded and poorly staffed.

In the end, American foreign policy opinion was mixed. Some favored the expansion of very general national interests; others urged a more systematic plan of acquisition and rule. Foreign policy decisions were neither uniform nor democratic; a small elite took the lead in shaping the course of US activities overseas and, eventually, their decisions led to conflict and conquest. By the early twentieth century, Jefferson's 'empire of liberty' had an international scope.

America Abroad, 1890–1914

The decade of the 1890s opened a more aggressive era in American ambitions overseas. One area of special interest was Hawaii. From the 1820s, when American missionaries began cultivation of the islands' souls, to the 1870s, when American corporations controlled cultivation of the islands' sugar cane, Hawaii fell increasingly under US influence. The sugar trade stayed healthy until 1890, when new tariffs gave the edge to *domestic* producers. Planters like Sanford B. Dole calculated that if they couldn't beat the United States, why not join them? Dole, other American planters, diplomats, ministers, and marines joined together in 1893 and overthrew the nationalist Queen Liliuokalani. President Cleveland looked warily on the proceedings, but by 1898, after another overseas venture half a world away, Hawaii was annexed. By 1900, it had become a US territory.

The other event in question was a war that erupted between Spain and the United States in 1898 over events in Cuba. In the 1850s, America had feared upheaval from Cuba posed by emancipation for black slaves. In the 1890s, America feared upheaval from Cuba posed by rebellion against Spanish rule. Uprisings on the island flared in the 1860s, 1870s, and again in 1895. Politicians and the press sympathized with rebel efforts to topple Spanish power, celebrated the martyred

Queen Liliuokalani of Hawaii

revolutionary José Martí, and condemned the policies of forced relocation and concentration camps instituted by Spanish commander, Valeriano Weyler.

Commercially, Cuba's violence threatened American trade and investments. Diplomatically, Cuba's volatility could prompt European intervention. President Cleveland urged Spain to modify its policies. His successor, William McKinley, confronted an increasingly tense situation by February 1898. The press leaked a Spanish diplomat's letter that sneered at reform and insulted the president. In mid-February, an explosion on the battleship *Maine*, anchored in Havana harbor, killed over 260 crewmembers. In the late twentieth century, careful inquiry blamed an engine room mishap, but in the late nineteenth century, popular opinion blamed the Spanish. McKinley urged Cuba's colonial rulers to make concessions to the rebels, but Spain resisted. By late April, Congress declared war against Spain, stating that the United

States had no desire to take control of Cuba 'except for the pacification thereof'.

The conflict that followed was quite brief but also quite successful for the United States. Fighting lasted four months, 400 Americans died in battle, and the struggle cost $250 million. All in all, Secretary of State John Hay reflected, it was 'a splendid little war'. The campaign in Cuba, however, was only part of the story. Spain was a weak but *worldwide* colonial power, and the United States aimed to pick off its possessions. The biggest prize fell to Commodore George Dewey; in May 1898, his Pacific naval squadron destroyed the Spanish fleet in Manila Bay. McKinley sent additional troops, and American forces took Manila in mid-August. Under the final peace terms, Spain gave up Cuba, ceded Puerto Rico and Guam, and handed over the Philippines to the United States for $20 million. Suddenly the heirs of an anti-colonial revolution at the end of the eighteenth century found themselves with an empire of their own at the end of the nineteenth century.

They also found themselves with an anti-colonial revolution, directed at the United States by Filipino rebels seeking independence. From 1899 to 1902, America became mired in its first land war in Asia. US leaders assumed that Filipinos, like Native Americans, were an inferior, ignorant, and ill-prepared people. 'They were unfit for self-government,' McKinley argued. 'There was nothing left for us to do but to take them all, and to educate the Filipinos, and uplift and civilize and Christianize them.' In the conflict that followed, 4,000 American soldiers perished, but the consequences for Filipinos were far more severe. The United States resorted to war tactics it had loudly condemned when practiced by Spain. Hundreds of thousands of Filipinos died from fighting, starvation, and disease. When the conflict ended, William Howard Taft became civilian governor, and the United States outlined the steps towards eventual Filipino self-rule. The process lasted over four decades: Philippine independence did not come until 1946.

The United States also maintained control over its other war trophies. In 1900, the United States created a colonial government for Puerto Rico; 17 years later, America declared the island an unincorporated territory and granted its people United States citizenship.

Under the terms of the Platt Amendment in 1901, Cuba remained only nominally independent. Its foreign policy decisions could not threaten US interests; it had to grant military bases to America; and Cubans had to recognize the right of the United States to intervene in their internal affairs (a privilege that the American military exercised in 1906, 1912, and 1917).

While the United States closed doors on full political independence for some, it tried to open doors of trade with others. A key interest was China, whose markets seemed promising but whose domination by European and Japanese powers seemed threatening. In 1899 and 1900, Secretary of State Hay issued two 'open door notes' to the key imperial players calling for free economic access to China and the preservation of China's 'territorial and administrative' integrity. Partial to profits and hostile to partitions, the United States stood behind its open door principles, but at a distance. Declarations were one thing, enforcement quite another.

US leaders were quite happy to do as they pleased closer to home, particularly as they tried to work out a quicker route to Asian markets. In 1901, a treaty with Britain allowed the United States to construct and operate a Central American canal linking the Atlantic and Pacific. In 1903, the United States bought the holdings of the French company that had tried unsuccessfully to build a canal through the Panamanian isthmus. American officials then leased the Canal Zone from Colombia, which controlled Panama. Everything fell into place, but then the deal fell apart when Colombia held out for more money. President Theodore Roosevelt did not look kindly on the tough bargaining, the French company feared the clearance sale would not go through, and Panamanians worried that the canal would end up somewhere else. The three parties teamed together to foment a revolution against Colombia. Panamanian rebels rose up in November 1903, an American naval vessel conveniently appeared to monitor events, the United States recognized the new Panamanian government, and, about two weeks after the skirmish began, Roosevelt had his lease in hand. Eleven years later, the Panama Canal opened.

Roosevelt intended to 'speak softly, but carry a big stick'. Although he actually spoke with something of a squeak, Roosevelt managed to achieve the 'stick' part, especially in Central America and the Caribbean. The region, he believed, was not a land of equals; leadership fell to the politically, economically, militarily, and racially superior United States. Its interests took precedence, its expectations set the standard for government behavior. The United States monitored its sphere of influence, kept those meddlesome Europeans out, and ensured that local countries conducted themselves in an orderly fashion. If they did not make 'good use' of their independence – if their misbehavior threatened 'the rights of the United States' or 'invited foreign aggression' – then the United States would intervene and correct the errors of their ways. The 'Roosevelt Corollary' to the Monroe Doctrine, outlined in 1904 and 1905, justified the nation's 'exercise of an international police power'.

Constables Roosevelt, Taft, and Wilson regularly walked the beat in Central America and the Caribbean. Whether containing insurgents (to ensure United States notions of political stability) or supervising economies (to keep European debt collectors from beating down the neighbors' doors), the United States intervened with a peculiar combination of troops and accountants in Nicaragua, Haiti, and the Dominican Republic in the opening decades of the twentieth century.

President Wilson eyed political turbulence in Mexico with an especially wary eye, leading to a complicated series of interventions. The Mexican Revolution of 1910–1911 brought Francisco Madero to power, but in 1913 supporters of General Victoriano Huerta murdered the president. While Europeans recognized Huerta, Wilson refused, siding instead with Venustiano Carranza's 'Constitutionalists' and pledging 'to teach the South American republics to elect good men'. In April 1914, after Mexican authorities arrested American sailors in Tampico and refused to bow and scrape in apology, Wilson took the incident as an assault on US 'dignity and authority'. He placed marines in Veracruz where fighting erupted and over 100 Mexican soldiers died. Carranza assumed power in August 1914 but had no desire to enroll in Professor Wilson's classes on good government. Wilson initially thought rebel leader Pancho Villa was a better ally, then reconsidered, and eventually recognized Carranza's government. Villa, feeling betrayed, launched attacks in 1916 on US interests and then on the United States itself, plundering and murdering Americans in a New Mexico border town. General John J. Pershing and 11,000 US troops hunted Villa down, but after ten fruitless months, the force returned home empty-handed. Wilson's Mexican adventures came to an end.

Swinging a policeman's club against weak neighbors, the United States posed as a courtly and dispassionate intermediary in disputes among the world's leading powers. Roosevelt mediated an end to the Russo-Japanese War in 1905, organized a conference to resolve colonial conflict between France and Germany in Morocco, and received the 1906 Nobel Peace Prize for his efforts. Willing to tip the scales of authority and influence close to home, the United States worked to restore the balance of power among major international players.

The nation's 'progressive' international agenda sought to instruct weak peoples in rational, universal standards of behavior while directing larger states toward the proper use of their enlarged power.[1] Whether acting as guide for the powerless or mediator for the powerful, the United States saw itself on a pivotal 'mission' to the world.

Facing the Great War, 1914–1917

Americans had their work cut out for them. European nations maintained standing armies of unprecedented size. Trained reservists stood at the ready. National interests played out around the world as Europeans extended their imperial reach over a fifth of the world's territories and a tenth of its population. Fearing encirclement, isolation, or impotence, major powers countered their foes and protected their flanks by forming opposing sets of alliances. Germany and Austria-Hungary created a Dual Alliance; with the addition of the Ottoman Empire, they formed the 'Central Powers'. Britain, France, and Russia established the Triple Entente; with the addition of Italy, they formed the 'Allies'. Strange bedfellows came together to offset a bewildering array of real and potential threats against one another's interests. The complex alliances and pledges of mutual assistance only heightened tensions, however, for the slightest spark could set off a huge conflagration. The most volatile source of spontaneous combustion was the intense and unpredictable force of nationalism, which ignited in late June 1914 after a Serbian nationalist assassinated Archduke Franz Ferdinand, heir to the Austro-Hungarian throne. Within five weeks, Europe was caught up in a general war, the first since the Napoleonic era. Precedents offered little guidance for what was to come. More people died in the Great War's four years than in all the wars of the previous four centuries.

As fighting erupted, Wilson announced that the United States had to maintain 'the true spirit of neutrality, which is the spirit of impartiality and fairness and friendliness to all concerned'. Passions among ethnic Americans tied to their warring homelands could divide the republic. The United States had to show itself 'a Nation fit beyond others to exhibit the fine poise of undisturbed judgment, the dignity of self-control, the efficiency of dispassionate action; a Nation ... which keeps herself fit and free to do what is honest and disinterested and truly serviceable for the peace of the world'. Extraordinary world events required exceptional American leadership.

Neutrality made sense for a number of reasons: the frightening events of 1914 convinced many that the best policy towards Europe was to have no policy; nonalignment kept the United States from being drawn into the vortex of war. Pacifist groups echoed the sentiment, appealing to negotiation over force. Wilson, who came into power in 1912 because of a split among Republicans, recognized that military intervention could unite his opponents in the next election. He managed to win a second term by a whisker, in part because of the slogan 'He kept us out of war'. Finally, the democratic-minded Wilson could hardly justify coming to the aid of a European alliance that included the autocratic regime of Tsar Nicholas II.

Genuine neutrality seemed reasonable but proved difficult. Ideologically, Wilson and his advisors admired the democratic habits of Britain and France over the militaristic habits of Germany. Emotionally, ethnic Americans found themselves torn: German-Americans (about 9 per cent of the population) often expressed support for the policies of their home country while Irish-Americans (over 4 per cent of the population) saw little reason for the United States to side with the despised British. Economically, US trade with France and Britain was greater in volume and value than that with Germany and its allies. Diplomatically, Wilson's *de facto* recognition of the British naval blockade of Germany demonstrated America's growing partiality in the conflict. Militarily, the president's support for a build-up of armed forces in late 1915 suggested his interest in a military solution; and technologically, Germany's reliance on submarine warfare made the preservation of neutral rights on the high seas seem like a quaint but outdated notion.

Military events in Europe and policy decisions by the Wilson administration drew the United States into war. The key factor was Germany's use, by February 1915, of the *unterseeboote* to counter Britain's naval blockade and to stop the flow of goods to the Allies. Germany warned of danger in the waters around the British Isles; all vessels, including the ships of neutrals, were fair game. When the British liner *Lusitania* went down in May 1915, killing nearly 1,200 passengers (including over 100 Americans), Wilson demanded recognition of neutral rights. Germany stepped back but, by February 1916, opened submarine warfare again against armed vessels. The French ship, *Sussex*, came under attack in March, injuring Americans on board. Germany again backed off after threats from Wilson, but in January 1917, unrestricted submarine warfare resumed, with American ships set in U-boat sights.

Two other events in early 1917 brought the United States closer to war. In February, British intelligence intercepted the 'Zimmerman telegram', a cable from the German government suggesting that if Mexico sided with Germany and attacked the United States, Mexico would regain the lands it lost in its 1846–1848 war with America. The telegram enraged the public and revealed how war in Europe threatened US security. Weeks later, a revolution in Russia ousted Tsar Nicholas II from power and the principal undemocratic member of the alliance left the scene, allowing Wilson to pursue pro-Allied assistance with a clearer conscience.

The United States already made loans to the Allies and traded in arms and supplies. Calls for a negotiated peace had failed and meanwhile, the war settled into a ghastly stalemate along thousands of miles of trenches. In April 1917, Wilson asked Congress to give the United States a role in the war-making. He was moved even more by a desire to have America shape the peace-making. 'The world', Wilson said, 'must be made safe for democracy'. With American assistance, the Allies would end the war; with American guidance, they would fashion a just and stable future.

The United States at War, 1917–1918

US entrance into the conflict required an enlarged military, mobilized resources, increased revenues, and greater federal powers. World-wide war required large-scale government. The expansion of national authority that guided Progressive reform in America would now work towards a new world order around the globe.

The first step was to create a strong military force. The United States entered the war with fewer than 200,000 servicemen; it ended the war with 25 times that number. A conscription act drafted three million; another two million volunteered. Forty per cent served in the American Expeditionary Force in France and were led by General Pershing, who had cut his teeth in clashes with Indians, Filipinos, and Mexicans. A disciplined commander, he trained troops thoroughly. Pershing did not deploy large numbers of American soldiers to the front until the spring of 1918 when, impatient with the defensive posture of Britain and France, he urged a more aggressive, offensive operation. Independent-minded, he rejected efforts to scatter his forces among Allied armies, leaving American troops under separate command.

On the seas, German submarines took a heavy toll on Allied shipping. On land, the Central Powers concentrated their forces on the Western front after Vladimir Lenin's Bolshevik government signed a separate peace treaty with Germany in March 1918. In both naval and ground operations, the presence of US forces turned the tide of the war. US destroyers helped reduce the number and effectiveness of U-boats by late 1917. American warships provided protection for supply convoys. The European Allies aided by American forces blocked German advances at Cantigny, Château-Thierry, and Belleau Wood from late May to late June. In July, the Allies began their own offensive operation. On September 26th, with a million troops under his command, Pershing launched the Meuse-Argonne offensive and the Allies drove their foe back. As Germany's military operations failed, civilian morale plummeted and war partners surrendered. The nation's officials agreed to an armistice that brought an end to war.

The Home Front

The scale of human and industrial resources needed for the war effort demanded an unprecedented coordination of American life. Historian David M. Kennedy notes that members of a 'strikingly voluntaristic and fragmented society . . . had to be made to perform in concert with their appointed parts'. The war served as a kind of national experiment in Progressive ideas of collective enterprise, centralized control, and expanded public power. Wilson steered a course 'between the shoals of unbridled *laissez-faire* and full-blown state economic control'.[2]

Government agencies directed key sectors of the economy. In manufacturing, the War Industries Board under financier Bernard Baruch made government purchases while supervising supplies, prices, and production. The Board both managed and cooperated with private concerns, generating lucrative contracts and relaxing anti-trust regulation; as a result, big business grew bigger. In agriculture, the Food Administration, led by an engineer named Herbert Hoover, expanded food supplies. Choosing market mechanisms over government coercion, Hoover favored high prices in order to spur production and voluntary cutbacks as a way to conserve resources. Agriculture grew more mechanized, output expanded, and farm incomes rose.

The war effort cost over $33 billion. A nation accustomed to balancing its budget found that income and outgoings went suddenly and wildly out of balance; the federal government spent three times more than it took in. The national debt, which stood at $3 billion as the war began, climbed to $27 billion by 1919. Part of the reason was that Wilson funded the conflict mainly through loans. War bonds covered two-thirds of the war's costs, taxes only one-third. In the inflationary spiral that followed, prices on a wide range of goods nearly doubled.

The war altered the circumstances of several groups in the United States. Union membership jumped 60 per cent as the National War

Labor Board protected workers' rights to organize. Women occupied a wider range of jobs as roughly a sixth of the work force left for military service; 25 per cent of war production workers were female. As industrial jobs expanded, up to half a million African Americans left the South and made their way to Northern cities. Midwest urban centers such Detroit, Chicago, Cleveland, and Gary witnessed a sharp rise in black populations, but East St. Louis, Chicago, New York, and Washington also witnessed the outbreak of violent race riots.

The federal government's control expanded over opinion as well as production. The Committee on Public Information served as a propaganda machine designed to demonize the enemy, Americanize the immigrant, and standardize public sentiment about the war. Those who remained unpersuaded could deal with the law. The Espionage Act of 1917 and the Sabotage and Sedition Acts of 1918 aimed not only at spies and saboteurs but also at anti-war dissent; the government prosecuted some 2,000 cases. Suspicion of radicals even continued after the war with the anti-Bolshevik 'Red Scare' of 1919–1920. In January 1920, the Attorney General launched raids in nearly three dozen cities, rounding up over 4,000 suspected radicals.

The Battle over Peace

Victorious Europeans wanted to enfeeble Germany and dismember its base of power, but Wilson envisioned a plan to end all wars, not just one war. Convinced that his proposal was right (and righteous), he found himself in conflict with Continental allies and Washington senators.

In January 1918, Wilson outlined what he saw as an enduring rather than a punitive peace that would remove 'the chief provocations to war'. His 'Fourteen Points' boiled down to five central commitments. Wilson advocated democracy over imperialism (by reducing colonialism and expanding self-determination), openness over secrecy (in the conduct of diplomatic affairs), freedom over restriction (in trade and on the seas), moral force over armed force (through demilitarization), and collectivity over national self-interest (by building world security through a co-operative 'League of Nations' rather than relying on balances of power). The proposal formed 'the moral climax of this, the culminating and final war for human liberty'.

Wilson brought his plan to the Paris Peace Conference in January 1919, confronting the alternative agenda of Britain, France, and Italy. Closed sessions – excluding both the Germans and the Soviets – took the place of open diplomacy. Appeals for free trade and open seas fell on deaf ears. Territorial settlements undercut principles of self-determination and colonialism was revised rather than eliminated under the system of 'mandates'. Disarmament applied to the vanquished, not the victors, and the European Allies planned to punish their foes by stripping them of territory and population, blaming the war on Germany, and demanding over \$30 billion in reparations. Wilson had never made acceptance of his peace principles a precondition for American military participation in the war. Now the European Allies forced him to make major concessions.

Wilson clung to the League of Nations. A collective security organization, he believed, could create stability out of a horrible war and a flawed peace. He hoped to win Senate approval of the peace treaty, which contained within it the League of Nations charter. In domestic political debates, too, Wilson stumbled badly. Although the Republicans won control of Congress in 1918, Wilson did not name any Republican senators to his advisory 'Peace Commission'. Snubbed party leaders were hardly in a cooperative mood with the president. Critics also pointed to the many ways Wilson had backed down from his 14-point program.

Most importantly, opponents charged that the peace treaty obligated the United States to obey the League's decisions. On this issue, Wilsonian idealism came up against an American tradition: freedom of action in foreign policy. Nonaligned, the United States independently chose when and where to intervene in the world. The League undermined national principles, argued Republican Senator William E. Borah. If the treaty were passed, America would surrender 'once and for all, the great policy of "no entangling alliances" upon which the strength of this Republic has been founded for 150 years'. Besides, the treaty conflicted 'with the right of our people to govern themselves free from all restraint, legal or moral, of foreign powers'. The concept of collective security that reassured Wilson outraged others who saw it as a challenge to American independence.

Critics called for changes in the League's charter. Wilson refused to bend and toured the nation promoting the Treaty and the League. Exhausted by his grueling schedule, he returned to Washington and suffered a massive stroke on 2 October 1919. He remained incapacitated for the final year and a half of his presidency – and more adamantly opposed to compromises on the treaty. In November, the Versailles agreement went down to defeat in the Senate. The United States eventually signed separate peace treaties with Germany, Austria, and Hungary in 1921.

The Great War revealed civilization's shocking capacity for inhumanity and left Americans pessimistic about the possibilities for rational, moral conduct in world affairs. Over 10 million people lay dead and another 20 million wounded. Peace talks revealed deep divisions among victorious Allies. The settlement generated deep hostility in Germany, fueling a sense of resentment and unjust punishment that Hitler later exploited. Talk of self-determination stirred nationalist leaders such as Ho Chi Minh and Mohandas K. Gandhi. Domestic debates over the League of Nations reinforced US commitments to a unilateral rather than a multilateral foreign policy, and the concluding acts of war and peace sowed the seeds of distrust between the Soviet Union and the West. Angered at Lenin for pulling out of the war, the Allies, including the United States, barred his government from peace talks and even invaded his nation with a joint military force in 1918 to support counter-revolutionaries. Western troops remained in the USSR until 1920.

The end of war produced a realignment of tensions, not their elimination. Wilson led the nation into war guided by Progressive aspirations. Unable to refashion the world in its own image and unable to achieve its own social goals, post-war America scrutinized both its ties with other nations and its informing principles of Progressivism. The appeal for a return to 'normalcy' would hold greater attraction than the clarion call for collective engagement.

CHAPTER ELEVEN

Economic Prosperity and Peril, 1920–1941

After the reform vigor and military horror of the century's first decades, Americans pulled back to a state of 'normalcy'. In practical terms, that meant reducing Progressive projects and expanding business activity. But the retreat from social engagement was tentative, largely because economic advance was so shallow. After markets collapsed at the end of the 1920s, the door to reform opened again in the 1930s. The result was the creation of a new 'norm' for America, one based on an unprecedented expansion of the federal government.

The Political Turn from Progressivism in the 1920s

Woodrow Wilson wanted the 1920 election to serve as 'a great and solemn referendum' on the peace treaty. The final tallies suggested a rejection rather than an affirmation of Wilsonian idealism. Republicans regained control of the federal government. The new president, Warren G. Harding, urged voters to step back from both international obligations and Progressive engagement. He announced

> 'America's present need is not heroics, but healing; not nostrums, but normalcy; not revolution, but restoration; not agitation, but adjustment; not surgery, but serenity; not the dramatic, but the dispassionate; not experiment, but equipoise; not submergence in internationality but sustainment in triumphant nationality.'

From 1921–1933, Republicans controlled the White House, first under Harding (until his death in 1923), then Calvin Coolidge, and finally Herbert Hoover. Except for a Democratic win in the House in

1930, Republicans also controlled Congress. And Republicans made eight appointments to the Supreme Court. While not renouncing 'progress', the party took a different route to that goal, requiring, as Harding might have said, not transformation but stability.

The Republican presidents were three very different personalities. Harding was a handsome, well-liked individual given to drink and dalliance who was limited both by his mediocre talents and his shady friends, three of whom brought scandal to executive agencies. Coolidge was a morally upright New England Puritan, so withdrawn in appearance that some speculated he had been weaned on a pickle, and so 'retiring' that he spent fully half of each day asleep. Hoover was an energetic, respected engineer and administrator who headed the wartime Food Administration and served as Secretary of Commerce for Harding and Coolidge.

However great the contrast in their traits, the presidents shared similar ideas about the proper course of government; Republicans challenged the collective principles of Progressivism. Hoover, the most reflective of the three, literally wrote the book on *American Individualism* in 1922. He contended that national greatness sprang from singular efforts. The American system rested on the notion that 'only through ordered liberty, freedom, and equal opportunity to the individual will his initiative and enterprise spur on the march of progress'.

Republicans also challenged Progressive notions of government intervention. Public agencies should not routinely remedy social problems, Harding argued, because 'all human ills are not curable by legislation'. A surfeit of statutes was 'no substitute for quality of citizenship'. Curiously anticipating John F. Kennedy's inaugural call four decades later, Harding asked for a political system in which 'a citizenship seeks what it may do for the government and country rather than what the country may do for individuals'. Coolidge also spoke against an over-reliance on government direction, arguing that 'industry, thrift, character, cannot be conferred by act or resolve. Government cannot relieve from toil'.

Republicans rejected Progressive demands that federal agencies defend the public interest against private interest. Hoover emphasized the *mutual* interests that tied public and private sectors together and explored how the government might assist rather than restrain business. His Commerce Department promoted 'associationalism'. Intent on improving market efficiency and order, Hoover believed that government should provide reliable economic statistics, show firms how to streamline their operations, help with foreign markets, and endorse co-operative business ventures. After all, as Coolidge remarked in 1925, 'the business of America is business'.

Republicans also disputed Progressive notions of an activist presidency. The chief executives of the 1920s did not vigorously lead national crusades or appeal to the public over the heads of other federal branches. Rather, they relied on guidance from their cabinets and allowed Republican Congresses to define legislative programs. Harding and Coolidge in particular tended to delegate rather than exercise power. The taciturn manner of 'Silent' Cal was, in that respect, less a

President Coolidge opens the 1924 Professional Baseball Season

national joke than an ironic 'performance' of a Republican political principle.

Promoting individualism, minimalism, and decentralization, the administrations revived Jeffersonian notions that that government is best which governs least. Domestically, Republicans contained federal spending, produced budget surpluses, trimmed the debt, lowered tax rates, reduced government regulation, and accepted corporate consolidation. Diplomatically, the administrations emulated the Jeffersonian conduct of foreign affairs through non-military means with little government direction. Harding hoped to rescue the United States both from 'the fevered delirium of war' and the 'divisionary and fruitless pursuit of peace through super government'. Republicans emphasized pacific and commercial measures. The administrations stayed out of the League of Nations, sponsored a 1921 conference to reduce naval arms, forged the 1928 Kellogg-Briand Pact to renounce war as an instrument of international policy, expanded markets abroad, raised tariffs, and pressed the Allies to repay the debts they owed America from the Great War.

Invoking familiar old political themes, Republicans held true to Harding's campaign promise of a 'return'; but culturally and economically, the nation was anything but 'normal'.

The Cultural Contradictions of the 1920s

In popular legend, Americans during the 'Roaring Twenties' defied convention by giving in to novel ideas and uninhibited indulgence. But the iconoclastic, unfettered, and secular trends embraced by some met with opposition from others repelled by the excesses and dangers of 'modernism.' The decade produced movements of both change and resistance.

World war sparked a crisis of confidence in the inevitability of progress. Many thinkers adopted a more skeptical pose suggested by the postulates of contemporary science, accepting principles of uncertainty in experience, the persistence of the irrational in human psychology, the relative (rather than absolute) nature of truth, and the perceived (rather than actual) nature of order. American literature expressed this sense of failed dreams and collective folly.

The despairing, questioning nature of post-war literature revealed itself in the work of several writers who left the United States to gain a perspective on their culture. Ezra Pound, T. S. Eliot, Ernest Hemingway, Katherine Anne Porter, John Dos Passos, Edna St. Vincent Millay, and others were members of what Gertrude Stein dubbed 'the lost generation'. Hemingway and Pound in particular turned a critical eye on literary conventions and turned their backs on the verbose, ornate, and didactic style of the late nineteenth century. A spare, elemental form of writing seemed appropriate for a world where noble ideals and grand structures of thought had collapsed. The expatriates' writing reflected a sense of loss and disorientation. Eliot's *The Waste Land* (1922) resonated with themes of desolation and ruin: 'What are the roots that clutch, what branches grow/Out of this stony rubbish?' Hemingway's *The Sun Also Rises* (1926) and *A Farewell to Arms* (1929) offered a stinging inspection of lives wounded by the war. As the narrator of the latter work observed, 'the things that were glorious had no glory and the sacrifices were like the stockyards of Chicago...'

While some writers grew disillusioned by the collapse of old axioms, others felt disenchanted by the rise of new obsessions. In *Tales of the Jazz Age* (1922), F. Scott Fitzgerald reflected on post-war prosperity: 'Never had there been such splendor in the great city, for the victorious war had brought plenty in its train.' His fiction explored the feverish pursuit of material well-being and luxurious excess, particularly in *The Great Gatsby* (1925). Describing the rise of a self-made man, Fitzgerald examined how the new wealth drained individual vitality and spirit. Unlike Eliot's image of a devastated world, the 'waste land' Fitzgerald created in *Gatsby* was a landfill, the decaying product of abundance rather than destruction.

Others envisioned a different type of barrenness, especially in small-town America. Sinclair Lewis's *Main Street* (1920) and *Babbitt* (1922), Sherwood Anderson's *Winesburg, Ohio* (1919), and H. L. Mencken's work in *The American Mercury* described smug complacency, mean-spirited narrowness, and thwarted dreams beneath the calm surface of the nation's heartland. As Anderson wrote of a character in *Winesburg*, 'a great restlessness was in her ... there was an uneasy desire for change, for some big definite movement to her life'. William Faulkner captured

F. Scott Fitzgerald

the interior dramas of the rural South. Beginning with *Sartoris* and *The Sound and the Fury* (1929), he created a series of works set in the fictional Yoknapatawpha County. With evocative imagery and narrative experimentation, Faulkner infused a simple Mississippi community with profound psychological complexity. His mythic characters struggled through a mass of family conflicts, class divisions, historical legacies, and racial tensions.

The 1920s also witnessed a flowering of African-American expression. In fiction and criticism, in anthologies such as *The New Negro*, and in journals such as *The Crisis*, participants in the 'Harlem Renaissance' explored the history and culture of blacks in America. Claude McKay examined African-American life in the North in *Home to Harlem* (1925). Jean Toomer's *Cane* (1923) contrasted Northern, urban blacks with Southern, rural communities. Zora Neale Hurston brought her anthropological study of African-American folkways to literature. Pulled from simple, rural roots to an urban, academic life, she felt 'like a brown bag of miscellany propped against a wall. Against a wall in company with other bags, white, red, and yellow.' Langston Hughes celebrated black identity in poetry that often challenged conventions of form and voice. 'The Negro Speaks of Rivers' (1920) offered a solemn summation of black heritage; 'The Weary Blues' (1923) provided a melancholy tone poem on suffering and endurance.

Black performers also expanded on America's original, indigenous contribution to music: jazz. Rooted in African-American musical forms such as spirituals, ragtime, and blues, jazz pieces often started with a steady rhythm and straightforward melody – before the real work began. Players moved the sound they had laid down in unexpected directions, shifting off the anticipated beat in a syncopated style, diverting from a lyrical path through 'scat', or extending a musical line to extremes. The key to jazz was its individualized, unpredictable improvisation on musical themes. Artists such as Jelly Roll Morton, Louis Armstrong, Fletcher Henderson, Duke Ellington, and Bessie Smith made music filled with surprise, discovery, and innovation.

While experimentation, invention, and challenge marked some forms of American expression, popular culture became more standardized. A wide variety of local customs still distinguished different regions of the country, but a more homogenous, *national* set of styles, vocabularies, and values spread across the United States. Mass culture developed with the rise of entertainment 'industries' that shaped the reading, listening, and viewing habits of Americans.

The 1920s witnessed a surge in 'mass circulation' magazines such as *The Saturday Evening Post*, *Good Housekeeping*, and *Collier's Weekly*, all of which spoke to readers in a steady, predictable editorial voice. A new venture called the 'Book-of-the-Month Club' helped shape national reading habits by spotlighting a particular literary work mailed to subscribers throughout the country. Members knew that their reading material was not peculiar but popular; the same sets of books rested on millions of bedside tables all over the nation.

Once people put the same novels down, they could turn to other uniform types of national entertainment. Commercial radio began in 1920, and by the second half of the decade the first 'networks' formed. The National Broadcasting Company (1926) and the Columbia Broadcasting System (1927) distributed fixed packages of programs to affiliates in every part of the country, providing listeners with a consistent, standardized mix of music, drama, comedy, and news.

When Americans left their homes for other forms of entertainment, one of the most popular destinations was the local movie theater. Viewers gazed at films produced by the 'dream factories' of America's motion picture industry. Film production centered in southern California while financing centered in New York City. Large studios made most of the films shown in the United States and also owned chains of theaters in which the movies played. The studios developed a 'star' system in which popular performers contracted with a firm and appeared in predictable 'vehicles' for their talent. High box office receipts grew even more with the addition of sound, an innovation that began with *The Jazz Singer* in 1927 when audiences heard Al Jolson say 'You ain't heard nothing yet'. By the close of the decade, the weekly audience for motion pictures in the United States was roughly equal to the nation's total population.

The novel and homogenous products of the 'mass media' did not entertain everyone. Eager acceptance by some played out against fear and resentment by others who hoped to restrain modern forces that insidiously undermined stable, traditional local values.

Some pinned the blame for the nation's presumed disorder and decay on 'un-American' groups. Supporters of 'nativist' causes assumed that those outside the mainstream of white, rural, native-born, Protestant America had imposed an alien system of values on the rest of the nation. True '100 per cent' Americans needed to contain the foreign threat and take back control of their society. Nativist sentiment stirred during the 1920–21 trial of two Italian immigrant anarchists, Nicola Sacco and Bartolomeo Vanzetti, convicted and later executed for murder and robbery. Nativist fears also escalated with the 1928 presidential campaign of Democrat Al Smith, an Irishman, from an immigrant family, raised in New York City, experienced in Tammany Hall politics, and, most alarming of all, a Roman Catholic.

A *legal* nativist effort, wrapped in the raiment of legislation, involved immigration restriction. The 1924 National Origins Act excluded East Asian immigrants from entry into the United States and set a quota on new immigration from southern and eastern Europe based on the 1890 census – taken before large numbers of Italians, Jews, and Slavs had entered the country. An *extra*-legal nativist campaign, wrapped in the garb of white robes and pointed hoods, involved the resurgence of the Ku Klux Klan. Weakened since the 1870s, the Klan came back to life in Georgia in 1915, the year D. W. Griffith released *The Birth of a Nation*, a film that celebrated the group's legacy. Klan members lashed out at Jews, Catholics, and immigrants, not just African Americans – and won support in the North and urban centers, not just the rural South. With a base of four million members by the mid-20s, prominent Klan leaders themselves fell victim to the temptations of sex and money that the organization so harshly condemned in modern society. The resulting scandals reduced the organization's size and appeal.

Campaigns to control America's habits accompanied efforts to shape its society. In January 1920, the Eighteenth Amendment prohibited the manufacture, distribution, and sale – but not the private consumption – of alcoholic beverages. Prohibition offered largely rural, native-born, Protestant 'dry' Americans a way of defending their cultural turf from the encroachments of largely urban, immigrant, Catholic 'wet' Americans. Prohibition was also one of the most visible legacies of Progressivism in the 1920s: the 'noble experiment' aimed at managing the socially dangerous and economically inefficient effects of drink.

Progressive in its lineage, Prohibition was Republican in its management. Minimalist-minded federal officials never provided sufficient funds to enforce the law. While alcohol consumption dropped, violations of the law increased. A liquor industry that was previously above-board came to be dominated by the underworld. Gangs of hoodlums expanded their pursuits into bootlegging, 'rationalizing' their activity along the lines of big business by consolidating operations, controlling the market, and literally killing off the competition through the development of 'organized' crime. Prohibition's unanticipated consequences led to its repeal when Democrats regained power in 1933.

Alongside other challenges to 'modern' forces, the 1920s witnessed the rise of 'fundamentalism', a militantly conservative branch of Protestantism that rejected liberal theology and tried to reorder a spiritually bankrupt society. Followers opposed reforms like that of the Social

Gospel which tried to reconcile traditional doctrine with the social and economic realities of the day. Fundamentalists insisted that the world had to conform to Scripture rather than forcing Scripture to conform to the world. The symbolic heart of the movement involved Darwinian theories of evolution, which fundamentalists saw as a denial of divine creation and Biblical inerrancy. Several Southern states forbade schools to teach evolution. A 1925 test case involving a Tennessee instructor, John T. Scopes, received national attention. The so-called 'Monkey Trial' offered an emotional, often circus-like debate on scientific versus religious principles. The legal proceedings in a hot, Tennessee courtroom embodied the cultural conflicts of a nation hurled into modernity while clinging to the security of the past.

Economic Rise

Known as a 'boom' time, the 1920s got off to a rough start. As post-war government spending dropped and overseas demand for US goods eased, the market slipped into a recession from 1920–1921. But by 1922, recovery was under way – and the economy took off.

The nation enjoyed considerable prosperity, marked by a rise in per capita income, steady productivity gains, a 40 per cent jump in gross national product, and the highest standard of living in the world, all accompanied by low unemployment, low inflation, and low interest rates. Consumer industries were particularly successful. Corporations applied the industrial know-how perfected at the turn of the century for 'capital goods' to the production of items aimed at the average person. The spark, so to speak, came from the expansion of electric power. By the end of the 1920s, most homes and industries ran on electricity. Wired Americans bought up the radios, refrigerators, washing machines, and vacuum cleaners that electrified factories churned out.

Consumer industries participated in another trend of the 1920s: corporate consolidation. The decade saw a merger wave rivaling that of the 1890s. Big businesses became bigger, led by firms such as General Motors, Chrysler, General Electric, Westinghouse, and US Rubber. As companies sold more products, controlled more markets, and made more profits, they expanded their manufacturing capacity even further to make a greater number of goods that they fully expected future consumers would buy. During the decade, the United States also became the world's largest creditor nation, with net credits rising by 58 per cent. Those who read the signals right reaped handsome rewards in the stock market, whose major indexes quadrupled from 1924 to 1929.

At the center of the economy stood the product that literally and figuratively drove the nation: the automobile. With greater efficiencies in production, cars became more affordable. At a time when the average industrial worker earned $1,300 a year, Ford's basic automobile cost less than $300. A toy of the rich became a possession of the many. In the 1920s, the number of cars in the United States increased by 250 per cent and by 1929, there were 26 million automobiles for 120 million people.

The car was the icon of the market and the culture; no consumer item had greater importance. One in 12 workers held jobs tied to the automobile industry. Car sales boosted production in steel, petroleum, chemicals, glass, and rubber. Higher car registrations also spurred highway construction. With legislation in 1916, 1921, and 1925, national and state governments created a network of linked, numbered roads identified by familiar black and white shields. One of the most famous, Route 66, ran, in the words of a popular song, 'from Chicago to L.A./over two thousand miles all the way'. By 1929, the government had built over 250,000 miles of modern highways, one and a half times more roadway than existed 20 years earlier.

Easy, rapid movement along new roads only added to the mystique of the car. In a society without a frontier, the open road offered an escape from other people and growing cities. In a culture increasingly standardized, homogenized, and predictable, the car gave new meaning to personal freedom and mobility. In a flamboyant era testing out the limits of permissible behavior, the privacy and intimacy of a car's interior rewrote the book on courtship.

Car sales also changed the rules of marketing. While Henry Ford cranked out lots of plain, black boxes on wheels at a low cost, his competitors at General Motors (GM) came up with a more colorful array of automotive products sold in a wholly new way. GM developed a diverse line of cars in different price ranges and introduced yearly model changes to keep enticing customers back into the showroom. GM not only manufactured cars; it manufactured the allure to keep individuals buying cars. Beyond satisfying needs, automobile companies and other industries in the 1920s shaped wants – or more precisely, the need to want. Big business created both consumer goods and a consumer culture; they surrounded Americans with appeals to buy, to buy more, and to keep buying. It became the paramount duty of citizens to consume the goods that the nation's economic machine produced; their purchases kept the new economy humming.

Of course, individuals might resist such messages and succumb to a bunch of tired old platitudes about frugality and simplicity. They might actually save their hard-earned money rather than part with it on a regular basis. Modern advertising could help break them of their backward habits. Advertising expenditures doubled during the 1920s, with campaigns that urged the public to submit to (rather than defer) personal gratification. And for those who whined that they did not have the cash to buy consumer goodies, installment purchase plans took away their last remaining flimsy excuse. Once used for extraordinary purchases, consumer credit became the popular way to buy popular items. Most cars, refrigerators, and even radios sold in the United States in the late 1920s were bought on installment plans. Consumer debt more than tripled in the decade, and the consumer credit industry became one of America's largest businesses.

Purchases were made painless, systematic, and predictable. Consuming became a habit: the more people fed it, the larger the economy grew. Some believed the United States had finally found its way out of catastrophic market swings. The dream of permanent growth seemed within reach.

Economic Fall

Unfortunately, a new nightmare was about to start, one that created the worst market calamity in the republic's history. The economy took a frightening four-year plunge from 1929–1933 and remained a wreck for the rest of the decade as the nation experienced the Great

Depression. How could something so disastrous come out of a market that seemed so promising? The answer is that the prosperity of the 1920s rested on a flawed economic base. The structure of the economy could not sustain the kind of expansion that business leaders and the public expected. The good times simply could not last.

The key problems were overproduction and underconsumption. The number of buyers for manufactured goods had just about peaked by the late 1920s. A consumer economy that rested on ever-expanding sales ran into a roadblock: there were not enough consumers. By 1927 and 1928, durable goods sales and construction starts began to level off and drop. It was not that Americans had had enough of material acquisition and suddenly went ascetic. Rather, too many individuals simply could not afford to buy more consumer goods.

The difficulties stemmed from income distribution and income growth. Throughout the decade, money concentrated in the hands of fewer people. By 1929, the top 1 per cent held almost one-sixth of all wealth; the top 5 per cent held one-quarter; the bottom 60 per cent divided up less than a quarter of national wealth. Two-thirds of American families did not earn enough to afford common necessities and simple comforts; the public simply did not have much money at its 'disposal'. Corporate gains in productivity and profits doubled or tripled the rate of increases in real wages. Industry geared up to produce more goods, but customers slowed their purchases. As inventories mounted, production fell. As production fell, layoffs rose. As layoffs rose, more workers were left without a paycheck and consumer demand declined even further.

Weakness in other parts of the economy only compounded income problems. Coal, railroads, and textiles did not share in the tremendous growth and profitability of the decade. Organized labor's ranks dropped by nearly 30 per cent. Banks faced instability with the failure of over 5,000 institutions in the 1920s. The worst sector was agriculture, stuck in recession since 1921. Farmers plowed wartime profits into more land and equipment, calculating that future sales would offset their heavier debts. But prices plummeted at the start of the decade and never fully recovered, leaving farmers in desperate straits. They were not alone. Internationally, the United States called for the repayment of war debts while also putting higher tariffs on European products. Continental trading partners had trouble coming up with the cash that Americans demanded – and trimmed their purchases of US goods. European nations 'solved' their problem by borrowing even more, digging themselves deeper into debt and becoming more dependent on American credit.

Many were left out of the prosperity of the period, but *some* people made lots of money. Unfortunately, the places where the wealthy spent their ill-gotten gains did not do much good for the broader economy. Sales of big-ticket, luxury items had little effect on overall demand in consumer industries. More troubling, however, was the money that went into speculation.

In the early 1920s, investors bought into the stock market on the plausible expectation that economic growth would translate into higher company profits and share prices. The cost of shares was reasonable relative to the earnings of companies, and the returns were handsome. From 1924 to 1929, the *New York Times* index of industrial stocks increased from 106 to 452, the volume of shares traded on the New York Stock Exchange ballooned four and a half times, and the total market value of stocks tripled between 1925 and 1929. Investors could get in on the action with as little as 10 per cent down; the rest came from expensive loans provided by brokers, who used the shares as collateral. Between 1926 and 1929, brokers' loans increased from $3.5 to $8.5 billion (at a time when the federal government spent about $3 billion per year).

By 1927 and 1928, stock prices bore little relation to business performance. Increasingly, buyers purchased equities, not as sound economic investments, but as wild speculative gambles, betting that what had gone up would keep going up. Wall Street became a wide-open casino, and a largely unregulated one at that. The federal government did little to monitor the activities of a market that absorbed so much attention and capital. In fact, the government probably made matters worse by easing credit and lowering tax rates, releasing more money into speculation.

By the autumn of 1929, the consumption that fueled prosperity had declined and key sectors of the economy barely limped along. In a weakened state, the Wall Street house of cards began to collapse; a series of falls took place. On 28 and 29 October, major indices lost a quarter of their value. Efforts to shore up the market failed, and the tumble in prices continued. General Electric (GE), which sold for nearly $400 per share in September, went for $168 in November. The collapse in prices continued for months and years and in 1932, shares of GE went for as little as $34. At its lowest depth in 1933, the Dow Jones industrial index had fallen 83 per cent, from 365 down to 63.

THE SCOPE OF THE DEPRESSION

The stock market crash of 1929 did not 'cause' the Depression. Rather, the collapse on Wall Street sprang from, and aggravated, the structural problems of America's 'boom' economy. A sounder, more balanced economy might have weathered the storm of 1929 a bit better, but an economy so flawed and uneven simply began to unravel.

The market crash wiped out capital and destroyed confidence. Stocks valued at $87 billion in 1929 were worth only $18 billion in 1932. Less than 1 per cent of the population held stocks, but the effects of the crash were widely felt. As prices collapsed, investors defaulted on loans to brokers; brokers, holding fairly worthless stocks as collateral, defaulted on loans to bankers; bankers lost the money they loaned to brokers as well as the funds they invested in the market. Strapped for cash, nearly 5,800 banks (with $3.5 billion in deposits) failed between 1929 and 1932. People who had never invested a dime in the stock market lost their savings. The banks that survived cut back available credit, and consumers reduced their purchases. Unable to raise money through bank loans or stock offerings and unable to sell their goods to customers, businesses tightened their belts, leading to more cutbacks, layoffs, and retrenchment. When the Federal Reserve Board responded by tightening (rather than loosening) credit, the crisis grew worse. The economy just kept sinking.

The collapse was unprecedented. From 1929–1933, the gross national product fell 46 per cent, the consumer price index dropped 25 per cent, and the wholesale price index tumbled 32 per cent. Farmers suffered even more: agricultural prices fell 60 per cent. A full quarter of the labor force was out of work by 1933 and unemployment did not return to pre-crash levels until 1942. A steady, unrelenting, and broad-based decline hit the economy. The horror of the Depression was not so much its length (which no one could accurately forecast) but its depth (which was visible to most Americans).

PRESIDENT HOOVER'S RESPONSE

Hoover had been in office only eight months when the market collapsed. In public opinion, he became vilified as cold, passive, and unresponsive. In fact, he took the federal government further than it had ever gone before in dealing with an economic catastrophe. He did act, but not as aggressively and continuously as possible.

Unlike his predecessors, Hoover did not view the depression as a 'natural' phenomenon which, like a bad cold, simply had to run its course. Unlike traditional theorists, he did not assume government intervention would worsen the situation. And unlike his Treasury Secretary, Andrew Mellon, Hoover did not believe that more failures would solve the depression. Mellon, picturing the collapse in Darwinian terms, claimed it would 'purge the rottenness out of the system' and give people an incentive to 'work harder, live a more moral life ... and enterprising people will pick up the wrecks from less competent people'. Hoover wanted to support moral duty, but not by compounding economic calamity.

Instead, Hoover was the first president to argue that the federal government had a responsibility to intervene in an economic emergency. He delivered reassuring (but ultimately incorrect) reports that recovery was just around the corner. He convened conferences with business and labor leaders, asking (but not ordering) that industries maintain jobs, wages, and production and that workers defer pay rises. He encouraged local government to support public building projects. The White House coordinated assistance efforts by private charities. Hoover tried to calm European fears by declaring a one-year moratorium on war debts and reparations payments. In all of these actions, the president took an active role in the economy but maintained his commitments to voluntarism, localism, decentralization, and international stability.

Hoover also took tentative steps in other directions. He proposed a large increase in funding for national public works projects, and supported a measure to protect homeowners from foreclosure. The federal government bought up farm surpluses (but did not limit production), and Hoover agreed to the creation of the $2 billion Reconstruction Finance Corporation that provided loans to banks and businesses (and later to local governments).

Hoover would go no further, however. Recalling the 1920–1921 recession, he believed the downturn would end soon without requiring an expansion of federal powers. Fearing an un-balanced budget, he objected to large-scale deficit spending. Dreading the moral and social effects of the 'dole', he rejected direct relief through federal 'handouts' to the unemployed. Revering private enterprise, he disapproved federal ownership, control, or management of the economy. Hoover assumed that as government control over the market expanded, individual freedom shrank. To preserve liberty, he could do no more against an economic collapse.

Others cared less for the fine points of political theory. The homeless sarcastically called their shantytowns 'Hoovervilles' and their open, empty pockets 'Hoover flags'. Farmers disrupted legal proceedings to stop foreclosures and dumped, burned, or held back agricultural products in an effort to stabilize prices. In the spring of 1932, 15,000 veterans of the Great War gathered in Washington asking for immediate payment of a military bonus scheduled for 1945. The 'Bonus Army' set up tents and shacks on the outskirts of the city. In late July, an impatient General Douglas MacArthur, sensing 'revolution' in the air, exceeded presidential orders and ousted the protesters from their encampment. Images of young soldiers attacking old soldiers appeared in papers, symbolizing for many the indifference of their government, and their president, to the suffering of common folk. Americans went to the polls a few months later, throwing out a party that had given them a raw deal and bringing in a party promising a new deal.

PRESIDENT ROOSEVELT'S RESPONSE

In terms of background, connections, experience, and personality, Franklin Delano Roosevelt was a formidable political force. Born to wealth and privilege in a distinguished New York clan, his distant cousin was Theodore Roosevelt, and his wife was TR's niece. He served as a New York State legislator, Wilson's assistant secretary of the navy, the Democratic Party's 1920 vice-presidential candidate, and governor of New York in 1928 and 1930. Stricken with polio in 1921, he rebuilt his strength, plunged back into public life, and remained an optimistic, energetic leader of his party and nation. Eyeing the White House, he surrounded himself with academics and professionals who served as an advisory 'brains trust'. In the summer of 1932, he received his party's nomination for president.

Hoover and Roosevelt were both committed to a balanced budget; neither had a well-conceived master plan for responding to the Depression; but on issues that caused Hoover to hesitate or bristle, Roosevelt forged ahead. As Governor, he promoted unemployment relief, public works, tougher child labor laws, pensions for the elderly, and union protection. Roosevelt exhibited a flare for action in place of Hoover's penchant for reflection.

Yet, during the 1932 campaign, it was difficult at times to tell where Roosevelt thought Hoover had gone wrong. Democrats lambasted the Republicans for their excessive spending, irresponsible budgets, and centralization of power; but Roosevelt's party called for centralized economic planning, large public works projects, relief for the unemployed, and 'distributing wealth and products more equitably'. There was one clear choice offered to voters, however: the Democrats wanted to drop prohibition.

Roosevelt received 57 per cent of the popular vote and 89 per cent of the electoral vote. Socialists, Communists, Prohibitionists, and others received 3 per cent of the popular vote. Even in the depths of economic crisis, Americans endorsed reformist rather than radical proposals.

The types of reforms they would experience were still up in the air. Roosevelt's responses to the Depression were jumbled and disjointed. Yet considering how poorly the economy fared under Hoover's rigid and coherent ideology, there was something to be said for flexibility and improvisation. In fairness, the new administration maintained some consistent standards for dealing with the Depression. Roosevelt was experimental and pragmatic, concerned less with abstract truths than with practical consequences, and his administration tackled economic problems by a combination of programs aimed at recovery, relief, and reform. The *strategies* for attaining these goals and the *scope* of the measures would change over time.

The First New Deal, 1933–1935

Historians often divide Roosevelt's programs into a 'First' and 'Second' New Deal. From 1933 to 1935, Roosevelt tried to take decisive action to stem national despair and halt further decline. The administration propped up weak institutions, assisted different sectors of the economy, emphasized co-operative action within the private sector, and experimented with centralized planning. Beginning in 1935, with mounting criticism from the right and left – and mounting concern about the 1936 election – the administration took a turn to the left, moving away from co-operative efforts and pushing towards greater federal power and responsibility.

The 'First' New Deal began with a flurry of legislative activity in the spring of 1933. Roosevelt's attention turned initially to the panicked banking and finance industry. After delivering an inaugural address that asserted 'the only thing we have to fear is fear itself', Roosevelt tried to ease public anxiety, not by nationalizing banks but by vouching for their soundness through federal regulation. A 'bank holiday' closed savings institutions for four days. Healthy banks reopened; weak institutions underwent reorganization under federal supervision. Bank failures plummeted, deposits rose, and financial confidence returned. The administration later passed legislation to insure deposits, halt speculative practices by bankers, regulate corporate securities, monitor the stock market, and take the United States off the gold standard.

A second group of measures helped relief agencies and created jobs. The Federal Emergency Relief Administration pumped $500 million in direct grants (rather than loans) to state and local governments. The Civilian Conservation Corps employed young men in forest, water, and soil projects. The short-lived Civil Works Administration provided federal jobs for four million people. The longer-term Public Works Administration built roads, bridges, tunnels, hospitals, housing, schools, courthouses, aircraft carriers, and other massive projects, 'priming the pump' of the economy through the agency's large-scale purchases and its huge payroll.

Another set of programs attacked agricultural problems. To manage the price and supply of farm goods, the Agricultural Adjustment Act (AAA) paid farmers to limit cultivation and slash production. To protect farms, the Farm Credit Act helped refinance mortgages on lands and homes. The measures represented a major change in American agriculture. Farmers who could not control production through individual or cooperative efforts accepted the direct and continuous management of the federal government to do the job. Down on the old Jeffersonian farm, the central government set up shop defining some of the basic conditions of agricultural life.

A fourth program focused on industry. The administration feared that individual businesses might try to cover themselves – and worsen the Depression – by shifting production schedules, cutting wages, firing workers, and slashing prices. The National Industrial Recovery Act (1933) (NIRA) brought delegates from different industries together to draw up 'codes of fair competition'. Business leaders helped to set maximum production schedules and minimum wages and hours; the National Recovery Administration (NRA) monitored the program. To some, the arrangement seemed an over cozy boon to big business, but the administration believed the benefits of large-scale corporations – in efficiency, distribution, employment, and pricing – outweighed the risks, especially at a time of nationwide economic emergency. Roosevelt was willing to trust the 'trusts', accepting the *cooperative* efforts and *voluntary* compliance of business.

Just in case the confidence was misplaced, the legislation provided for the creation of government-sector jobs. The act also helped organized labor. Section 7(a) of the NIRA stated that 'employees shall have the right to organize and bargain collectively through representatives of their own choosing'. Although the automobile and steel industries proved tough nuts to crack, overall union membership jumped from 3 to 4.5 million in just two years. Before Roosevelt entered the White House, less than 12 per cent of the nation's labor force was unionized. When he died in 1945, the figure increased to 35.5 per cent. While allowing businesses to protect their interests in an economic emergency, Roosevelt felt that labor organizations would help workers guard their interests as well.

Congress also combined public works, conservation, recovery, and pump-priming with one other project: regional planning. The Tennessee Valley Authority (TVA) aimed at controlling the destructiveness of the Tennessee River while providing power, plenty, and a new way of life for residents of its seven-state valley – all under the direction of the federal government. The TVA constructed dams and electric plants, provided cheap power, promoted land conservation, produced fertilizers, encouraged agricultural and industrial development, and even provided educational, recreational, and public health facilities. It sought to transform an area of the country ravaged by natural catastrophes and economic hardship. The TVA was a laboratory in which the federal government tinkered with markets and re-engineered a society.

The federal government had, of course, already tried its hand at social experimentation – in the 1800s with Native Americans. Roosevelt's advisors tried to reform the work earlier administrations had botched so badly. One change was already in place: in 1924, Congress conferred citizenship on Indians born in the United States. A decade later, Commissioner of Indian Affairs John Collier sponsored the Indian Reorganization Act. Economically, the measure stopped the policy of allotment by restoring control of lands to tribes and providing funds to buy back lands lost in the previous half century. Politically, the act challenged traditions of subjugation by calling for the reestablishment of tribal governments under constitutions that federal authorities would recognize. Culturally, the new law reversed the policy of forced assimilation by promoting the study, preservation, and development of Indian culture.

The recovery and reform efforts of the First New Deal ran into many problems. Some agencies dispensed money slowly. Some hurt the interests of small businesses, small farmers, and sharecroppers. Others ran up against the Constitutional objections of the Supreme Court. Most importantly, the economy gained little strength. Bank failures declined, and the precipitous plunge in employment, wages, and prices finally stopped. But all three rates stayed far below pre-crash levels.

Even nature seemed to conspire against recovery when, in 1931, the rains stopped falling regularly in the southern plains. A severe drought, high winds, and intense heat ravaged parts of Kansas, Oklahoma, Colorado, New Mexico, and Texas, creating a 'Dust Bowl' that lasted throughout the decade. The expansion of agriculture in the fragile area had, as Donald Worster notes, upset the region's delicate balance. The 'Dust Bowl' encompassed 50 million acres of land, almost half of which lost at least two inches of topsoil.[1] Hundreds of thousands left the area in search of a better life. John Steinbeck passionately told their story in *The Grapes of Wrath* (1939). John Ford's film adaptation added a visual depth to the tale of the Joad family on their trek from the scorched Plains to the promised land of California.

The New Deal was buffeted not only by nature but also by a wide

Migrant mother
After 1936 photograph by Dorothea Lange

range of critics. Foes on the right denounced policies of centralization and socialism. Opponents on the left called for radical changes in the capitalist system. And popular movements from across the political spectrum devised schemes to boost consumption and guarantee incomes – or simply blame the nation's woes on corporate, financial, and even Jewish interests. Despite the controversies, Democrats widened their hold on Congress in the 1934 elections and pushed their reform agenda further.

The Second New Deal, 1935–1939

Roosevelt told Congress he planned to weed out the 'overprivileged,' assist the 'underprivileged,' and provide 'security' for all citizens. In a flurry of legislation known as the 'Second' New Deal, Democrats passed measures to control, uplift, and protect, launching the nation an even more ambitious program of reform and social justice.

To check the 'overprivileged,' Roosevelt increased tax rates and expanded federal regulation, enlarging its power over banks, utilities, and transportation. To help the 'underprivileged,' the administration circumvented Supreme Court rulings that had gone against the interests of laborers and farmers. One measure expanded workers' rights to unionize. Another put agricultural production limits back in place. Democrats also assisted sharecroppers and tenant farmers.

The key measure for the underprivileged was an emergency relief act. Congress funded the bill with $5 billion, a staggering sum in a nation accustomed to federal budgets of $3–4 billion a year for *all* spending. The act created the Works Progress Administration which, over eight years, at a cost of over $11 billion, put eight million people to work on federal projects that expanded the nation's infrastructure *and* supported its cultural life. Federal relief moved to a higher and broader level.

Having lifted up the underprivileged, the federal government saw to it that they did not fall down again. In an unprecedented move, Roosevelt created 'security against the major hazards of life' through the 1935 Social Security Act. One part provided 'old age insurance,' a federal plan funded by taxes on both employees and employers. A second part provided 'unemployment insurance,' a federal-state effort funded by a tax on employers. A third part provided 'benefits for children, for mothers, [and] for the handicapped.'

The legislation offered partial rather than full protection. It began rather than completed 'a structure intended to lessen the force of possible future depressions.' Despite its limits, the measure marked a sharp break from tradition in a political order – and a national culture – that idealized self-help, personal initiative, and government limits. Individuals no longer had to fall back entirely on their own resources when dealing with the 'vicissitudes of life'; the national government would step in to assist them. Social Security, FDR declared, would 'take care of human needs and at the same time provide the United States an economic structure of vastly greater soundness.'

Roosevelt won reelection in 1936 with even larger percentages of the popular and electoral votes. His party gained more seats in Congress. Victorious Democrats then moved even further to build economic security, passing bills on public housing and a minimum wage.

Having secured strongholds in the executive and legislative branches, Roosevelt set his sights on an elusive prize, the Supreme Court, a bastion of conservatism that challenged New Deal programs and threatened future policies. In Jacksonian form, Roosevelt went after a power center that seemed to defy the people's will. He proposed increasing the number of federal judges, adding one for every sitting judge over 70 years old, with a maximum of six new Supreme Court appointments. The plan was quickly condemned as a 'court-packing' scheme. FDR lost face devising a strategy that, in the end, proved unnecessary. Justices began ruling in favor of his programs; and from 1937 to 1939, Roosevelt was able to make four Court appointments.

FDR's 'courting' cost him considerable political capital. Those on the right were wary of expanded federal authority and Roosevelt's enlarged political ambitions. The President's grip on conservatives, especially Southern Democrats, weakened. The party lost seats in the 1938 election, and its internal cohesion began to break down.

Losses in 1938 resulted from other sources as well. Tightened fiscal and monetary policies led to a recession in 1937. Industrial production dropped over 33 percent; unemployment rose to 20 percent. The rise of expansionist regimes in Europe and Asia only compounded economic woes. The combination of political blunders, party infighting, economic recession, and growing world crises drained the energy out of the New Deal. The drive toward domestic reform began to sputter.

Roosevelt's programs still made two major changes in American life. First, the federal government took responsibility for intervening in the economy at all times, not just during a crisis. Its agencies would rescue, protect, shape, regulate, and stimulate the market, guaranteeing both economic performance and individual well-being. The New Deal, in other words, marked the beginning of welfare state capitalism in the US. Second, as an active player, the federal government began to figure prominently in the daily lives of citizens. Before the 1930s, federal power was largely distant and removed, barely affecting most of the day-to-day decisions people made. After the 1930s, the federal government played a greater role in a greater number of personal choices, ranging from work to housing to health to transportation to retirement. Big government became a fixture in American life.

There were limits to centralization. Private ownership remained sacrosanct. National health insurance did not materialize. *Joint* federal-state efforts underwrote unemployment insurance. And, in deference to Southern Democratic principles of 'local control,' Roosevelt did not press for significant change in civil rights. Federal job programs frequently discriminated against people of color. Public housing was usually segregated. Relief payments occasionally varied by race. And Social Security did not protect workers in many menial occupations, often the only jobs whites permitted blacks and Mexican Americans to hold. On matters of civil rights, discrimination, and equality, the administration's programs offered only incremental progress.

Roosevelt's programs kept the nation from sinking deeper into an economic quagmire, but recovery was slow, uneven, and partial. The answer to economic calamity *did* come through massive government spending and extraordinary market control. But the necessary infusion of money and extension of authority was on an order unimaginable (and unacceptable) to most in the early 1930s. The Depression finally came to a close not when the nation solved dislocations at home but when it engaged in a war abroad.

CHAPTER TWELVE

From World War to Cold War, 1941–1961

The United States was never completely 'isolationist' in foreign affairs. The nation pursued its overseas policies intensely and ambitiously, doing so with a fairly free hand, unencumbered by responsibilities to others, hesitant to step into complicated power disputes, checked by its own military weakness, and guided by what its leaders saw as high moral principles.

By the mid-twentieth century, all that remained of the traditional foreign policy was its moral certitude. The United States intervened regularly and forcefully at points around the globe; it tied its interests to those of other nations through elaborate alliances; and it commanded military forces of unprecedented size in a perpetual state of readiness. America's rise from regional to global power grew largely out of a conflict that it tried to avoid.

Foreign Policy Sentiments in the 1930s

Two themes dominated American foreign policy thinking for much of the 1930s. The first was a focus on recovery at home – not engagement overseas, not the protection of diplomatic ideals, not the uplift of other peoples. Political leaders and the general public did not even view a large-scale military build-up as a way out of the market's collapse.

The second theme was a widespread sense of disenchantment and even betrayal over US involvement in the Great War. A war that claimed such a ghastly toll for such a muddled peace seemed a dreadful error. The experience confirmed to many that America should stay out of brutal European quarrels and maintain an independent, unilateral course of action in the world. Critics on the right decried the war's tendency to expand national authority while those on the left bemoaned the war's postponement of needed reforms. Activists organized peace societies. Popular books and films, such as *All Quiet on the Western Front* (and even the Marx Brothers' anti-militaristic *Duck Soup*) portrayed the folly of war. European allies who defaulted on war debts added to the bitterness. And in the mid-30s, Senate hearings suggested (but did not prove) that self-interested bankers and munitions makers led the nation into war. A grim cynicism about international commitments pervaded American opinion. As late as the autumn of 1939, 60 per cent or more of Americans felt their nation's participation in the last war was a misguided error.

Responding to suspicions of collective security, the United States stayed out of the League of Nations. Acknowledging mutual interests in trade and Asian stability, America recognized the USSR in 1933. Hoping that free commerce might alleviate political tensions and economic distress, Roosevelt's administration promoted lower tariffs. Stepping back from direct military intervention in Latin America, Hoover and Roosevelt pursued what the latter called the 'Good Neighbor Policy' in the Western Hemisphere, expanding US economic interests and creating ties to dictatorial regimes while granting that 'no state has the right to intervene in the external or internal affairs of another'. Trying to avoid the entrapments of war, Congress passed Neutrality Acts to prohibit Americans from providing belligerents with arms (1935) or loans (1936) and requiring cash for other goods carried away on the purchasers' own vessels (1937). Pursuing an independent course, American policy tried to steer clear of unanticipated and unwanted conflicts.

The United States Edges Towards Involvement

The United States had figured out how to avoid the entanglements that led to involvement in the Great War – only to find itself drawn slowly into a new conflict. Its cautious policy of independence and non-alignment proved difficult to maintain as militaristic, nationalistic, and expansionistic governments in the Far East and Europe engaged in acts of aggression threatening peace on three continents. Japan, Italy, and Germany forcibly extended control over other societies to ensure their own economic security, to reclaim national honor, and to lay the foundation for a new order. The three powers gazed expectantly on the future, confident that a glorious military struggle would break the constraints of the recent past. The United States focused apprehensively on the past, certain that a tragic military struggle would repeat itself in the near future.

The chronicle of conquest around the world moved with increasing speed and scope. In 1931, Japan occupied Manchuria. In 1933, Adolf Hitler became chancellor of Germany. In 1935, Germany withdrew from the League of Nations and announced a program of rearmament; on 3 October, Italy attacked Ethiopia. In 1936, Germany occupied the Rhineland; civil war against the Spanish Republic erupted in July led by fascists under Francisco Franco (and soon supported by Mussolini and Hitler); and Germany and Italy agreed to the Rome-Berlin Axis Pact in October. In 1937, Japan began a full-scale war with China and signed the Anti-Comintern Pact with Italy and Germany outlining a united diplomatic front against international communism. In 1938, after announcing his plans for *Lebensraum* for the German people, Hitler annexed Austria and occupied the Sudetenland; at home, the Nazis, who had formalized anti-Semitism in law three years earlier, launched more direct persecutions of Jews, culminating in the fury of *Kristallnacht* on 9 November. In 1939, Italy moved into Albania; Hitler took the remainder of Czechoslovakia, signed a non-aggression pact with the Soviets, and, on the first of September, invaded Poland.

The principles of collective security that promised peace after 1918 failed to halt the aggression. The League's condemnations and sanctions changed nothing. While the Soviets expressed alarm at the rise of Nazi Germany, Britain and France did not respond decisively to the expansion around them. Militarily, neither nation was prepared to act boldly; diplomatically, neither was inclined to take resolute action.

The major democracy on the other side of the Atlantic was in much the same situation. Roosevelt did not have the political backing, the military force, or the legal basis to offer more than token opposition to aggression. His personal roots were in Wilsonian internationalism, but his sense of responsibility to the world paled in comparison to the commitments he felt at home in Depression America. Besides, voters did not want to see their nation dragged into another war. US defenses had weakened, and neutrality legislation did not allow the president to distinguish aggressors from victims. Roosevelt accepted the policy of appeasement that Neville Chamberlain had hailed in the autumn of 1938 as the way to bring 'peace in our time'. Yet, Roosevelt, like his counterparts in Britain and France, was troubled by armed expansion and sensed a threat to American security. He did not know where aggression would lead. He conveyed his concerns to a Congress and public that did not want to listen.

By the late 1930s, a pattern had emerged in Roosevelt's foreign policy. He stayed slightly ahead of popular opinion and cautiously nudged the public to accept the ever-more activist foreign policy he came to embrace. The process, clearer in hindsight, moved in roughly three stages.

First, from 1937 to 1938, Roosevelt accepted neutrality but urged greater preparedness. In October 1937, Japan's warfare in China served as the occasion for recommending a 'quarantine' on the 'epidemic of world lawlessness'. Trying to 'minimize our risk of involvement', Roosevelt recognized that the United States 'cannot have complete protection in a world of disorder'. In private, he denounced the 'bandits' leading Japan, Germany, and Italy. In public, he persuaded Congress in 1938 to expand military spending and aircraft production. At the year's end, a Latin America conference announced a joint commitment to protect the hemisphere from Axis aggression. Roosevelt believed the public would accept little more, especially because Britain and France had not yet taken forceful steps themselves to stop aggression.

In the next stage of his developing foreign policy, from 1939 to early 1941, Roosevelt outlined a three-part approach to international security. First, he requested military assistance for Britain and France, suggesting that, if well armed, they could stop German expansion. Secondly, he called for greater military preparedness, suggesting that a strong defense would deter threats to the United States. Thirdly, he insisted that the United States would stay out of any fighting. After the

Nazi invasion of Poland, Roosevelt, like Wilson in 1914, reaffirmed neutrality; but, unlike Wilson, he believed he could *not* 'ask that every American remain neutral in thought'. By the early autumn, a hemispheric agreement outlined a 300-mile security zone around the Americas, prohibiting belligerent ships from conducting warfare. In November, neutrality restrictions eased, allowing the United States to provide arms to Britain and France on a cash-and-carry basis. In the spring of 1940, Germany's *Blitzkrieg* into Denmark, Norway, Belgium, the Netherlands, and France prompted Roosevelt to step up military preparedness and, for the first time in American history, conduct a peacetime military draft. In September 1940, as England stood alone, the United States 'swapped' old naval destroyers for British air and naval bases.

Roosevelt's opponent in the November 1940 election, Republican Wendell Willkie, warned voters that Roosevelt would lead the nation into war. He denied the charge, defeated Willkie, and won an unprecedented third term in office. He then urged Congress to expand US military assistance even further. Since America could not extend loans to the United Kingdom for arms purchases, Roosevelt convinced Congress in March 1941 to lend or lease supplies to Britain (and China). The president's policy of supplying as much aid as possible short of war led the United States away from a stance of neutrality to a position, by mid-1940–1941, of non-belligerency.

By mid-1941, in a third set of responses, Roosevelt came to believe that overseas aid and domestic preparedness were insufficient; American participation in the war was probably necessary. US actions made the prospect all the more likely, although Roosevelt did not reveal the danger to the public. A practical problem presented itself: how would America actually get war materials to their destination? In April, Roosevelt extended US naval patrols into the hazardous North Atlantic and also passed intelligence information on to the Allies. In July 1941, after Hitler's invasion of the Soviet Union, Roosevelt placed American troops in Iceland. In August, he met with British Prime Minister Winston Churchill and drew up the 'Atlantic Charter', outlining the aims of the war and the shape of the post-war world. By September, having extended its aid, its vessels, and its commitments, the United

States found itself in an undeclared naval war with Germany. Clashes occurred in September and October, and in November, Roosevelt extended Lend-Lease aid to the Soviets. Congress then allowed merchant vessels to arm and sail into war zones.

Several key points stand out in the curious turns in US foreign policy from 1937 to 1941. A minority of Americans were 'literalists' on neutrality; only a small number demanded that the nation remain completely aloof and non-preferential. Most accepted a 'broad' reading of neutrality, rejecting US military participation while sympathizing with democracies and Allied aid. The president read neutrality even more 'loosely': he moved from impartiality to partiality to fortification to provocation, demonstrating, as Churchill suggested, a desire to wage but not declare war. Roosevelt focused on the conflict in Europe, trying to avoid a fight in the Pacific, but circumstances in Asia eventually precipitated a US declaration of war.

United States Entrance into War

While Britain, France, the USSR, and the United States concentrated their attention on Europe, the Japanese government pursued its expansion in the Far East. Control over China formed one part of a 'Greater East Asia Co-Prosperity Sphere' designed to liberate Asian peoples from Western colonialism, establish Japanese dominance, provide reliable markets, and guarantee a steady supply of natural resources. The United States objected to Japan's military moves into China as a violation of 'Open Door' principles. With the prospect of Japanese expansion into the Asian colonies of European nations, the Roosevelt administration grew even more alarmed.

The United States responded economically rather than militarily, and in the summer of 1939, announced plans to cancel a 1911 trade agreement with Japan. Negotiations broke down as Japan rejected US demands for a withdrawal from China. In July 1940, the administration embargoed aviation fuel and scrap metal sales to Japan. When the Japanese occupied northern Indochina and signed the Tripartite Agreement with Germany and Italy, the United States created a broader embargo, and increased aid to China. After Japan completed its occupation of French Indochina in July 1941, the United States froze Japanese assets and stopped most commerce, including the trade in oil.

The prime minister, Prince Konoye, chose a path of continued negotiation, but Roosevelt insisted that Japan withdraw from occupied areas. The hard-line general, Hideki Tojo, replaced Konoye in October 1941. While the pretense of negotiations continued, neither side expected a favorable outcome. The United States pressed for China's sovereignty and Open Door principles; Japanese military leaders proceeded with the war plans they had begun preparing in September.

Having broken Japan's diplomatic code in 1940, the United States knew an attack was imminent but did not know where it would occur. The Philippines and British and Dutch possessions in Southeast Asia seemed likely targets, but advisors assumed that the Japanese did not have the intention, capacity, or ingenuity to strike American installations. On Sunday, 7 December, they were taken by surprise as Japan's air and naval forces attacked Pearl Harbor in Hawaii, America's key Pacific base. After two hours, 2,400 Americans lay dead and nearly 1,200 wounded, some 200 aircraft were damaged or destroyed, and nearly 20 vessels, including battleships, cruisers, and destroyers, were badly damaged or sunk. Japan followed up with attacks on Malaya, Hong Kong, Guam, the Philippines, Wake Island, and Midway.

Standing before Congress the next day, President Roosevelt solemnly reflected on the events of 7 December, 'a date which will live in infamy'. Congress issued a declaration of war and three days later, Germany and Italy declared war on the United States. For Americans, who were now strongly unified after years of debate, the Second World War had begun.

The Allied Effort

The conflict presented similarities with the Great War. Germany was the key foe; the United States fought along with Britain, Russia, and Free France; fighting raged in Europe years before the United States committed troops; and the Allies were in desperate straits, badly needing American supplies and personnel. But the new contest proceeded in different directions according to unfamiliar sets of rules: the United States fought in two theaters rather than one; instead of entering a stalemate, America's enemies were on the offensive; the war was not likely to end quickly; and disagreements over war strategy and post-war conditions deeply divided the 'Allies'.

The 'Grand Alliance' (the United States, USSR, and Britain chief among them) agreed that Germany posed the major military threat. Planning focused on Europe; the Pacific was secondary. But the Allies disagreed on their approach. Stalin urged the United States and Britain to open a second front in Europe to draw off German forces concentrated against the Soviet Union. Roosevelt also hoped to launch a European offensive by late 1942. Churchill disagreed: a premature strike by unprepared Allies could repeat the horror of World War I. He believed the Allies had to build their strength gradually, pound Germany by air, and hit Nazi power at its Mediterranean points of weakness rather than its Continental center of strength. Churchill eventually won out. The United Kingdom and United States focused first on Operation Torch, attacking German positions in North Africa.

In January 1942, the 26 nations fighting the Axis signed a 'Declaration of the United Nations' restating the Atlantic Charter principles of self-determination, free trade, disarmament, collective security, and the renunciation of territorial gains through war. The Soviets promised to 'adapt' the ideals to pressing conditions. Anglo-American leaders also jettisoned commitments when circumstances warranted.

The Allies agreed more on what they opposed than on what they supported. They saw the Axis as a dangerous, expansionist-minded, uncontrollable force threatening their fundamental interests and security. Short term, they differed over strategy; long term, they differed over the future shape of the world. To stay united, they had to stay focused on defeating the enemy.

The War in Europe

The first half of 1942 presented a grim picture to the Allies. Hitler held most of western Europe. In the east, Nazi forces took the Crimea and advanced towards Stalingrad. In North Africa, General Erwin Rommel moved east across Libya, imperiling Cairo and the Suez Canal. On the seas, Nazi submarines heavily damaged Allied shipping. U-boats even patrolled close to the US coast. Germany had quickly – and literally – brought the war to America's shores.

The second half of 1942 brought better news to the Allies. Soviet forces stopped Hitler's advance in the Battle of Stalingrad and gained victory over Nazi troops by February 1943. On the seas, improved radar detection and code breaking led to a drop in Allied shipping losses. In the Mediterranean, the British victory at El-Alamein preceded by three days the Anglo-American landings in Vichy-controlled Morocco and Algeria. Dwight Eisenhower served as commander in chief of American forces, chosen for the job by virtue of his organizational skills and personal tact. Together, Eisenhower in the west and General Bernard Montgomery in the east slowly squeezed German forces in their southernmost stronghold.

The year 1942 was pivotal in one other way: German leaders formalized a new stage of national policy toward the Jews, whom they had already denounced, discriminated against, and persecuted. In January, the Wannsee Conference systematized the extermination of the Jews; all told, the Nazis killed 12 million 'undesirables', half of whom were Jews. By early 1942, the American press began to report the news in small, scattered stories and by November, the State Department confirmed the atrocities.

America's response was limited and minimal, shaped by four key factors. First, fearful of creating more competitors for scarce jobs, Congress defeated efforts to raise immigration quotas for fleeing refugees. Secondly, the immigrants involved were Jews, and in a nation where anti-Semitism ran deep (in employment, education, housing, and government), the possibility of relaxing policy was highly unlikely. Thirdly, many assumed the stories from Europe were far-fetched, reminiscent of World War I tales about German atrocities that later proved false. Fourthly, even after confirming the existence of death camps, the Allies did not try to destroy the facilities or rescue their prisoners; such actions would presumably have diverted limited military resources from more urgent targets. In 1944, Roosevelt did establish the War Refugee Board to help some 200,000 Jews and 20,000 non-Jews in Europe. In general, however, the US response was not to save the victims but, as historian David S. Wyman has argued, to abandon them.[1]

Roosevelt and Churchill met in Casablanca in January 1943 and came to two key decisions. The first, looking to the end of the war, demanded the 'unconditional surrender' of Axis forces. The second, looking at the next step in the war, determined that the Allies would not take forces into France but into Sicily and then northward through Italy.

American and British troops moved across North Africa and took Tunis in May 1943. In July, they invaded Sicily, where Axis control collapsed within five weeks. Mussolini was toppled from power and imprisoned but later rescued by Nazi forces. The new government surrendered on 3 September as Allied troops moved into the southern part of the Italian mainland, but it took another nine, difficult months before the Allies occupied Rome in June 1944. Fighting continued for another year as troops moved north from the capital. The Allies slowly won control over the Mediterranean and forced Hitler to pull some of his forces out of western and eastern Europe.

In the summer and autumn of 1943, as Axis positions in the south weakened, Soviet troops in the east mounted an offensive drive after their victory at Stalingrad. They defeated Nazi forces at Kursk (in July) and Kiev (in November), forcing Germany into retreat. In the Atlantic, British and American crews harassed Nazi submarines, allowing the Allies safer transport of soldiers and war materials to Europe. And over the skies of Germany, American pilots joined British flyers in 1943 conducting strategic bombing of military and industrial targets and cities. Two and a half million tons of bombs fell, inflicting nearly a million and a half casualties.

As the tide of war turned, Allied leaders met in Tehran in November 1943. Churchill, Stalin, and Roosevelt agreed to open a second front in the spring of 1944 by invading occupied France across the English Channel. The Soviets would mount their own spring offensive in the east and enter the Pacific war once the fighting in Europe ended.

Eisenhower, the Supreme Commander of the Allied Expeditionary Force, coordinated the invasion. 'Operation Overlord', the joint American, British, and Canadian offensive, was the largest seaborne invasion in history. In England, three million soldiers assembled. Over 5,000 ships carried the first troops and tens of thousands of vehicles across the Channel to the beaches of Normandy. During the first hours of D-Day, 6 June, paratroopers dropped behind German lines. Bombardment from planes and ships followed. The first waves of 150,000 soldiers, most of them new to combat, came onto the beaches in the morning and slowly overcame German defenses. The battle scene, especially at 'Omaha' Beach, was harrowing and horrifying. There, and at four other landing sites, the Allies suffered some 9,000 casualties in the initial assault. By day's end, ships transported a quarter of a million soldiers to Normandy; within weeks, well over a million troops moved inland. A second invasion in southern France took place in mid-

D-Day

August. The Allies liberated Paris on 25 August; by mid-September, they controlled the rest of France and Belgium.

With Allied troops advancing, Roosevelt faced another election at home. Democrats worried about the Congressional gains of Republicans, the unpopularity of the vice-president, Henry A. Wallace, and the poor health of the president. The party dropped Wallace from the ticket in favor of a less contentious Democrat, Missouri Senator Harry S. Truman. Roosevelt handily defeated the Republican candidate, Governor Thomas E. Dewey of New York, but by the lowest popular and electoral vote percentages of his four presidential campaigns.

In Europe, Allied hopes for a swift end to the war were dashed as Hitler counterattacked. The Battle of the Bulge in the Ardennes Forest raged from mid-December 1944 to the end of January when over a million Allied and Axis troops fought one another and inflicted 200,000 casualties. No Yank soldiers had ever seen anything like it; the Bulge was the costliest battle in American military history, but it was also Germany's last, large-scale military action in the war. As the Reich faced defeat in the west, Soviet forces continued pushing through Eastern Europe.

In February 1945, Roosevelt, Churchill, and Stalin met at Yalta to discuss Europe's future, the Pacific conflict, and the post-war world. Stalin enjoyed considerable bargaining power in the talks. His nation dominated eastern Europe; he intended to keep the region under Soviet control to prevent any future invasions; and the United States and United Kingdom needed Russian assistance to defeat Japan. The Allies' relative power positions largely dictated the outcome of the talks. Berlin would become a partitioned city within a partitioned nation, both divided into sectors controlled by the Allies. The Soviets vaguely pledged (and then sternly refused) to allow 'democratic' elections in the lands they held. Stalin would enter the Pacific war but the USSR would receive territorial and political concessions in the East. Finally the Allies outlined a 'United Nations' organization to serve as an agency of collective security. Yalta's agreements were limited, not utopian, practical more than principled, flawed rather than perfected. Some charge that Roosevelt planted the seeds of the Cold War on the shores of the Black Sea; others argue that, realistically, there was little more he could have achieved at the time.

By spring, Allies in the west crossed the Rhine while Soviet troops entered Germany from the east. Nazi defenses rapidly collapsed, but Roosevelt did not live to see the end of the war. On 12 April 1945, he suffered a fatal stroke and Harry S. Truman took the oath of office as president. Eighteen days later, another leader who, like Roosevelt, had risen to the summit of national power in early 1933, also died. On 30 April, in a Berlin bunker, Adolf Hitler took his own life. On 8 May 1945, after almost six years of war, the fighting ended with Allied victory in Europe.

The War in the Pacific

As in Europe, the first half of 1942 proved calamitous for Allied forces in the Pacific Theatre. By May, a rapid series of advances gave Japan control of Malaya, Thailand, Burma, Hong Kong, the Dutch East Indies, the Gilbert and Solomon Islands, and the Philippines. The Japanese Empire ruled over the entire Western Pacific south of the Aleutian Islands, north of Australia, and west of the 180th meridian, plus all of Southeast Asia. But this would be the extent of Japan's triumph; the empire's expansion ended by mid-year.

In the Allies' secondary theater of war, Americans bore most of the fighting. While much of its Pacific fleet was lost or damaged at Pearl Harbor, US aircraft carriers and fuel supplies remained intact. Five months after the surprise attack, American forces stopped Japanese expansion south towards Australia at the Battle of the Coral Sea (May 1942), and in June, the United States stopped Japanese expansion east towards Hawaii at the Battle of Midway. Japan's offensive failures also left its fleet seriously damaged.

The United States then aimed at the Solomon Islands where, on Guadalcanal, the Japanese began constructing an air base in June 1942. In fierce land and sea battles waged from August to February 1943, the Japanese were finally ousted and their navy so hobbled that it could no longer conduct offensive missions.

In 1943 and 1944, the Allies conducted a dual offensive drive designed to advance simultaneously from the south and the east. Forces did not take every Japanese position; rather, in an 'island-hopping' strategy, commanders skipped over or bypassed some enemy strongholds, moved beyond them, left them behind Allied lines, and cut them off from Japanese supplies.

One offensive drive struck across the Southwest Pacific. There, forces dominated by the Army and commanded by General Douglas MacArthur moved from the Solomon Islands and New Guinea to the Philippines. Since March 1942, MacArthur had been in Australia, having left the Philippines after Japan's invasion. His forces advanced to northeastern New Guinea by September 1943 and secured the entire territory in July 1944. By October, MacArthur prepared to honor his pledge to return to the Philippines. On the 20th, the Army landed on Leyte Island. Japanese forces moved in and, from the 23rd to the 26th, the largest naval battle in history was fought in Leyte Gulf. The fighting also introduced the Allies to *kamikaze* suicide attacks. When the battle ended, Japan had lost most of its remaining fleet. MacArthur's advance in the Philippines continued for five months and by March 1945, the Army had taken the main island of Luzon.

The other offensive drive of 1943–1944 struck across the Central Pacific. There, forces dominated by the Marines and commanded by Admiral Chester Nimitz moved westward from Hawaii across the major island chains. Nimitz began in the Gilbert Islands where his troops met heavy resistance, especially at Tarawa. By November 1943, troops secured the islands, built an airstrip, and began bombing the next objective, the Marshall Islands. Nimitz took that chain by February 1944, built another airstrip, and started bombing the Mariana Islands. Battles raged on the Marianas in the summer of 1944 and a furious naval encounter in mid-June, the Battle of the Philippine Sea, accompanied the fighting. Mariana airstrips not only prepared for the next move against the Caroline Islands; the airfields also allowed long-range, B–29 'Superfortress' aircraft to begin regular bombing runs over Japan. With its naval and air forces weakened and its empire shrinking, Japan faced steady, systematic attacks on its home cities and industries.

Allied forces now prepared for the concluding and most ominous phase of the war: the invasion of Japan. In the first half of 1945, attempts to secure two more islands as air bases met with intense Japanese resistance. On Iwo Jima, in February and March, over 6,000 Americans and 21,000 Japanese died. On Okinawa, from April through June, the toll was higher: 12,500 American deaths, 100,000 Japanese deaths, and over 80,000 civilian deaths. The fierceness of the combat, after more than three years of war, filled military advisers with dread: Iwo Jima and Okinawa seemed to offer ghastly previews of what was to come in an invasion of Japan itself. The Allies planned a November 1945 invasion on Kyushu followed by a 1946 invasion of Honshu. Estimates pointed to a million US casualties, and ten times as many Japanese casualties. The projection was staggering, even though the Allies had all but destroyed the enemy's air and naval power, blocked its trade, and inflicted 900,000 casualties through bombing runs. Planners expected the horrifying level of bloodletting to continue in the Pacific Theater.

They did not expect a terrible new form of warfare to emerge in the Pacific Theater, an approach that came from the physicist's laboratory rather than the strategist's map room. Since 1941, federal researchers in the $2 billion 'Manhattan Project' had raced against German scientists to create an atomic weapon of mass destruction. Unable to complete their work by V-E Day, the US research team successfully detonated a test weapon on 16 July 1945. They had material for two more bombs – that might or might not fire properly. President Truman decided to use the weapons against Japan if, by 3 August, its government refused a final demand for surrender, one that now included a dire warning of 'prompt and utter destruction'. The date passed and the military proceeded with orders to drop the bombs. The first atomic weapon fell on Hiroshima on 6 August; the second hit Nagasaki on 9 August. On 14 August, after intense debates among internal factions and frantic exchanges with outside diplomats, the Japanese government accepted terms of surrender that ended the fighting and allowed the emperor to remain on the throne under the supervision of the supreme Allied commander. A formal signing ceremony on 2 September ended World War II.

The decision to use atomic weapons was one of the most momentous, and controversial, events in the twentieth century. Three considerations shaped the US decision, involving military policy, foreign policy, and the state of moral judgment by 1945. Strategically, the United States developed the weapon in order to use it; when completed, it would be employed against Germany and Japan. The Manhattan Project was an investment in applied, rather than theoretical, physics. After the July test revealed the device's awesome power, some researchers urged caution and reconsideration. Military advisors, looking around at Japanese resistance and looking ahead to a costly invasion, urged deployment rather than delay. Truman thought of the American lives he would save by ending the war quickly; he saw the bomb as a godsend, not a curse.

The device was more than a show of force against the Japanese, it was also a show of determination against the Soviets. The United States shared research with Britain but kept information about the project from Stalin (although, not even Vice President Truman knew of the secret). In the summer of 1945, Truman and his advisors recognized that the bomb could serve as a reminder that the United States intended to keep the ambitions of the USSR in check. Atomic weaponry would presumably strengthen America's hand in shaping the postwar world.

Few top advisors expressed reservations about the destructive capacity of the device, reflecting, perhaps, the moral callousness that shaped decision making on all sides after years of war. Death counts in battles remained high; graphic details of the Holocaust became known after the liberation of death camps; the war continually tore at the lives of non-combatants. In the Pacific, a two-day firebombing of Tokyo in March 1945 killed over 80,000. In Europe, bombing raids on German cities may have killed over half a million civilians. The bombs dropped over Hiroshima and Nagasaki claimed 120,000–180,000 lives with another 100,000 injured. The *mode* of inflicting death (through atomic weapons) was new; the *extent* of inflicting death was not.

In the end, the war took over 400,000 American lives; the full casualty figure came to one million. Only the Civil War had witnessed a larger loss of life. The death toll for other nations was even greater, none higher than the Soviet Union where 20 million people died. Historians estimate that the Second World War claimed a total of 40–50 million lives, half of them civilians, a level of carnage that the world had never before witnessed.

The War at Home

THE ECONOMY

While transforming the shape of the world overseas, World War II also altered life in the United States. The conflict ended the Depression. The economic crisis faded because of an unimaginable level of federal spending that not only revived but ignited the marketplace. The economic fortunes of the nation continued into the twenty-first century, creating what Americans had never before experienced: more than six straight decades of prosperity uninterrupted by depression.

Statistics tell a remarkable story about the federal government and the economy during the war years. War production costs totaled nearly $200 billion. During the war years, the number of civilian employees on the federal payroll tripled; the national debt grew sixfold; federal spending rose nearly ten times; the budget deficit jumped 15 times higher. All of this represented a dramatic change from the previous decade. Between 1933 and 1939, federal spending averaged $7 billion a year while annual deficits averaged $2.6 billion – amounts that were not enough to break the back of the Depression. From 1940–1945, spending averaged $53 billion a year and annual deficits averaged nearly $30 billion – amounts that brought the nation out of economic collapse. The federal government spent twice as much in the first half of the 1940s as it had in the nation's previous 15 decades.

The gross national product more than doubled from 1940–1945. Per capita income also doubled and income disparities declined. As 15 million people entered the military and as production orders rose, unemployment dropped from 14 per cent to under 2 per cent. Union membership climbed more than a third. War production involved a quarter of all economic activity in 1941, a third by 1942, and two-thirds by 1943.

Growth did not end economic problems but often turned them upside down. The nation faced rapid expansion rather than rapid contraction, labor shortages rather than labor surpluses, and price increases rather than price decreases. Several federal agencies guided the process, and tried to contain the turmoil. The War Production Board outlined the shift from consumer to military production. The National War Labor Board regulated wages, hours, and working conditions. The Office of Price Administration monitored the cost and consumption of products by initiating price limits and rationing scarce goods, and tax increases also checked inflation. Nearly four times more Americans had to file federal tax returns, launching yet another tradition of modern life. Taxes covered 45 per cent of the war's costs, loans 55 per cent. The combination of revenues and economic controls kept wartime inflation at around 30 per cent, half the rate of the First World War.

Despite a different set of market problems, several larger trends continued. The federal government became an even more important player in the economy, deficit spending lifted the economy from its slump, the size of government and its supervision of daily life expanded; and big business grew even bigger as the largest industries dominated wartime production. America's industrial output rose, and its industrial facilities escaped damage during the war. Already an economic giant, the United States grew even more powerful through the war.

SOCIETY

In countless small ways, millions of Americans made daily contributions to the effort behind 'the good war'. Support for the war came in the form of buying bonds, planting a victory garden, observing 'meatless Tuesdays', donating blood, or collecting items for scrap. Parents and wives with loved ones in the military displayed small banners in their front windows with a star for each soldier in their family. Communities honored those who served and commemorated those who had fallen. The gestures were sometimes significant, sometimes merely symbolic, but almost always heartfelt and genuine. Looking back on the period, older Americans often reflect on the strong sense of unity and common purpose they perceived around them during the war.

To a degree, popular culture helped shape feelings of harmony and commitment. Although information from the fighting front was usually censored and filtered, radio programmers filled nearly a third of their air time with news reports about the war. References to the conflict appeared in comic books, advertising, dramas, billboards, and the ever-present war bond drives. Music and movies did not always offer an 'escape' from the story of the war but often reflected in different ways on the experience. Sometimes the expression was proud and triumphant, as in a song like 'Goodbye Mama, I'm Off to Yokohama' or films such as *Hitler's Madman* and *Back to Bataan*. On occasion the approach was humorous as in Spike Jones's 'Der Führer's Face', Ernst Lubitsch's *To Be or Not to Be*, or Preston Sturges's *Hail the Conquering Hero*. Often the mood created was sad and poignant, as in tunes such as 'I'll Be Seeing You' and 'White Christmas' or movies like *The Fighting Sullivans* or *Tender Comrade*. And at times a bit of complexity might even be presented as in 'For All We Know (We May Never Meet Again)', Michael Curtiz's *Casablanca* and Alfred Hitchcock's *Lifeboat*. Then again, there were times when a commitment to the war effort allowed all sorts of liberties as when Twentieth Century Fox pitted the detective of 221b Baker Street against Nazis in *Sherlock Holmes and the Secret Weapon*.

Whatever the popularity of different diversions, nothing in American popular culture during the war years matched the appeal and frenzy created by the person known simply as 'The Voice'. Frank Sinatra started as a featured singer with Harry James, continued with Tommy Dorsey, and then ventured out on his own to become the biggest entertainer in America. He learned from Bing Crosby's example how the microphone allowed vocalists to tone down their presentation several notches, how the song could be simpler, less stylized, more natural, and how audiences could focus on the singer standing up front rather than the band playing in the back. Sinatra went beyond Crosby, however, in his tender, resonant phrasing, the subtle shifts he made in notes, beats, and lyrics, and the complex interplay he created between himself and his accompanists. Sinatra made a song 'his'. And he made millions his fans, especially young women who flocked to his concerts and bought up his recordings. For six decades, Sinatra not only performed songs but topped the song charts. Like no one else, he defined American popular music during the war years, and for much of the twentieth century.

When records were back in their sleeves, radios turned off, movie theaters closed, fundraisers finished, and ceremonies ended, the day-to-day impact of the war was felt throughout the nation. World War II brought opportunity for some and hardship for others. In economic terms, the war opened up new doors for women and African Americans. In security terms, the war closed off the civil liberties of Japanese-Americans.

New opportunities opened for women in the military beyond nursing and clerical jobs. The armed forces formed special units for women including the Army 'WACs', Navy 'WAVEs', and the Women's Army Service Pilots (or 'WASPs'). Women were barred from combat duty, although nurses were sometimes brought to front-line action. Most of the 350,000 women who served during the war engaged in a wide range of support and administrative tasks.

With so many men in the service, new opportunities for women also opened in civilian jobs. Women made up less than a quarter of the total work force before the war; during the war, they composed over a third. In some ways, the expanded role of women at work pointed to significant changes. As the war continued, the word went out from political and economic centers that women were welcome and needed in the workplace. Industrial tasks, especially at defense plants, were now seen as open, suitable, and acceptable for women. Even the profile of the 'typical' woman worker changed considerably from the pre-war years. By 1944 and 1945, most female workers were older, married women, unlike their average younger and single counterparts at the start of the decade. In other ways, however, the experiences of women in the work force only echoed familiar refrains about their 'place' and 'sphere'. Most employers viewed the hiring of women as a temporary phenomenon that would end when men came home from the war. Most work tasks were categorized and assigned according to gender. Women received about a third less pay than men for the same work. Government and industry often promoted jobs for women as extensions of housework and family responsibilities, describing tools and machines as larger versions of home appliances and portraying defense work as a way of providing for husbands and sons in the service. And veneration of women as mothers caring for their offspring at home meant that child care facilities for defense workers were usually limited and underfunded.

The war resonated in a special way for people of color in the United

States. The Aryan doctrines of Nazism equating national greatness with racial purity served as a potent reminder that the United States needed to do more than defeat a military machine abroad; it also had to overcome deep-seated prejudices at home. Most African Americans viewed the war effort as a chance to prove their loyalty and individual worth to a society that had long belittled both. Nearly a million blacks served in the military during the war, encountering a world as segregated as in civilian life. The armed forces desegregated officer training, allowed blacks to serve as pilots, and permitted African Americans to serve in combat units. But for the most part, blacks found themselves in separate units, with separate barracks, and even segregated blood supplies.

On the home front, the exclusion of blacks from most war production jobs led labor leader A. Philip Randolph to threaten a mass protest march on Washington in 1941. Roosevelt responded with an executive order in June 1941 that tied defense contracts to nondiscriminatory hiring and set up a Fair Employment Practices Committee to oversee employment practices. To expand food production, the federal government also instituted a *bracero* program to bring more than 200,000 Mexican workers across the border to do farm labor.

The possibility of jobs led to another great migration: 750,000–1.5 million blacks left the South for the West, Midwest, and Northeast. Most moved to cities where they faced the hostility of whites. In 1943, riots broke out in over 40 US cities; the bloodiest took place in Detroit, leaving 34 dead. Black advocacy groups rose to counter segregation and discrimination. The Congress of Racial Equality, for example, formed in 1942. The 30-year old National Association for the Advancement of Colored People (NAACP) saw a ninefold increase in its membership. The NAACP created the 'Double V' campaign to remind the nation of its military *and* social problems, calling for a 'Double Victory' of democracy, both 'Abroad [and] At Home'.

Fervent support for the war inspired great personal sacrifice but also generated hysteria against one particular group, Japanese-Americans. Having endured discrimination for decades in the Pacific states where most lived, Japanese-Americans encountered new dangers after Pearl Harbor when they faced charges of disloyalty, treason, and threats to national security. Although most of the 127,000 Japanese-Americans were citizens, one military leader warned that their 'racial strains are undiluted' and 'there are indications that these are organized and ready for concerted action at a favorable opportunity'. Investigations revealed no such evidence of espionage or subversion. Yet, in February 1942, Roosevelt signed an 'Executive Order Authorizing the Secretary of War to Prescribe Military Areas' where nearly all Japanese-American residents of the West Coast states were relocated. That meant liquidating their property and possessions immediately, suffering $400-500 million in losses. The order also meant living for 2½–3 years in one of ten spare, enclosed, guarded internment camps set up in interior areas of the United States. The policy confined a total of 112,000 Japanese-Americans. Some young males offered their services to the military where they fought with distinction in the Italian campaign; some received temporary leave for agricultural work; but most remained imprisoned during the war. The Supreme Court upheld the policy in 1944 and not until the 1980s did the government issue apologies and monetary compensation to those who had been held in the camps.

The delay in expressing official regrets was distressing, but illustrated how difficult it has been for US leaders to think beyond the categories established in World War II. The struggle has stood as a benchmark in the American mind for judging the 'rightness' and 'wrongness' of things. It is a standard by which the nation continued to measure its actions in the world, as in the way policy leaders validated a military response to genocide in the Balkans in 1999. The Second World War had a profound effect on the conduct of American lives, the content of American values, and the construction of American memory.

The Roots of the Cold War

Having shaped popular thinking and altered the nature of combat, the war also redefined the basic structures of economic and political power. War left Europe's major powers weak if not crippled. In 1945, only one participant in the struggle stood strong: the United States. As the war ended, the United States produced fully half of the world's goods and services; it was the richest, most productive, most prosperous, and most powerful country on Earth. The only other player on the world scene whose power came close – by virtue of its size, population, natural wealth, and military force – was the Union of Soviet Socialist Republics. Both societies were relative newcomers to international politics, but in their hands the fate of the world appeared to rest.

They were, of course, allies. Perhaps the commitment against fascism forged in time of war should have strengthened their bonds in time of peace, but the war's 'Grand Alliance' was more a marriage of convenience than of affection. Military co-operation did not mark the culmination of a developing friendship; it was a temporary lull in an otherwise tense relationship. The 'normal' state between the two was one of mutual suspicion and animosity. When the war ended, and even before, tensions did not suddenly begin but merely resumed. In a world of complex geo-political relations, the Cold War fostered a stark, dualistic picture of the struggle between communism and capitalism, state control and individual rights, the East and the West.

At the heart of Soviet thinking lay concerns over security. Over a century and a half, its people suffered three major invasions across the convenient pathway of Eastern Europe. The last, by Hitler, exacted a horrible toll: one in nine people died in the Great Patriotic War. The United States seemed oblivious to this startling fact; the Soviets could only imagine how Americans would respond had they suffered such catastrophic losses. To prevent future threats, the Soviets had to prevent the resurgence of hostile powers on their borders, shape the political destiny of countries to the east, and create a security zone for the USSR. Capitalism's aggressive course also justified the need for a buffer. Western nations were bent on enlarging their economic control of the globe. The United States, in particular, intended to enter nations devastated by war and, operating under the guise of a benevolent liberator, bind foreign peoples to the American market. In response, the Soviets supported the development of a revolutionary consciousness among oppressed and subjugated nations. Stalin and his heirs believed that Marxist-Leninist principles would release humanity from the predatory and repressive conditions under which they lived. Concern about internal safety, external threats, and historical dynamics guided Soviet policy.

American policymakers held their own informing assumptions. Chief among these was a sense of the incompatibility of Soviet and American systems. The USSR formed an authoritarian political order and a state-owned economy that robbed individuals of personal rights and property. The US, on the other hand, valued a constitutionally limited political system and privately controlled economy that provided individual opportunity and political guarantees. The contrast between the two recalled the struggle between power and liberty that had long dominated American political culture. US leaders also assumed that the USSR sought hegemony over others, not merely security for itself. Soviet rulers intended ruthlessly to expand their rigid system by exploiting post-war despair, promoting instability, and centrally directing world revolution. Those who shaped US policy viewed the Soviet Union in the totalitarian and militaristic categories of Nazi Germany. Stalin seemed to be another Hitler who annihilated opponents, consolidated power, enlarged armies, broke promises, and pursued victims. Other nations could not appease such aggression but needed to stop its advance. In the end, the United States created the mirror image of the Soviets' worldview. Americans, too, feared for their internal security, perceived ominous external threats, and scrutinized the familiar patterns of history.

Each side assumed that recent history confirmed its worst fears. The Soviets believed that the West, led by the United States, despised the Bolshevik Revolution, had invaded the workers' state after World War I, and isolated the USSR in the world community. More recently, Western powers failed to heed Stalin's warnings about the Third Reich. They watched passively as Hitler slaughtered the Russian people; they delayed a second front until mid-1944; they objected to the Soviets' legitimate security needs; and they kept atomic secrets from their wartime ally.

US leaders contended that the Bolshevik Revolution terrorized political opponents at home, sparked instability in Europe, and betrayed the Allied cause by withdrawing from the Great War, allowing Germany to focus its military might on the Western front.

The Soviets then sponsored world revolution through the Third Communist International, purged internal enemies, entered into a pact with Hitler, and invaded their neighbors. By the mid-40s, the USSR began to establish brutal, dictatorial regimes in East Europe.

Each nation believed that history pointed to a predictable and threatening pattern of behavior by the other. Post-war events only intensified their mutual suspicions and fears.

International Flashpoints, 1945–1953

From the 1940s into the 1950s, the East and West confronted one another in a number of crises, showdowns, and shooting wars in numerous parts of the world.

European and Middle Eastern tensions in 1945–1946 gave American leaders a sense of the Soviets' post-war intentions. Stalin appeared to renege on the Yalta agreements by refusing to allow open, democratic politics in Poland in 1945. The following year, the Soviets balked at pulling troops out of Iran, which they jointly occupied during the war with British and American forces. US threats finally led to a Soviet withdrawal. The incidents confirmed Truman's sense that he had to use tough talk and determined action against the Soviets. Roosevelt might have tried 'handling' Stalin through negotiation and compromise, but Truman's direct, hard-line approach reflected the different nature of his worldview – and the shorter fuse of his personality. He agreed with Churchill's 1946 warning that 'an Iron Curtain has descended across the Continent'.

The following year, US leaders clarified their approach to the Soviet Union in three policy statements. The first, known as the 'Truman Doctrine' (March 1947) condemned the 'totalitarian regimes forced upon' Eastern Europe and declared that the United States would 'support free peoples who are resisting attempted subjugation by armed minorities or by outside pressures'. America, in other words, would act as a policeman not only in the Western Hemisphere but also around the world to 'assist free people to work out their own destinies in their own way'.

The second policy, known as the 'Marshall Plan' (June 1947), focused on post-war Europe's economic problems and the potential appeal of communism in a world of 'hunger, poverty, desperation, and chaos'. Secretary of State George C. Marshall proposed massive US economic aid to the Continent to 'permit the emergence of political and social conditions in which free institutions can exist'. In return, America would get reliable friends and good customers. The United States offered aid to the Soviet bloc, too, but the USSR refused the plan (as the Truman administration guessed it would), denouncing it as a devious attempt to bind otherwise independent people to the United States. From 1948–1951, the United States funneled $13 billion into Western Europe, increasing productivity, raising standards of living, and containing inflation.

The third policy statement, known as 'containment' (July 1947), aimed at checking Soviet ambitions. Writing in *Foreign Affairs*, George F. Kennan of the State Department advised the United States to match the fixed, steady resolve of Soviet leaders, who remained confident of capitalism's 'eventual fall'. America needed to commit to 'a long-term, patient but firm and vigilant containment of Russian expansive tendencies'. Swagger and bravado would not solve international crises. Instead, the United States should rely on 'the adroit and vigilant application of counter-force at a series of constantly shifting geographical and political points'. For the next four decades, containment served as an informing principle of American foreign policy.

European economic revival included a prosperous Germany. By 1947–1948, US, British, and French officials moved towards unification of the country into a West German Federal Republic. The Soviets, angered that the *West* had reneged on Yalta, retaliated in June 1948 by blocking ground transportation through the Russian zone into Berlin. US policy leaders toyed with atomic strikes and considered armed convoys but decided finally to fly supplies into the city. The joint US-UK 'Berlin Airlift' ferried between 1.5 and 2 million tons of goods to West Berliners over 11 months. Stalin, like Western leaders, feared the use of military options in the crisis. He did not stop the flights and eventually lifted the blockade in May 1949.

Although the Truman Administration threw its support behind

containment, the policy failed in Hungary and Czechoslovakia as communists took power in 1947 and 1948. In 1949, the United States endorsed one further strategy for checking Soviet designs: a military pact with Western European nations. The 12 countries of the North Atlantic Treaty Organization agreed to view an attack on any member nation as an attack on all. For the first time in its history, the United States entered a military alliance in peacetime; and for the first time, the nation engaged in a mutual defense alliance with European nations. America formally closed the books on 160 years of independence and unilateralism in the conduct of foreign policy.

The United States did not expect to force communism into retreat; but it did expect to hold its own and prevent other areas from 'falling' to Marxist-Leninist control. Three events in 1949 and 1950 indicated that all was not going according to plan. First, Truman acknowledged in September 1949 that the Soviets had successfully detonated an atomic bomb. America's monopoly over nuclear weapons ended, as did the peculiar leverage the nation believed it enjoyed over Soviet policy. US leaders responded with research on a more powerful weapon, the hydrogen bomb, and started investigating how the Russians had learned about atomic secrets.

Secondly, in October, China's Nationalist government under Jiang Jieshi, a wartime ally of the United States, lost its civil war with communist forces led by Mao Zedong and Zhou Enlai. While some policymakers saw Mao as an independent leader for whom Stalin had little love (and even less trust), most believed that the establishment of the People's Republic of China expanded the domain of a united, monolithic communist front. Debates swirled in the United States over who 'lost' China. Sensing an urgent need to stop communist insurgency throughout the Far East, the administration supported the French in their fight against guerrillas struggling for independence in the colony of Indochina. In February 1950, the United States sent France $18 million in military aid to help turn back Vietminh forces led by a fervent nationalist and ideological communist, Ho Chi Minh. The United States had begun its 25 year effort to stop communism in Vietnam.

The president's National Security Council echoed the call for greater reliance on military responses to communism. In April 1950, the NSC's 'Memorandum 68' advised that the federal government should nearly quadruple the defense budget, build up the nation's conventional military forces, expand its atomic arsenal, and extend its alliances. Subtle political, economic, and diplomatic policies needed to give way to military might.

A third set of events, in June 1950, made militarization easier to promote. The trigger point was Korea, an area that seemed marginal to US security interests in Asia. 'Temporarily' divided in 1945 at the 38th parallel, the Soviets backed the North's communist government under Kim Il Sung while the United States supported the South's pro-Western (but dictatorial) government under Syngman Rhee. On June 24, the North launched an invasion of the South. The North may have intended to reunite the nation or to punish wartime collaborators in the South; the attack may have been just one stage in a civil war; perhaps

Korean War Scene

the North assumed the United States would not retaliate. Historians raise a number of possible explanations. It does appear that Stalin accepted, but did not instigate, the invasion. Truman, however, assumed the invasion was a Soviet-inspired effort to expand communism and test US resolve. The president called for a UN 'police action'. With the Soviets conveniently boycotting the Security Council, the UN intervened. General Douglas MacArthur made one more return to Asia to lead an international (though overwhelmingly American) military force against North Korea.

The fighting swung back and forth from June 1950–March 1951. First, the North advanced swiftly, pushing its opponents far south to Pusan. Then, in mid-September, MacArthur guided his forces behind enemy lines with a landing at Inchon and within six weeks moved north to the Chinese border. Chinese troops launched their own offensive drive in November, pushing UN soldiers below the 38th parallel. By March 1951, MacArthur moved his forces back to the dividing line. A stalemate ensued and a new battle broke out – between Truman and MacArthur. The president wanted to contain the enemy and negotiate a settlement; the general wanted to eliminate the enemy and carry the war into China if necessary. Their strategic disagreement went public and MacArthur won popular support but, by April, found himself relieved of his command. The squabble complicated an already tangled military campaign.

Peace talks that began in July 1951 dragged on for two years as the fighting continued. By the time an armistice was reached in July 1953, more than 54,000 Americans had died and over 100,000 were wounded. The Korean death toll was over two million. The conflict was the first of many occasions when the Cold War turned hot, and the United States committed troops in the battle against communist expansion. The struggle demonstrated the president's expanded powers over foreign policy, illustrating how the nation could engage in fighting without a Congressional declaration of war. The Korean conflict also posed an exercise in national frustration: the country that defeated the Axis could not topple North Korea. And the war helped seal the political fate of Democrats who, in the 1952 election, lost the presidency, the Senate, and the House.

Eisenhower's Policies of Containment, 1953–1961

The new president was a familiar and comforting face to Americans. During Dwight Eisenhower's two terms, he carried a familiar and comforting foreign policy message about containment. But Republicans hoped to achieve that goal in bolder, more powerful, more economical, more selective, and less obvious ways than the previous administration.

The administration's boldness came from the heightened rhetoric of its secretary of state, John Foster Dulles. A deeply religious and morally rigorous individual, Dulles divided the world into forces of good and evil. Instead of simply hindering America's foes, he advocated their defeat. Instead of trying to contain communism, he speculated on the 'liberation' of captive nations and a 'roll back' of Red power. And instead of shrinking from confrontation, Dulles advised a policy of 'brinksmanship' to show down (rather than back down from) communist threats.

John Foster Dulles

In a world where the atomic monopoly was now an oligopoly, Dulles and Eisenhower argued for a more powerful response to security threats by expanding America's nuclear stockpile and refining its weapons' guidance systems. The United States would meet force with massive retaliation, guaranteeing an attacking enemy its own 'Mutually Assured Destruction'. The administration insisted there was a method to the atomic MAD-ness: a nuclear arsenal of sufficient size, range, and dependability would dissuade others from using their own weapons.

In addition, Eisenhower pressed for more affordable security. Advanced weapons, his secretary of defense argued, provided 'more bang for the buck'. More mutual defense pacts would pool existing military resources. The administration's 'new look' in foreign policy sought to economize on costs while heightening national defense.

Eisenhower also favored a more discriminating foreign policy that allowed the United States to respond to world events on a 'sub-atomic' level. The United States should cajole some leaders but lay down the law with others; force might settle some disputes, but talk might resolve others; some events deserved immediate attention while others were too insignificant or too inflammatory to pursue. By picking its fights more carefully, the nation stood to gain the most and waste the least.

Finally, the new administration pursued some foreign policy goals out of the spotlight, preferring covert action over high-profile ventures. The Central Intelligence Agency (CIA), founded in 1947 and headed by John Foster Dulles's brother, Allen, assumed a leading role. Charged with gathering and assessing information, the CIA supported and refined military campaigns, or substituted for them. Its operatives did more than passively observe events; agents actively shaped the outcome by bribing officials, funding opposition forces, training troops, subverting political processes, and even toppling regimes. CIA projects offered another way to trim security costs by responding selectively to trouble spots and defeating the enemy from within.

Much of the administration's early overseas work was not highly 'visible'. In 1953, the CIA organized opposition to Iran's Prime Minister, Mohammed Mossadegh, who threatened Western interests by nationalizing oil fields. The shah of Iran, Mohammed Reza Pahlavi, replaced Mossadegh and ruled (with US support) for the next 26 years.

In 1954, the CIA also led a coup against Guatemala's president, Jacobo Arbenz Guzmán, whose land reform policies challenged the property interests of corporations such as the United Fruit Company.

That same year, the CIA assumed a larger role in Vietnam. US aid in the region steadily increased as the fight against nationalist forces steadily deteriorated. By 1954, when the French pulled out, America footed three-quarters of the bill for the struggle against the Vietminh. Eisenhower would not commit US troops, believing war would prove as disastrous for America as it had for France, but he feared that communist control would lead to the collapse of other societies in the region. His 'domino' theory led to greater support for anti-communist forces in the area. Agreements reached in 1954 divided Vietnam in two and called for reunification after elections in 1956. The United States did not sign the accord but helped install the South Vietnamese government of Ngo Dinh Diem and supported Diem through the Southeast Asia Treaty Organization, a military pact created with Britain, Australia, the Philippines, Thailand, and other nations. The CIA also assisted, helping to train Diem's army and police.

Diem needed all the help he could get. Nationalist-minded but not reform-minded, a Catholic in a Buddhist society, tough on opponents but tolerant of widespread corruption, Diem did not enjoy broad-based, popular backing. When the scheduled 1956 elections came around, Eisenhower knew that North Vietnam's leader, Ho Chi Minh, was likely to win. Rather than see communists installed in power, the United States and Diem simply blocked the election. As Diem continued his unpopular rule, US money kept flowing, and resistance to Diem kept mounting.

In Eastern Europe, Eisenhower refrained from intervention. On two occasions the administration did not pursue Dulles' 'roll-back' policy. When East German workers mounted demonstrations against their government in 1953 and Hungarian 'freedom fighters' organized against Soviet rule in 1956, the United States did not rally behind the popular protest, in large part because Eisenhower feared the Soviets would respond with large-scale military force.

Eisenhower also chose caution rather than conflict when war broke out in the Middle East in 1956. Egypt's President Gamal Abdel Nasser, having failed to secure American aid for the Aswan Dam project, nationalized the Suez Canal and planned to use its revenues in place of US funds. British, French, and Israeli forces responded with attacks on Egypt in October. Fearing possible Soviet reprisals (and angered at Allies who had left the United States in the dark about their plans), Eisenhower condemned the military action. In 1957, after the armies withdrew, the president announced his 'Eisenhower Doctrine' offering military aid to nations in the region who were trying to stop communist expansion.

Eisenhower pursued flexible and selective policies, in part because of changes in the Soviet Union. After Stalin's death in 1953 and a subsequent Kremlin power struggle, Nikita Khrushchev consolidated authority in Moscow. He suggested his interest in a cold war 'thaw' by denouncing Stalin's brutal crimes, helping end Austria's joint occupation, and speaking of 'peaceful co-existence' with the West. Leaders of the USSR and the West followed up by holding a Geneva summit in 1955. Eisenhower proposed an 'open skies' plan to monitor nuclear weaponry and military capacity. Talks on arms inspection continued and in 1958, Khrushchev announced a halt in above-ground nuclear testing. Russo-American cultural exchanges took place and it appeared that the bitter distrust of the Stalinist era might have passed.

Not all signs were favorable, however. In 1957, Americans learned that the Soviets successfully placed the first satellite, *Sputnik*, into orbit. Many feared that the USSR now enjoyed a technological lead over the United States, that the Soviets' scientific edge heightened their military threat, and that a 'missile gap' between the powers had widened. In 1959, communist threats to America's spacious skies were compounded by a new danger on the nation's Gulf shore. Long-standing obsessions with Cuba took a new turn when Fidel Castro's guerilla forces successfully toppled the regime of dictator Fulgencio Batista. Although hailed by some as a heroic reformer, the administration assumed that Castro was already in Moscow's clutches; and perhaps Washington's withdrawal of economic aid from Cuba helped push Castro closer to the Soviets. In the past, the United States had feared emancipation, Spanish tyranny, and anarchy in Cuba; now the nation worried about Marxist-Leninist revolutionaries 90 miles from Florida.

Nevertheless, Eisenhower and Khrushchev hoped to reconcile their differences. They scheduled a Paris summit for mid-May 1960 and a presidential visit to the Soviet Union. However on May Day, the Soviets downed an American U-2 spy plane flying over their air space. The United States first denied the intelligence-gathering purpose of the flight and then admitted that the reconnaissance had been going on for years. Khrushchev cancelled both the summit and the visit. Eisenhower's presidency closed with diplomatic embarrassment and frustration rather than hope.

In the end, the Republican president had refined rather then rejected his Democratic predecessor's diplomatic principles. Containment was a *bipartisan* goal and remained the centerpiece of American foreign policy for much of the post-World War II era. The United States maintained global commitments, endorsed collective security, and supported a massive defense establishment. Just as Eisenhower did not renounce the foreign policy objectives laid out by Democrats, he did not seek to dismantle the basic framework of domestic policy. The welfare state created in the Depression continued to operate in a modern, more prosperous, and more youthful America.

CHAPTER THIRTEEN

The Military State and the Welfare State,
1945–1980

The years from 1945–1980 are often associated with consumer binges, sprawling suburbs, big cars, glowing televisions, changing mores, mass protests, blaring rock, and blasting rockets. On the surface, it seems so different from what came before, as if Americans broke from the past and launched into what John F. Kennedy labeled the 'new frontier'.

On closer view, the period was shaped by memories of depression and war. The legacy of failure and fighting lingered, and voters endorsed policies designed to avoid another economic catastrophe at home and another global catastrophe abroad. They supported the maintenance of a welfare state, creating a massive, permanent build-up of the federal government. And they supported military readiness, creating a massive, permanent build-up of the armed forces.

Such popular commitments also produced unexpected consequences. An economic system that celebrated affluence and growth eventually confronted the reality of poverty and finite resources. A

Gas Guzzler

political system that endured crash and combat could barely contain domestic protest. And a military system that defeated opponents in two corners of the world during the 1940s faced an intractable foe in one corner of Southeast Asia during the 1960s and 1970s. A nation driven by boundless expectations encountered troubling and unanticipated limits.

Post–War Boom(s)

America's economic prospects at the end of World War II initially appeared quite bleak. President Truman worried that the end of war might trigger the start of economic calamity. Federal spending plummeted, defense production dropped, consumer industries retooled, and millions of service people prepared to return to civilian life. It looked as if a massive collapse might occur. Truman demobilized the military quickly so that soldiers could return to their families, but he deregulated the economy gradually so that the federal government could contain any sudden threats to prosperity. The president allowed contracts to expire, relaxed wage controls, pulled back price controls – and then waited to see what would happen.

The results were remarkable. Americans had saved $140 billion during the war years, but had few consumer goods to buy with all the loot. After the war, they went on a spending spree. In short order, the nation faced a new set of problems: shortages of desirable items, rising prices for consumer goods, and waves of strikes by organized labor. The president's handling – or mishandling – of the economy angered voters, led to Republican Congressional victories in November of 1946, and gave rise to the slogan, 'to err is Truman'.

As soldiers returned home from war, and as a decade and a half of crises passed, delay in gratifying other kinds of wants also came to an end. Beginning in 1946, the birthrate began to soar, creating a demographic surge that accompanied (and fed) economic expansion. A population that rose only 7 per cent during the 1930s jumped 15 per cent in the 1940s, nearly 20 per cent in the 1950s, and over 13 per cent in the 1960s. Newborns accounted for most of the increase. The peak came in 1957, when over four million children were born – one every seven seconds. Unlike Europeans, who witnessed a brief rise in the birthrate after the war, Americans experienced something quite different: for two decades, the nation went through a sustained 'baby boom'.

Supplied with more money and bigger households, Americans who changed *how* they lived also changed *where* they lived. From 1940 to 1970, just under a third of Americans remained urban dwellers. The percentage of rural residents fell, from half to less than a third of the population. But the percentage of those on the fringes of cities jumped, from a fifth to well over a third of all Americans. They created yet another 'booming' sector of national life: the suburbs.

A major geographic shift also took place: the growth of the 'Sunbelt'. Populations in the West, Southwest, and South climbed in the decades after the war. As the population of New York City leveled off, and Chicago, Philadelphia, and Boston all declined, the number of residents in Los Angeles (LA), Dallas, Phoenix, Atlanta, and Miami rose steadily. LA was America's fourth largest city in 1950, third largest in 1970, and second largest in 1990. By the early 1960s, California replaced New York as the nation's most populous state.

The expansion of the post-war economy was remarkable. From 1945–1950, the total sum of all goods and services produced in the United States grew by about 25 per cent. The gross domestic product jumped 80 per cent in the 1950s, 83 per cent in the 1960s, and nearly 150 per cent in the 1970s. The total increase from 1945 to 1980 was over elevenfold. The gains were not all eaten up by higher prices. The 'real', inflation-adjusted sum of national production rose over 55 per cent between 1945 and 1960. Even in the 'inflated' 1960s and 1970s, the gross domestic product more than doubled.

Real personal income rose 25 per cent between 1945 and 1960. Over the next two decades, the figure increased 70 per cent. Three-fifths of Americans were in the 'middle class'. By 1960, 60 per cent were homeowners, up from 40 per cent before the war. Automobile sales quadrupled from 1945 to 1955, and purchases of refrigerators, washing machines, dishwashers, ovens, and, especially, televisions soared. The nation boasted the most wealth, the strongest productivity, and the highest standard of living in the world. A quarter century after the war, the United States was a giant production and consumption machine. With 6 per cent of the world's population, it made and used

66 per cent of the world's goods. Writing in 1954, historian David M. Potter described Americans as 'People of Plenty'.

CAUSES OF THE ECONOMIC BOOM

Consumer buying powered the boom, accounting for up to two-thirds of the gross domestic product. More people had more 'discretionary' income for purchases, and, in 1950, customers found a new way to pay for goods without cash when Diners Club introduced the first credit card. Explanations of the economic boom, like tales of Western settlement, often focus on individual determination, private ventures, and personal choices, but the underlying conditions that guided the marketplace grew in great part from *public* rather than private decisions.

To a considerable extent, the boom was a gross domestic product of federal policy. One reason was that the government was a bigger customer. By the early 1950s, federal spending accounted for almost 20 per cent of all goods and services produced in the United States, up from 1 per cent in the late 1920s. Government was also a major employer; by 1970, nearly one in five non-farm employees worked for government. The federal government stabilized the economy through its social welfare programs, putting a modest but reliable stream of money into the hands of many who might otherwise not 'consume' at all. Finally, federal authorities continuously monitored the marketplace, keeping statistical tabs on its performance, adjusting its money supply, and regulating key sectors like banking and security.

The government activity that had perhaps the greatest impact on post-war domestic affairs involved issues that seemingly affected *other* people: national defense policy. Federal authorities first reduced the military, then reorganized it, then enlarged it to meet the needs of a new, globalist foreign policy – all of which altered the circumstances of life within the United States.

The Effects of Military Demobilization

Concerned about 12 million soldiers suddenly returning to the job market, and troubled by memories of Depression-era Bonus Marchers, Congress passed the 'GI Bill' in 1944. For job-seeking veterans, the bill provided preferential treatment in federal civil service exams. For the academically minded, the act picked up the charge for a college education. For house-hunting GI's, the bill created low-cost mortgages.

The GI Bill helped individual veterans while managing the larger, post-war economy, and provided many with secure government employment. By encouraging others to pursue higher education, the bill reduced the flood of workers seeking jobs; educational aid spurred growth on campuses, laying the foundation for US academic leadership after the war. University graduates moved largely into white-collar jobs, earning higher incomes and paying more taxes to the government that put them in college in the first place. The bill's home mortgage program also boosted the post-war construction industry.

Not all Americans shared equally in the benefits, however. Women were encouraged to leave their wartime work, focus on domestic matters, and 'open up' employment for returning veterans. But by early 1947, the number of working women returned to wartime highs alhough the slots women filled usually paid far less than the jobs they had held during the war. African-Americans who received veterans benefits still found themselves restricted by discriminatory practices. Segregation in education, housing, and employment continued despite their service in time of war. Whatever the limits of the GI Bill, most of its better-educated, better-paid, and better-consuming recipients kept feeding national economic expansion for decades to come.

Besides releasing soldiers from service, the federal government also had to work out what to do with all the manufacturing capacity it had built up during the war. The 'arsenal of democracy' held what amounted to a 'going out of business' sale. Private corporations bought most of the factories and equipment built with public funds during the war, typically at or below cost. By providing cheap, efficient, up-to-date machinery and plants for American business, the government extended one more form of assistance to the nation's 'free' enterprise system.

The Effects of Military Reorganization

Having scaled down the military, the government then restructured it. The National Security Act of 1947 unified the armed forces into the

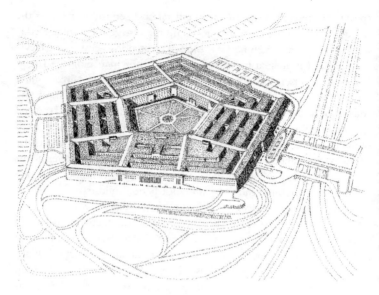

The Pentagon

'National Military Establishment' (later called the Department of Defense) and centered operations in the Pentagon, which was then the world's largest office building. The act created the National Security Council to advise the president and the Central Intelligence Agency (CIA) to gather information on foreign activities.

While demobilization led to many *economic* changes, military reorganization had important *political* consequences. The most significant was the expansion of presidential power. The new streamlined, centralized defense administration reported directly to the commander-in-chief. The National Security Council, presided over by the president, located in the White House, and staffed by military and diplomatic personnel, allowed agencies 'to cooperate more effectively in matters involving national security'. Presidents could respond more quickly and directly to international events, with fewer opportunities for Congressional involvement. The CIA only strengthened the executive's hand: the agency reported to the National Security Council which, in turn, reported to the president. The 1947 act defined the CIA's security mission in broad terms; later legislation freed the agency from public scrutiny and accountability. Its operations expanded in the 1950s and 1960s, going beyond intelligence gathering to include covert military operations overseas and spying at home – all under presidential management.

For decades, Progressives advocated presidential leadership as a way to unite a diverse, fragmented nation. At times, executive power grew because of a president's personality, outlook, and ambition. At times, national emergencies led presidents to exercise greater authority. The National Security Act, however, helped institutionalize a stronger presidency in the modern United States.

The Effects of Containment Policy

As World War II ended, leaders scaled back the armed forces. As the Cold War escalated, the size and strength of the military grew once again. Beginning in 1951, the federal government launched massive programs to strengthen the US military. For a decade, rising defense costs accounted on average for six of every ten dollars spent in the national budget. The government's greatest single task was to keep 1.5 million troops deployed in over 100 countries with all the latest weapons. Military spending accounted for 10 per cent of the value of everything Americans produced during the early economic boom. Anything that soaked up most of the budget of the nation's largest single customer was bound to have spillover effects in the economy and society.

Military spending that stood at $9 billion in 1948 ballooned to $53 billion by 1953. From 1954–1961, under President Eisenhower, national defense costs averaged over $46 billion a year. Under Presidents Kennedy and Johnson in the 1960s, military budgets ranged from $50–80 billion per year. Under Republican presidents, Nixon and Ford, the range was from $76–100 billion per year. And under Democrat Jimmy Carter, spending stood at $100-150 billion per year. At its height, the Department of Defense employed 4.5 million people, nearly as many workers as the 30 largest corporations in America combined.[1]

What the military bought, how it made purchases, and where it left its money all had major consequences for the economy. In established industries such as aircraft manufacturing, major companies received 60–90 per cent of their business from defense spending. In emerging industries, the Defense Department spent much of its money buying cutting-edge products to ensure America's lead in the firepower and technology of warfare. As a result, most of the nation's top growth industries from 1950–1966 were in fields that relied heavily on military purchases.[2] Government spending, rather than consumer spending alone, boosted those sectors of the economy that enjoyed the greatest post-war expansion.

The electronics industry was one of the biggest winners. Defense agencies hoping to track trajectories and break codes helped develop the earliest computers, such as the Electronic Numerical Integrator and Calculator (ENIAC) built in 1946. Research into transistors, integrated circuits, and microchips, all supported by military spending, led to further advances. Computer hardware and software continued to serve as hot growth markets, owing their start, not to unconventional young capitalists, but to straight-laced military commanders. Even the internet was a product of the Cold War, developed first by the Advanced Research Projects Agency to maintain military communications during enemy attack. The agency first demonstrated its ARPANET in 1968. One year later, a network linked four universities in California and Utah. By 1992, the 'World Wide Web' was born, and a technological innovation designed to let generals keep nuclear missiles on course became used by teenagers to order home-delivery of pizzas.

The Defense Department also stayed ahead of the enemy by sponsoring 'R & D', research and development. The Atomic Energy Commission (1946) and the National Science Foundation (1950) promoted both scientific progress and national defense. After the launch of 'Sputnik' in 1957, the United States launched the National Aeronautics and Space Administration (NASA) in 1958. Spending on space exploration increased eighty-fold in a ten-year period, and some two million people depended on NASA for their livelihoods. Overall, federal agencies provided most of the 'R & D' money in post-war America, and most federal research dollars went to defense and space

'Moon Landing'

projects. US leadership in scientific research depended primarily on the security needs of the nation rather than on the entrepreneurial dreams of private investors.

Defense policy also contributed to some of the larger demographic shifts in national life after World War II. Americans turned to the Sunbelt not just to get a better tan but also because those were the areas where the military spent most of its money and created well-paying, middle-class employment. States such as California, Washington, and Texas – and cities such as Los Angeles, Seattle, and San Diego – owed much of their post-war success to defense expenditures.[3]

Containment policy also stimulated other trends in the economy. By pumping aid into Europe, the Marshall Plan helped check communism while widening markets for American goods. By giving most military contracts to America's largest companies, the Defense Department fed corporate consolidation. And by placing ex-military leaders such as Omar Bradley and Douglas MacArthur on boards of directors, corporations kept a strong personal tie between the Pentagon and their own operations.

The link between defense and business led Eisenhower to note one other post-war trend: the rise of a large, peacetime military *and* a vast, permanent armaments industry. Neither had existed before in the nation's history; their 'conjunction', Ike warned in 1961, was fraught with danger. 'The acquisition of unwarranted influence, whether sought or unsought, by the military-industrial complex' posed a serious threat to freedom. 'The potential', Eisenhower said, 'for the disastrous rise of misplaced power exists and will persist.' Defense issues that fueled economic prosperity could also endanger 'our liberties and democratic processes'.

The Red Scare

The nation had already witnessed the kind of political peril that could flow from a 'warfare' state. From 1945–1954, the United States was gripped by a second 'Red Scare', one far more extensive and systematic than the episode following World War I. Many feared that Soviet agents and their allies had penetrated deeply into American life, undermining US security from within while nations abroad fell to communism.

The era's hysteria is easy to condemn but difficult to explain. The crusade was not simply the work of a few high-profile figures but was also shaped by large numbers of political, diplomatic, religious, and labor leaders. Moderates and liberals joined conservatives in the effort, and while those who led the charge created arguments filled with hyperbole, distortion, and lies, there were sufficient pieces of evidence to make their appeals seem plausible and persuasive.

The small US Communist Party of the 1930s was far more marginal than menacing, but its leaders built fuzzy alliances with others on the left in anti-fascist campaigns. By the mid-1940s, individuals with present (or past) membership (or mere 'ties') to the Party – the connections were often construed as 'liberally' as the ideologies – held posts in labor and a small number of government slots. Before the end of World War II, reports surfaced about espionage and illegal activities for the Soviet cause. In 1945, news broke about classified documents in the hands of a leftist magazine; in 1946, Canadian authorities uncovered a Soviet spy ring. In 1948, Congress learned of a former State Department employee accused of providing the Soviets with secret documents. The same year, Soviet agents received sensitive information about FBI counter-espionage measures. In 1950, the British arrested Klaus Fuchs for passing atomic secrets to the Soviets. US officials arrested Julius and Ethel Rosenberg in connection with the case, convicted the couple, and executed them in 1953. News about Soviet atomic tests, communist victory in China, and North Korean attacks made the espionage stories even more alarming. Some assumed that America's enemies had triumphed because anti-American conspiracies had flourished.

Before the war, Congress expressed its concern over subversion through the House Un-American Activities Committee (HUAC) and the 1940 Smith Act, which made it illegal to advocate the forceful overthrow of the US government. After the war, the crackdown expanded. In 1947, President Truman launched loyalty checks on all federal employees, leading to over 2,000 resignations and 212 firings. State governments joined in the effort. Also in 1947, HUAC investigated members of the movie industry about communist penetration of show business, and jailed the 'Hollywood Ten' for failing to 'cooperate' with investigators looking for more suspects. In 1948, members of HUAC, led by Congressman Richard M. Nixon, opened the sensational case of Alger Hiss, a former Roosevelt advisor and State Department official, charged with passing secret documents to the Soviets in the 1930s. Democrats came to Hiss's defense but found themselves in difficult political straits two years later when he was found guilty of perjury. Meanwhile, beginning in 1948, the Justice Department indicted (and later convicted) American communists for violations of the Smith Act. Truman expanded federal house cleaning in 1950 by allowing sensitive national agencies to dismiss employees who were simply *deemed* security risks. Eisenhower entered office in 1953 and increased the rate of firings. In a series of internal security measures passed from 1950–1954, Democratic and Republican Congresses expanded federal crackdowns on Communist Party members and their organization.

The period's heightened anxiety and perceived threats created conditions ripe for political demagoguery. Days after Hiss's conviction and the Fuchs arrest in early 1950, an obscure Republican senator from Wisconsin, Joseph R. McCarthy, told a West Virginia group that he had a list of 205 State Department employees who were card-carrying communists. The senator later changed the count to 81 – and then to 57. McCarthy could have come up with any number, for he held no evidence, proof, or documentation. All he had were headline-grabbing charges, wild claims, and an inflammatory issue that launched him on a meteoric rise to fame and power.

As chair of the Senate Committee on Government Operations, McCarthy investigated the workings and employees of federal agencies. His charges were simple: communists had secretly infiltrated the government. His methods were also simple: McCarthy was skilled in defamation rather than demonstration, smears instead of substance, fabrication over fact. The charges he raised turned out to be as flabby as the Senator's paunch, but most politicians hesitated to criticize him, fearing he might go after them next. Even Eisenhower refrained from confronting his fellow Republican, claiming he did not want to sink to McCarthy's level but recognizing it was helpful to have a pit bull on the loose, attacking political opponents.

Emboldened by publicity, McCarthy went after big game and charged that the Army itself harbored nests of communist spies and sympathizers. The 'Army-McCarthy hearings' of 1954 televised the Senator's accusations as well as his aggressive, reckless tactics. In the end, he proved nothing about others' traitorous activities but demonstrated much about his own political opportunism. The Senate censured McCarthy in December 1954 and he died in 1957.

Since 1995, disclosures from American and Russian archives suggest that an active but limited Soviet spy network operated in the United States during the 1930s and 1940s and that the espionage efforts included Hiss and the Rosenbergs. The extent of their involvement, the value of their information, the motives behind their behavior, and the consequences of their actions all remain in dispute, but several points remain clear. In the decade following the war, Americans were obsessed with national security and internal enemies. The crisis permitted an extraordinary expansion of federal authority. Government investigations probed deeply into the actions *and* opinions of citizens; authorities weakened Constitutional safeguards in order to strengthen defenses against subversion; and dissent itself became subject to scrutiny and punishment. In a 1951 Supreme Court decision, Justice William O. Douglas wrote that Marxist-Leninism had not taken hold in the United States because it was subject to open discussion and inquiry: 'Free speech has destroyed it as an effective political party'. Ironically, Douglas noted, the most zealous prosecutors of the Red Scare undermined the most effective tool of anti-communism.

Putting the Military Establishment to Work: The Kennedy Years

A bipartisan commitment to containment and military expansion continued in the Kennedy administration – with a slight twist. Kennedy and his advisors were troubled by what they saw as Eisenhower's heavy-handed and ineffective foreign policy. When threatened, the United States seemingly had no choice but to respond militarily with a massive atomic punch. To steer clear of such a catastrophe, Ike had presumably *avoided* conflict. Kennedy, however, intended to expand foreign policy options, in Robert D. Schulzinger's words, by better *managing* conflict.[4]

One approach was economic: fighting communism with butter rather than guns through the Peace Corps and the Alliance for Progress. A second approach was a 'flexible response' strategy that replied to security threats through 'limited' nuclear strikes and varying levels of non-nuclear combat. A third approach was to take Cold War conflict out of this world by engaging the Soviets in a 'space race', scientifically demonstrating the superiority of the American way by reaching for the moon – where human beings first stepped on 20 July 1969.

However strong his desire to break from the previous administration, Kennedy was still tied to Eisenhower's foreign strategies and headaches. He approved a CIA plan hatched under Ike to remove Castro from power with an invasion force composed of Cuban exiles. The botched effort, launched in April 1961 at the Bay of Pigs, was an embarrassing failure for Kennedy. Undeterred, the CIA kept trying to kill the Cuban leader, using chemicals, pills, bombs, and even mobsters. Castro, annoyed at those meddling Yankees, convinced Khrushchev to extend greater military aid to Cuba: the subtle Soviets installed offensive nuclear missiles on the island. The United States got wind of the build-up in mid-1962 and had evidence of the installations by the autumn. Despite the fact that similar nuclear installations had been set up by the United States in Turkey to hit Russia, Kennedy insisted on removal of the weapons from Cuba. Rejecting preemptive air strikes, he imposed an air and naval blockade on Cuba on 22 October 1962. Several terrifying days passed before the Soviets responded. On 26 October, Khrushchev agreed to remove the missiles if the United States promised not to invade Cuba. The next day, he demanded that the United States remove its missiles from Turkey. Kennedy overlooked the second request, agreed to the first, and defused the standoff. By mid-1963, the two powers agreed to ban atmospheric tests of nuclear weapons.

The United States had earlier confronted a *Russian*-built blockade in another lingering trouble spot, Berlin. Khrushchev insisted on recognition of East and West Germany and also wanted to stop the flight of East Berliners to the Western sector. Kennedy responded by calling for a defense build-up. Khrushchev replied in August 1961 with a wall that cut East Berlin off from West Berlin. The structure became the emblem of Cold War conflict, but one not provocative enough to fight over. While Kennedy visited the site to declare solidarity with Berliners, his rhetoric and his audience's enthusiasm were not enough to make a chink in the barrier.

A third chronic problem was Vietnam. Like Eisenhower, Kennedy saw South Vietnam as a test of American will, insisted that Asian nations would not 'fall' to communism, and propped up the disreputable regime of Ngo Dinh Diem. By 1959, a growing insurgent movement in South Vietnam began receiving supplies from Ho Chi Minh's government in the North. The following year, the 'National Liberation Front', directed out of Hanoi, began a wider war of resistance in the South. Kennedy responded by fighting Vietnamese communists on their own ground with their own tactics. In 1961, he deployed 500 military 'advisors' from a new, counterinsurgency unit called the 'Green Berets'. Within two years, troop levels climbed to 16,000, and their 'advice' expanded from training, to intelligence-gathering, to combat. Protest from communists and non-communists in South Vietnam also widened as did the dissatisfaction of South Vietnamese army leaders with the Diem government. The United States tacitly supported the decision of 'ARVN' commanders to oust Diem. On 1 November 1963, Diem's own military captured and then promptly executed him. Debate still rages over whether or not Washington knew the coup would take such a deadly turn. There turned out to be little time for reflection on the outcome, however, as three weeks later, John F. Kennedy lay dead from an assassin's bullet in Dallas, Texas.

The Vietnam War Widens, 1964–1968

Lyndon Johnson continued Kennedy's legacy by standing firm on globalism, militarism, and containment. While limiting the spread of nuclear weapons (through new arms treaties) and intervening in Latin America (by sending Marines into the Dominican Republic in 1965), Johnson's main foreign policy concern was Southeast Asia. As Vietcong guerillas in the South and North Vietnamese forces out of Hanoi stepped up their fighting, Johnson revised overall US strategy: he placed increasing military pressure on the North (so it could not continue its support of insurgency in the South), escalated US involvement in the fighting (but not to such an extent that the Chinese or Soviets might directly intervene), and fought a war of attrition (to deplete the ranks of Southern rebels and Northern troops). Johnson 'Americanized' the war in Vietnam.

In pursuit of the first goal, American destroyers assisted the South Vietnamese navy. In August 1964, two US ships reported that North Vietnamese vessels had fired on them. Johnson condemned the 'open aggression', ordered air attacks on the North, and won a broad expansion of presidential war-making powers from Congress in the 'Gulf of Tonkin Resolution'. Authorized 'to take all necessary measures to repel any armed attack against the forces of the United States and to prevent further aggression', Johnson used the resolution in lieu of a declaration of war to expand the fighting. In pursuit of that second goal, he placed troops on the ground and bombers in the skies beginning in 1965. By 1968, half a million US troops were stationed in Vietnam expanding their offensive operations. Systematic and sustained bombings of the North began, and eventually, the tonnage of bombs dropped in the Vietnam War exceeded the level of US bombings in World War II. The enlarged air and ground war contributed to Johnson's third goal by increasing the 'body counts' of North Vietnamese and Vietcong troops.

But the counts also showed that 250–300 Americans died each week. Television brought the grinding and horrifying conflict into living rooms nightly, and by 1968, more Americans were asking if the war was working, if it was worth it, or if it was warranted. A military effort so carefully conceived seemed terribly flawed. Massive firepower seemed to have little effect on a rural, agrarian opponent. In guerilla fighting, US soldiers could not easily distinguish friend from foe. Enemy forces fought at times and places of their own choosing. The commitment of insurgents and of the North appeared stronger than the resolve of the South. The South's military took a secondary role in their own war; unpopular political leaders moved in and out of public office from 1963–1967. American troops (younger than their World War II counterparts, drawn more heavily from working class and minority groups, and more often drafted than enlisted) were caught in a war that was at once fierce, tedious, and surreal. Protest against American policy sharply divided a society that recalled its sense of unity during World War II. And just as the United States spoke of containing the enemy, the North Vietnamese and Vietcong launched surprisingly strong attacks in January 1968 during Tet, the lunar new year. Within two months, Johnson decided not to expand the number of American ground troops. He initiated a partial halt to bombings, called for peace talks, and pulled himself out of the 1968 presidential election.

THE VIETNAM WAR 'CONTRACTS', 1968–1975

The winner of that race, Richard Nixon, had a 'secret plan' to end the war while still maintaining 'peace with honor' and an independent, non-communist South Vietnam. The strategy was two-fold: a deliberate and overt move to reduce the number of American troops while strengthening South Vietnamese forces; and an equally deliberate but more covert effort to expand the air war against the North and the ground war into Cambodia and Laos.

Nixon reduced US troops from 540,000 to 40,000; ARVN forces expanded to over a million; and Nixon also ordered stepped up air attacks. From 1969–1972, a greater tonnage of bombs were dropped from American planes than under Johnson's command. Air strikes over Cambodia remained hidden from Congress and the public, and in 1970, Nixon moved ground forces into Cambodia to root out the enemy. With fewer troops, the United States conducted a geographically wider war.

During the 'de-escalation', 20,000 more Americans died, as did an unknown number of Vietnamese. South Vietnamese forces kept losing to their opponents, war protest in the United States expanded, and a negotiated settlement proved elusive. Meanwhile, Nixon and Secretary of State Henry Kissinger ventured down a number of unexpected and unusual foreign policy paths.

In 1969, the 'Nixon Doctrine' affirmed America's world-wide security interests and treaty agreements but declared that in local conflicts, 'we shall look to the nation directly threatened to assume the primary responsibility of providing the manpower for its defense'. The United States stayed on global alert but served only as a partial participant in others' military campaigns.

Nixon and Kissinger also moved in a different direction with America's superpower super-rivals, experimenting with a 'softer' line toward the USSR and the People's Republic of China. By 1971 and 1972, their policy of 'détente' sought to ease international tensions, while playing off the friction and mutual suspicion that had become part of Sino-Soviet relations.

With the USSR, Nixon witnessed accords between the two Germanys, planned a joint space venture, limited strategic nuclear weapons, reached trade agreements, and toured Moscow. With China, the administration opened private talks, signed new trade accords, and approved some high-profile ping pong matches. Nixon visited China in 1972 and, in one of the most incongruous photo opportunities of the century, exchanged hearty handshakes with Mao Zedong. In 1979, the United States and the People's Republic of China established full diplomatic relations.

All the while, negotiations to end the Vietnam War continued. When talks dragged, the United States turned up the military heat. North Vietnam replied with a large offensive operation in the spring of 1972; the United States responded with mines and bombs. Negotiations resumed by autumn but stalled in December. The United States then launched a massive 'Christmas bombing' campaign. Within days, talks resumed and in January 1973 all sides reached a cease-fire agreement. The United States would withdraw in two months; North Vietnamese troops remained in place; South Vietnam continued to receive American economic aid; and complex political arrangements would, theoretically, conclude the struggle peacefully. More fighting, however, ended the conflict; in 1975, a Northern offensive secured the remainder of South Vietnam. On 30 April, helicopters flew the last Americans and a few of their South Vietnamese allies out the US embassy in Saigon.

For a quarter of a century, the United States tried to contain communism in Vietnam, first by aiding the French, then by supporting a pro-Western government. Johnson expanded the war to secure American objectives and to prevent Soviet or Chinese intervention. Nixon contracted the war to secure American objectives and to prevent a rising tide of domestic protest. But 58,000 American lives and $150 billion did not achieve what foreign policy architects intended. The United States ended its longest war and faced its most agonizing defeat.

Post-Vietnam

Considering how long the Vietnam War had occupied US attention, the conflict mattered remarkably little by the time of the presidential campaign of 1976. According to the cliché of the day, Americans tried 'to put Vietnam behind them'. Leaders and the public generally accepted the need to reassess, and scale back, their foreign commitments. Perhaps the United States had overextended itself and, in the future, could not be on call in all places at all times to protect all interests.

Nixon's diplomatic agenda lived on in his successor. Gerald Ford urged Congress to extend more aid to the government of South Vietnam in the months before its final collapse. He continued talks with the Panamanian government about transferring control of the Panama Canal. He also tried to pursue the course of détente that Nixon had explored in the early 1970s. And in 1975, Western powers and the USSR signed the Helsinki Accords formalizing post-World War II boundaries and establishing guidelines for the protection of basic human rights.

Ford's successor, Jimmy Carter, hoped to guide foreign affairs by idealism rather than force. The United States, he insisted, could still lead the world, but not through power or coercion. Rather, national interests were best served by championing human rights, acting as a broker for peace, and providing assistance to those in need. Instead of containing security threats or balancing power centers, the President felt that US foreign policy should primarily pursue 'world order'.

Carter demonstrated his preference for morality over muscle in several ways. The administration criticized South African apartheid and Soviet repression of Jews and other dissidents. Officials cut or withheld aid from undemocratic governments in Chile, Argentina, Uruguay, and Ethiopia. A new Bureau of Human Rights reported on the status of freedom in different nations; a 1978 treaty transferred control of the Panama Canal Zone; and in 1979, the United States accepted the outcome of the leftist, Sandinista revolution in Nicaragua against a long-standing, but dictatorial, ally. The administration also crafted a second strategic arms limitation treaty with the Soviets. Carter brought the leaders of Egypt and Israel together to resolve decades of hostility in the Middle East. Their 1979 treaty established full diplomatic relations between the two nations and transferred the Israeli-held Sinai Peninsula back to Egypt. The 'Camp David' agreement opened up an ongoing peace 'process' that continued into the next century.

Carter's idealistic course remained muddy, however. In the Middle East, he did not secure guarantees for Palestinian rights. In Nicaragua, insurrectionary activity by Sandinistas pushed the administration to cut aid programs. And the president seemed to pursue an arbitrary approach to human rights, scolding some nations while overlooking the flagrant abuses of others.

Two events in late 1979 derailed both Carter's foreign policy and his presidency. In Iran, Islamic fundamentalists rose up against the American-backed Shah, Mohammed Reza Pahlavi. Angered at the Shah's admission to the U.S., militants in Teheran stormed the United States embassy in November and seized over 50 staffers, holding them hostage for over a year. A second crisis began in late December when Soviet troops invaded Afghanistan to put down resistance by conservative Muslims. Condemning the action, the president instituted economic sanctions against the USSR, withdrew the strategic arms treaty from the Senate, and pulled out of the 1980 Olympics in Moscow. But public opinion found Carter's actions insufficient and held him responsible for a world of expanded Cold War tensions and diminished American prestige.

Since 1945, foreign policy leaders had viewed the world with a combination of concern and confidence, fearful of threats to US security but certain that America could stop its enemies. As the 1980s began, the high price of militarization and the human cost of warfare seemed to have yielded meager returns abroad and deep division at home. After 30 years of Cold War, all the nation had to show for its efforts seemed to be the containment of *American* power and prestige.

The Welfare State: Domestic Issues

Since the Revolution, Americans have debated their founding notions of power and liberty, arguing for and against expansions of national authority. From the Federalists to the Jeffersonians and on to the Civil War, Reconstruction, Progressivism, and the New Deal, citizens wondered if they could trust the enlargement of power, monitor its course, contain its faults, and maintain their freedoms. After 1945, would the nation want to continue living under an active, interventionist federal government, even after terrible economic and military crises had passed? Most politically active, patriotically bound, and traditionally minded Americans answered 'yes'.

Under Hoover, the federal government assumed responsibility for solving national economic emergencies. Under Roosevelt, the federal government assumed responsibility for maintaining national economic health. Under Truman and his successors, the federal government has acted as a permanent player, monitoring, regulating, and guaranteeing the nation's economic performance – and serving as a permanent manager of the market's social consequences. From the post-war period on, welfare state capitalism has become part of the fabric of American life.

Bitter arguments raged over the costs, complications, and consequences of the project, but, overall, discussion took place within fairly well-defined bounds. The debate was usually not an either-or question of retaining or dismantling the welfare state. Most have agreed on the former position. Instead, for almost six decades, the debate has revolved around a more specific point: should the nation expand the welfare state or limit it to its present scope?

From 1945–1980, the welfare state debate took place in a political system where Democrats and Republicans split the presidency. The former held the White House under Truman (1945–1953), Kennedy (1961–1963), Johnson (1963–1969), and Carter (1977–1981). The Republicans, known as the Grand Old Party (GOP) controlled the post under Eisenhower (1953–1961), Nixon (1969–1974), and Ford (1974–1977). Democrats also secured eight Supreme Court appointments, the Republicans ten.

While competition for the presidency and the Court remained fairly even, Democrats dominated the House and Senate, controlling the legislature for 16 of the period's 18 Congressional sessions. Half the time, a Democratic president worked with a Democratic Congress; only once (1953–1955) did a Republican president enjoy a Republican Congress. While the GOP found popular presidential candidates during the era, most voters went Democratic when it came to picking lawmakers. And throughout the 1970s, most Democrats favored expanding the welfare state – albeit in fits and starts.

Truman's 'Fair Deal'

Harry S. Truman weighed in on the side of expansion. He tried to make New Deal programs broader and more inclusive, partly out of ideological conviction, partly out of political calculation. Truman felt that federal management of the economy was essential to ensure prosperity and to maintain his party's coalition of voters.

Truman labeled his plan the 'Fair Deal'. He expanded on the 'New Deal' by asking for increases in Social Security coverage, the minimum wage, and public housing. He went beyond Roosevelt by creating new programs for economic progress and social justice. Truman called for full employment, national health insurance, federal aid to education, and civil rights reforms.

Republicans, who controlled Congress from 1947–1949 hoped, instead, to lead a swing against the New Deal. One of their measures was the Taft-Hartley Act of 1947, which was designed to limit the power and organizing ability of labor unions. Another was the 22nd Amendment to the Constitution, which, by prohibiting anyone from being elected to the presidency more than twice, tried to ensure that there could never be another reign like Roosevelt's.

Democrats took back control of Congress in 1949, but Truman did not fare much better with them. Party members agreed on the need to magnify existing New Deal programs but hesitated to lead a federal charge into other areas of American life. The Employment Act of 1946, however, did make federal management of the economy a permanent matter of law rather than a variable matter of policy. The national government would fine-tune the performance of the economy whether the market overheated or underperformed. A new Council of Economic Advisers guided presidents on ways to stabilize and expand the economy.

Truman also appointed committees to examine the status of African Americans. Their reports called for equality in education, desegregation of the military (begun in 1948), and federal leadership against segregation and civil rights violations. Through legal channels, the Justice Department pursued cases aiding minority groups. Through legislative channels, Truman pursued proposals to end lynching, assure voting rights, and guarantee housing and employment opportunities. But Southern Democrats aligned with Republicans to block the measures.

Truman pushed civil rights issues further than any administration since Reconstruction and used the White House as a 'bully pulpit' to promote causes of justice and equity. As a presidential activist, a defender of the welfare state, and an advocate of federal programs for economic growth and social change, Truman was very much in the mold of his predecessor. Unlike Roosevelt, he did not win Congressional approval for many of his ideas. It would be another decade and a half before political leaders took up his liberal agenda again.

Eisenhower and the 'Business' of Government

Riding on his military record, his centrist positions, and his affable manner, Dwight D. Eisenhower (Ike) handily defeated his Democratic opponent for the presidency, Adlai Stevenson, both in 1952 and 1956. Some Republicans hoped to use the victory to turn back the clock on welfare state capitalism, but the new president (and most of the country) did not call for retreat. In the jargon of foreign policy, Ike preferred the containment of federal activism to a roll-back.

Labeling himself a 'modern' Republican committed to 'dynamic conservatism', the president claimed to be 'conservative when it came to money and liberal when it comes to human beings'. He intended to maintain the status quo, trim expenses, and allow the administration of government to catch up with the new responsibilities of government.

Ike was not cut from the 'activist' mold of Teddy or Franklin Roosevelt, but neither was he a passive figure like Harding or Coolidge. He adopted more of a 'hidden-hand' approach to the presidency. Eisenhower preferred working behind the scenes, implementing rather than initiating policy, and he delegated authority to advisors around him. He avoided public showdowns and patiently built consensus, especially with a Congress dominated by Democrats for most of his presidency. Presidential restraint was part of his larger campaign for government restraint, and one of the ways he parted company with the politics of the previous two decades.[5]

One way the administration contained activism was to make yet another shift in Indian policy, touting the change as a way to cut both costs and controls. After decades of New Deal programs designed to protect the interests, identity, and sovereignty of tribes, Republicans chose a different path. The administration sought to terminate treaty rights and the reservation system, limit tribal sovereignty, and relocate native peoples off traditional lands into the heart of mainstream, urban America. Eisenhower saw the strategy as a way to end dependence and to speed assimilation. As historian David R. Lewis notes, 'Congress intended to get out of the Indian business'.[6] Promising to 'free' Indians from federal control, the program allowed officials to relieve themselves of what they felt was an unnecessary expense, and also permitted private enterprises to exploit native resources with greater ease.

Eisenhower also stepped back from presidential activism in the area of civil rights. He argued that *compulsory* measures would not change engrained habits of racism. He would not use his office even to *persuade* white Americans to alter their prejudices. He let others take the lead. One of the most prominent figures was Earl Warren, Chief Justice of the Supreme Court. In the landmark 1954 case, *Brown v. Board of Education*, the Court ruled against segregation in public education. The decision argued that 'separate educational facilities are inherently unequal', creating in minority students 'a feeling of inferiority ... that may affect their hearts and minds in a way unlikely ever to be undone', and violating 'the equal protection of the laws guaranteed by the Fourteenth Amendment'. In 1955, the Court ruled that desegregation must advance 'with all deliberate speed'. But throughout the South, states moved with all deliberate lethargy, and Eisenhower moved with deliberate passivity in enforcing the decision. By 1957, however, in the face of white threats against African-American youngsters trying to attend Central High School in Little Rock, Arkansas, the president finally acted, sending in federal troops (and federalizing the state's National Guard) to guarantee the safety of black students. For the first time since Reconstruction ended in 1877, the nation used its armed forces to protect the rights of African Americans. The same year,

Eisenhower endorsed the first Civil Rights Act in eight decades, designed to safeguard voting rights. Clear in its objectives but weak in its enforcement, the measure marked a turn in national policies on race.

While trimming executive initiative and some federal programs, Eisenhower enlarged other functions of government. The administration created the Department of Health, Education, and Welfare and hiked unemployment benefits, Social Security coverage, and the minimum wage. Republicans sponsored massive public works projects such the 2,400-mile-long St. Lawrence Seaway. The administration also launched the interstate highway system in 1956. Economically, new nationwide highways would accelerate the movement of goods and people. Militarily, the roads would expedite the movement of missiles and equipment – and speed the evacuation of cities that might come under nuclear attack. For national commerce, national security, and national convenience, Congress budgeted over $30 billion to build over 40,000 miles of highways, paving enough land to cover an area the size of West Virginia.

Ike initially held down the costs of government, but by the time he left office, spending levels were 30 per cent higher than when he entered. The federal social welfare workforce doubled. And the administration ran budget deficits in five of its eight years. Still, the nation enjoyed peace, modest growth, and low inflation.

Eisenhower's presidency did not magnify or shrink the welfare state but *consolidated* a half-century of Progressive reforms. The moderation, caution, and measure hit a responsive chord in the electorate, weary from two decades of crises at home and abroad. While many approved the respite from engagement and reform, complacency also bred neglect, most often of groups who could least afford to be overlooked. For them, a measure of flash, energy, and enthusiasm inspired hope, not dread.

Kennedy and the 'New Frontier'

John Fitzgerald Kennedy's campaign for the presidency promised boldness, dynamism, and energy, everything a retiring president in his early 70s had not delivered, everything an aspiring president in his early

40s confidently projected. Kennedy's opponent, Vice-President Nixon looked back on Eisenhower's rule; Kennedy looked forward to a 'New Frontier'. He charged that Eisenhower and Nixon had not spurred the economy fast enough, expanded the welfare state wide enough, used the presidency strongly enough, or stockpiled nuclear weapons high enough. It was time for something new – in leadership, style, rhetoric, and direction. Whether policy would change remained up in the air, but it certainly *sounded* as if that would happen.

There was much that was different about Kennedy. He was young; he was Catholic; he was charismatic, especially in the cool medium of television. And he drew his advisors largely from the academic world rather than the corporate community, creating a White House staffed more by 'whiz kids' than biz kids. Still, Kennedy tended to be another vague centrist. He had had an undistinguished career in Congress where he had not vigorously supported the promise of civil rights or vigorously fought the threat of McCarthyism. His presidential campaign, his inaugural address, and his first years in office pointed to a keen interest in foreign policy. On the domestic front, he spoke more about the need to expand existing social programs than to create new ones. In fairness, however, Kennedy had not received the kind of popular vote majority in 1960 that would have provided a 'mandate' for change, and he had to deal with a Congress that, while nominally Democratic, tended to be ideologically conservative-to-moderate.

Kennedy clearly intended to revive one progressive principle: an active presidency. He relished the vigorous, challenging, conspicuous leadership that the presidency could provide, and hoped to use the office to focus attention on national concerns, to inspire creative thinking about the future, and to energize a country that seemed to have flown on auto-pilot for eight years. The White House itself served as a focal point of activity and possibility. The galas, the glamour, the lore, the luminaries, the beguiling rhetoric, and the media glitz all served to keep eyes riveted on the person in the Oval Office. Image mattered; style counted.

In domestic affairs, Kennedy concentrated on economic growth. Relying on market mechanisms more than government agencies, he believed that economic expansion would raise incomes and opportunities. He called for cuts in tariffs and taxes and anticipated that Americans with more money in their pockets would presumably buy their way to prosperity for all. The economy rose at a faster pace than it had under Eisenhower while inflation remained low, but federal spending and budget deficits also increased.

By the autumn of 1963, a president who celebrated activism had scored only modest legislative gains. Broader benefits in Social Security, unemployment, and housing had all been passed; educational and medical proposals failed. Kennedy started to move towards legislation on civil rights and poverty, but remained hampered by conservative Democrats. To shore up Southern support, he traveled to Dallas, Texas, with his wife, Jacqueline. On 22 November 1963, as the couple rode in an open-car motorcade past friendly crowds, shots rang out. Decades have passed, but older Americans still carry vivid memories of where they were when they heard that the president had been shot and killed. For four dramatic days, the nation came to a halt. Americans watched the reports from Dallas, the mourning in Washington, the murder of the president's accused killer, and the funeral procession to Arlington National Cemetery. Eyes that focused for a thousand days on a vibrant, energetic leader now gazed at the casket of a slain president.

Johnson's 'Great Society'

Vice-President Lyndon Baines Johnson took up the work Kennedy left unfinished. Johnson was also a presidential activist but one without Kennedy's grace, wit, or refinement. He drew on other talents. Johnson got things done; he passionately loved politics; and he won compromises from contentious players. He was also a Texan, with a closer personal connection to Southern members of Congress. A former Senate majority leader, he was knowledgeable about the ways to move legislation through government, and was a hard-nosed wheeler-dealer who glad-handed, arm-twisted, threatened, and cajoled the people's representatives. He trounced conservative Barry Goldwater in the 1964 presidential election with the greatest popular vote margin in US history. He was a Democrat deeply committed to the completion of New and Fair Deals, and he could invoke the memory of a fallen president to win support for his programs.

Johnson moved quickly on his agenda. He began with economic growth, pushing Kennedy's tax cut. The goal was to trim federal revenues and raise the federal deficit in the short run, and enjoy an eventual up-turn in the economy in the long run.

Johnson's larger goal was to expand progressive reform through programs of social justice. He first addressed racial equality. The Civil Rights Act of 1964 banned discrimination in jobs and public accommodations, withheld federal funds from public agencies that refused to comply, and authorized the Justice Department to investigate racial inequities. In addition, the 24th Amendment outlawed the poll taxes that whites had long used to prevent blacks from voting.

Johnson's second initiative was a 'war on poverty'. The federal government already had the responsibility for relieving economic emergencies and providing 'economic well-being and prosperity'. The Economic Opportunity Act of 1964 outlined a third task: 'to eliminate the paradox of poverty in the midst of plenty'. The drive for equality and opportunity, both for minorities and the poor, formed the basis of Johnson's 'Great Society' program.

Coming off his 1964 victory, Johnson worked on a legislative program rivaling Roosevelt's first 100 days in office. One set of bills attacked poverty through financial aid, job training, educational opportunities, and 'community action' programs. A second addressed issues of equality through Voting Rights and Civil Rights Acts. A third measure provided national health insurance for the elderly (Medicare) and the indigent (Medicaid). A fourth act established broad federal aid to education. A fifth package of bills addressed environmental protection. Johnson later moved the judicial branch in a more liberal direction by nominating Abe Fortas and Thurgood Marshall (the first African-American justice) to the Supreme Court.

The Great Society marked the greatest expansion of federal authority and responsibility in a third of a century. To a considerable extent, it worked. The percentage of Americans living in poverty was cut almost in half. The percentage of African Americans registered to vote in the South nearly doubled during the 1960s. The economy grew at a faster rate than in the 1950s. The expansion helped in part to pay for new programs (which Johnson was loath to fund through higher taxes). More dollars went to social needs: under Johnson, about a third of government spending addressed 'human resources' compared to a quarter of Eisenhower's outlays.

Johnson's programs had severe limits as well as severe critics. One major failing was that the Great Society did little to alter the *distribution* of income in the United States. A second problem, that Johnson came to recognize after 1966, was that the domestic war against poverty had to play second fiddle to the foreign war in Vietnam. The Southeast Asian conflict absorbed far greater sums of money (and, eventually, more Presidential attention) than social causes at home. A third problem was that the costs of new domestic programs skyrocketed. As federal spending grew, so did inflation, budget deficits – and political opposition.

Democrats were deeply divided among themselves: three party members launched their own presidential campaigns; and the Democrats' 1968 convention in Chicago led to shoving matches inside the hall and street riots outside. Opponents on the right condemned a more powerful, centralized federal government and questioned the presumed advantages Washington bestowed on economically disadvantaged groups. As early as 1966, a conservative-to-moderate majority dominated Congress, adding one more obstacle to the expansion of the Great Society.

Johnson's political stock fell so low – and the divisiveness he generated rose so high – that he decided not to run for re-election. One president fell victim to a bullet. Another fell victim to political discord. The next White House occupant eventually fell victim to the twin demons of power and paranoia. Just as federal activism and presidential authority seemed to have reached their zenith, the structure of public confidence in the national government began to crumble.

Nixon's 'New Federalism'

In his political career, Richard Nixon took on prominent liberals and trounced on civil liberties. He argued that Americans had grown too dependent on government. He promised to take power from Washington and distribute it throughout the nation. He appealed to conservative Southerners and blue-collar workers. It might seem to follow that he was a rabid reactionary in terms of social policy. But Nixon *expanded* federal power and proposed changes that would have moved welfare state capitalism *beyond* the New Deal and the Great Society. As in his personality and foreign policy, Nixon was a man of contradiction and paradox. As Congressional investigators came to learn, it was difficult to pin the president down.

Nixon targeted his 1968 campaign at the so-called 'silent majority', Americans presumably tired of over-governance by federal agencies, overindulgence of dissenters, criminals, and the poor, and oversight of their own needs and interests. He became president, but with a minority of the popular vote, a Democratically controlled Congress, and in the midst of widespread domestic protest. These were hardly ideal circumstances for a politician who had long displayed bitterness, distrust, and suspicion towards those who challenged him. However, Nixon often managed to work with Congress rather than defying its will, and tried to woo Democrats by maintaining the services and programs they supported. He defused protest by scaling back United States involvement in Vietnam, but when political opposition became too much of a problem, Nixon and his cronies turned up the heat on critics through illegal means. It was this last 'coping' mechanism that led to his downfall – but not before his sweeping re-election in 1972.

Nixon called for a 'New Federalism' in the United States. He pointed to 'the limits of what government can do alone' and warned that there was not 'a purely governmental solution for every problem'. He would neither demolish nor enlarge the existing welfare state but, instead asked Americans to take greater individual and community responsibility for their destiny. Yet for every step Nixon took in that direction, he took at least one stride back.

One way to implement the 'New Federalism' was to halt the growth of the federal government. However, federal programs such as Social Security, Food Stamps, housing subsidies, the Job Corps, and educational loans all expanded under Nixon's tenure.

A second way to contain federal authority (and win Southern white support) was through civil rights policy. Convinced that the pursuit of racial justice expanded government control over daily life, the administration challenged extensions of voting rights, blocked plans for school desegregation, and opposed forced busing of students to promote integration. Yet the White House supported hiring-quotas for minorities and created programs to aid minority businesses.

A third way to control federal power was to create a Supreme Court that challenged 'judicial activism'. Nixon secured four Court appointments. His nominees argued for a limited Court, one that *interpreted* rather than *made* law. The Court did grant more police authority against criminals and more community power against pornography. It also ruled in favor of a woman's right to an abortion, in support of those facing racial discrimination, against state death penalty laws – and against Nixon himself as he tried to protect 'executive privilege'.

A fourth theme of the 'New Federalism' was to disperse power and decision-making more broadly throughout the nation. One key measure was 'revenue sharing'. Federal officials would provide the money for the social program; state and local officials would decide where to spend it. But while the fiscal power of communities grew, the regulatory power of the federal government expanded even more, in new agencies that monitored workers' conditions, consumers' purchases, and environmental quality. Communities gained more control over tax dollars, but wound up with less choice in other types of decisions.

Another proposal for distributing power involved welfare reform. Nixon sensed that bureaucratic and inefficient federal social programs funneled too much money to administrators and too little to the needy – whose only incentive was to stay on welfare. The President proposed a 'Family Assistance Plan' through which the federal government provided money and recipients spent it as they thought best. There were fewer regulations, less red tape, and more incentives to put people to work – a conservative's idea of heaven. Unless, of course, one viewed it another way. Nixon's plan provided nothing less than a guaranteed annual income from the federal government. Those on the right could not live with the idea; those on the left thought the program was underfunded. A proposal that would have taken a giant leap beyond the existing welfare state – inspired by that world-famous liberal, Richard Nixon – died in Congress.

Nixon did not have much to show for all his talk about limiting the federal government. Federal spending (and total deficits) increased more than in the Johnson years. Presidential 'activism' also expanded. In foreign policy, Nixon engaged in secret activities, enlarging and contracting conflict as he saw fit with little Congressional and public oversight. In domestic policy, Nixon also moved 'energetically'. When Congress appropriated more for programs than he deemed acceptable, Nixon 'impounded' the funds, refusing to spend what legislators had approved. And in the face of recession and inflation in the early 1970s, Nixon imposed wage, price, and rent controls, a move Americans had not seen since the end of World War II.

But Nixon's most aggressive (and reckless) expansion of presidential powers came in the way he and aides handled their so-called 'enemies', a group that included radical activists, non-violent dissenters, political rivals, and policy critics. Nixon saw the nation on the edge of collapse, destabilized by internal foes who threatened national security. From 1969–1971, the White House tried to stop opponents with illegal wiretaps, break-ins, and plans to disrupt domestic protest. By 1972, Nixon's suspicions even extended to Democratic challengers for the presidency. The White House funded 'dirty tricks' to foul up opponents' campaigns; in June, a 'plumbers' unit (designed to stop information 'leaks') broke into the Democratic National Committee's headquarters in the Watergate complex in Washington.

Within days of the break in, Nixon tried to block the investigation, buy off the burglars, and cover-up White House involvement. It took two years to come up with the facts. Throughout the process, the President denied personal involvement, 'stonewalled' investigators, dismissed adversaries, and blocked release of Watergate tapes. The probe gradually disclosed a pattern of domestic spying, sabotage, illegal fundraising, hush money, perjury, burglary, and conspiracy, all in the name of 'national security' and 'executive privilege'. The House Judiciary Committee approved three articles of impeachment in July 1974, charging that Nixon obstructed justice, abused presidential powers, and acted with contempt towards Congress. Rather than face House approval of the articles – and a Senate trial – Nixon resigned on 9 August, succeeded in office by Gerald R. Ford. Richard Nixon rose to national prominence in the 1940s by feeding off fears of 'security'. His personal obsession with the same issue led to his fall a quarter century later.

Ford, Carter and the Diminished Presidency

In the wake of Vietnam and Watergate, Congress responded to popular suspicions of the executive office – and tried to reclaim its own power – by passing measures to check 'activist' presidents. Laws restricted a president's ability to wage war without Congressional approval, limited the White House from impounding funds authorized by the House and Senate, controlled the unwarranted use of untraceable campaign money, monitored activities of the FBI and CIA, and opened government documents to public scrutiny.

The very ways in which Presidents Gerald Ford and Jimmy Carter presented themselves to the public revealed their appreciation of changes in the executive branch. When Nixon's successor took office in 1974, he played on both history and car models by acknowledging, 'I'm a Ford, not a Lincoln'. The new president offered simplicity rather than stature, humility not hubris, congeniality over constructiveness. There was nothing distinctive or distinguished about him. But in the mid-70s that was a plus; Ford seemed perfectly suited for a limited task. He came out of the House, the body closest to the people; he served as 'minority leader', guiding despondent Republicans who had *not* exercised decisive power in over two decades. Ford acted more as a caretaker helping a debilitated federal system through a crisis of public confidence.

The graceless Ford, who quickly gained a comic reputation for physical clumsiness, stumbled politically by pardoning Richard Nixon. He floundered legislatively by irritating Congressional Democrats with a series of vetoes. And he bumbled economically by failing to check inflation and ease recession.

In the 1976 election, where nearly half the eligible voters failed to show up at the polls, Ford was narrowly defeated by Jimmy Carter. While Ford suggested that his greatest strength was his lack of strength, Carter claimed bragging rights to another virtue: he was no Washington 'insider'. Nope, Jimmy (not James) was just a reg'lar ol' Georgia peanut farmer, a political outsider who served as governor, a trustworthy fellow who sullied his hands by putting in a crop rather than by planting partisan intrigue. He even promised that he would never lie to the nation, a startling proposition for a person moving into an office occupied by a long line of deceivers, dissemblers, and one unindicted co-conspirator. Democrats were in for another surprise: Carter also stood apart from almost all the established patterns of Washington life. The schmoozing and finagling of DC politics was not his style. Instead, the president tended to distance himself from the old power brokers and put his trust in friends and allies from Georgia. Carter never established a good working relationship with the Democratic Congress.

Though a Southern Democrat, Carter was no LBJ. He stepped back from both an activist presidency and a robust reform agenda. Although he added cabinet posts for education and energy and brought more women and minorities into White House leadership positions, Carter did not broadly extend social services. Instead, he broke from Progressive tradition by launching the de-regulation of several industries, *reducing* federal supervision of private enterprises.

The economy bedeviled Carter more than politics, however. Interest rates reached 20 per cent, hurting both spending and investment. Carter took the heat for an economy mired in recession, a domestic policy left without direction, and a foreign policy that seemed to leave the United States 'hostage' to fundamentalist toughs. The best thing for his personal reputation was his defeat in the 1980 election. As citizen Carter, he engaged in a life of humanitarian service and international peacemaking, becoming the nation's most distinguished *ex*-President.

Still, both Ford and Carter achieved an ironic measure of success by how little they accomplished. Their restraint helped redress the balance of power in the federal government – and also cut down the number of calamities executives caused. Less *was* more. But for two decades, from 1961–1981, no president served two full terms in office. Voter participation dropped. And the absence of executive leadership contributed to a policy drift that Congress did not resolve. While the main pillars of New Deal liberalism remained in place, ambitious foreign policies, aggressive market expansion, visionary reforms, and bold leadership remained in check. Problems of finite resources, poisonous wastes, industrial decline, financial stagnation, and dispirited public sentiment left some to bemoan the fate of the United States in an 'age of limits'. A gnawing, anti-Progressive suspicion spread that government, so long considered the solution to national problems, might, after all, *not* work.

Voices of America: African Americans

While a broad consensus supported an enlarged welfare state and military state, other voices called attention to the nation's neglected concerns, asserting that the quest for national security could not ignore or derail the drive for popular freedom, equality, and power.

African Americans stood at the forefront of this struggle in the post-war period. Since the turn of the century, in the work of Booker T. Washington and W.E.B. DuBois, in the court cases of the National Association for the Advancement of Colored People (NAACP), and in the political pressure applied by labor leaders such as A. Philip Randolph, African Americans took on long-standing traditions of racism by invoking long-standing traditions of liberty and equality. Opponents slowed, limited, or obstructed political and legislative change, however. As the *Brown v. Board of Education* decision demonstrated, the *formulation* of a ruling was one thing, *implementation* quite another. Two years after the Court handed down its opinion, not one black child in the Deep South attended school with whites.

By the mid-1950s, African-American activism had undergone a subtle and significant change, brought to national attention by the simple action of an ordinary woman in a small Southern city. In December 1955, in Montgomery, Alabama, 42-year-old Rosa Parks refused to give up her bus seat to a white as required by law. She was arrested. Blacks boycotted the bus system, brought suit, and won a favorable Supreme Court decision. The events in Montgomery moved black protest in a different direction, building a wider, more intense, and more diverse campaign for racial justice. Parks was a local leader, not a national leader. Her supporters were common people, not prominent celebrities; her actions took place first on the streets, not in the halls of government or justice. Her approach was to defy the law and take the consequences, not to organize nationwide, petition officials, or gather lawyers. The boycott effort was guided by a local minister who would soon redefine the quest for equality.

Reverend Martin Luther King, Jr. had recently come to Montgomery as a pastor. He directed the bus boycott, bringing a commitment to nonviolence inspired by Gandhi and a commitment to service inspired by the Social Gospel. In the face of oppression, he called for passive resistance and disobedience to civil authorities, urging African Americans to wield love rather than force as a way to create social change. To inspire his followers, he drew on passionate and evocative oratory. To steer the movement, he helped organize the Southern Christian Leadership Conference and, later, the Student Non-Violent Coordinating Committee. For over a decade, he was the face, the voice, and the spirit of the civil rights movement.

King spelled out his approach in a 1963 letter, written from a jail cell in Birmingham, Alabama, where he was arrested after leading protest demonstrations. The powerless, he argued, had few resources against the powerful. Violent confrontation was not sanctioned by Scripture. Patience and endurance were ineffective. Negotiation was fruitless since those holding authority and privilege had no compelling reason to alter their ways. Change might come, however, through 'tension', by generating, through non-violent means of direct action, a crisis that drew attention to injustice and compelled those in power to confront their own assumptions and policies. A disciplined, 'self-purified' community of protest could prick the conscience (and the interests) of society. Blacks *will* take action, King noted: 'The question is not whether we will be extremists, but what kind of extremists we will be. Will we be extremists for hate or for love?'

King's campaigns of peaceful provocation spread out of Montgomery to include sit-ins at segregated lunch counters, 'freedom rides' against discrimination, voter registration drives, and marches against inequality. In August 1963, a quarter of a million marchers in Washington heard King speak of his dream of human brotherhood. The movement helped secure laws that built up voting rights and broke down segregation. But protests also met with violence through the terror of the Ku Klux Klan, bombings of black churches and homes, and the killings of African American leaders including, on 4 April 1968, King himself.

The civil rights movement also encountered division among African Americans. Some grew disenchanted with King's moral strategy, arguing that it offered no escape from the cycle of poverty, no answer to *informal* patterns of segregation, no release from menial jobs, shabby housing, or substandard education, and no realistic alternative to the lives most blacks lived *outside* of the South. Some disagreed with King's goal of integration, arguing that blacks had to cut themselves off from whites who were hopelessly infected by racism. Some disagreed with King's non-violence, arguing about the need for vigorous self-defense against a hostile society.

One sign of growing rifts came in waves of urban rioting during the mid-1960s in New York, Los Angeles, Chicago, Newark, and Detroit. A second division came with the growing appeal of black 'separatist' groups such as the Nation of Islam which, under the dynamic leadership of Malcolm X, urged blacks to develop their own resources, defenses, and community strength against the brutality of whites. A third division came with the rise of the 'black power' movement in the later 1960s. Shifting from King's moral tone and the Nation of Islam's religious voice, black power advocates such as Stokely Carmichael promoted a cultural and political message emphasizing racial pride, solidarity, and power.

By the end of the 1970s, one other, economic line of division emerged as the ranks of the African American middle class expanded. Incomes rose during the 1970s and by the end of the decade a third of all blacks were part of the middle class. Nearly half of all African American workers held 'white-collar' jobs by 1990. In the same year, 12 per cent of all university students were African American, a figure roughly equal to the percentage of blacks in the US population. Black suburban populations also increased as individuals moved out of the inner city. They often left behind another African-American community trapped by the overwhelming presence of poverty, crime, and drugs and the faintest hopes of opportunity and release. As Clayborne Carson wrote in 1976, 'the battle against racism has widened rather than narrowed the class divisions among blacks'. Two years later, William Julius Wilson observed that 'class has become more important than race in determining black life-chances'.[7] Economic condition generated greater diversity among African Americans.

Hispanic Americans and Native Americans

The civil rights movement demonstrated to many minority communities the value of actively organizing and defending a group's common concerns. The lesson was learned by Hispanic Americans whose population rose sharply after World War II. Mexican-American workers entered the United States in large numbers during the war in response to labor shortages. More came to the Southwest to work on post-war water projects. Puerto Ricans settled in increasing numbers in the Northeast. After Castro's rise to power, over 300,000 Cubans entered the United States during the 1960s, often settling in Florida. Between 1960 and 1995, the Hispanic American population grew nearly ninefold to 26 million.

Hispanic Americans were often subordinated into continuing poverty and marginalized through discrimination. Separated from one another by culture, history, and region, it also proved difficult to find common ethnic ground. Puerto Ricans, while the poorest of the group, came into the United States as citizens because of the peculiar political status of their home island. Among Cuban Americans, leadership often fell to the educated, professional groups who fled Castro. Their economic success in the United States, and the vitality of Cuban-American communities, created a voting bloc wooed by both political parties. Mexican Americans were often lured to the United States by job prospects, were exploited as cheap factory and field workers, and at the same time pursued by immigration and naturalization officials cracking down on illegal aliens. The Mexican-American Political

Association, La Raza Unida, and Cesar Chavez's United Farm Workers provided organizational means of countering the problems that Mexican Americans confronted.

The interests, claims, and tribal unity of Native Americans weakened in the 1950s as Republicans withdrew long-standing federal services. Democrats in the 1960s changed course and terminated 'termination'. But even 'Great Society' programs proved inadequate, and Indians faced the worst poverty, the highest unemployment, and the poorest living conditions in the United States.

Some Indian leaders responded with cultural efforts to reclaim their heritage, preserving tribal languages, ceremonies, and religions as ways of revitalizing Indian life. Best-selling books such as N. Scott Momaday's *House Made of Dawn*, Vine DeLoria Jr's *Custer Died for Your Sins*, and Dee Brown's *Bury My Heart at Wounded Knee* brought native readings of American life to large popular audiences. Others relied on political strategies for changing public policy. Congress passed the Indian Civil Rights Act of 1968, which extended many guarantees of the Bill of Rights to reservations while acknowledging tribal sovereignty, and the Indian Self-Determination Act of 1974, which gave tribes greater control over social and educational programs on their reservations. Some native peoples emphasized legal approaches to reform. The Native American Rights Fund, in particular, focused on upholding treaties, reclaiming lost lands, expanding self-determination, and guaranteeing Indian sovereignty. Other groups, like the American Indian Movement (AIM), advocated a more militant course of action. AIM's agitational program led to a highly publicized occupation of Alcatraz Island off San Francisco, demonstrations at the Bureau of Indian Affairs in Washington, and a deadly confrontation with FBI agents at Wounded Knee in South Dakota. The organization's call for 'Red Power' echoed those who championed the causes of 'Brown Power' and 'Black Power'.

Racial and ethnic communities often described themselves as part of the 'other' America that mainstream groups kept out of sight and out of mind. Where the powerless identified a crisis, the powerful saw no problem. Those on the margins saw a society that had broken apart and failed; those on the inside saw a society that served all and functioned smoothly. Currents of bitter, rancorous division stirred beneath the apparent surface calm of American life.

The Renewal of Women's Movements

The contrast that American minorities drew between superficial serenity and underlying discontent spoke to America's majority as well. In her provocative, 1963 book *The Feminine Mystique*, Betty Friedan took up a problem that many not only failed to *see* but also refused to *say*, a problem 'that has no name'. Friedan argued that post-war culture prescribed home and family as the focus of female experience. It seemed to matter little that women felt constrained by these expectations, that the percentage of women in the labor force kept rising, and that pre-war culture often held up a remarkably different ideal of independent and self-reliant women. The 'modern' world taught that women could 'find fulfillment only in sexual passivity, male domination, and nurturing maternal love'. Friedan argued that there was a wide gap 'between the reality of our lives as women and the image to which we are trying to conform'. A culture that claimed to satisfy women's needs left them, instead, confined, dependent, and powerless.[8]

By the 1970s, the nation had witnessed a remarkable renewal of feminist thought in the United States, the likes of which had not been seen in the half century since the 19th Amendment granted women's suffrage. Part of the work of women's rights movements was to open up discussion, to let women talk about their lives and name the problem 'that has no name'. The 'consciousness raising' that took place through small groups, large rallies, and published works served as both a strategy and a goal of the movement. A second part of reform activity involved organization. One important group, founded in 1966, was the National Organization for Women (NOW) whose goal was to allow women 'full participation in the mainstream of American society NOW, exercising all the privileges and responsibilities thereof in truly equal partnership with men'. Public demonstrations formed a third part of the movements' activities, whether in headline-grabbing protests against beauty pageants or more historically minded celebrations of the

Seneca Falls Convention or the suffrage campaign. Political activism was a fourth component of women's movements, promoted in large part by the National Women's Political Caucus and led by scores of women elected to positions in the House, Senate, and state government. Legislation formed yet another part of the work of women's groups. State and national laws tackled problems of equal pay, fair credit, educational programs, and employment opportunities.

Controversies within and outside of women's movements surfaced by the early 1970s. In 1972, Congress passed a proposed 'Equal Rights Amendment' to the Constitution prohibiting the denial or abridgement of equal rights under the law 'on account of sex'. Nearly three dozen states approved the amendment, but the measure fell short of the three-quarters majority needed for ratification. In 1973, the Supreme Court ruled in favor of women's reproductive rights and their rights to privacy. *Roe v. Wade* legalized abortion in the first trimester. While feminists hailed the ruling, the decision galvanized conservative religious and political groups who condemned abortion along with other social and legal reforms sponsored by women's groups. The movement also split into different directions, as advocates of 'women's rights' focused their efforts on legal channels of change and proponents of 'women's liberation' created more radical agendas to transform society. Finally, groups such as NOW tried to hold together women who, while bound by gender, often found themselves separated along lines of race and class.

The Culture of Youth

A different source of division, marked by a 'generation gap', separated the children of depression and war from the children of affluence. A younger generation – like other groups in the post-war United States – developed a sense of their distinctive identity and pressed for their own 'liberation'. An older generation that managed to live through world conflagration and sought the simple joys of hearth and home, literally bred a whole new set of conflicts for themselves.

The rise in the post-war birthrate meant that, demographically speaking, modern America looked a bit more like traditional America:

the nation became younger. By 1970, more than half the population was under 28. After that point, age started to creep up on Americans; as the century closed, the median national age was a ripe 35. But for about 20 years, the nation recaptured its vigorous, energetic (some might say puerile) character from a bygone day.

The 'traditional' nature of post-war youth was limited to statistics, however; by almost every other measurement, 'baby boomers' defied convention. Parents gave it their best shot from 1945 to 1965, providing the comfort of private homes and backyards, building new schools, and worshipping (in unprecedented numbers) in churches and synagogues. What they got for all their stabilizing effort was a generation of youth that often seemed unruly, defiant, and unpredictable.

Young people were certainly a distinct group. So many were born in such a short space of time. Unlike earlier in the century, most children and teenagers spent most of the day together in school, reinforcing a sense of group identity. They formed a major market in the economy. And a distinctive subculture catered to young people, setting them apart in appearance, language, and, culture. 'Beat' writers such as Allen Ginsberg and Jack Kerouac celebrated a spirit of spontaneity, sensuality, and iconoclasm – and indicted a society of security and order that created empty, lifeless prisons for its inhabitants. Youth films such as *Rebel Without a Cause* played off the box office power of 24-year-old James Dean; *The Wild One* featured a motorcycle-riding Marlon Brando; and *The Blackboard Jungle* examined problems of 'juvenile delinquency'.

Blackboard Jungle brought something new to movies: a rock 'n roll soundtrack. Director Richard Brooks used the song *Rock Around the Clock* as a counterpoint to the action on the screen, bringing to an even larger audience a new sound that changed the nation's musical taste. Rooted in African American rhythm and blues, rock music was hard-driving, cool, swaggering, suggestive, and sexy, especially when performed by its premier artist, Elvis Presley. In just three years, from 1956–1958, Presley released 14 million-selling albums. Into the 21st century, rock music, rock artists, and rock formats dominated the airwaves and record charts in the United States – and provided one of the nation's leading cultural exports.

Elvis Presley

In the 1960s and 1970s, eight million young people left home and high school and headed to American colleges. Experimenting with sex, drugs, and more issue-oriented rock 'n roll, activists turned campuses into centers of protest, reform, and rebellion. The 'Students for a Democratic Society' (SDS) declared in 1962 that they were a 'generation, bred in at least modest comfort, housed now in universities, looking uncomfortably to the world we inherit.' Troubled by racial hatred, Cold War tension, technological destruction, overpopulation, and imperialism, SDS members became the advance guard of radical protest against the Vietnam War. They were helped in part by the success of the 'Free Speech Movement' at the University of California at Berkeley in 1964 which opened campuses for political activities. By the late 1960s, universities across the United States (as in Europe and Asia) witnessed steady protests against military policies and economic depredations. Strikes, vandalism, and even bombings hit campuses. In

May 1970, six students were killed at two universities in protests sparked by the United States invasion of Cambodia.

At the same time, a politicized 'counterculture' developed. Theodore Roszak wrote that the interests of young people in the 'psychology of alienation, oriental mysticism, psychedelic drugs, and communitarian experiments comprise a cultural constellation that radically diverges from values and assumptions that have been in the mainstream of our society at least since the Scientific Revolution.'[9] By celebrating a world of natural rhythms, personal pleasures, and spiritual transcendence, a generation that defined itself as distinctive developed an alternative 'lifestyle' to complement its singular identity.

The young, along with African Americans, Hispanic Americans, Native Americans, and women, all challenged the notion that the United States was a 'melting pot' in which people of different backgrounds lost their identities and formed a homogenous 'American' whole. Instead, the United States remained, as Walt Whitman wrote in 1855, a 'nation of nations'. At its root, the country was plural rather than singular, diverse rather than uniform. From the beginning of the New Republic through the Civil War, Americans debated whether the United States was essentially one or many. By the late twentieth century, that important *political* question had become the central *cultural* question of American life.

CHAPTER FOURTEEN

The Close of the Twentieth Century,
1980–2000

By 1980, it seemed to many that the international powerhouse of the postwar era had exhausted itself through executive incompetence, market calamities, and foreign policy failures. America appeared drained of strong and coherent leadership. A grinding, stagnating wage-price spiral continued. And the United States looked on as religious radicals held its diplomats hostage and an old enemy expanded its domain in Central Asia.

By 2000, the fortunes of the nation had undergone a considerable change. A people who had grown wary of the White House grew fond of two later inhabitants, even when those presidents squandered their popularity with blunders and scandals. A nation caught in the grip of Cold War for half a century caught its breath when its main rival crumbled from within, and an economy drained by recession and inflation enjoyed unprecedented peacetime expansion. As the new century opened, the United States had once again become a world leader – in part through its own successes, in part through others' failures. But having 'won' so many contests at home and abroad, Americans found themselves stumbling to define their future course.

Conservatism in the Late Twentieth Century

However entrenched the welfare state had become, strong currents of conservatism remained rooted in American political thought. Part of the appeal sprang from a long historical tradition of Jeffersonianism that idealized a limited state, valued individual liberty, and suspected centralized power. Part of the appeal came from economic arguments that

371

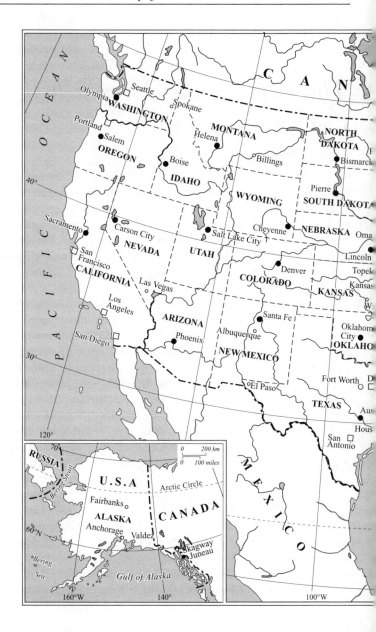

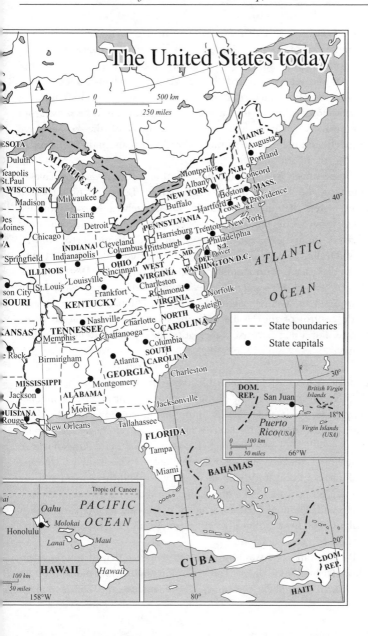

The United States today

market forces (rather than government management) offered the best guarantee of prosperity. Conservatism also drew strength from contemporary moral arguments, especially from fundamentalist groups such as the self-proclaimed 'Moral Majority', which criticized permissive sexual conduct, rising rates of divorce and abortion, feminism, and homosexuality. A fourth source of rightist influence arose from demographic changes, especially the growth of the conservative 'Sunbelt' and the decline of more liberal urban and industrial areas of the Northeast and Midwest 'Rustbelt'.

Conservatism had a strong ideological base, but it did not have an appealing popular face. In 1964, right-winger Barry Goldwater scared more voters than he attracted. In 1968, Richard Nixon mouthed conservative pieties but adopted moderate-to-liberal policies. The most effective modern voice of conservatism was a former actor, former New Dealer, political convert, and twice-elected California governor, Ronald Reagan, who trounced Jimmy Carter in the 1980 election. Reagan served as president for two terms and was succeeded by his vice-president, George Bush. Republicans chipped away at Democratic control of the House and, for six years, they controlled the Senate. For a dozen years, conservative ideas held sway in the White House.

The Republican Party's popular approval grew in part from Carter's popular disapproval. His 'favorable' ratings in opinion polls were lower than Nixon's at the height of the Watergate scandal. The Democrats failed at recovery, and a fear of continuing inflation began to hold the same popular dread as the specter of 'depression' four decades earlier. But Republicans had something else working for them: Reagan was an appealing candidate. He was a likeable fellow who flashed a winning smile, told a good story, and successfully worked the camera and the crowds. Reagan also had a simple message that won the admiration of voters with a limited attention span and even less tolerance for complex analysis. For most politically active Americans (a shrinking number) Reagan had the 'right' stuff.

Reagan's message was more conservative than that of any president since Harding or Coolidge. The expansion of government had brought Americans into their present mess, he argued; the contraction of government (at least in domestic programs) would end their predicament. Reagan renounced the Progressive political tradition: government, he assumed, was part of the problem, not part of the solution. True to his word, the new president took steps to reduce federal power. Deviating from his word, Reagan reinvigorated both national defense and executive leadership.

'Morning in America': Reagan's Policies

Reagan's campaign proclaimed it was, once again, 'morning in America'. Prosperity, the ads suggested, would replace failure; international prestige would supplant international weakness; patriotism would overcome cynicism; hope would conquer despair. All it took was a restoration of individualism over collectivism, private enterprise over state control, armed might over military meekness, and strong traditional values over a muddled modern relativism.

Economically, Reagan pledged to liberate private enterprise and roll back the welfare state. The best way to open up the market place and put a curb on government, he reasoned, was to reduce the flow of revenue to Washington. Tax reductions would put more money in the pockets of people and businesses and less in the hands of spendthrift bureaucrats. The private sector would use the extra money to buy consumer goods; those with big tax breaks would make large economic investments, which would expand the economy and create more jobs. More jobs meant more income. More income led to more spending. More spending gave an incentive for even more investment. And the whole 'trickle-down' process would keep going, providing growth, employment, purchasing power, and, over time, even a bit more tax revenue down the line for government. At the same time, Reagan wanted markets to get on with the work of generating wealth. He intended to cut the 'red tape' that ensnarled business in paperwork, discouraged risk taking, and left the United States less competitive against other, less regulated producers.

Republicans instituted 'supply-side' economics in three ways. First, Congress reduced taxes. Over three years, taxes for individuals fell by 25 per cent. Secondly, Congress reduced spending. Legislators trimmed money earmarked for transportation, natural resources, commerce, and housing, slashed spending on education, training, employment, and social service, and gutted a wide range of energy projects. Thirdly, federal regulators reduced regulation. Government cut back its monitoring of business consolidation, the stock market, broadcasting, the environment, consumer products, health, and safety.

Judicially, Reagan sought to 'get the government off the backs' of the American people by creating a federal court system geared toward 'restraint', led by judges who supported the constitutionally limited task of interpreting law rather the constitutionally broad view of making policy. The president made four Supreme Court appointments, including Sandra Day O'Connor, the first woman to sit on the Court. Though the Court did not sharply reverse earlier decisions, its opinions shifted to the right, particularly in cases that involved abortion rights, affirmative action, the death sentence, and discrimination. Reagan also had the opportunity to appoint more than half the total number of judges in federal district courts and courts of appeal, shaping the judicial system in the twentieth century to an extent matched only by Franklin Roosevelt.

Militarily, a passion for strength over restraint gripped the administration. Reagan held that the delicacy of détente would not restore the nation's prominence or refashion the world to its liking. The times required the boldness of a buildup. He vowed to modernize the military. He pledged to support 'freedom fighters' around the globe. And he insisted the United States would prevail in any possible nuclear conflict, rejecting 'mutually assured destruction' in favor of 'victory'.

None of those goals came cheap. National defense spending nearly doubled under Reagan, rising from $157 billion to $303 billion. Reversing a trend since the late-1960s, military programs absorbed a growing rather than declining percentage of all federal dollars, rising from 23 per cent of spending to 28 per cent (while spending on human resources dropped from 53 per cent of government spending to 48 per cent). The most ambitious (or, as some thought, the most questionable) project was the 'Strategic Defense Initiative', designed to create a shield around the United States to destroy incoming nuclear missiles. However suspect the research effort, Congress still poured money into the project at the start of the 21st century.

Diplomatically, Reagan defended American goals of individual and market freedom while condemning the USSR as an 'evil empire' intent on destabilizing democracies, inciting revolution, and enslaving people to the state. In his stark, dualistic, bipolar breakdown of the forces of good and ill, Reagan returned to the heightened rhetoric and confrontational tone of the early Cold War. The president dealt with the Soviets through a tough war of words, a hard line on arms negotiations, and a steady expansion of United States military power. Arms control stalled as the military deployed new missiles in Western America (and Western Europe) and Reagan announced his Strategic Defense Initiative. Towards Third World countries, especially in Central America and the Caribbean, the 'Reagan Doctrine' pledged support for anti-communist movements. In 1981, the administration began funding and training Nicaraguan 'contras' opposed to the Sandinista government. The United States also aided repressive, right-wing leaders in El Salvador trying to contain domestic revolution. And in the autumn of 1983, United States forces landed on the Caribbean island of Granada to oust a leftist government. Towards Middle Eastern nations, Reagan began his presidency on a high note: on inauguration day, Iranian fundamentalists released the American hostages in Tehran. In 1982, Reagan deployed United States 'peacekeepers' to Lebanon, joining other international troops. But after the barracks bombing the following year, the administration pulled forces out in 1984, unable to secure or even clarify its objectives in the region. In 1985, Lebanese terrorists seized American hostages. In 1986, the United States launched air strikes at Libya in order to punish – or perhaps 'take out' – its leader, Muammar al-Qaddafi, for his support of terrorism.

The Consequences of Reagan's Domestic Policies

Reagan scored enough economic victories, in categories that mattered to the bulk of voting Americans, to secure a second term in office in the 1984 election. But he did not get off to the best start. One year after the tax and spending cuts of 1981, the nation fell into the worst recession since the 1930s. Unemployment rose to nearly 11 per cent, the highest since 1940. Yet, by late 1983, a strong recovery was in place. The Federal Reserve pursued 'tight' money policies, oil producers lost their grip on the cost of crude oil, military spending began boosting some sectors of the economy, and the recession kept a curb on prices.

There was good news ahead. The bogeyman of the modern economy, inflation, began to break down. In Reagan's first year, the cost of living rose 9 per cent; after that, it averaged 4 per cent, a huge drop from the 12–13 per cent rates in Carter's last two years. A seemingly insurmountable problem finally came under control. Interest rates and unemployment were both cut in half, spurring consumer purchases and business investment. The economy created over 14 million new jobs, and real disposable income rose 27 per cent. The gross domestic product, even adjusted for inflation, jumped over 28 per cent. The stock market's key indicator, the Dow Jones industrial index, doubled as insecurity left the securities market. By the late 1990s, stocks and bonds formed the largest single component of Americans' net worth. By 2000, the Dow index had risen tenfold.

Then there was the bad news. While *total* wealth increased, the *division* of wealth became less equitable. The top one percent of Americans held a fifth of national wealth in the late 1970s, but over a third by the late 1980s. The richest tenth of Americans controlled two-thirds of all private wealth by the time Reagan left office. The top fifth of all households enjoyed a rising share of aggregate income; the bottom four-fifths saw their share fall. Simply put, the rich got richer and the poor got poorer. America's poverty rate had increased, starting in the Carter years. By 1983, over 15 per cent of Americans lived in poverty, the highest level since the 1960s. When Reagan left office, the percentage in poverty stood where it did when he entered; his administration had not improved the lives of the poorest. Most of the jobs added to the economy were low-paying. Manufacturing jobs kept declining as corporations sought cheaper labor overseas. 'Blue collar' employment for those with various levels of skill and education became scarcer, and the percentage of organized workers, with sound wages and benefits, continued a decline that had begun in the early 1970s. Over one-third of the labor force was unionized in 1945 but only about one-sixth by the late 1980s. Prosperity, in other words, came to some, not all.

Just as disturbing were the government's reckless habits. The president's conservatism did not extend to fiscal behavior. When it came to spending more than the government had, Reagan made Roosevelt look like a cheapskate. Budget deficits peaked, standing at $79 billion when Reagan took office and nearly doubling by the time he left. Even generous 'adjusted' measurements pointed to deficits that reached the highest levels since the spending spree of World War II. On top of that, the gross federal debt nearly tripled in Reagan's two terms. Interest payments that had eaten up 10 cents of every federal dollar in 1981 took nearly 15 cents eight years later. In addition, as jobs and manufacturing went overseas, so did the dollar. Trade deficits quadrupled during the 1980s (in a nation that had achieved trade surpluses since the 1880s). As a result, the world's largest creditor nation for much of the century became the world's largest debtor nation. An alarmed stock market halted its upward leap in October 1987 when the Dow Jones average fell 22 per cent, its worst one day drop in nearly three-quarters of a century. The market value of equities fell half a trillion dollars in a single trading session.

The sleaziness of Reagan's underlings only added to Republican woes. Recurring charges of bribery, illegal lobbying, conspiracy, and influence peddling followed administration officials. Reagan solidly won re-election for himself in 1984, but his fellow Republicans never gained control of the House. In 1986, they even lost control of the Senate, leaving the president with a Democratic Congress in his last two years in office. Reagan had much to show for his presidency but much to confess to as well. Like the Republican presidents of the 1920s, he had presided over a boom, but one marked as much by its unevenness as by its size.

The Consequences of Reagan's Foreign Policies

The outcome of Reagan's international strategies was hardly what most expected when he first entered office. Despite his tough line towards the Soviets, Reagan warmed up to new Kremlin leaders by the late-

1980s. And for all his energetic talk about overseas objectives, law and order, and the condemnation of international terrorism, Reagan wound up bewildered and bedeviled by a scandal involving arms, hostages, terrorists, and violations of US law.

The transformation of the USSR in the 1980s continues to spark debate. Reagan's defenders contend that the President's tough foreign policy reined in Soviet ambitions, his support of 'freedom fighters' boosted the morale of anti-communists, and his military build-up forced the Kremlin into a competition they could neither win nor afford. Hemmed in, retreating, and bankrupted, the Soviet Union gave up its aggressive, expansionist designs. Other historians focus less on causes from *without* and emphasize circumstances *within* the USSR to explain its remarkable changes. After three aged Kremlin leaders died in quick succession from 1982–1985, Soviet policy was in disarray and opportunities for a new cadre of officials opened wider. A 'younger' group of leaders, headed by Mikhail Gorbachev, were part of a tech-nocratic, postwar generation suspicious of Stalinism, concerned about economic inefficiencies, troubled over military influence, frustrated by a stalemate in Afghanistan, and eager to contain internal divisions. Assuming power in 1985, Gorbachev engaged in *perestroika* and *glasnost*, reforming the Soviet economic structure while opening its political order to greater debate.

Whatever the causes of change in the Soviet Union, the results led to a thaw in the Cold War. Reagan and Gorbachev met four times between 1985 and 1988. After reaching a stalemate on arms reductions, they agreed to ban intermediate range nuclear missiles in Europe in 1987, an accord that was unprecedented in 30 years of nuclear nego-tiation. In 1988, the Soviets began to pull their troops out of Afgha-nistan. Friendly visits by Gorbachev to the United States and Reagan to Moscow capped the superpower 'love fest'. Reagan, and his successor, George Bush, hoped to keep the nation focused on the new and warmer relations with the empire formerly known as evil.

Instead, attention increasingly turned to a foreign policy scandal known as 'Iran-Contra'. In the mid-1980s, the administration faced three lingering dilemmas. One involved Nicaragua: Congress pro-hibited further aid to the contras' war against the Sandinista government. A second involved hostages: Americans were still held by Lebanese terrorists. A third involved Iran, under the Ayatollah Khomeini: still on bad terms with the United States, the Iranians were at war with Iraq and tied to radical fundamentalist groups in Lebanon. Officials of the CIA and the National Security Council (NSC) devised a 'solution' to all three problems. The United States could build good will with moderate factions in Iran, sell them arms to use in their war against Iraq, hint that Iran should pressure the Lebanese to release hostages, and use the profits from arms sales to fund the contra effort. Of course, all this was done secretly. Of course, 'bargaining' with terrorists was against stated administration policy, and, of course, aid to the contras violated the law. But it seemed worth the effort to build a bridge to Iran, free American prisoners, and roll back communism. The scheme began unraveling in the autumn of 1986, and Congress launched an investigation. Key figures in the scandal, particularly Lieutenant Colonel Oliver North, an NSC aide, destroyed documents and lied to Congress. The secretaries of defense and state stated that they had opposed the arms sale and related deceptions. The CIA director died before investigators could understand his full role in the matter, and Reagan's political reputation was badly damaged.

Just before the scandal broke, a major business magazine hailed Reagan's management style, applauding the way the president concerned himself with the broad outlines of policy, relied on the judgment of trusted assistants, and set them off to complete their appointed tasks with little interference. After Iran-Contra, the approach seemed dangerously disengaged. Reagan stated that he approved the arms sale, insisted it was only meant to cajole Iran, denied he 'dealt' with terrorists, forgot key details of high-level meetings, and acknowledged that he was in the dark about plans to break and circumvent the law. The president's inattentiveness to details gave him the precious legal gift of 'deniability'. His secretive advisors had run the show, leaving their boss in the dark, misleading Congress, and ignoring the public. The illegal exercise of executive power sprang, oddly enough, from a 'hands-off' rather than a 'hands-on' president.

Despite questionable leadership, questionable ethics, and questionable prosperity, Reagan remained enormously popular, and might have won a third term had not Republicans in the late 1940s cooked up an amendment to prevent that from happening. If the fine points of policy left much to be desired, the big picture Reagan drew for the American people won tremendous support. By counseling confidence over anxiety, individualism over statism, enterprise over regulation, and world leadership over diplomatic caution, the president shifted the course of politics, and forced Democrats to rethink their own strategies for winning the White House.

The New World Order and the Bush Presidency

In the 1988 elections, Democrats maintained their control in Congress; but Reagan's vice president, George Bush, continued the Republicans' hold on the Oval Office. Bush was born to a privileged family, and his good fortune followed him politically when he assumed the legacy of Ronald Reagan. But his 'inheritance' proved a blessing and a curse. Bush benefited from the improving state of world affairs, but he was done in by the worsening state of domestic affairs.

For four decades, across nine administrations, the United States lived and breathed containment. The commitment defined its international strategies, guided its military development, led to two costly wars, claimed over 100,000 American lives, generated alarm among its people, and helped limit the resources available for domestic development. And then the adversary America tried to confound and confine suddenly collapsed. From 1989 through 1991, elections in the Soviet Union, democratic movements in Eastern Europe, the fall of the Berlin Wall, German reunification, Baltic independence, and formation of the Commonwealth of Independent States created what Bush called a 'new world order'. The Cold War that had given such clear focus and direction to United States foreign policy came to an end. Without a sharply defined 'enemy', the old reference points and rallying cries lost their punch. During the 1990s, national leaders tried, with limited success, to define a guiding foreign policy principle to replace the one that passed away.

The former Soviet Union was still beset with political, economic, ethnic, and military instability. But President Bush felt reasonably certain that its republics posed no more than a rhetorical threat to United States interests. America could operate with a bit freer hand in world affairs.

Bush's foreign policy initiatives moved in three directions. The first involved military de-escalation. American and Russian negotiators agreed to reduce (rather than merely limit) strategic nuclear arms and to cut troop levels in Europe. The second policy involved regional intervention. In late 1989, the United States invaded Panama in order to end the rule of General Manuel Antonio Noriega who, in a career of distinguished public service, rigged elections, survived a coup, worked for the CIA *and* Castro, and evaded drug trafficking and racketeering charges.

A third initiative focused on an economic threat to valuable resources and a political threat to sovereign allies. Iraqi President Saddam Hussein, whom the United States had supported in his war

Gulf War

with Iran, invaded oil-rich Kuwait in August 1990. Iraqi forces then prepared to attack Saudi Arabia. Acting unilaterally, Bush deployed US troops to the Persian Gulf. Acting multilaterally, he coordinated international criticism of the Iraqis and forged a multinational military force. The United Nations (UN) imposed economic sanctions on Iraq, sent military forces to the region, and issued an ultimatum for Iraqi withdrawal by mid-January. Acting politically, Bush secured Congressional authorization to use military force in the area. On January 16, and for the next 40 days, coalition forces from 28 nations launched air attacks on Iraq and its troop positions in Kuwait. On February 24, the ground war began, and in 100 hours the allies ousted Hussein's forces from Kuwait. Over half a million US troops served in the war; 300 died. Hussein remained in power, and the United States did not move in to assist opposition forces it had earlier encouraged. But in the eyes of most Americans, the United States had successfully organized and concluded an international military campaign, carried out with strategic flair, technological know-how, and political muscle.

The Weak Domestic Order

Bush reaped huge rewards from the Gulf War. His approval ratings soared to near 90 per cent. Parades for returning veterans expressed a fervent patriotism almost unimaginable in the 1970s. The president seemed headed for a second term, but Bush failed to win re-election in large part because he rested on his overseas laurels and left domestic affairs in a muddle. Forced to work with a Democratic Congress, he also found himself in a legislative stalemate. Victory in the Persian Gulf in 1991 was not enough to bring victory on Election Day in 1992.

Bush pledged to continue Reagan's policies, asking Americans to read his lips when he told them 'no new taxes'. Not tax *reductions* – deficits and debts would not allow that – but no *higher* taxes. Bush also promised a 'kinder and gentler' America: Reaganism with a heart. And indeed, the share of federal spending for defense dropped to about 20 per cent while 'human resource' spending rose to almost 60 per cent. Legislation was passed on civil rights, the disabled, and clean air. Bush appointed Colin Powell to head the Joint Chiefs of Staff, the first

African American to hold the post, and nominated the second black justice to the Supreme Court, Clarence Thomas.

What did Americans get from their kinder and gentler president? An economic report that was 'kind of' gentle. The gross domestic product edged up 20 per cent and stocks zoomed 50 per cent higher, but, overall, the 1980s boom began to stall and sink. Bush's term began with a crisis in 'saving and loans' institutions, brought on by deregulation and speculative investments, and brought to an end by hundreds of billions of federal dollars. Just as the financial mess eased, a recession hit, lasting from 1990–1992. Unemployment rose to 7.5 per cent. The poverty rate grew to over 15 per cent. Only the top 20 per cent of Americans saw their share of the nation's wealth increase under Bush's administration; the remaining 80 per cent found that their portion declined. Real median income, generally rising in the 1980s, *fell*. Inflation pushed upward, slowed only by recession. The budget deficit increased 67 per cent, and the federal debt climbed 50 per cent by the end of Bush's term.

As for the 'heart' of domestic policy, Bush recommended that social compassion (like the creation of wealth) ought to be more of a private affair. He encouraged a spirit of voluntarism through the poetically named 'Thousand Points of Light' program which spotlighted people who worked without federal guidance or funds to improve the conditions of American life. The examples were genuine, just, and inspiring, but Bush's overall strategy was vaguely Hooverian, suggesting that the answer to massive social problems lay in small-scale private efforts. The campaign's individual, independent, and localist message harkened back to traditional but inadequate reform efforts of an earlier day.

Bush's effort to include a variety of groups in the work of government also ran into difficulties with his nomination of Clarence Thomas to the Supreme Court. Instead of applause, the recommendation drew jeers. The conservative nominee raised the ire of the NAACP and other organizations, which feared that Justice Thomas would reverse judicial gains of the past four decades. Feminist groups voiced concern about charges that Thomas had sexually harassed a former assistant, law professor Anita Hill. Senators finally approved the nomination, but only after the administration endured a difficult, unintended, and wrenching controversy.

What did Americans get from their no-new-taxes president? New taxes. Stymied by rising deficits and debts, the president agreed to a 1990 budget plan with Congress that required, among other things, new revenues. Bush suffered a 'double whammy' from the measure. Not only had he taken back his word, but also the new taxes did not help ease the budget deficits that followed.

Most often, Bush seemed to have no strategy for attacking domestic issues. When he took a clear position (like the tax pledge), he later backtracked. The leader who showed such clear concentration and command in a war against a foreign enemy appeared confused and less engaged in attacks on domestic problems. Bush's inability to reverse the economic downslide left him weakened in the 1992 campaign against a politically aware opponent.

The Triumph of the Center: The Clinton Presidency

Bush's Democratic challenger for the presidency, Bill Clinton of Arkansas, focused on one issue: campaign office signs read 'It's the economy, stupid'. Democrats hoped that if the election centered on the recession, Bush's foreign policy reputation would matter little.

Clinton guessed right. The former governor won the 1992 election in a three-way race. He bested the Republican, Bush, who courted the right wing of his party. Clinton also defeated an independent, the simultaneously folksy and quirky H. Ross Perot, who campaigned, pulled out, and campaigned again, all without good explanation, all based on an appeal to his presumed financial expertise. The interesting election brought more Americans to the polls, but they split their choices. Clinton received only 43 per cent of the popular vote, making him a 'minority' candidate with no clear mandate from the electorate (a title he kept after his re-election in 1996). But his fellow Democrats dominated both houses of Congress in 1993 and 1994, the first time a president's party had formed the majority in the House and Senate since the Carter years.

Clinton carefully, consciously, and feverishly presented himself to the American people as a 'centrist'. He was part of the 'Democratic Leadership Council', a group impatient with old political formulas, and tired of hearing that they were fiscally irresponsible, economically backward, beholden to special interests, and unresponsive to changing markets. Clinton's 'new Democrats' learned hard lessons from Reagan and Bush. Republicans lambasted the logic of the New Deal and Great Society, and they seemed to have a point: the left's old guard was more adept at defending than re-evaluating the liberal line. A little reassessment couldn't hurt, Clinton thought. Toss out some failed programs, add some imaginative new ones, keep the Republicans from stealing all the thunder on cultural and moral issues, and demonstrate how they had failed to live up to their promises. That might be a formula for success.

It was the course Clinton followed. To those on the right, he vowed to overhaul welfare, reduce trade barriers, fight crime, rebuild competitiveness, and restore fiscal responsibility. To those on the left, he promised affordable health care, taxes on the rich, environmental protection, the defense of abortion rights, and an end to economic polarization. To those in between, he pledged education improvements, technological innovation, a middle-class tax break, and a plan to rebuild the nation's decaying highways, tunnels, and bridges.

At his worst, Clinton tried to be all things to all people, paying more attention to opinion polls than to coherent strategies and disciplined management. At his best, Clinton offered an alternative for those tired of partisan gridlock, unresponsive government, and worn-out formulas. He tied Bush with the right, distanced himself from the left, sympathized with reformers like Perot, and then helped himself to a heaping portion of what remained: the vast American center.

On one point Clinton was clear: he did not share the Reagan-Bush disdain for government. The president loved politics, threw himself into campaigning, worked the crowds, devoted himself to public service, and remained confident that government was, after all, the last, best hope for progress and justice. After years of tired and stale Republican rule, a young Clinton in 1992 (like a young Kennedy in 1960), took on the old-timers and promised to re-invigorate government, stimulate growth, alter programs, trim expenses, and cut deficits.

Unfortunately, Clinton proved 'Kennedy-esque' in one other way: his fondness for risky personal behavior. In the 1992 campaign, Clinton offered lame excuses for his draft status during the Vietnam War, and his inhalation status when experimenting with marijuana. Early in his presidency, he and his wife faced charges of financial chicanery in a failed Arkansas land deal, a body of cases known as 'Whitewater' that continued through 1999. Even worse, Clinton had to account for his inveterate womanizing. His scandalous behavior with a list of women (in both consenting and sexual harassing situations), fed the rumor mills, nearly derailed his candidacy, constrained the agenda for his second term, and led to his impeachment in 1998.

The 'character issue' dogged Clinton, earning him the nickname 'Slick Willie'. Failed political issues also followed the president. Although working with his own party in Congress, Clinton found Democrats hard to tame and Republicans hard to bear. His health care proposal, designed to contain costs and broaden coverage for those with little or no medical protection, would have dramatically expanded the umbrella of federal social programs for the first time in nearly three decades. But opponents warned of the plan's cost and effectiveness and its enlargement of federal power. They defeated the measure. A pledge to end a ban on homosexuals in the military ended in a watered-down compromise. The plan for a middle-class tax cut collapsed, and a few botched presidential appointments added to White House woes.

Clinton managed some successes. Economically, he and Congress worked out a deficit-reduction plan that combined spending cuts and tax rises; the administration pushed through a free trade agreement with Canada and Mexico; and Clinton expanded tax credits for low-income workers. Socially, the administration supported abortion rights and won passage of bills dealing with gun control, crime prevention, and family leave programs. Politically, Clinton filled the cabinet and other offices with appointees drawn from a range of racial and ethnic groups, making government reflect the composition of American society. And judicially, the president secured a long-awaited Democratic goal: not one but two Supreme Court appointments.

Clinton's mixed political performance and his questionable personal affairs contributed to Democratic losses in the 1994 elections. Voters who had soured on Bush had not turned their backs on conservatism. Starting in 1995, through 2000, Republicans held majorities in both houses of Congress. Led by conservative Newt Gingrich, the new Speaker of the House, they made a 'Contract with America' to cut taxes and social spending, expand the military, get tough with crime, limit Congressional terms, and pass balanced-budget and anti-abortion amendments. Gingrich's forces were so anti-statist that when a budget agreement failed in 1995, Republican leaders simply let much of the federal government shut down – twice.

The following year, however, all sides agreed on at least one issue: an overhaul of the welfare system. The new plan focused nominally on 'personal responsibility' and 'work opportunity'. This meant that one's economic condition was, to a great extent, one's own problem, and loafers need not apply. Rather than centralizing welfare aid in Washington, the bill dispersed responsibility across the states. Rather than expanding or maintaining funding, the measure reduced welfare spending. Rather than providing open-ended assistance, the new law limited the time recipients could obtain aid and required the able-bodied to work.

Gingrich and his friends eventually played their anti-government card too hard and too long, and the Speaker's popularity plummeted after the government shutdowns. In the presidential election of 1996, Clinton defeated a centrist Republican candidate, Senator Robert Dole of Kansas. In 1997, Gingrich was reprimanded by Congress for financial improprieties, and after the 1998 elections, in which Republicans lost Congressional seats, he retired from the House.

Meanwhile Clinton reaped the political rewards of an improving economy. Inflation peaked at a modest 3.3 per cent and slid below 2 per cent in the closing years of the decade. Real median income, which fell under Bush, rose under Clinton. For the first time since the mid-1970s, the share of wealth controlled by the top 20 per cent of Americans declined, and the share held by the lowest 60 per cent increased. During Clinton's first term, the poverty rate fell, and unemployment dropped under 5 per cent. The major index of industrial stocks tripled from 1993-1999.

The most remarkable change came in the budget. In 1993, the

federal government was $255 billion in deficit. Six years later, Clinton and Congress found themselves debating how to handle a budget surplus, the first in three decades. In the new budgetary order, the military's share of federal spending dropped to 15 per cent while human resources rose to 63 per cent, turning the ratios from the early 1950s on their heads. Expanded incomes, lower inflation, higher employment, and black ink in the ledger books led to a new kind of debate: what would the government do with all its money? Spend it on needed programs or reduce it by cutting taxes?

Clinton had built a strong base of support for himself by 1997 and needed every percentage point of it as he made his way through a tangle of scandals over a two year period. One issue involved political fundraising, including charges that big donors received choice White House lodging, and choice plots in federal cemeteries, for their contributions. Foreign nationals and even Chinese military officers also allegedly provided illegal money. A second issue was the continuing Whitewater probe under the direction of a special prosecutor, Kenneth Starr.

Starr expanded his investigation in January 1998 and began looking into charges that Clinton had obstructed justice in a sexual harassment suit brought against him by a former Arkansas state employee, Paula Jones. Her attorneys investigated reports that the president had had improper relations with other women. One of those questioned, a White House intern named Monica Lewinsky, denied a sexual relation with the president. Clinton denied it, too, in both sworn testimony and in a finger-wagging public address. Jones's suit was thrown out of court, but Starr kept up his investigation of possible cover-up, obstruction, and perjury charges against the president. Clinton's August 1998 testimony before a grand jury relied on carefully parsed, hair-splitting legalese; to the public, he admitted an inappropriate relation with Lewinsky but, technically, not a sexual one. He acknowledged that his behavior was wrong, and that he had tried afterwards to protect himself and his family from embarrassment.

The Special Prosecutor's report to the House focused not on Whitewater or fundraising but on sexual improprieties and charges of perjury, witness tampering, and obstruction of justice. The House

Monica Lewinsky

Judiciary Committee began proceedings against the president in November 1998. In December, the full House formally impeached him – that is, voted to charge Clinton with perjury and obstruction of justice. A trial followed in the Senate in early 1999. While most members questioned the president's behavior and personal morality, they did not believe that his actions, however deplorable, rose to the level of impeachable offenses worthy of conviction and removal from office. The public tended to agree, and criticized the techniques used by Starr and Republican Congressmen. In the end, no one came out of the mess looking good. A chastened Clinton tried to restore his family life, pulled back from contentious political debate, and used what authority was left in his office to call national attention back to questions of poverty and health care.

Foreign Policy in the 1990s

Internationally, the United States remained an active, powerful, interventionist player in search of a policy. Like Bush, Clinton failed to define a steady, guiding principle behind America's overseas actions; foreign policy was not his strong suit anyway. Voters recognized the gap in his resumé and did not hold it against him. Perhaps their support for a president with so little interest or expertise in global events was as telling a comment as any about the drift in foreign policy.

The administration's course of action was difficult to determine at times. In Africa, Clinton pulled US forces out of Somalia when political questions complicated famine relief efforts, and the United States refrained from interfering in Rwanda despite widespread massacres. Closer to home, however, Clinton was ready to send US forces into Haiti to restore a democratically elected government, though, at the last minute, Haitian generals stepped down and averted an invasion. Problems of terrorism hit home in 1993 with the bombing of New York's World Trade Center and in 1995 with a bombing at a federal building in Oklahoma City. The administration stepped up investigations of home-grown terrorists, especially those involved with anti-government, white supremicist, and radical religious causes, but the administration's strategy did not include 'preemptive' military strikes or covert campaigns against international terrorists.

Clinton hoped that the focus of American foreign policy could rest on economic routes to peace. Recalling diplomatic themes from before the 1930s, Clinton pushed for reductions in trade barriers in the hope that nations with plentiful markets and supplies would be less likely to resort to force as a way to guarantee their security. In 1994, new trade agreements with Canada and Mexico went into effect, and Clinton also approved new tariff-reducing guidelines formed by the world-wide General Agreement on Tariffs and Trade. The administration hoped that American exports and investments would face as little containment as possible.

The president quickly learned, however, that rational economic calculation only goes so far in explaining human behavior. The main problems he faced in foreign policy grew from nationalism, ethnicity, and religion rather than markets. Fortunately, negotiations eased some disputes. In the Middle East, the administration helped broker a 1993 agreement between Israel and the Palestine Liberation Organization. In 1994, Israel and Jordan signed a formal peace treaty. In April 1998, after Clinton sent former Senator George Mitchell to chair peace talks for

Northern Ireland, delegates from the United Kingdom, the Irish Republic, the Ulster Unionist Party, the Social Democratic and Labor Party, and Sinn Fein signed the 'Good Friday' accords.

Unfortunately, negotiations failed in one other case. Clinton's greatest foreign policy crisis came in post-Cold War Yugoslavia. Beginning in 1991, as the formerly united state broke apart, Serbians warred with Croats and Bosnians over land, power, and long-standing ethnic hatreds. Serbian President Slobodan Milosevic funneled arms to fighters engaged in 'ethnic cleansing', a policy of attack, imprisonment, torture, and execution directed chiefly against Bosnian Muslims. Evidence of atrocities surfaced in 1992; the UN and NATO intervened to force a peace in the region. Finally, in late 1995, the Clinton administration brought leaders of the warring factions together in Dayton, Ohio; in December, they reached an accord. US troops went to Bosnia to serve as part of a NATO peacekeeping contingent.

By July 1997, Milosevic became President of the Federal Republic of Yugoslavia. He focused his attention on rebel activity in Kosovo province, and again the international community raised charges of genocidal ethnic cleansing by Serb forces, this time against ethnic Albanians. In 1998, the United States and NATO Allies called for a halt to the killing. When Milosevic ignored their demands, a 78-day Allied bombing campaign began in the spring of 1999, directed at Serb forces on the ground in Kosovo and Yugoslavia and at the capital city of Belgrade.

Clinton equated Milosevic's actions with those of Hitler's 'Final Solution'. The president argued that America had a moral duty to intervene; those who idly watched the slaughter were accomplices to it. Clinton's strategy was risky and open-ended; there was no clear timetable for the attacks, only a demand that Serb forces withdraw. Russia expressed grave concerns about the bombings, and misdirected allied missiles fell on the Chinese Embassy in Belgrade, killing staff members and heightening Sino-American tensions. After two-and-a half months of intensive bombings, Milosevic agreed to the Allies' demands. The Serbian military pulled out of Kosovo and the military campaign came to an end.

Conclusion

By the end of the 1970s, America's political leaders lacked wide public support, its economy suffered stagnation, inflation, and rising debts, and its foreign policies endured failure and frustration. By the end of the 1990s, a considerable turnaround had taken place. Reagan, Bush, and Clinton each enjoyed a level of public support that chief executives of the 1970s could have only dreamed about. Whatever their political slant (and personal peccadilloes), the three reinvigorated the White House as an office of national leadership. In a political universe of 'divided government', Republican chief executives forced to work with Democratic Congresses and a Democratic president forced to work with Republican legislators rearranged the basic ground rules of New Deal liberalism and the role of the state in America's economic and social order. Their policies freed the economy (for the time, at least) from the old fear of grinding depression and the more recent dread of uncontrollable inflation. By the end of the century, egregious disparities of wealth and rising rates of poverty slowly began to ease. Rates of crime in the United States fell significantly and cities such as New York became safer places for their residents. Productivity increases brought about by advanced computer technology and management changes kept America more competitive internationally. The cautious (at times, even passive) role the United States assumed while communism broke apart led both to an easing of Cold War tensions and a recalculation of 'globalist' strategies. The greatest fear brought about by the new millennium had more to do with calendar-changing computer devastation than with apocalyptic nuclear desolation. As one public policy analyst said, 'all the big issues that used to divide the left and right – the cold war, inflation, crime, welfare – have just collapsed as partisan issues'.[1] In their place, a vast, consensual 'center' seemed to hold.

Sources of division remained, however. Politically, as candidates headed to a safe middle ground, their crowded and blurred central field opened the door for more focused appeals on the left and right. Internationally, leaders did not decisively answer how, where, when, or even if, the United States would exercise the power it had built up so massively over half a century. For a people long-accustomed to ideas of global intervention and broad security interests, the presence of a 'demonic' superpower breathing down their necks since 1945 may not have been *calming*; but it was, at least, *convenient* in defining foreign policy. Economically, the productivity gains that revived the United States in the 1990s appeared hard to maintain into the new century. European unification and Asian recovery indicated strong international competition ahead. Socially, the life chances of whites in the United States were still starkly different from those of African Americans, Hispanics, and Native Americans. In terms of income, housing, education, impoverishment, health care, and the criminal justice system, the gap separating whites and other Americans had narrowed at an excruciatingly slow pace. As manufacturing employment and union membership declined, some of the economic paths minorities had taken to the middle-class narrowed even further, and analysts questioned if an 'information gap' would increasingly separate affluent and 'wired' white households from poorer families left out of the computer revolution.

In a variety of ways, the American drive to control power, protect liberty, and pursue equality continued as strenuously – and unpredictably – as it had for over two centuries. In the twenty-first century, the quest is one followed by a nation that finds itself economically more complex, internationally more ambivalent, and culturally more diverse.

Notes

Notes

Notes

Notes on Sources

CHAPTER ONE
1 *The World Almanac and Book of Facts, 1999* (Mahwah, New Jersey, 1998) p.556.

CHAPTER TWO
1 Michel-Guillaume-Jean de Crèvecoeur, 'Letter III', *Letters from an American Farmer* (1782), in Nina Baym et al., eds., *The Norton Anthology of American Literature*, 3d ed., vol. I (New York: W.W. Norton & Co., 1989), p.561.
2 Thomas Paine, *Common Sense* (1776) (Middlesex, England: Pelican Books, 1979), p.120.

CHAPTER FOUR
1 Robert V. Remini, *The Jacksonian Era* (Arlington Heights, IL: Harlan Davidson, Inc., 1989), pp.23–39.
2 Philip Weeks proposes the categories of 'gradualist' and 'separationist' in *Farewell, My Nation: The American Indian and the United States, 1820–1890* (Arlington Heights, IL: Harlan Davidson, Inc., 1990), pp.11–33.

CHAPTER FIVE
1 William L. Barney, *The Passage of the Republic: An Interdisciplinary History of Nineteenth-Century America* (Lexington, Mass.: D.C. Heath and Company, 1987), p.48.
2 David Brion Davis, in Bernard Bailyn, *et al.*, *The Great Republic: A History of the American People*, 2 vols. (Lexington, Mass.: D.C. Heath and Company, 1985), I:288.
3 Barney, *Passage of the Republic*, p.29.
4 William J. Cooper, *Liberty and Slavery: Southern Politics to 1860* (New York: Knopf, 1983) pp.14, 30–31, 269.
5 Albert J. Raboteau, *Slave Religion: The Invisible Institution of the South* (New York: Oxford University Press, 1980).

CHAPTER SIX

1 Larzer Ziff, *Literary Democracy: The Declaration of Cultural Independence in America* (New York: Penguin Books, 1981), p.vii.; Joseph J. Ellis, *After the Revolution: Profiles of Early American Culture* (New York: W.W. Norton & Co., 1979), p.xi.

2 Ellis, *After the Revolution*, pp.3–21.

3 *Ibid*, p.47.

4 George M. Marsden, *Religion and American Culture* (New York: Harcourt Brace Jovanovich, 1990), p.50.

5 Nathan O. Hatch, *The Democratization of American Christianity* (New Haven: Yale University Press, 1989), p.5.

CHAPTER SEVEN

1 William Wiecek, *The Sources of Antislavery Constitutionalism in America, 1760–1848* (Ithaca: Cornell University Press, 1977), p.277.

2 Quoted in Wiecek, *Antislavery Constitutionalism*, p.277.

3 *Ibid*, p.277.

4 Philip S. Foner, ed., *The Life and Writings of Frederick Douglass*, 5 vols. (New York: International Publishers, 1975), 5:524.

CHAPTER EIGHT

1 David M. Potter, *The Impending Crisis, 1848–1861*, completed and edited by Don E. Fehrenbacher (New York: Harper & Row, 1976), p.479.

2 James M. McPherson, *What They Fought For: 1861–1865* (New York: Anchor Books, 1995), pp.4–6, 27.

3 *Ibid*, pp.9–14, 25, 27–30, 40–41.

4 William Gillette, *Retreat from Reconstruction, 1869–1879* (Baton Rouge: Louisiana State University Press, 1979), p.191.

5 Leon F. Litwack, *Been in the Storm So Long: The Aftermath of Slavery* (New York: Vintage Books, 1980), pp.167–205.

6 *Ibid*, p.228.

7 *Ibid*, pp.292–326.

8 *Ibid*, pp.229–61.

9 William L. Barney, *The Passage of the Republic: An Interdisciplinary History of Nineteenth-Century America* (Lexington, Mass.: D.C. Heath and Company, 1987), p.251.

10 C. Vann Woodward, 'Birth of a Nation', *The New York Review of Books* (20 November 1980), p.50.

11 Eric Foner, *Nothing but Freedom: Emancipation and Its Legacy* (Baton Rouge: Louisiana State University Press, 1983), p.40.

CHAPTER NINE
1 William L. Barney, *The Passage of the Republic: An Interdisciplinary History of Nineteenth-Century America* (Lexington, Mass.: D.C. Heath & Company, 1987), pp.293–95.
2 The term referred to a minstrel tune.

CHAPTER TEN
1 Robert Dallek, *The American Style of Foreign Policy: Cultural Politics and Foreign Affairs* (New York: New American Library, 1983), pp.40–41, 68.
2 David M. Kennedy, *Over Here: The First World War and American Society* (New York: Oxford University Press, 1980), pp.vii, 127–28.

CHAPTER ELEVEN
1 Donald G. Worster, *Dust Bowl: The Southern Plains in the 1930s* (New York: Oxford University Press, 1979), pp.5, 13, 29.

CHAPTER TWELVE
1 See David S. Wyman, *The Abandonment of the Jews: America and the Holocaust 1941–1945* (New York: Pantheon Books, 1984).

CHAPTER THIRTEEN
1 William E. Leuchtenburg, *A Troubled Feast: American Society Since 1945* (Boston: Little, Brown and Company, 1983), p.26.
2 James Gilbert, *Another Chance: Postwar America, 1945–1968* (New York: Knopf, 1981), p.167–68.
3 Richard S. Kirkendall, *A Global Power: America Since the Age of Roosevelt*, 2d ed. (New York: Knopf, 1980), p.116.
4 Robert D. Schulzinger, *American Diplomacy in the Twentieth Century*, 3d ed. (New York: Oxford University Press, 1994), p.266.
5 Fred I. Greenstein, *The Hidden-Hand Presidency: Eisenhower as Leader* (New York: Basic Books, 1982.
6 David Rich Lewis, 'Still Native: The Significance of Native Americans in the History of the Twentieth-Century American West', in Clyde A. Milner II, ed., *A New Significance: Re-envisioning the History of the American West* (New York: Oxford University Press, 1996), p.224.
7 Clayborne Carson, 'Black Power after Ten Years', *The Nation* (14 August 1976); William Julius Wilson, *The Declining Significance of Race: Blacks and Changing American Institutions* (Chicago: University of Chicago Press, 1978), p.150.
8 Betty Friedan, *The Feminine Mystique* (New York: Dell Publishing, 1974), pp.7, 11, 37.
9 Theodore Roszak, *The Making of a Counter Culture: Reflections on the Tech-*

nocratic Society and Its Youghful Opposition (Garden City, New York: Anchor Books, 1969), p.xii.

CHAPTER FOURTEEN
1 Francis Fukuyama, quoted in 'Left and Right are Crossing Paths', *New York Times* (11 July 1999).

Presidents of the United States

President	Years served	Party	
1. George Washington	1789–1797		
2. John Adams	1797–1801	F	(Federalist)
3. Thomas Jefferson	1801–1809	DR	(Democratic-Republican)
4. James Madison	1809–1817	DR	
5. James Monroe	1817–1825	DR	
6. John Q. Adams	1825–1829	DR	
7. Andrew Jackson	1829–1837	D	(Democrat)
8. Martin Van Buren	1837–1841	D	
9. William H. Harrison	1841	W	(Whig)
10. John Tyler	1841–1845	W/D	
11. James K. Polk	1845–1849	D	
12. Zachary Taylor	1849–1850	W	
13. Millard Fillmore	1850–1853	W	
14. Franklin Pierce	1853–1857	D	
15. James Buchanan	1857–1861	D	
16. Abraham Lincoln	1861–1865	R	(Republican)
17. Andrew Johnson	1865–1869	D/U	(Unionist)
18. Ulysses S. Grant	1869–1877	R	
19. Rutherford B. Hayes	1877–1881	R	
20. James A. Garfield	1881	R	
21. Chester A. Arthur	1881–1885	R	
22. Grover Cleveland	1885–1889	D	
23. Benjamin Harrison	1889–1893	R	
24. Grover Cleveland	1893–1897	D	
25. William McKinley	1897–1901	R	
26. Theodore Roosevelt	1901–1909	R	
27. William H. Taft	1909–1913	R	
28. Woodrow Wilson	1913–1921	D	
29. Warren G. Harding	1921–1923	R	

30. Calvin Coolidge	1923–1929	R
31. Herbert C. Hoover	1929–1933	R
32. Franklin D. Roosevelt	1933–1945	D
33. Harry S. Truman	1945–1953	D
34. Dwight D. Eisenhower	1953–1961	R
35. John F. Kennedy	1961–1963	D
36. Lyndon B. Johnson	1963–1969	D
37. Richard M. Nixon	1969–1974	R
38. Gerald R. Ford	1974–1977	R
39. James E. Carter Jr.	1977–1981	D
40. Ronald W. Reagan	1981–1989	R
41. George H. Bush	1989–1993	R
42. William J. Clinton	1993–2001	D

Population Growth by Decade

Year	Population	Percent Increase
1610	350	
1620	2,300	557.1
1630	4,600	100.0
1640	26,600	478.3
1650	50,400	90.8
1660	75,100	49.0
1670	111,900	49.0
1680	151,500	35.4
1690	210,400	38.9
1700	250,000	19.2
1710	331,700	32.2
1720	466,200	40.5
1730	629,400	35.0
1740	905,600	43.9
1750	1,170,800	29.3
1760	1,593,600	36.1
1770	2,148,100	34.8
1780	2,780,400	29.4
1790	3,929,214	41.3
1800	5,308,483	35.1
1810	7,239,861	36.4
1820	9,636,453	33.1
1830	12,866,702	33.5
1840	17,063,353	32.7
1850	23,191,876	35.9
1860	31,443,321	35.6
1870	38,558,371	26.6
1880	50,189,209	26.0
1890	62,979,766	25.5

1900	76,212,168	20.7
1910	92,228,496	21.0
1920	106,021,537	14.9
1930	123,202,624	16.1
1940	132,164,569	7.2
1950	151,325,798	14.5
1960	179,323,175	18.5
1970	203,302,031	13.4
1980	226,542,199	11.4
1990	248,718,301	9.8
(2000)	(est. 275,000,000)	(10.4)

Figures from 1610–1780 are estimates, drawn from British North American colonies in the present-day United States.

Figures from 1790–2000 are drawn from statistics compiled by national census reports.

For the most part, these figures do not include the Native American population. The first census to attempt such a count found 125,719 Native Americans in 1890.

Sources: *Historical Statistics of the United States, Colonial Times to 1970* (1975)
Statistical Abstract of the United States (1999)

Chronology of Major Events

BC

14,000–10,000	Estimated period when first human beings set foot in North America
10,000–9000	Paleo-Indians
8000–1500	Archaic Indians
5000	Agricultural practices develop in Western Hemisphere
1500	Poverty Point culture (present-day Louisiana)
500–500AD	Adena-Hopewell culture (present-day Midwest)

AD

100–1300	Anasazi culture (present-day Southwest)
800–1500	Mississippian culture
1325–1521	Aztec (Mexica) culture
1492	Columbus lands in America
1519	Cortés lands in Mexico
1534	Cartier's exploration of the St. Lawrence River
1539	Expeditions of DeSoto and Coronado begin
1565	Founding of St. Augustine by Spain
1585–1587	Raleigh's colony at Roanoke Island
1607	Founding of Jamestown by England
1608	Founding of Québec by France
1610	Founding of Santa Fe by Spain
1617	Trade in Virginia tobacco begins
1619	First Africans brought to Virginia
1620	Founding of Plymouth Colony by Pilgrims; *Mayflower Compact*
1624	Dutch settlement on Manhattan Island
1630	Puritans settle in Massachusetts Bay Colony
1636	Founding of first college in America (Harvard)
1662	Virginia law makes slavery hereditary
1664	English take control of New Netherland

1675	King Philip's War
1676	Bacon's Rebellion
1681	William Penn granted land for establishment of colony
1692	Salem witchcraft trials
1701	Founding of Yale
1718	Founding of New Orleans by France
1720s–1740s	Religious revivals known as the 'Great Awakening'
1756–1763	Seven Years War (French and Indian War)
1760	George III becomes king
1765	Stamp Act
1769	Colonization of California by Spain begins
1770	'Boston Massacre'
1773	Boston 'Tea Party'
1774	Intolerable Acts
	First Continental Congress convenes
1775	Battles of Lexington and Concord; start of the American Revolution
	Second Continental Congress
1776	Thomas Paine's *Common Sense*
	Declaration of Independence
1777	Drafting of Articles of Confederation
1778	France enters Revolutionary War on the side of Americans
1781	Ratification of the Articles of Confederation
	Surrender of Cornwallis at Yorktown
1783	Treaty of Paris concludes the Revolutionary War
1787	Constitution drafted at the Philadelphia Convention
1788	Constitution ratified
1789	Washington inaugurated first president of the new republic
1791	Bill of Rights (first ten amendments) becomes part of the Constitution
	Alexander Hamilton's *Report on Manufactures*
1793	Invention of the cotton gin
1794	Whiskey Rebellion
1796	Washington's farewell address
1798	'XYZ Affair'
	Alien and Sedition Acts
1800	Washington, DC becomes capital of the United States
1803	Louisiana Purchase
	Marbury v. Madison decision by the Supreme Court declares legislation passed by Congress unconstitutional
1804–1806	Lewis and Clark expedition
1807	Robert Fulton builds steamboat, *Clermont*
	Embargo Act

1812–1814	War of 1812 with Great Britain
1820	Missouri Compromise
1823	Monroe Doctrine
1825	Opening of the Erie Canal
1829	David Walker's *Appeal*, calling for abolition of slavery
1831	Founding of the *Liberator*, abolitionist newspaper
	Nat Turner's slave rebellion, Virginia
1833	Nullification Crisis
1837	John Deere's steel plow
1838	'Trail of Tears' (Indian Removal)
1844	Invention of telegraph
1846–1848	Mexican-American War
1848	Women's rights convention, Seneca Falls, New York
1849	California gold rush
1850	Compromise of 1850 (including Fugitive Slave Act)
1852	Harriet Beecher Stowe's *Uncle Tom's Cabin*
1854	Kansas-Nebraska Act
1857	*Dred Scott v. Sanford* (slavery expansion and status of African Americans)
1859	John Brown's raid on Harpers Ferry
1860	Abraham Lincoln elected president
	South Carolina becomes first state to secede from the Union
1861	Confederate States of America formed
	Attack on Fort Sumter, Charleston harbor, South Carolina
1861–1865	The Civil War
1863	*Emancipation Proclamation*
	Battles of Gettysburg and Vicksburg, turning points in the Civil War
1865	Assassination of Abraham Lincoln
	13th Amendment (ends slavery)
1868	Impeachment of President Andrew Johnson; acquitted in Senate trial
1869	Completion of transcontinental railroad
1876	Invention of the telephone
	Defeat of General George Armstrong Custer at Battle of Little Bighorn
1877	'Compromise' brings an end to Reconstruction
1879	Invention of electric light bulb
1886	Statue of Liberty dedicated in New York City harbor; gift from France
	Plessy v. Ferguson (Court decision on segregation)
1898	Spanish-American War

1901	Completion of immigration processing depot on Ellis Island, New York
1903	Flight by the Wright Brothers
1909	Production of first Model T by Ford Motor Company
	Founding of National Association for the Advancement of Colored People
1914	Opening of the Panama Canal
	World War I begins in Europe
1917–1918	US participation in World War I
1919	18th Amendment (prohibition)
1920	19th Amendment (women's suffrage)
	Commercial radio broadcasting begins
1927	Charles Lindbergh's solo flight from New York to Paris
	The Jazz Singer, the first talking motion picture
1929	Stock market crash; start of the Great Depression
1933	Beginning of Franklin D. Roosevelt's 'New Deal'
	US recognizes USSR
	Repeal of prohibition
1935	Social Security Act
1939	World War II begins in Europe
1941	Attack on Pearl Harbor, Hawaii
1941–1945	US participation in World War II
1942	Founding of Congress of Racial Equality
1947	Truman Doctrine; Marshall Plan; containment policy
1948	Development of the transistor
	Network television programming begins
1949	Establishment of NATO
1950	US aid to the French in Indochina begins
	Diner's Club introduces the first credit card
1950–1953	Korean War
1954	Geneva accords on Vietnam; US aid to South Vietnam begins
	Army-McCarthy Hearings
	Brown v. Board of Education (Court decision on desegregation)
1955–1956	Bus boycott in Montgomery, Alabama
1956	Construction of interstate highway system begins
1957	Crisis in Little Rock over school desegregation
	Founding of Southern Christian Leadership Conference
1960	U-2 spy plan shot down over USSR
1961	First US manned space flight
1962	First US manned orbital flight
	Cuban missile crisis

1963	Civil rights March on Washington
	Founding of United Farm Workers by Cesar Chavez
	Assassination of John F. Kennedy
1964	Free Speech Movement, University of California at Berkeley
	Gulf of Tonkin Resolution.
1965–1966	Lyndon B. Johnson's 'Great Society' programs
1966	Founding of National Organization for Women
	Founding of Black Panther Party
1968	First demonstration of a computer 'network'
	Founding of the American Indian Movement
	Assassination of Martin Luther King, Jr.
	Assassination of Robert F. Kennedy
1969	Americans walk on the moon
1970	Creation of Environmental Protection Agency
1971	Development of the microprocessor
1972	Founding of *Ms.* magazine
	Richard Nixon visits China
1973	Cease fire agreement in Vietnam; US forces leave South Vietnam
	Oil embargo
	Roe v. Wade (Court decision legalizes abortion)
1974	Richard Nixon resigns from the presidency after Watergate investigation
1975	Fall of Saigon; end of the Vietnam War
1976	Sale of first personal home computer by Apple
1979	Full diplomatic relations established between the US and the People's Republic of China
1980–1981	Hostage crisis in Iran
1981	First reported case of AIDS in the US
1989	Fall of the Berlin Wall
1991	Persian Gulf War
	Dissolution of the Soviet Union
1992	Creation of the World Wide Web
1995	Terrorist bombing of Murrah Federal Building in Oklahoma City
1998	Impeachment of President Bill Clinton
1999	NATO air war in Kosovo
	Senate acquits President Clinton
2000	Microsoft appeals judge's order to break up the corporation for anti-trust violations
	Furor over return of six-year-old 'boat boy' Elián González, to Cuba

Further Reading

AMBROSE, STEPHEN E., *Eisenhower* (New York, 1983)

AMBROSE, STEPHEN E., *Rise to Globalism: American Foreign Policy Since 1938*, 7th rev. edn. (New York, 1993)

AMBROSE, STEPHEN E., *Undaunted Courage: Meriwether Lewis, Thomas Jefferson, and the Opening of the American West* (New York, 1996)

BERLIN, IRA, *Many Thousands Gone: The First Two Centuries of Slavery in North America* (Cambridge, Mass., 1998)

BRANCH, TAYLOR, *Parting the Waters: America in the King Years, 1954–63* (New York, 1988)

BRANCH, TAYLOR, *Pillar of Fire: America in the King Years, 1963–65* (New York, 1998)

BURROWS, EDWIN G., MIKE WALLACE, *Gotham: A History of New York City to 1898* (New York, 1999)

CORDES, KATHLEEN A. and JANE LAMMERS, *America's National Historic Trails* (Norman, Okla., 1999)

CRONON, WILLIAM, *Changes in the Land: Indians, Colonists, and the Ecology of New England* (New York, 1983)

CRONON, WILLIAM, *Nature's Metropolis: Chicago and the Great West* (New York, 1992)

DALLEK, ROBERT, *The American Style of Foreign Policy: Cultural Politics and Foreign Affairs* (New York, 1983)

DELANY, SARAH L., A. ELIZABETH DELANY, AMY HILL HEARTH, *Having Our Say: The Delany Sisters' First 100 Years* (New York, 1994)

DEMOS, JOHN, *The Unredeemed Captive: A Family Story from Early America* (New York, 1994)

FONER, ERIC, *The Story of American Freedom* (New York 1998)

GENOVESE, EUGENE D., *Roll, Jordan, Roll: The World the Slaves Made* (New York, 1974)

GOODWIN, DORIS KEARNS, *The Fitzgeralds and the Kennedys* (New York, 1987)

GOODWIN, DORIS KEARNS, *Lyndon Johnson and the American Dream* (New York, 1976)

GOODWIN, DORIS KEARNS, *No Ordinary Time: Franklin and Eleanor Roosevelt, The Home Front in World War II* (New York, 1994)

HAWKE, DAVID FREEMAN, *Everyday Life in Early America* (New York, 1988)

HINE, DARLENE CLARK and KATHLEEN THOMPSON, *A Shining Thread of Hope : The History of Black Women in America* (New York, 1998)

HUGHES, ROBERT, *American Visions: The Epic History of Art in America* (New York, 1997)

JOHNSON, PAUL, *A History of the American People* (New York, 1997)

KAMMEN, MICHAEL, *American Culture, American Tastes: Social Change and the 20th Century* (New York, 1999)

KRAUT, ALAN M., *The Huddled Masses: The Immigrant in American Society, 1880– 1921* (Arlington Heights, Il., 1982)

LARKIN, JACK, *The Reshaping of Everyday Life, 1790–1840* (New York, 1989)

LIMERICK, PATRICIA NELSON, *The Legacy of Conquest: The Unbroken Past of the American West* (New York, 1987)

McCULLOUGH, DAVID, *The Path Between the Seas: The Creation of the Panama Canal, 1870–1914* (New York, 1977)

McCULLOUGH, DAVID, *Truman* (New York, 1992)

McPHEE, JOHN A., *Coming into the Country* (New York, 1977)

McPHERSON, JAMES M., *Battle Cry of Freedom: The Civil War Era* (New York, 1988)

McPHERSON, JAMES M., *For Cause and Comrades: Why Men Fought in the Civil War* (New York, 1997)

MARTY, MARTIN E., *Pilgrims in Their Own Land: 500 Years of Religion in America* (Boston, 1984)

MIDDLEKAUFF, ROBERT, *The Glorious Cause: The American Revolution, 1763– 1789* (New York, 1982)

MILNER, CLYDE A., II, CAROL A. O'CONNOR, MARTHA A. SANDWEISS (eds.), *The Oxford History of the American West* (New York, 1994)

MOODY, ANNE, *Coming of Age in Mississippi* (New York, 1968)

MORGAN, EDMUND S., *American Slavery, American Freedom: The Ordeal of Colonial Virginia* (New York, 1975)

NORTON, MARY BETH, *Liberty's Daughters: The Revolutionary Experience of American Women, 1750–1800* (Boston, 1980)

OATES, STEPHEN B., *With Malice Toward None: A Life of Abraham Lincoln* (New York, 1977)

POTTER, DAVID M., completed and edited by Don E. Fehrenbacher, *The Impending Crisis, 1848–1861* (New York, 1976)

REISNER, MARC, *Cadillac Desert: The American West and Its Disappearing Water,* rev. ed. (New York, 1993)

SCHLERETH, THOMAS J., *Victorian America: Transformations in Everyday Life, 1876– 1915* (New York, 1991)

SHEEHAN, NEIL, *A Bright and Shining Lie: John Paul Vann and America in Vietnam* (New York, 1989)

TAKAKI, RONALD, *A Different Mirror: A History of Multicultural America* (Boston 1994)

TERKEL, STUDS, *Hard Times: An Oral History of the Great Depression* (New York, 1970)

THOMAS, EMORY M., *The Confederate Nation, 1861–1865* (New York, 1979)

ULRICH, LAUREL THATCHER, *A Midwife's Tale: The Life of Martha Ballard, Based on Her Diary, 1785–1812* (New York, 1990)

VIORST, MILTON, *Fire in the Streets: America in the 1960s* (New York, 1979)

WALTERS, RONALD G., *American Reformers, 1815–1860*, rev. edn. (New York, 1997)

WILLS, GARRY, *A Necessary Evil: A History of American Distrust of Government* (New York, 1999)

WILLS, GARRY, *Lincoln at Gettysburg: The Words That Remade America* (New York, 1992)

WOOD, GORDON S. *The Radicalism of the American Revolution* (New York, 1991)

WOODWARD, C. VANN, *The Strange Career of Jim Crow*, 3d rev. edn. (New York, 1974)

ZINN, HOWARD, *A People's History of the United States: 1492–Present*, rev. edn. (New York, 1999)

Internet Resources

Note: Web site addresses frequently change, especially on commercial (com) sites. Government (gov) and organizational (org) sites tend to keep the same address. If a site does not appear using the address below, go to an internet search engine (such as altavista.com/yahoo.com/metacrawler.com) and enter the name of the site you wish to find.

General historical reference

Library of Congress: www.loc.gov
>For the text of the Constitution and the Bill of Rights, see:
>lcweb2.loc.gov/const/const.html

National Archives: www.nara.gov
>For the text of the Declaration, Constitution, and Bill of Rights, see:
>www.nara.gov/exhall/charters/constitution/conmain.html

Virtual Library, University of Kansas: www.ukans.edu/history/VL/USA/

Other services:
>The History Channel: www.thehistorychannel.com
>>This cable television service provides an entertaining web site, much of it tied to the company's programming. Its 'exhibits' are particularly interesting and useful.

>The History Net: www.thehistorynet.com
>>The web site also offers a wide variety of subjects and resources.

>Public Broadcasting Service: www.pbs.org/wgbh/amex/
>>The web site for *The American Experience* series of documentaries. Go to the site's 'archives' for material on television programs broadcast in this distinguished and varied series.

>*American Heritage*: www.americanheritage.com
>>A popular and well-written periodical, aimed at a general audience, devoted to topics in American history. The web site has an archive with some past articles from the magazine.

General reference for travellers

Historical travel

The National Parks Foundation: www.nationalparks.org

The National Park Foundation offers special pages on its web site with links to particular historical travel interests:

African American History: www.cr.nps.gov/aahistory/bhm-sites.htm

Archeology, paleontology: www.nationalparks.org/guide/special-interest-2.htm

Battlefields: www.nationalparks.org/guide/special-interest-3.htm

Civil War: www.nationalparks.org/guide/special-interest-4.htm

Hispanic heritage: www.nationalparks.org/guide/special-interest-5.htm

Presidential history: www.nationalparks.org/guide/special-interest-6.htm

Women's history: www.nationalparks.org/guide/special-interest-8.htm

Other topics: www.nationalparks.org/new_special%20interest_1.htm

History Travel: www.historytravel.com

See, in particular, its page for varied and interesting historical itineraries throughout the US, including topics such as 'women's historical sites' and 'literary sites for book lovers': www.historytravel.com/features/

The History Net: www.thehistorynet.com/THNarchives/HistoricTravel/

For an archived list of articles on historical travel, see:

www.thehistorynet.com/THNarchives/HistoricTravel/articles_index.htm

Civil War Traveler: www.civilwartraveler.com

Information on key Civil War sites plus tours, maps, calendars of events.

National Trust for Historic Preservation: www.nthp.org

The site offers travel programs as well as a list of historic inns and hotels for travellers.

Maps

Mapquest: www.mapquest.com

National Park Service: www.nps.gov/parklists/TI_maps.htm

Roadways

National Scenic Byways Online: www.byways.org

The Federal Highway Administration's website with information and itineraries for over 50 'All-American Roads' and 'National Scenic Byways,' plus a complete listing of 500 state and federally designated byways, listed by name and by state.

Calendar of historical events taking place in the United States

www.thehistorynet.com/calendar/events.htm

www.geocities.com/~livinghistory/event00.htm

Companies offering general information on travel in the United States

Travelocity: www.travelocity.com

See Travelocity's 'Destination Guide' for the USA in general (and for particular cities and states).

USA Travel: www.usatourist.com
  A site designed with foreign visitors in mind.
Lonely Planet: www.lonelyplanet.com
  Blunt, practical, down-to-earth advice on travel.
Lycos: www.travel.lycos.com/Destinations/North_America/USA/
  Plenty of information on travel in America, organized by state. A good deal of practical travel information, too, for those arriving in the USA from abroad.
City Spin: www.cityspin.com
City Search: www.citysearch.com
  Offering a variety of sites focused on states and cities in the USA
Weather reports
  National Weather Service: www.wrh.noaa.gov/wrhq/nwspage.html
  The Weather Channel: www.weather.com

National Park Service: www.nps.gov/index.html

Categories: The National Park Service (created in 1916) offers a wide range of natural, historical, scientific, and cultural resources for travellers. The NPS refers to its park sites according to different categories (see below). A guide to the names is found at: www.nps.gov/legacy/nomenclature.html

National Battlefields	National Parkways
National Battlefield Parks	National Preserves
National Battlefield Site	National Recreation Areas
National Historic Sites	National Reserve
National Historical Parks	National Rivers
National Lakeshores	National Scenic Trails
National Memorials	National Seashores
National Military Parks	National Wild and Scenic Rivers
National Monuments	International Historic Site
National Parks	Other parks

MAPS

For digital maps of National Park Service resources, see www.nps.gov/carto/
In addition, go to: www.nps.gov/parklists/TI_maps.htm

HISTORICAL SITES

The National Park Service conveniently groups its resources according to a wide range of historical categories. A sample of the categories appears below. For a complete list, see: www.cr.nps.gov/history/catsig/catsig.htm

African American Heritage; Alaska Native Heritage; American Indian Heritage; Architecture; Asian American Heritage; Civil War; Hispanic Heritage; Landscape; Maritime; Military; Pacific Islander Heritage; Presidential; Revolutionary War; Social and Humanitarian Movements; Women's History/Women's Rights; World War II

NATIONAL HISTORIC LANDMARKS

'National Historic Landmarks' (NHL) include tribal communities, battlefields, buildings, landmarks, and landscapes. See list of examples below.
The NHL home page is located at: www2.cr.nps.gov/nhl/virtvist.htm

Arizona: Pueblo Grande Ruin and Irrigation Sites

Arkansas: Fort Smith

California: Alcatraz; Presidio of San Francisco

Connecticut: Connecticut State Capitol; Mark Twain Home

District of Columbia: US Department of the Treasury; Library of Congress; Smithsonian Institution; Pension Building (National Building Museum); United States Capitol; The White House

Florida: Dixie Coca-Cola Bottling Company Plant; New Echota

Hawaii: USS *Arizona*

Illinois: Lincoln Home

Indiana: Levi Coffin House

Iowa: Hoover Birthplace

Maryland: Baltimore and Ohio Transportation Museum; Clara Barton House

Massachusetts: John and John Quincy Adams Birthplace; Emily Dickinson Home; New Bedford Historic District

Missouri: Gateway Arch; Scott Joplin Residence

Montana: Pictograph Cave

Nevada: Virginia City

New Jersey: Sandy Hook Lighthouse

New Mexico: Trinity Site

New York: Susan B. Anthony House; Brooklyn Bridge; Carnegie Hall; Central Park; Empire State Building; Fort Ticonderoga; John D. Rockefeller Estate (Kykuit); Sunnyside; and Van Cortland Manor; Metropolitan Museum of Art; Oneida Community Mansion House; United States Military Academy

North Carolina: Bentonville Battlefield; Thomas Wolfe Memorial

Pennsylvania: Carpenter's Hall; Delaware and Hudson Canal; Drake Oil Well; Eastern State Penitentiary; Fonthill; Mercer Museum; Moravian Pottery and Tile Works

Rhode Island: The Breakers

South Carolina: Drayton Hall

Texas: Fort Concho

Virginia: Cape Henry Lighthouse; Christ Church; Gadsby's Tavern; Gunston Hall; Monticello; Stratford Hall

Wisconsin: Taliesin

MAJOR NATIONAL PARKS

These large natural areas are among the best known (and most heavily visited) places in the National Park Service.

Alaska: Denali; Gates of the Arctic; Glacier Bay

Arizona: Grand Canyon; Petrified Forest

California: Joshua Tree; Kings Canyon; Redwood; Sequoia; Yosemite

California/Nevada: Death Valley

Colorado: Mesa Verde; Rocky Mountain

Florida: Dry Tortugas, Everglades

Hawaii: Haleakala; Hawaii Volcanoes

Kentucky: Mammoth Cave

Montana: Glacier

New Mexico: Carlsbad Caverns

North Dakota: Theodore Roosevelt

South Dakota: Badlands; Wind Cave

Tennessee/North Carolina: Great Smoky Mountains

Texas: Big Bend; Guadalupe Mountains

Utah: Arches; Bryce Canyon; Canyonlands; Capitol Reef; Zion

Virginia: Shenandoah

Washington: Mount Rainier, North Cascades, Olympic

Wyoming: Grand Teton

Wyoming/Montana/Idaho: Yellowstone

TRAILS

The National Park Service offers descriptions to its park trails and long distance trails at the following web address: www.nps.gov/trails/

You can also find more specific information at the site for:

Major, long-distance, 'scenic' trails such as:

Appalachian National Scenic Trail

Ice Age National Scenic Trail

Natchez Trace National Scenic Trail

Major, long-distance, 'historic' and 'heritage' trails such as:

California National Historic Trail

Freedom Trail, Boston

Juan Bautista de Anza National Historic Trail

Lewis & Clark National Historic Trail

Mormon Pioneer National Historic Trail

New Jersey Coastal Heritage Trail

Nez Perce National Historic Trail

North Country National Scenic Trail

Oregon National Historic Trail

Overmountain Victory National Historic Trail

Pony Express National Historic Trail
Potomac Heritage National Scenic Trail
Santa Fe National Historic Trail
Trail of Tears National Historic Trail

(A commercial site offering further information on National Scenic and Historic Trails can be found at: www.gorp.com/gorp/resource/us_trail/nattrail.htm)

National Register of Historic Places www.cr.nps.gov/nr/index.htm

The web site lists buildings placed on the National Register. The site also offers suggestions for those who wish to visit the designated buildings. Click on the special area for 'Travel Itineraries'. To access the site, go to: www.cr.nps.gov/nr/tourism.html The itineraries offered include:

Cities/States:	Baltimore	Kingston, NY
	Charleston, SC	Seattle
	Chicago	Central Vermont
	Detroit	Washington, DC.
Themes:	Aboard the Underground Railroad	
	Places Where Women Made History	
	We Shall Overcome: Historic Places of the Civil Rights Movement	

World Heritage Sites in the USA

The United Nations agency UNESCO has designated places around the globe with special natural, historical, and cultural significance as 'World Heritage Sites'. The full listing of sites (and further information) may be found at the homepage for UNESCO's project: www.unesco.org/whc/nwhc/pages/sites/main.htm

An alternative web address is: www.nationalparks.org/guide/special-interest-9.htm

State	World Heritage Site
Arizona:	Grand Canyon National Park
California:	Redwood National Park
California:	Yosemite National Park
Colorado:	Mesa Verde National Park
Florida:	Everglades National Park
Hawaii:	Hawaii Volcanoes National Park
Illinois:	Cahokia Mounds State Historic Site
Kentucky:	Mammoth Cave National Park
New Mexico:	Carlsbad Caverns National Park

New Mexico:	Chaco Culture National Historic Park
New Mexico:	Pueblo de Taos
New York:	Statue of Liberty
North Carolina/ Tennessee:	Great Smoky Mountains National Park
Pennsylvania:	Independence Hall
Puerto Rico:	San Juan National Historic Site and La Fortaleza
Virginia:	Monticello, and the University of Virginia
Washington:	Olympic National Park
Wyoming:	Yellowstone National Park

The natural environment

Audubon Society: www.audubon.org/
National Forest Service: www.fs.fed.us/
   In autumn months, the service's web page offers information on autumn foliage in the USA.
Nature Conservancy: www.tnc.org/frames/index.html?/infield/index.html
Sierra Club: www.sierraclub.org

Living history

'Living history' sites throughout the U.S. bring history to life by offering a wide range of museums, historical farms, reenactments, interpretative demonstrations, and folklore programs. For guides to key living history locations, see:
Living History Association: www.geocities.com/~livinghistory/
Living history museums: www.voicenet.com/~frstprsn/alhfam/fpsites.htm

Historical Gazetteer

Numbers in bold refer to main text

Asheville, North Carolina. *Biltmore Estate* (1895): the largest home in the U.S., built for George Vanderbilt. Design by Richard Morris Hunt; landscaping by Frederick Law Olmsted. **233**

Alabama, *Selma-to-Montgomery March National Historic Trail and All-American Road;* route of 1965 voting rights march. **361–363**

Alamo, San Antonio, Texas. Mission remembered as the place where Texas independence forces faced a nearly two-week siege by Mexican troops. On 6 March 1836, General Santa Anna's army defeated the Texans, killing almost all of them. Also in San Antonio: *San Antonio Missions National Historical Park:* Four Spanish missions, built from 1755–1782. **164**

Amherst, Massachusetts. *Emily Dickinson Home;* where the 19th century poet lived most of her life. Located 20 miles north of Springfield. **152–153**

Annapolis, Maryland. Originally settled in 1649; became the capital of colonial Maryland in 1694. Located 32 miles east of Washington, DC. *Banneker-Douglass Museum:* the 1874 Mt. Moriah African Methodist Episcopalian Church. *Hammond-Harwood*

House: 1774 example of Georgian architecture. *Maynard-Burgess House:* home to two 19th-century African-American families. *Maryland Statehouse:* late 18th century structure; from 1783–1784 served as the nation's capitol. *William Paca House and Garden:* 1765 Georgian home. *St. John's College:* founded in 1696; third oldest college in America. *United States Naval Academy:* First established in 1845 as the 'Naval School'. **20–21**

Atlanta, Georgia. Established in 1827 as 'Terminus', the town served as the southern endpoint of a railroad. In 1845, the city was rechristened 'Atlanta', named after a rail line. Perhaps one day the town will be renamed 'Hartsfield', in honor of its more recent, air transportation link, the busiest airport in the United States. *Atlanta University Center Historic District:* Includes three campuses (Morehouse College, Spelman College, Atlanta University) that played important roles in the civil rights movement. *CNN Center:* Home base of Cable News Network and Turner Broadcasting. *Fox Theater:* Ornate 1920s movie palace. *Martin Luther King, Jr. National Historic Site:* East of downtown Atlanta, the site includes the birthplace of the civil rights reformer as well as Ebenezer Baptist Church, where King, his father, and his grandfather all served. Also, King's burial site. *Margaret Mitchell House and Museum:* home of the author of *Gone with the Wind. Swan House:* 1928 mansion designed by local architect Philip Trammell Shutze. *Tullie Smith Farm, Atlanta History Center:* plantation home from the 1840s. *World of Coca-Cola:* The history of a soft drink – and a major part of American popular culture's 'coca-colonization' of the world. *Wren's Nest House Museum:* Home of Southern regionalist writer, Joel Chandler Harris. **199, 201, 329**

Auburn, Indiana: *Auburn-Cord-Duesenberg Museum;* Displays of automobiles from a northeast Indiana manufacturer in the 1920s and 1930s. Located 130 miles northeast of Indianapolis. **226, 278–279**

Aztec, New Mexico: *Aztec Ruins National Monument;* artifacts of Pueblo cultures from the 12th through 13th centuries. Located 31 miles south-southwest of Durango, Colorado. **8, 10**

Baranof Island, Alaska: *Sitka National Historical Park;* buildings and cultural artifacts from the Haida and Tlingit Indians as well as Russian settlers. Located 100 miles south of Juneau (by air). **12**

Battle sites

Revolutionary War:
Bunker Hill Monument (See 'Boston').

Cowpens National Battlefield, Chesnee, South Carolina: January 1781 victory of American troops over British forces. Located 20 miles northeast of Spartanburg. *Fort Moultrie*, Charleston, South Carolina: Site of an early American victory against Britain, one week before the Declaration of Independence. Eighty-five years later, forces in this fort fired on Fort Sumter, launching the Civil War. Also the burial place of Seminole leader, Osceola. *Guilford Courthouse National Military Park*, Greensboro, North Carolina: March 1781 battle between forces under Nathanael Greene and Cornwallis inflicted heavy losses on the latter's army. *Kings Mountain National Military Park*, Blacksburg, South Carolina: 1780 battle that served as a turning point in the Southern campaign. Located 30 miles northeast of Spartanburg. (The path of Patriot soldiers to this battle site may be traced today over the National Park Service's *'Overmountain Victory National Historic Trail'*.) *Minute Man National Historical Park*, Concord, Massachusetts: A 5½-mile trail winds from Lexington to Concord, retracing the events of 19 April 1775 that marked the start of the American Revolution. *Morristown National Historical Park*, Morristown, New Jersey: Washington's headquarters, 1779–1780. Located 20 miles west of Newark. *Saratoga National Historical Park*, Stillwater, New York: Where American forces under Gates defeated Burgoyne's troops in October 1777. Located approximately 30 miles north of Albany. *Valley Forge National Historical Park*, Valley Forge, Pennsylvania: site where Washington's troops made winter quarters in 1777–1778. Located 18 miles west of Philadelphia. *Yorktown Battlefield*, Colonial National Historical Park, Yorktown, Virginia: The site where British commander Cornwallis surrendered his troops in October 1781 in the closing battle of the American Revolution. Located 12 miles east of Williamsburg. **50, 52–60**

War of 1812:
Battle of New Orleans (Chalmette Battlefield and National Cemetery), Chalmette, Louisiana: site of the battle fought on 8 January 1815, when Andrew Jackson's troops defeated British forces under Sir Edward M. Pakenham's command. Located 6 miles southeast of New Orleans. *Fort McHenry National Monument and Historic Shrine*, Baltimore, Maryland: The Baltimore harbor fort, built from 1794-1803, came under British attack in September 1814. During the bombardment, Francis Scott Key composed 'The Star-Spangled Banner', adopted as the national anthem in 1931. *Horseshoe Bend National Military Park*, Daviston, Alabama: Site of a bloody battle fought between Red Stick Creek Indians and troops commanded by Andrew Jackson. Located in east central Alabama, 20 miles east of Alexander City. *Perry's Victory and International Peace Memorial*, Put-in-Bay, South Bass Island, Ohio: Marks Oliver Hazard Perry's victory in the Battle of Lake Erie, 10 September 1813. The 'memorial' is a tower offering a spectacular view of Lake Erie. Located 35 miles east of Toledo. **91–95**

Mexican-American War:
Palo Alto Battlefield National Historic Site, Cameron County, Texas: Site of fighting in May 1846. Located near Brownsville. **163–165**

Civil War:
Andersonville National Historic Site, Andersonville, Georgia: Camp where Confederate troops held Union prisoners of war, 13,000 of whom died. Located 60 miles southwest of Macon. *Antietam National Battlefield*, Sharpsburg, Maryland: Where the bloodiest single day of fighting in the Civil War took place, 17 September 1862. Located approximately 70 miles northwest of Washington, DC. *Appomattox Court House National Historical Park*, Appomattox, Virginia: Where Lee surrendered to Grant in April 1865 to end the Civil War. Located 75 miles west of Richmond. *Chickamauga and Chattanooga National Military Park*, Fort Oglethorpe, Georgia, and Chattanooga, Tennessee. Commemorates battles fought between September and November of 1863, the former a Confederate victory, the latter a Union victory. *Fort Donelson National Battlefield*, Dover, Tennessee: Site of February 1862 victory by troops under Ulysses S. Grant, who began their penetration of the upper western portion of the Confederacy. Located approximately 80 miles northwest of Nash-

ville. *Fort Moultrie:* (See *Revolutionary War*) *Fort Pulaski National Monument,* near Tybee Island, Georgia: First occupied by Confederate forces; taken by Union troops. Located 17 miles east of Savannah. *Fort Sumter National Monument,* Charleston, South Carolina: Where the Civil War began in April 1861 when Confederate forces shelled the Union-held island fortress. *Fredericksburg and Spotsylvania County Battlefields Memorial National Military Park,* Fredericksburg, Virginia: The large park commemorates four of the war's bloody encounters: the Confederate victories at Fredericksburg (December 1862), Chancellorsville (May 1863) and the Battle of the Wilderness (May 1864) and the Union victory at Spotsylvania Court House (May 1864). Located 57 miles north of Richmond, 48 miles southwest of Washington, DC. *Gettysburg National Military Park,* Gettysburg, Pennsylvania: During the first three days of July 1863, the war's deadliest battle took place in this quiet Pennsylvania town. Union forces turned back Lee's invading army. Four months later, Lincoln delivered his 'Gettysburg Address' at the site. Located 77 miles north of Washington, DC, 50 miles northwest of Baltimore. *Harpers Ferry National Historical Park,* Harpers Ferry, Virginia: The site of John Brown's raid in October 1859. Located 65 miles northwest of Washington DC. *Manassas National Battlefield Park,* Manassas, Virginia: Scene of two Confederate victories (in July 1861 and August 1862) which left more than 4,000 dead and 28,000 total

casualties. Located 25 miles southwest of Washington, DC. *Monocacy National Battlefield,* Frederick, Maryland: Part of a July 1864 Confederate effort to threaten Washington, DC. Located 45 miles northwest of the nation's capital. *Pea Ridge National Military Park,* Pea Ridge, Arkansas: The Union's March 1862 victory at this site in northwest Arkansas helped federal forces maintain their hold of the border state of Missouri. Located 92 miles north-northeast of Fort Smith. *Petersburg National Battlefield,* Petersburg, Virginia: Site of Union siege that lasted from June 1864 to April 1865, resulting in harrowing trench warfare. Located 23 miles south of Richmond. *Shiloh National Military Park,* Shiloh, Tennessee: April 1862 battle in the war's Western Theater that resulted in a Union victory, at a ghastly human cost. Located approximately 100 miles east of Memphis. *Vicksburg National Military Park,* Vicksburg, Mississippi: Grant's Union forces laid siege on the Confederate garrison in Vicksburg from late May to early July 1863. The Southern stronghold fell on the Fourth of July, one day after the Confederate defeat at Gettysburg. **183–203**

Native Americans:
Horseshoe Bend National Military Park (See *War of 1812*). *Little Bighorn Battlefield National Monument,* Crow Agency, Montana: June 1876 battle between Indian forces and Custer's Seventh Cavalry. Located 62 miles east-southeast of Billings. *Tippecanoe*

Battlefield, Battle Ground, Indiana: site of fighting between followers of Shawnee leaders Tecumseh and Tenskwatawa and white soldiers led by General William Henry Harrison, November 1811. Located 70 miles northwest of Indianapolis. *Wounded Knee Memorial*, Pine Ridge, South Dakota: Site of Army massacre of Sioux tribesmen in December 1890. Located 80 miles southeast of Rapid City. **92, 102–103, 247–251, 365**

Bering Land Bridge National Preserve, western Alaska: For the truly committed historical traveller; where the first human beings in the Western Hemisphere probably strolled. Located over 100 miles north of Nome, but only 55 miles east of Siberia. **8**

Boston, Massachusetts: Founded in 1630, Boston is a center of history, business, finance, education, and culture, all in a fairly dense and compact city made up of distinct and appealing neighborhoods. One of the best ways to explore the city's historic sites is to follow 'The Freedom Trail', a 2½ mile course marked by a painted red line (and red brick). The sites include: *Boston Common:* Acquired by city founders in 1634. *Boston Massacre Site:* Confrontation between British troops and American protestors on 5 March 1770. *Bunker Hill Monument:* Revolutionary battle fought on 17 June 1775. *Charlestown Navy Yard (1800–1974):* One of the nation's earliest naval shipyards, where visitors will find the Navy's oldest commissioned warship, the USS *Constitution* (1797), popularly known as 'Old Ironsides'. *Faneuil Hall (1742):* Center of Revolutionary (and post-Revolutionary) public debate in Boston. *Old North Church (1723):* On 18 April 1775, lanterns indicated the approach of British forces. *Old South Meeting House (1729):* Where protestors gathered before 'throwing' the Boston Tea Party on 16 December 1773. *Old State House (1713):* Center of Boston's colonial government. *Paul Revere House (1680):* Owned by the patriot in the last three decades of the 18th century. Other Boston historical sites include: Beacon Hill, the fashionable residential area for the city's elite 'Brahmins', and Harvard University (in Cambridge), the first college in America. **46–48, 53–54, 117**

Cahokia Mounds, A 2,200-acre state historic site, located east of St. Louis, Missouri. Inhabited by tribes from 700–1400. Sixty-eight mounds preserved. **10**

Cambridge, Massachusetts: *Longfellow National Historic Site;* home of poet Henry Wadsworth Longfellow. **145–155**

Cape Canaveral, Florida: *Cape Canaveral/Kennedy Space Center;* an odd pairing of wild life and technological wizardry: *Kennedy Space Center:* where human space flights are prepared and launched (and often land). *Canaveral National Seashore/Merritt Island National Wildlife Refuge:* After getting one's fill of the future at the Kennedy Space Center, the seashore and reserve pull visitors back to the past, especially at Turtle Mound State Memorial where one can stand atop a 50-foot mound from an Indian culture. In the flat landscape of Florida, it is quite a site. **334, 335, 339**

Cartersville, Georgia: *Etowah Indian Mounds State Historic Site;* Mississippian mounds over 60 feet high from a culture that inhabited the area from 950–1550. Located 40 miles northwest of Atlanta. **10, 11**

Charleston, South Carolina: Founded by English colonists in 1670 and capital of the Carolina colony, the city expanded from the growing trade in rice, indigo – and, later, cotton and slaves. Charleston also served as a political center of states' rights and, later, secessionism. The city's historic district contains over 1400 noteworthy structures. Some highlights include: *William Enston Home:* late 19th-century community for the aged and infirm. *Fort Sumter National Monument:* (See **Battle Sites**, *Civil War*). *Kahal Kadosh Beth Elohim Synagogue (1840):* congregation founded in 1749. *Joseph Manigault House (1803):* Federal style (See also the 1808 Nathaniel Russell House). *Market Hall and Sheds (1840–1841):* Greek Revival commercial center. *Old Bethel United Methodist Church (1807):* First used by an integrated congregation. Then moved and given to African Americans for their use (1852). Whites built themselves a new church. *Old Slave Mart (1859):* site of slave auctions. *Powder Magazine (1713):* storage location for the colonial city's gunpowder. *St. Mary's Roman Catholic Church (1839):* Classical Revival style church. *St. Michael's Episcopal Church:* mid-18th century landmark, with a pew used by George Washington. *St. Philip's Episcopal Church (1838):* noted for its tall steeple and the luminaries in its cemetery. *United States Custom House:* begun in 1853 but not completed until after Reconstruction. **58, 142, 181–182**

Charlottesville, Virginia: *Monticello;* Thomas Jefferson's Classical Revival home, begun in 1768. Construction, and remodeling, completed by 1809. *University of Virginia;* scholarly community designed by Thomas Jefferson and chartered in 1819. **77–91, 102, 131**

Chicago: Called the 'Windy City', the 'Second City', and (for poet Carl Sandburg) the 'city of big shoulders', Chicago was first settled in 1779 as a trading post and incorporated as a town in 1833. A destructive fire in 1871 killed hundreds and left a third of Chicagoans homeless. Two decades later, the city rebuilt itself into a major commercial, manufacturing, and residential center. In contemporary Chicago, one finds fine examples of 'Chicago School' architecture, as well as outdoor sculptures by Picasso, Chagall, Miro, Oldenburg, and Calder. *Auditorium Building (1889):* A grand and ornate gem on South Michigan Avenue by architects Louis H. Sullivan and Dankmar Adler. *Carson, Pirie, Scott and Company Store (1899–1904):* Designed by Louis Sullivan; addition by Daniel H. Burnham. *Chicago Fire Site:* Origin of the destructive fire of 8–10 October 1871 in the barn of the O'Leary family. The blaze destroyed much of downtown Chicago and killed 1 per cent of its population. Located at Dekoven and Jefferson Streets. *Chicago Theater (1921):* An elaborate movie palace, with a distinctive marquee. *Grant Park:* Magnificent municipal park built along Lake Michigan after the fire of 1871. *Haymarket Square:* Site of labor rally, and violence, on 4 May 1886. Located near Desplaines and Randolph. *Ernest Hemingway Museum and Birthplace:* Located in the suburb of Oak Park. *Hull House:* The South Halsted site of Jane Addams' settlement house reform (begun in 1889). *Monadnock Building (1891):* Designed by Daniel H. Burnham and John Root. *Pullman (1880–1894):* Planned community in south Chicago built for the railroad car company of the same name, containing manufacturing plants, workers' housing, and civic facilities. *Reliance Building (1890–1895):* Designed by Burnham and Root. *Robie House (1909):* Prairie-style home designed by Frank Lloyd Wright. *Rookery Building (1888):* Designed by Burnham and Root. *Unity Temple (1906):* Designed by Frank Lloyd Wright in Oak Park, Illinois. *Water Tower:* Along with the Chicago Pumping Station, these were the only structures in the main Michigan Avenue area to survive the fire of 1871. *Ida B. Wells House:* Home of the civil rights leader home from 1919 to 1930. *Frank Lloyd Wright Home (1889–1898):* The architect's home and studio, located west of downtown Chicago in Oak Park. **110, 118, 171, 232**

Chillicothe, Ohio: *Hopewell Culture National Historical Park;* 2,000 year-old earthworks of the Hopewell Culture. Located 50 miles south of Columbus. **9**

Chinle, Arizona: *Canyon de Chelly National Monument;* contains the ruins of Native American homes built from 350-1300. Located 100 miles northwest of Gallup, New Mexico. **10**

Cody, Wyoming: *Buffalo Bill Historical Center;* four museums with collections of Plains Indians artifacts, firearms, Western art, and materials related to the life and times of William F. 'Buffalo Bill' Cody. Located 52 miles east of Yellowstone National Park. **11–12**

Concord, Massachusetts: A center for both military and literary history. *Emerson House:* residence of Ralph Waldo Emerson for half a century. *Minute Man National Historical Park:* (See **Battle Sites**, *Revolutionary War*). *The Old Manse:* home of Nathaniel Hawthorne and Ralph Waldo Emerson. *Orchard House:* home of *Little Women* author Louisa May Alcott from 1858–1877. *Sleepy Hollow Cemetery:* the final resting place of Ralph Waldo Emerson, Henry David Thoreau, Nathaniel Hawthorne, and Bronson Alcott. *Walden Pond:* where Thoreau got back to basics. *The Wayside (1714):* home occupied by the Alcotts, Hawthorne, and Margaret Sidney. **50, 130, 145–155**

Connor Prairie, Fishers, Indiana: living history museum northeast of Indianapolis, Indiana, focusing on community life in the Old Northwest in the 1820s and 1830s. **109–112, 118–120**

Cooperstown, New York: *National Baseball Hall of Fame;* shrine to the great American sport, located in the home town of 19th-century author James Fenimore Cooper. Located 65 miles west of Albany. **150**

Cumberland Island National Seashore, near St. Marys, Georgia: Linked with the history of native peoples, Spanish missionaries, British settlers, American developers, and ex-slaves, the island is home to numerous sites listed on the National Register of Historic Places. Located on the Georgia coast, 35 miles south of Brunswick and 40 miles north of Jacksonville, Florida.

Daytona Beach, Florida: *Mary McLeod Bethune Home;* home of the prominent African American educator and New Deal administrator. **292**

Del Norte and Humboldt Counties, California (headquarters in Crescent City): *Redwood National and State Parks;* a World Heritage Site biological preserve featuring old growth coast redwood forest, and the world's tallest tree, standing nearly 368 feet tall. Located on the Pacific coast of far northern California. **2–3**

Detroit, Michigan: Founded by the French in 1701, Detroit's fortunes revolved first around furs, then grains, and then factories – especially the kind that churned out automobiles. *General Motors Building:* Architect Albert Kahn's 1923 structure. *Henry Ford Museum and Greenfield Village*, Dearborn, Michigan: History, as seen by Henry Ford. Designed to commemorate his own youth, the technical marvels of the day, and the triumphs of the American experience. A wide range of artifacts and historical buildings. *Highland Park Ford Plant*, Highland Park, Michigan: The factory where Henry Ford launched the moving assembly line. *Mies van der Rohe Residential District:* A planned,

post-World War II community with buildings designed by the famous architect. *River Rouge Plant, Dearborn*, Michigan: Henry Ford's integrated manufacturing plant that produced steel and glass, and put all the parts together to make cars. **118, 226, 232**

Epps, Louisiana: *Poverty Point National Monument;* 3,000-year-old earth works of prehistoric native cultures. Located 50 miles northwest of Vicksburg, Mississippi. **9**

Erie Canal, upstate New York: The opening of the 363-mile canal in 1825 linked the Atlantic Coast and the Old Northwest, lowered freight rates, expanded trade among Americans, made New York City the busiest US port, boosted Western settlement, and started a canal-building craze in the young nation. Key sites visible today, traveling from east to west, include: *Vischer Ferry Nature Preserve*, Clifton Park. *Schoharie Crossing State Historic Site*, Fort Hunter. *Erie Canal Village*, Rome. *Old Erie Canal State Park and Canastota Canal Town Museum*, Canastota. *Chittenango Landing Canal Boat Museum*, Chittenango. *Erie Canal Museum*, Syracuse. *Medina Terminal Canal State Park*, Medina. *Erie Canal Heritage Center*, Lockport. **113**

Eunice, Louisiana: *Prairie Acadian Cultural Center;* interpretive center with demonstrations performances, and displays of 'Cajun' culture, telling the story of Acadians who settled in Louisiana after their mid-18th-century removal from Nova Scotia. Located approximately 80 miles west of Baton Rouge. Other National Park Service sites for Acadian culture:

Acadian Cultural Center, Lafayette, Louisiana. *Wetlands Acadian Cultural Center*, Thibodaux, Louisiana.

Evansville, Indiana. *Angel Mounds State Historic Site*, home to a Mississippian native culture from 1100–1450 along the banks of the Ohio River. Located 168 miles south-southwest of Indianapolis. **9–10**

Grand Canyon, Arizona: *Grand Canyon National Park;* displays what 6–10 million years of erosion can do. The Colorado River has carved out a breathtaking, mile-deep canyon in northern Arizona. Located 80 miles north-northwest of Flagstaff. **3**

Great Barrington, Massachusetts: *W.E.B. Du Bois Boyhood Homesite National Historic Landmark;* ruins of the home where DuBois lived as a child, 40 miles west of Springfield. **242**

Greensboro, North Carolina: *F.W. Woolworth Building;* 1960 sit-in demonstration at store's lunch counter to protest racial segregation. **361–363**

Gustavus, Alaska: *Glacier Bay National Park and Preserve;* over 3 million acres of park land, featuring the spectacle of retreating glaciers. Most visitors arrive on cruise ships. By air, 65 miles west-northwest of Juneau. **4, 8, 12**

Hartford, Connecticut: *Mark Twain House;* home of the famous author from 1874–1891. Located 119 miles northeast of New York City. **254**

Hermitage, Tennessee: *Andrew Jackson home, The Hermitage;* 1836 mansion that was home to the seventh president and 140 slaves. Located 12 miles east of Nashville. **99–107**

Hodgenville, Kentucky: *Abraham*

Lincoln Birthplace National Historic Site; 50 miles south of Louisville. **177–208**

Honaunau, Hawaii: *Pu'uhonua o Honaunau National Historical Park;* preserved and reconstructed sites, featuring royal grounds and the pu'uhonua (a historic sacred refuge). Located on the west-southwest side of the island of Hawaii. **2, 5, 254, 255**

Hyde Park, New York: *Franklin D. Roosevelt Home National Historic Site;* site of 'Springwood', FDR's home. Also, the adjoining Presidential Museum and Library. Located 91 miles north of New York City. **284–305**

Independence, California: *Manzanar National Historic Site;* site of a Japanese-American internment camp during World War II. Located in east-central California, 40 miles south of Bishop. **313–314**

Jamestown, Virginia: The first permanent English settlement in North America (1607). The Colonial National Historical Park sits on the site of the original settlement. 'Jamestown Settlement' is a living history museum offering a recreation of Jamestown life. Located 6 miles southeast of Williamsburg. **20**

Jekyll Island, Georgia: *Jekyll Island Historic District;* originally home to Indian tribes, then the possession of a French family, and then, in the late 19th century, a 'club' for many of America's super-rich. The houses of J.P. Morgan, Goodyear, the Rockefellers, and others are open for visitors. Located southeast of Brunswick.

Kawaihae, Hawaii: *Pu'ukohola Heiau National Historic Site;* site of temple constructed in the early 1790s.

Located on the north-northwest side of the island of Hawaii. **2, 5, 254–255**

Key West, Florida: *Key West Historic District;* American settlers came after the transfer of the territory from Spain (1819). The historic district boasts distinctive architecture from the past three centuries. Located on the western edge of the Florida Keys, 160 miles southwest of Miami. *Ernest Hemingway Home and Museum:* The author moved into this 1851 home in 1931 and lived there during most of the 30s. *Fort Jefferson* (1846), Dry Tortugas National Park: Located 68 miles west of Key West. **95, 272**

Kill Devil Hills, North Carolina: *Wright Brothers National Memorial;* site of the brothers' flight on 17 December 1903. Located 214 miles east of Raleigh. **408**

Lake Havasu City, Arizona: *London Bridge;* Thames River crossing sold in 1968 and reconstructed in 1971 in the desert southwest. Located 200 miles northwest of Phoenix.

Las Vegas, Nevada: A formerly sleepy town in southern Nevada transformed in 1931 by the power of money (legalized gambling) and electricity (the Hoover dam) and now the epitome of American excess. *Flamingo Hotel and Casino:* Built by mobster Benjamin 'Bugsy' Siegel in 1946. The present owners thoughtfully set up a memorial plaque for Mr. Siegel in the gardens. *Moulin Rouge Hotel:* In 1955, when Vegas hotels were racially segregated (and African American performers could not stay in the places where they entertained), the Moulin Rouge offered a novel idea: an *integrated* resort.

Lincoln City, Indiana: *Abraham Lincoln Boyhood National Memorial;* farm on which Lincoln lived from 1816–1830. Located approximately 35 miles east of Evansville. **177–208**

Little Rock, Arkansas: *Little Rock Central High School National Historic Site;* site of 1957 confrontation between federal and state authorities over school desegregation. **217, 350**

Los Angeles: Founded in 1781 as 'El Pueblo de Nuestra Señora la Reina de Los Angeles de Porciúncula', LA has existed under Spanish, Mexican, and (since 1848) US rule. Starting with under 100 residents, LA is now home to over 3½ million, about 1 in 10 Californians. Known popularly for its sun and fun, the city and county are among the hardest working in the nation, serving as a center of manufacturing and home to one of America's busiest ports. *Angels Flight:* A restored funicular, billing itself as the 'Shortest Railway in the World', at the corner of Third and Hill; built in 1901, closed in 1969, restored in 1996. *Autry Museum of Western Heritage:* Collections focus on the history of the American West. *Chinese Theater:* Spectacular theater created by Sid Grauman which opened in 1927. Blocks of cement in front have footprints and signatures of movie stars. *Disneyland* (Anaheim): The first of the world's Disney theme parks; opened in 1955. *Gamble House:* One of the finest examples of Arts and Crafts design in the USA, created in 1908 by Charles Sumner Greene and Henry Mather Greene. *Hollywood Sign:* Originally constructed in 1923 to advertise a real estate development called 'Hollywoodland'. Since 1945, its 50-foot letters have simply spelled out 'Hollywood'. *La Brea Tar Pits:* One comes across odd things in downtown LA – but Pleistocene vertebrates? Yes, these and other kinds of plant and insect organisms have been found in the gooey asphalt. *Mission San Fernando Rey de España:* Spanish mission founded in 1797. *Movie palaces on South Broadway:* Palace Theater (1911), State Theater (1921), Orpheum Theater (1926). *Olvera Street:* The oldest part of LA, rescued by city officials in the late 1920s. Its historic buildings, market place, music, and cafes draw many visitors. *Queen Mary* (Long Beach, CA): The beautiful ship, launched in 1934, is now docked in Long Beach; open as a museum and hotel. *Studio tours:* Universal Studios provides a major theme park; Paramount and Warner Brothers offer a better sense of the nuts and bolts of filmmaking. *Union Station:* Completed in 1939, the Moorish and Spanish style building is still a center of rail travel for Southern California. **3, 17, 275, 329, 335**

Lowell, Massachusetts: *Lowell National Historical Park;* mills, canals, and boardinghouses that tell the story of America's industrial revolution, and the young women and immigrants whose labor made it possible. Located 32 miles northwest of Boston. **115–116**

Memphis, Tennessee: *Graceland;* Elvis Presley's magnificently overstated home. **367–370**

Mesa Verde, Colorado: *Mesa Verde National Park;* a major archeological site, Mesa Verde contains the artifacts of Pueblo peoples who inhabited the area from the 7th through the 14th centuries. Key attraction: the 'cliff dwellings'. Located 35 miles west of Durango. **10–11**

Miami, Florida: Acquired from Spain in 1819, the city was incorporated in 1896. That year, businessman Henry M. Flagler brought in rail transportation, improved the harbor, built a hotel, and began promoting Florida as a winter mecca. A spectacular land boom followed in the 1920s. Today, the city is a year-round resort, and a major commercial, industrial, and population center. *The Breakers* (Palm Beach): Palatial 1926 hotel fashioned after Rome's Villa Medici. *Miami Beach Art Deco District:* An eye-popping, exuberant, and fanciful parade of Art Deco architectural forms in hotels, businesses, and residences. *Vizcaya:* A National Historic landmark, built in 1916 for James Deering, in an ornate Italian Renaissance mode. Lavish gardens add to the spectacle. **95, 277–279**

Missions of California: Between 1769 and 1823, the Franciscan order (under the initial direction of Father Junipero Serra) founded 21 missions. Built along California's El Camino Real ('King's Highway'), paralleling today's US 101, the missions stretch from San Diego north to San Francisco. The missions (with founding date and location) are: *La Exaltación de la Santa Cruz*, 1791, Santa Cruz. *La Purísima Concepción de María Santísima*, 1787, Lompac. *Nuestra Señora de la Soledad*, 1791, Soledad. *San Antonio de Padua*, 1771, Jolon. *San Buenaventura*, 1782, Ventura. *San Carlos Borroméo de*

Carmelo, 1770, Carmel. *San Diego de Alcalá*, 1769, San Diego. *San Fernando Rey de España*, 1797, Mission Hills. *San Francisco de Asís*, 1776, San Francisco. *San Francisco de Solano*, 1823, Sonoma. *San Gabriel Arcángel*, 1771, San Gabriel. *San José*, 1797, Fremont. *San Juan Bautista*, 1797, San Juan Bautista. *San Juan Capistrano*, 1776, San Juan Capistrano. *San Luis Obispo de Tolosa*, 1772, San Luis Obispo. *San Luis Rey de Francia*, 1798, San Luis Rey. *San Miguel Arcángel*, 1797, San Miguel. *San Rafael Arcángel*, 1817, San Rafael. *Santa Barbara*, 1786, Santa Barbara. *Santa Clara de Asís*, 1777, Santa Clara. *Santa Inés*, 1804, Solvang. **17**

Montgomery, Alabama: *Dexter Avenue King Memorial Baptist Church National Historic Landmark;* the nerve-center of the 1955–1956 bus boycott; Martin Luther King, Jr. served as minister from 1954–1960. **361–363**

Monument Valley, Utah: *Monument Valley Navajo Tribal Park;* scenic, stark, and much-photographed site of mesas, buttes, and desert in southeast Utah and northeast Arizona, along US 163. Contained within the Navajo Indian Reservation. **3**

Mount Rushmore National Memorial: The busts of Washington, Jefferson, Lincoln, and Theodore Roosevelt, sculpted by Gutzon Borglum from 1927 to 1941 in the Black Hills of South Dakota. Located 20 miles southwest of Rapid City. **107**

Mystic, Connecticut: *Mystic Seaport;* recreation of a Northeast seafaring center. A major maritime museum. Located 8 miles east of New London. **25**

Natchez, Mississippi: Spectacular antebellum mansions are open for tours in what was, at one time, the richest county in the USA. Among the grandest homes are Stanton Hall, Longwood, Rosalie, Melrose Estate, and Monmouth. **137**

New Orleans, Louisiana: Founded in 1718, the city has existed under French, Spanish, and (after 1803) US rule. The flags have changed over time, but the flow of goods from the Mississippi River and the Gulf of Mexico has remained constant. So, too, has the city's exuberant culture, a product of New Orleans's multi-racial and multi-ethnic population. The city's French Quarter ('Vieux Carré') is a National Historic District, with examples of Spanish and French architecture. The more 'American' Garden District is a former 'suburb', rich in examples of Andrew Jackson Downing's designs. *Acadian culture:* (see Eunice, Prairie Acadian Cultural Center). *The Arsenal:* built in 1839. *The Cabildo:* center of Spanish government, built from 1795–99. *Chalmette Battlefield and National Cemetery* (see **Battle Sites**, *War of 1812*). *Historic homes:* Beauregard-Keyes House (1826); Gallier House (1857); Hermann-Grima House (1831); Madame John's Legacy (1789); Pontalba Buildings (1850). *Mardi Gras:* The wildest annual public festival in the USA, when parades, music, and wicked merriment fill the streets in the days before Lent. *New Orleans Jazz National Historical Park:* dedicated to the preservation of jazz. *Old US Mint* (1835): Greek Revival building. *The Presbytere* (1813): commercial and municipal structure. *Saint Louis Cathedral:* built from 1789–1794. **18, 90, 93, 169, 194**

Newport, Rhode Island. *The Breakers* (1895); summer home of Cornelius Vanderbilt II, designed by Richard Morris Hunt. **233**

New York: Since 1810, New York has been the largest city in the USA, currently with more than 7 million residents. In 1609, Henry Hudson sailed into its harbor. The Dutch created the first permanent settlement in 1624. Forty years later, England seized the colony. Control passed to Americans after Independence. The city served as the nation's capital for a brief period. Since 1898, the entity known as New York City has been composed of five boroughs: Manhattan (Manhattan Island), Staten Island, Brooklyn and Queens (both on Long Island), and the Bronx (the city's one connection to mainland America). *Apollo Theater* (1913): Famous Harlem theatre on 125th Street. *Brooklyn Bridge* (1883): Designed by John A. Roebling and Washington A. Roebling. *Carnegie Hall:* Concert hall completed in 1891 by chief architect William Burnet Tuthill. *Cathedral Church of St. John the Divine:* Begun in 1892, the world's largest cathedral. *Central Park:* Frederick Law Olmsted's 840-acre urban masterpiece (Olmsted also designed the 526-acre Prospect Park in Brooklyn). *Chrysler Building:* Architect William Van Alen's 1930 structure lost the height derby to the Empire State Building in a matter of months, but it beats its New York skyline rival in the design category.

An Art Deco jewel. *City Hall:* Constructed from 1805–1812 in the Federal style. *The Cloisters:* On the upper west side of Manhattan in Fort Tryon Park, the museum features Romanesque and Gothic art in a facility built out of parts from French monasteries. *Coney Island:* Late 19th-early 20th-century amusement park on the shore of southern Brooklyn. *Ellis Island Immigration Museum:* The processing station through which 12 million immigrants entered the United States from 1892–1954. *Empire State Building:* From 1931 to 1972, Shreve, Lamb, and Harmon's structure was the tallest building in the world (1,250 feet). A monument to engineering innovation, and to economic defiance (since the building rose while the market plunged in the early years of the Great Depression). *Federal Hall National Memorial:* Site where the Stamp Act Congress, the Continental Congress, and the first Congress of the new republic met. Here, Washington took the oath of office as first president. Present structure completed in 1842. *Grand Central Terminal:* Magnificent Beaux-Arts style structure completed in 1913. *Lower East Side Tenement Museum* (99 Orchard Street): Restored tenement housing used by different immigrant groups from the 1870s through the 1930s. *New York Stock Exchange* (1903): The Vatican of capitalism. *Edgar Allan Poe Cottage (circa 1812):* One of the last places a person would expect to find in the Bronx. The author's home from 1846–1849. *Radio City Music Hall (1932):* 6,000-seat Art Deco palace, recently restored. *South Street Seaport Museum:* An 11-block historic district in the southeastern tip of Manhattan Island, the center of a once-flourishing East River port and now home to a half-dozen historic ships and restored commercial architecture. *Saint Patrick's Cathedral:* Built from 1858–1874 by architect James Renwick, a Gothic oasis at a fashionable Fifth Avenue address. *Statue of Liberty*, Liberty Island: Donated by France, designed by Frederic-Auguste Bartholdi, placed in New York City harbor, supported by Gustave Eiffel's frame, dedicated by President Grover Cleveland in 1886, inscribed with a poem by Emma Lazarus, and renovated in the 1980s. *United Nations:* Headquarters of the world body, begun in 1949 under chief architect Wallace K. Harrison. *United States Custom House (1907):* Site at 'Bowling Green' where supposedly, in 1626, Peter Minuit purchased Manhattan from native peoples. Presently houses the National Museum of the American Indian (George Gustav Heye Center). **19, 24, 54–56, 74, 113, 117, 228–231, 329, 394**

Old Sturbridge Village, Massachusetts: A recreation of New England rural life in the 1830s. Located approximately 65 miles west of Boston. **109–112, 118–120**

Oyster Bay, New York: *Theodore Roosevelt Home, Sagamore Hill National Historic Site;* TR's home from 1886–1919. Located 45 miles east of New York City on Long Island. **242–244, 258–260**

Pearl Harbor, Hawaii: Northwest of Honolulu, the site evokes the beginning and the end of World War II. The USS *Arizona* Memorial stands above the sunken battleship where 1,177 crewmen died during the Japanese attack on 7 December 1941. The Battleship *Missouri* Memorial commemorates the vessel on which surrender terms were signed, ending the war. **299**

Petrified Forest National Park, Arizona: Petrified wood, a Painted Desert, fossil finds, archeological sites, and other visually stunning attractions. Located 117 miles east of Flagstaff. **3**

Philadelphia, Pennsylvania: A settlement conceived in idealistic (and geometric) terms, William Penn arranged his 'city of brotherly love' in a precise grid pattern to allow for openness, greenery, and orderly growth. Penn arrived in 1682. By 1700, the urban area had 4,400 residents; as the new republic began, it was the premier city in the USA. Its famous residents (such as Benjamin Franklin) and famous events (such as the drafting of the Declaration and Constitution) made Philadelphia a symbol of American republican life. Independence National Historical Park (billed as the 'most historic square mile' in the USA) contains over a dozen sites, structures, and artifacts linked to the nation's founding, including: *Carpenters' Hall (1770):* Meeting place of the First Continental Congress. *Congress Hall (1789):* Where the US Congress met from 1790–1800. *Independence Hall* (or, the 'State House') (1756): Here, the Second Continental Congress met (1775) and founders adopted the Declaration of Independence (1776), designed the flag (1777), wrote the Articles of Confederation (1777), and drafted the Constitution (1787). *Old City Hall* (1791): where the US Supreme Court sat from 1791–1800. *Second Bank of the United States* (1824): a graceful building that served its national banking function for only a brief period, before Andrew Jackson decided to shut the whole thing down. **49, 56, 57, 64, 118, 329**

Plantations: Travellers may visit a large number of antebellum plantations throughout the South. Some are publicly owned historical sites; others are privately owned, available for tours and, in many instances, lodging. Some examples are:

Florida

Kingsley Plantation, Fort George Island: An antebellum plantation, with the main house and slave quarters. Located approximately 15 miles east of Jacksonville.

Georgia

Hamilton Plantation, St. Simons Island: contains slave cabins from the first third of the 19th century. Located east of Brunswick. *Hofwyl-Broadfield Plantation, near Darien:* Example of an antebellum rice plantation. Located 5 miles south of Darien, 15 miles northeast of Brunswick. *Wormsloe State Historic Site, Savannah:* 1737 plantation with a lovely oak-lined drive. *Archibald Smith Plantation Home, Roswell:* 1845 home plus outbuildings. Located 24 miles northwest of Atlanta *Stately Oaks Plantation, Jonesboro:* 1839 Greek Revival mansion, 20 miles south of Atlanta.

Louisiana

Cane River Creole National Historical Park and Heritage Area, Natchez (near Natchitoches): Buildings from two cotton plantations, Magnolia (1835) and Oakland (1821). Located 250 miles northwest of New Orleans. *Destrehan Plantation, Destrehan:* Home built in 1787 and remodeled by 1840, 16 miles east of New Orleans. *Houmas House, Darrow:* 1840 Greek Revival mansion; 30 miles southeast of Baton Rouge. *Laura Plantation, Vacherie:* 1805 Creole sugar plantation, with main house and slave quarters, 42 miles west of New Orleans. *Nottoway Plantation, Plaquemine:* 1859 Greek revival structure, 20 miles south of Baton Rouge. *Oak Alley Plantation, Vacherie:* 1839 home, 42 miles west of New Orleans. *Rosedown Plantation, St. Francisville:* 1835 mansion (with wings added). Located 30 miles north-northwest of Baton Rouge.

Mississippi

Melrose Estate, Natchez National Historical Park, Natchez: 1847 Greek revival mansion plus outbuildings on a historic cotton plantation. *Oak Square Plantation, Port Gibson:* Cotton plantation; 1850 Greek revival home; midway between Vicksburg and Natchez. *Rosswood Plantation, Lorman:* 1857 mansion, 35 miles northeast of Natchez.

South Carolina

Boone Hall Plantation, Mt. Pleasant: Estate dates back to 1680s; original mansion destroyed by fire. Located 5 miles east of Charleston. *Drayton Hall, Charleston:* 1742 mansion on the Ashley River. *Hampton Plantation, McClellanville:* mid-18th-century rice and indigo plantation, approximately 40 miles northeast of Charleston.

Hopsewee Plantation, Georgetown County: 1740 rice plantation, 45 miles northeast of Charleston.

Virginia

Carter's Grove, near Grove: 1753 home, 6 miles from Williamsburg. *Charles City plantations, approximately 30 miles southeast of Richmond: Berkeley:* 1726 mansion on the James River; birthplace of President William Henry Harrison. *Sherwood Forest:* Home to Presidents William Henry Harrison and John Tyler. Landscaping designed by Andrew Jackson Downing. *Shirley Plantation:* 1738 mansion; a National Historic Landmark. *Westover:* Georgian masterpiece from 1730. **131–143**

Plymouth, Massachusetts: *Plimouth Plantation;* a living history museum, located near (not on) the site of the original Pilgrim settlement, recapturing village life in 1627. Located 35 miles southeast of Boston. **20–22**

Promontory, Utah: *Golden Spike National Historic Site;* site where the Central Pacific and Union Pacific were linked to form the nation's first transcontinental railroad on 10 May 1869. Located 84 miles north-northwest of Salt Lake City. **114, 171**

Roanoke Island, North Carolina: *Fort Raleigh National Historic Site;* site of Sir Walter Raleigh's 'lost colony', 1585–1587. Located 90 miles southeast of Norfolk, Virginia. **19**

Rochester, New York. *Susan B. Anthony House*, Rochester, home of the prominent women's rights advocate. **126–128**

Saint Augustine, Florida: The oldest, continuously-occupied city in the USA. In 1513, Ponce de León

arrived. In 1565, the Spanish military founded the city. *Castillo de San Marcos National Monument:* Spanish coastal fort, begun in 1672. *Hotel Ponce de León:* One of many Florida creations by the late 19th-century businessman, Henry Flagler. Designed in 1887 in the Spanish Renaissance style. *St. Augustine Town Plan Historic District:* Filled with private, public, and religious structures from the early 18th through the late 19th centuries, including a home built in 1706 and the Basilica Cathedral of St. Augustine from the late 18th century. **17**

Salem, Massachusetts: Northeast of Boston, Salem was founded in 1626. It made its other-worldly mark with the witch craze of 1692–1693, and its commercial mark with the maritime trade. A number of museums display materials related to the witch frenzy. Other sites include: The Custom House (1819): where Nathaniel Hawthorne worked; described in the opening of *The Scarlet Letter. The House of the Seven Gables (1668):* inspiration for Hawthorne's romance of the same name. *Salem Maritime National Historic Site:* features waterfront historical structures that recall the city's maritime trade. **21, 23, 25, 154**

San Francisco, California: One of the most exciting and cosmopolitan cities in the United States, San Francisco started out in a much more staid fashion, with the establishment of a Spanish military post and mission in 1776. The town remained a small settlement until it was transformed by the worldly allure of gold (and, later, silver). Rebuilt after the 1906 earthquake and fire, the city expanded into a center of West Coast commerce, industry, and finance. *Alcatraz:* Originally, a military installation that served as a fort and prison (1850–1933); then a federal penitentiary (1934–1963). *Cable cars:* Service began in 1873. *City Lights Bookstore:* Founded by beat poet Lawrence Ferlinghetti in 1953. *Coit Tower (1934):* On Telegraph Hill, offering wonderful views of the Bay. *Golden Gate Bridge (1937):* 4,200-foot span painted a distinctive orange vermilion color. *Haight-Ashbury:* Working class neighborhood that became a favorite haunt of the counter-culture from the 1950s through the 1960s. *Mission Dolores (Mission San Francisco de Asís) (1776):* The city's oldest intact structure. *Palace of Fine Arts:* Created for the 1915 Panama-Pacific International Exposition. *The Presidio:* A Spanish, then Mexican, then US military post since 1776; now a national park. *San Francisco Maritime National Historical Park:* Maritime museum, ship tours, crafts demonstrations; located on Fisherman's Wharf. **3, 166**

San Juan, Puerto Rico: *San Juan National Historic Site;* city founded in 1521. A World Heritage Site that includes fortifications built by the Spanish to guard Old San Juan (Castillo de San Felipe del Morro on the west, Castillo de San Cristóbal Fort on the east). Other sites include: *Caparra Ruins:* first settlement by Juan Ponce de León in 1508. *Casa Rosada (1812):* military structure. *Casa Blanca (1521):* built for Juan Ponce de León. *Catedral de San Juan:* construction on

the original cathedral began in 1540. *City walls:* nearly 3½ miles of walls that ring the city; construction began in the 1630s. *La Fortaleza:* early fortification (constructed from 1533–1540); later, governor's residence. *Iglesia de San José:* begun in 1532 by Dominican friars; built in Spanish Gothic design. **15–18, 257, 364**

San Juan County, New Mexico: *Chaco Culture National Historical Park;* Chaco Canyon is a remote destination in today's world, but from the 9th through 13th centuries, it was a center of Pueblo culture. Over 1100 ruins. Located in northwestern New Mexico, approximately 85 miles northeast of Gallup. **10**

San Simeon, California: Newspaper tycoon William Randolph Hearst's monumental estate on the Pacific Coast. The man and his home were both larger than life; little wonder that Orson Welles thought the subject matter fit for a movie (*Citizen Kane*). Located midway between Santa Cruz and Santa Barbara.

Santa Fe, New Mexico: Founded by Spanish officials in 1610, the city became a center of imperial administration, missionary activity, and commercial trade. The central plaza has served as the city's hub for nearly four centuries. *Cathedral of St. Francis (1886):* Romanesque church that stands apart from the area's predominant adobe motifs. *Loretto Chapel:* Gothic Revival church built from 1873–1878 with a remarkable winding wooden staircase. *Palace of the Governors (circa 1610):* oldest, continuously used public building in the USA. *The Plaza:* where two historic roads, El Camino Real (to Mexico City) and the Sante Fe Trail (to Independence, Missouri) end. *San Miguel Mission:* originally built in the early 17th century; rebuilt in 1710; restored in 1955. Nearby: Los Alamos National Laboratory, center for the Manhattan Project's research on the atomic bomb (35 miles northwest). **17, 164, 307–308**

Savannah, Georgia: James Oglethorpe laid out the city in 1733 on a grid plan with public squares interspersed. Two historic districts contain: *Savannah Historic District:* homes from the late 18th through the early 20th centuries. Of particular interest: Owens-Thomas House, 1819. *Savannah Victorian Historic District:* homes from the late 19th century. *Nearby:* Wormsloe Plantation (See **Plantations**); Fort Pulaski National Monument (see **Battle Sites**, *Civil War*). **24, 58, 201, 203**

Scottsdale, Arizona: *Taliesin West;* Frank Lloyd Wright's desert complex of residences, offices, and studios, begun in 1937. Located 13 miles from Scottsdale.

Seattle, Washington: *Pioneer Square-Skid Road Historic District;* area built up after the Great Fire of 1889; expanded during the Klondike gold rush of the late 19th century. *Pioneer Building (1892):* Romanesque centerpiece of the historic district. Nearby: eight blocks northwest of Pioneer Square, customers still swarm to Pike Place Public Market Historic District, established in 1907 (now a 7-acre shopping area). **3, 335**

Seneca Falls, New York: *Women's Rights National Historical Park;* the park commemorates leaders of the women's rights movement in the mid-nineteenth century. Includes the home of Elizabeth Cady Stanton and the Wesleyan Chapel where the Seneca Falls convention was held in 1848. Located 40 miles west-south-west of Syracuse. **127–128**

Serpent Mound State Museum, near Elmville, Ohio: Earthen works of the Adena native culture. Located 60 miles east of Cincinnati. **9–10**

Springfield, Illinois: *Abraham Lincoln Home National Historic Site;* Lincoln's residence from 1844–1861. **177–182**

Spring Green, Wisconsin: *Taliesin;* architect Frank Lloyd Wright's home and studio from 1911–1959. Located 40 miles west of Madison.

Stanton, North Dakota: *Knife River Indian Villages National Historic Site;* focus on Plains Indian culture. Located 60 miles north-northwest of Bismarck. **11, 12**

Taos, New Mexico: *Taos Pueblo;* settled since the 1600s. Located 65 miles north-northeast of Santa Fe. **10, 12**

Tarrytown, New York: *Washington Irving home, Sunnyside;* the author's home from 1835–1859. Located 20 miles north of Manhattan. **150**

Tonalea, Arizona: *Navajo National Monument;* features rugged trails and ancient Anasazi ruins. Located 130 miles northeast of Flagstaff. **10**

Topeka, Kansas: *Brown v. Board of Education National Historic Site;* Monroe Elementary School, attended by young Linda Brown, whose case led to a landmark Supreme Court decision on desegregation in 1954. **350, 361**

Tuskegee Institute, Alabama: *Tuskegee*

Institute National Historic Site; African-American school headed by Booker T. Washington in 1881. Agricultural research conducted by George Washington Carver. Located 35 miles east of Montgomery. **241–242**

Utopian communities: For those who think of the USA only in terms of 'rugged individualism', a tour of restored communitarian experiments may be interesting. Some key sites include: *Amana Colonies, Amana, Iowa:* A German society that settled in Iowa in the 1850s and maintained its communal order until 1932. Located 17 miles southwest of Cedar Rapids. *Bishop Hill, Bishop Hill, Illinois:* Organized by Swedish religious dissenters from 1846–1861. Located 160 miles west-southwest of Chicago. *Ephrata Cloister, Ephrata, Pennsylvania:* Established in 1732 by Conrad Beissel and his followers. Located 65 miles northwest of Philadelphia. *The Fruitlands Museum Historic District, Harvard, Massachusetts:* Site of Bronson Alcott's transcendental experiment in communal living. *New Harmony, New Harmony, Indiana:* Site of antebellum utopian experiments by the religious Harmony Society (led by George Rapp) and by more secular-minded reformers (led by Robert Owen). Located 170 miles southwest of Indianapolis. *Old Aurora Colony Museum, Aurora, Oregon:* A German communal society in the Pacific Northwest, approximately 25 miles south of Portland. *Old Economy Village, Ambridge, Pennsylvania:* A Harmonist community built in 1824 (and dissolved in 1905). Located approximately 20 miles northwest of Pittsburgh. *Oneida Community Mansion House, Oneida, New York:* Perfectionist community inspired by John Humphrey Noyes. Located 28 miles east of Syracuse. *Shaker Villages:* visitors may tour restored communities of the followers of Mother Ann Lee at Canterbury Shaker Village, Canterbury, New Hampshire; Hancock Shaker Village, Pittsfield Massachusetts; Harvard Shaker Village Historic District, Harvard, Massachusetts; Sabbathday. Lake Shaker Village, New Gloucester, Maine; Shaker Village of Pleasant Hill, Harrodsburg, Kentucky; Watervliet Shaker Historic District, Colonie, New York. *Zoar Village State Memorial, Zoar, Ohio:* ten miles south of Canton, Ohio, the site of a German Separatist communal society from 1817–1898. **128–131**

Washington, DC: Created as the nation's capital in 1800 after a political deal made in 1790, the District of Columbia was laid out by Pierre Charles L'Enfant to echo the architectural look of ancient Greece and Rome. Sandwiched in between Maryland and Virginia, the city is a center of power, administration, and tourism. *White House:* Built between 1791 and 1800 and designed by James Hoban, the building at 1600 Pennsylvania Avenue NW has housed every president since John Adams. Ingloriously torched by the British during the War of 1812. *United States Capitol:* Home to the legislative branch of the federal government, containing both the Senate (north wing) and the House of Representatives (south wing). Originally designed by Dr. William Thornton and begun in 1793, the building was completed in 1826. Since then, there have been several additions, extensions, and renovations, the latest in the early 1990s. *Supreme Court:* Originally, justices met in the halls of Congress (1801–1935) because there simply were not funds provided for a separate facility. By the late 1920s, Congress decided to produce the money for a Supreme Court building, which opened across the street from the Capitol in 1935. *Washington Monument:* Begun in 1848, work on the memorial to the first president proceeded fitfully until construction resumed 30 years later. The 555-foot obelisk opened to the public a decade after that, in 1888. *Lincoln Memorial:* Built between 1914 and 1922, designed by Henry Bacon, and modeled after the Greek Parthenon, the building's 36 columns symbolize the number of states in the Union in 1865. Inside sits the magnificent figure of the seated Lincoln created by Daniel Chester French. *Thomas Jefferson Memorial:* Built between 1938 and 1943, designed by John Russell Pope, and modeled after the Roman Pantheon, the memorial honors the author of the Declaration of Independence. *Holocaust Memorial Museum:* A dramatic and eloquent center dedicated to victims of the Holocaust during the 1930s and 1940s in Europe. *Vietnam Veterans Memorial:* A heavily visited and profoundly moving memorial with the names of the war dead inscribed on a black granite wall. *National Archives:* Houses the key documents in US history including the Declaration of

Independence, the Constitution, and the Bill of Rights. *Frederick Douglass National Historic Site:* The home of the prominent African American reformer from 1877–1895. *Ford's Theatre National Historic Site:* Site of Lincoln's assassination on 14 April 1865. *Chesapeake and Ohio Canal:* The 185 mile-long canal, built from 1828–1850, stretches from Georgetown west to Cumberland, Maryland.

In the vicinity of Washington, DC: *Arlington National Cemetery:* The burial ground for a quarter of a million American veterans. Located on the estate of Mary Ann Randolph Custis, wife of Robert E. Lee. The couple lived at the Arlington House estate for three decades. They left in 1861. After confiscating the property, the Union began burying its dead at Arlington in 1864. Also the burial site of John F. Kennedy. *Pentagon:* The Department of Defense's home base—and one of the largest office buildings in the world. *Mount Vernon:* The estate of George Washington; located 16 miles south of the nation's capital. **77–78, 93, 155, 166, 189–191**

West Point, New York: site of a key Revolutionary war fortress and, since its establishment in 1802, the United States Military Academy. Located 63 miles north of Manhattan.

Wichita, Kansas: *Old Cowtown;* depicts Wichita in the last quarter of the nineteenth century. **171–173**

Williamsburg, Virginia: Eighteenth-century life in Virginia's colonial capital comes alive in this large complex of restored buildings and recreations, 120 miles south of Washington, DC. **19–20**

Index

abolitionism 124–125, 175
activism, government
  Hoover 269–70, 283–284;
  opposition to 220–221, 224,
  268–71, 355, 356, 360–361,
  374–379; Progressivism 236–237;
  F. Roosevelt 285–293; T.
  Roosevelt 242–244; Wilson
  244–246; *see also* conservatism,
  military, presidency, welfare state
  capitalism
Adams, John 59, 74, 81, 85–89, 98
Adams, John Quincy 95, 99, 100, 106
Addams, Jane 238–239, 254
African Americans
  accommodation vs. agitation
  240–242; and abolition 125, 167;
  and Bush 384–386; and
  Constitutional Convention
  65–66; and Eisenhower 350–351;
  and G. I. Bill 331; and L. Johnson
  354; and Kennedy 352; and
  Lincoln 184; and Nixon 356–357;
  and Progressivism 240–242; and
  F. Roosevelt 292; and Truman
  348–349; and World War I 265;
  and World War II 312–313; black
  codes 137, 209; black power 363;
  black separatism 363; civil rights
  movement 361–363; class division
  363–364; colonization 124–125;

culture 152, 273–274;
emancipation 195–197, 212–213;
farm organizations 234; free
136–137; Freedman's Bureau 209,
212; fugitive slaves 167; in Civil
War 196–197, 213; in colonial
America 32, 37; labor contracts
214; land 213–214; lynching 241;
NAACP 242, 313, 361; political
office 215; religion 160–161,
214–215, 363; sharecropping 214,
241; women 213; urbanization
265, 313; voting rights 39, 98,
208, 209, 211–212, 241,
362–363; *see also* amendments (13,
14, 15, 24), civil rights, Civil
Rights Acts, Ku Klux Klan,
Reconstruction, segregation,
slaves, slavery
Alamo, the 164
Alaska 2, 5–6, 254
amendments 70–71
  Bill of Rights 75–76; 5th 174, 175;
  12th 86; 13th 196, 209; 14th
  209–210, 211, 217, 224, 350; 15th
  211–212, 217; 18th 240, 276, 285;
  19th 127–128, 239–240, 366;
  22nd 348; 24th 354; Equal Rights
  367
Anti-Federalists 67, 68, 72
anti-imperialism 254, 265–267

A TRAVELLER'S HISTORY OF AUSTRALIA

John H. Chambers

'Here ... *Australia whose chequered past merits more than "convicts find gold then government", is laid open deftly, and we are effortlessly brought from 53,000 BC to the present day'* **The Observer**

'*Dr Chambers is a first-rate storyteller . . . will be used for year to come when other, weightier tomes are tossed away'* **The Examiner (Tasmania)**

A *Traveller's History of Australia* is essential reading for tourists, or anyone interested in its history, who wishes to enjoy the amazing diversity of Australia. This book gives a complete account of that great southern democracy from the arrival of the earliest Aborigines some fifty or sixty thousand years ago, to the preparations for the Sydney Olympics in the year 2000.

The ancient Aboriginal way of life is described; the vast deserts and fertile coastal plains, treacherous climate and peculiar marsupial animals; early European sightings; and the establishment of the British convict colony in 1788 which dragged the continent into the modern world. The nineteenth century saw the exploration of and pastoral expansion across the vast inland, the frenzied gold rushes and self-government for the six colonies, as well as growth of the great cities.

The dynamic story of Australia is continued into the twentieth century with its role in two world wars, the post-war discoveries of huge mineral deposits, and the influx of Southern European migrants who changed the country's ethnic make-up. Australia's courting of Asia in recent decades, the return of vast areas of land to the Aborigines and its confidant cultural vibrancy in wine, food, film and art are all analysed in the final chapter.

A Historical Gazeteer highlights the chief places of interest for tourists. The book concludes with two intriguing Appendices – why boomerangs return and the peculiarities of kangaroo physiology.

A TRAVELLER'S HISTORY OF CHINA

Stephen G. Haw

'Haw manages to get 2 million years in 300 pages – and he does it without gimmicks or colour pictures. An excellent addition to a series which is already invaluable. Whether you're travelling or not.' **The Guardian (London)**

A Traveller's History of China provides a concise but fascinating journey from the country's earliest beginnings right up to the creation of the economic powerhouse that is today's China. Stephen Haw carries the reader back in time to the prehistoric civilizations of 4,000 years ago, and from there to the centuries of China's silk trade with the less-developed countries of Europe. Some of the most significant inventions of the pre-modern world, including paper, gunpowder and the magnetic compass originated in China and were transmitted to the West. The author describes the glories of the Tang and Song dynasties which saw the creation of the great Chinese cities to the period of its decline and the efforts of Europe to conquer and subdue this giant land. It covers the tumult and triumphs of the Chinese revolution and the dramatic changes in political policies since the late 1970s which have now made it one of the world's fastest-developing countries.

A TRAVELLER'S HISTORY OF INDIA

SinhaRajah Tammita-Delgoda

'For anyone . . . planning a trip to India, the latest in the excellent Traveller's History series . . . provides a useful grounding for those whose curiosity exceeds the time available for research.' **The London Evening Standard**

India is heir to one of the world's oldest and richest civilizations and the origin of many of the ideas, philosophies and movements which have shaped the destiny of humankind.

For the traveller, India is both an inspiration and a challenge. The sheer wealth of Indian culture has fascinated generations of visitors. We see the sweeping panorama of Indian history, from the ancient origins of Hinduism, Jainism, Buddhism, and the other great religions, through the tumultuous political history of India's epic struggle against colonialism, to the ravages of Partition, Non-Alignment, and finally the emergence of India as a powerful modern state still grounded in the literature and culture of an ancient land. *A Traveller's History of India* covers the whole scope of India's past and present history and allows the reader to make sense of what they see in a way that no other guide book can.

A TRAVELLER'S HISTORY OF GREECE

Timothy Boatswain and Colin Nicolson

The many facets of Greece are presented in this unique book.

In *A Traveller's History of Greece*, the reader is provided with an authoritative general history of Greece from its earlier beginnings down to the present day. It covers in a clear and comprehensive manner the classical past, the conflict with Persia, the conquest by the Romans, the Byzantine era and the occupation by the Turks; the struggle for Independence and the turbulence of recent years, right up to current events.

This history will help the visitor make sense of modern Greece against the background of its diverse heritage. A Gazetteer, cross-referenced with the main text highlights the importance of sites, towns and ancient battlefields. A Chronology details the significant dates and a brief survey of the artistic styles of each period is given. Illustrated with maps and line drawings *A Traveller's History of Greece* is an invaluable companion for your holiday.

A TRAVELLER'S HISTORY OF ITALY

Valerio Lintner

In *A Traveller's History of Italy* the author analyses the development of the Italian people from pre-historic times right through to the imaginative, resourceful and fiercely independent Italians we know today.

All of the major periods of Italian history are dealt with, including the Etruscans, the Romans, the communes and the city states which spawned the glories of the Renaissance. In more modern times, Unification and the development and regeneration of the Liberal state into Fascism are covered, as well as the rise of Italy to the position it currently enjoys as a leading member of the European Community.

The Gazetteer, which is cross-referenced to the main text, highlights sites, towns, churches and cathedrals of historical importance for the visitor.

A TRAVELLER'S HISTORY OF JAPAN

Richard Tames

Whether you are going to Japan on business, to study, to teach or simply on holiday, you know that you are going to a country which really does merit the title 'unique'. A century ago the first modern guidebook to Japan warned the visitor that 'he … who should essay to travel without having learnt a word concerning Japan's past, would still run the risk of forming opinions ludicrously erroneous.' This is still sound advice.

A Traveller's History of Japan not only offers the reader a chronological outline of the nation's development but also provides an invaluable introduction to its language, literature and arts, from *kabuki to karaoke*. Political, social and industrial history and economics are also well covered; this clearly written history explains how a country embedded in the traditions of Shinto, Shoguns and Samurai has achieved stupendous economic growth and dominance in the twentieth century.

There is a Historical Gazetteer, cross-referenced to the main text and particular attention is paid to the classic historical sites which feature on any visitor's itinerary. Special emphasis is given to the writings and reactions of travellers through the centuries.

A TRAVELLER'S HISTORY OF TURKEY

Richard Stoneman

A Traveller's History of Turkey offers a full and accurate portrait of the region from Prehistory right up to the present day. Particular emphasis is given to those aspects of history which have left their mark in the sites and monuments that are still visible today.

Modern Turkey is the creation of the present century, but at least seven ancient civilisations had their homes in the region. Turkey has also formed a significant part of several empires – those of Persia, Rome and Byzantium, before becoming the centre of the opulent Ottoman Empire. All of these great cultures have left their marks on the landscape, architecture and art of Turkey – a place of bewildering facets where East meets West with a flourish.

Richard Stoneman's concise and readable account covers everything including the legendary Flood of Noah, the early civilisation of Çatal Hüyük seven thousand years before Christ, the treasures of Troy, Alexander the Great, the Romans, Selcuks, Byzantines and the Golden Age of the Sultans to the twentieth century's great changes wrought by Kemal Atatürk and the strong position Turkey now holds in the world community.

A TRAVELLER'S HISTORY OF FRANCE

Robert Cole

"Undoubtedly the best way to prepare for a trip to France is to bone up on some history. The Traveller's History of France by Robert Cole is concise and gives the essential facts in a very readable form" **The Independent on Sunday**

"Hundreds of thousands of travellers, visit France each year. The glories of the French countryside, the essential harmony of much of French architecture, the wealth of historical remains and associations, the enormous variety of experience that France offers, act as a perennial and irresistible attraction. For these visitors this lively and useful guide provides the essential clues to an understanding of France's past, and present, in entertaining and sometimes surprising detail"
From the Preface by the Series Editor, Denis Judd.

In *A Traveller's History of France*, the reader is provided with a comprehensive and yet very enjoyable, general history of France, from earliest times to the present day.

An extensive Gazetteer which is cross-referenced with the main text pinpoints the historical importance of sites and towns. Illustrated with maps and line drawings *A Traveller's History of France* will add to the enjoyment of every holidaymaker who likes to do more than lie on a beach.

A TRAVELLER'S HISTORY OF PARIS

Robert Cole

". . . an excellent resource . . . Robert Cole presents a complete picture of this historic city . . ." **Small Press**

Paris, in many people's thoughts, is the epitome of the perfect city – beautiful, romantic and imbued with vitality and culture. It is a wonderful place to visit and to live.

Packed with fact, anecdote and insight. *A Traveller's History of Paris* offers a complete history of Paris and the people who have shaped its destiny, from its earliest settlement as the Roman village of *Lutetia Parisiorum* with a few hundred inhabitants, to 20 centuries later when Paris is a city of well over 2 million – nearly one-fifth of the population of France.

This handy paperback is fully indexed and includes a Chronology of Major Events, a section on Notre-Dame and historic churches. Modernism. Paris parks, bridges, cemeteries, museums and galleries, the Metro and The Environs. Illustrated with line drawings and historical maps, this is an invaluable book for all visitors to read and enjoy.

A TRAVELLER'S HISTORY OF ENGLAND

Christopher Daniell

A Traveller's History of England gives a comprehensive and enjoyable survey of England's past from prehistoric times right through to the 1990s.

All the major periods of English history are dealt with, including the Roman occupation, and the invasions of the Anglo-Saxons, Vikings and Normans, and the power struggles of the medieval kings. The Reformation, the Renaissance and the Civil War are discussed, as well as the consequences of the Industrial Revolution and urbanism, and the establishment of an Empire which encompassed a quarter of the human race. In this century the Empire has been transformed into the Commonwealth, two victorious, but costly, World Wars have been fought, the Welfare State was established, and membership of the European Union was finally achieved.

Illustrated throughout with maps and line drawings, *A Traveller's History of England* offers an insight into the country's past and present and is an invaluable companion for all those who want to know more about a nation whose impact upon the rest of the world has been profound.

A TRAVELLER'S HISTORY OF LONDON

Richard Tames

A full and comprehensive historical background to the capital's past which covers the period from London's first beginnings, right up to the present day – from *Londinium* and *Lundenwic* to Docklands' development. London has always been an international city and visitors from all over the world have recorded their impressions and these views have been drawn on extensively throughout this book.

At different points in London's 2000-year history, it has been praised for its elegance and civility and damned for its riots, rudeness, fogs and squalor. Visitors and London's own residents will enjoy discovering more about the city from this fascinating book.

There are special sections on the Cathedrals, Royal Palaces, Parks and Gardens, Railway Termini, The Underground, Bridges, Cemeteries, Museums and Galleries, The London Year as well as a full Chronology of Major Events, Maps and Index.

A TRAVELLER'S HISTORY OF SCOTLAND

Andrew Fisher

'. . . the book is an extremely enjoyable journey through our nation's past.'

A Traveller's History of Scotland begins with Scotland's first people and their culture. Before the Vikings in 900 it was a land of romantic kingdoms and saints, gradually overtaken by more pragmatic struggles for power. Centuries of strife lead up to the turbulent years of Mary Queen of Scots, the Calvinistic legacy of Knox, and the bitterness of final defeat.

The dreams of the Jacobites are contrasted with the cruel reality of the end of the Stuarts and the Act of Union with England. Scotland now saw an age of industry and despoilation. The result was much emigration and an obsession with the nation's past which glorified the legends of the Highlander and the Clans. In this century, the loss of identity and drift to the south have been followed by a new surge of national pride with higher aspirations for the future. In the millenium the effects of devolution and a separate Scottish parliament are eagerly awaited.

A Traveller's History of Scotland explains the roots of Scottish history and is an invaluable companion for visitors.

A TRAVELLER'S HISTORY OF IRELAND

Peter Neville

A Traveller's History of Ireland gives a full and accurate portrait of Ireland from Prehistory right up to the 1990s.

Hundreds of thousands of tourists visit Ireland every year drawn by the landscape, the people and the underlying atmosphere created by its rich heritage.

The story opens with mysterious early Celtic Ireland where no Roman stood, through Saint Patrick's mission to Ireland which began the process of making it 'an island of saints', to the struggle with Viking and Irish enemies alike.

It moves through the arrival of the Norman 'Strongbow' in the twelfth century, and the beginnings of the difficult and tragic Anglo-Irish relationship. Great historical figures like Hugh O'Neill, Cromwell, and Jonathan Swift figure as well as ordinary people like the Londonderry 'apprentice boys; who helped change the course of Irish history. Then into modern times with the great revolts of 1798, the horrors of the Potato Famine and the careers of the leading constitutional nationalists, O'Connell and Parnell. The book ends with a description of modern Ireland, and of its two separate Catholic Nationalist and Protestant Unionist traditions.

A TRAVELLER'S HISTORY OF THE CARIBBEAN

James Ferguson

A concise and authoritative history of the entire region covering the larger nations of the Bahamas, Cuba, Jamaica, Haiti, the Dominican Republic, Puerto Rico and Trinidad and Tobago as well as the smaller islands of the Eastern Caribbean and the French, British and Dutch territories.

The Caribbean, a region of spectacular natural beauty, has a turbulent history of colonialism, slavery and resistance in which people from all continents have played their part. Described by Columbus as an earthly paradise, the Caribbean has long enticed foreigners with its promise of wealth. From the gold-seeking exploits of the Spanish conquistadors to modern-day tourist cruises, the islands have exerted a fascination on generations of visitors.

Tracing the islands' path from slavery to revolution and independence, *A Traveller's History of the Caribbean* looks at the history of countries as different as Cuba, Jamaica and Haiti, explaining their diversity and their common experiences. It reveals a region in which a tumulous past has created a culturally vibrant and intriguing present.

A TRAVELLER'S HISTORY OF NORTH AFRICA

Barnaby Rogerson

"Remarkable – Barnaby Rogerson has succeeded in isolating all the different strands of North African history and weaving them into a clear and comprehensive narrative. No one interested in the Maghreb can afford to be without this book.' **– John Julius Norwich**

This Traveller's History covers the countries of Morocco, Tunisia, Libya and Algeria and is written by an expert on the area. It endeavours to provide a concise and readable history of the region's journey from its earliest beginnings right up to the politics and life of the present day.

North Africa is an island surrounded by three seas, the Mediterranean, the Atlantic and to the south by the sand sea of the Sahara. It has seen wave upon wave of invasion break on its rocky shores. From the Carthaginians in the fifth century BC to the French in the twentieth century, the North African people have assimilated what suits them and remained resiliently aloof to what does not.

Onto this complex cultural background *A Traveller's History of North Africa* weaves a cast of memorable characters. Dido, the lovelorn Queen of Carthage, Hannibal, the general's general and St Augustine all play their part, as do such lesser-known luminaries as the Berber queen Kahina and the horseback Muslim conqueror Oqba Ibn Nafi'.

For travellers on the ground or students at their desks, this handy paperback will prove invaluable for sorting out the Almohads from the Almoravids and for explaining the dazzling wealth and art of Roman North Africa.

A TRAVELLER'S HISTORY OF SPAIN

Juan Lalaguna

Spain's vibrant and colourful past is as exciting to discover as is taking a fresh look at the upheavals of the twentieth century. *A Traveller's History of Spain* will unlock the secrets of the country, its people and culture for the interested traveller.

Juan Lalaguna takes you on a journey from the earliest settlements on the Iberian peninsula, through the influences of the Romans, the Goths and the Muslims, the traumas of expansion and the end of Empire, the surge for national identity – right up to the current dilemmas that face post-Franco Spain.

A Traveller's History of Spain is an essential companion for your trip to Spain.

To order your free 32-page full-color
Interlink catalog specializing in world travel, world literature
in translation, and world history and politics, please call us at
1-800-238-LINK
or write to us at the following address:
Interlink Publishing
46 Crosby Street, Northampton, MA 01060
Tel: (413) 582-7054   Fax: (413) 582-7057
e-mail: info@interlinkbooks.com
website: www.interlinkbooks.com